C000221755

LIFE

—IS A—

GAME

Mev Dinc

"The inspirational success story of
a legendary game developer!"

Unless otherwise indicated, or else rights for games and visual elements included within the book belong to their respective copyright holders, other than those which are owned/produced by the author.

Copyright © 2021 by Mevlut Dinc

All rights reserved. No part of this book may be reproduced or used in any manner without written permission of the copyright owner except for the use of quotations in a book review.

First Edition

Book design by Publishing Push

ISBNs:
Paperback 978-1-914078-59-0
eBook 978-1-914078-60-6

To Mum, Dad, Janet, Nejati, Gulsun and Sila

Barcelona, London, Istanbul, 2016-2020

The video clip contained in the QR code below is from a Gaming Panel in Istanbul (November 2012), discussing the possibility of *Creating A Global Gaming Company* from Turkey.

Participants include Mev Dinc, Sidar Sahin (CEO of Peak Games) and Erdem Celik.

It contains Sidar's opening remarks about me and my contribution to the Turkish Game Industry.

Zynga bought Peak Games for 1.8 billion USD in 2020!

Please access the video by imply reading the QR code with your mobile phone's camera or installing a QR code reader application.

Mev Dinc, Sidar Sahin & Erdem Celik

About the Author

Mev Dinc (aka Mevlut Dinc)

Mev Dinc is an award winning veteran video games developer and BAFTA member. Mev began to learn games programming back in 1983 in England, and established his reputation very quickly for both programming and game design. Furthermore, he won numerous nominations and awards from the specialist press for his work, in particular, for 'Enduro Racer' and 'Last Ninja 2'.

More awards followed at his Vivid Image Developments Studio, which he co-founded with John Twiddy and Hugh Riley in 1988. 'Time Machine' (1990) - the Most Original Game), 'First Samurai' (1991) – Arcade Game of the Year, and the hugely successful 'Street Racer' on the Super Nintendo console. Amazingly, Intel used Dinc's Actor Game Engine Technology Demo in its Worldwide promotions of the Pentium 4 processor in 2000.

Considered as the Founding Father of the Turkish video games industry, Dinc returned to his native Turkey to lead and help establish the Turkish Gaming Sector in 2000 after 21 years in the UK. He founded the first professional games development studio 'Sobee Studios' at the end of 2000. Mev rapidly set up a very talented local team producing high quality original games. He went on to produce Turkey's first and biggest MMO (Massively Multi-player Online) title 'Istanbul Kiyamet Vakti'. It was first published in 2006 and is still active after 14 years! Soon after, he developed the world's first 11 vs 11 online soccer game, 'I Can Football' (2009). Followed by 'SuperCan', Turkey's first superhero kid which quickly reached millions of users.

Sobee became a 100% Turk Telekom owned company in 2009, which Mev continued to manage until May 2013. Sobee's acquisition by Turk Telekom is the first sale of a gaming company in Turkey.

I Can Football won the Best Content Award in the 2010 London World Communication Awards. It also won the Technology Award from The Scientific and Technological Research Council of Turkey (TUBITAK).

Mev is also the founder and the first elected president of the world's first Turkish Digital Games Federation.

Quotes

Michael J. Holley (Author of Plaster Scene, The Dead Man's Curse)

"I'm so gripped by this book and I even know how it ends!!!

I am extremely humbled by everything I have read so far; from your childhood in the village, to the riots at university, to how you and Janet even got together, to moving to England without any English, to getting the job at STC... blown away.

It feels like a Dickensian story that actually touches my life. And I had no idea of so much of your story. This must be made into a film."

Jon Hare (Sensible Software):

"Both Mev and I did some of our early games in the mid-80s. His early programming success came with Last Ninja 2, which went on to become one of the great 8-bit series. Following this, Mev's Vivid Image went on to be one of the top British 16 Bit game developers, this time with original games like Street Racer and First Samurai.

Our shared loves of football and games have been constant themes in our times together, he even played football for our Sensible Software team back in the 90s.

I am proud of him for using his experience and knowledge as part of the gaming scene in the UK to become the founding father of the games industry in his native country of Turkey. Cheers to you Mev!!"

Charles Cecil (Revolution Software, Activision):

When I arrived to run Activision's UK development studio in 1988, my team spoke in hallowed tones about a brilliant young programmer who created innovative, beautiful, expertly crafted games. When I met Mev, shortly into my tenure, I found that their description was accurate - he is one of those rare developers that is both hugely talented and a pleasure to work with. Mev left the UK to kick-start and help establish the Turkish gaming sector. Someone I both admire and hold as a dear friend, Mev has had a fascinating life with plenty of great stories to tell.

Jon Dean (Activision, EA Sports):

"Everyone loves Mev, with good reason. He greets you with a smile and is always pleased to see you. Generous and insightful, he makes for great conversation and great company. He is also wicked smart, hard-working and a talented programmer who is passionate about going back and helping the next generation of game designers and programmers.

I have had the privilege to have known him for pretty much my entire career, lucky enough to have produced some of his games and had him bail me out by rescuing a few of my off-the-rails projects.

Mev is a legend!"

Rod Cousens (Activision, Acclaim)

"The context was the heady days of the emergence of videogames starting to give way to demands for greater sophistication and disciplines. It was against this background that I first met Mev. He hadn't long arrived at our shores and was eager to find work and make sense of the chaos in which he found himself. He brought a dedicated work ethic, which was beyond reproach.

As an external contractor he integrated well with those within the company who then embraced him and he became the preferred go to Programmer. But he was that and more. He was talented and creative, contributing to the design process, before going on to establish his own business and IP. He forged long held friendships in the industry, which still stand out today, earning respect, credibility and admiration from those around him. We may have given him a break in the first instance, but he then ran with it and turned it into something.

Having learnt, built contacts and knowledge, he returned to his homeland of Turkey where he pioneered and trail blazed video games in the country and is rightly recognised for doing so. It is well deserved. His manner is endearing, as is his warmth and I am fortunate to count him as a dear and valued friend."

Paul Gardner (Partner, Wiggin UK)

"I first came across Mev in the late 1980s while working as a junior lawyer for a games publisher. The publisher had been through a number of bad experiences with games developers; some were prima donnas, some were hopelessly unreliable and some were simply unable to deliver what they had promised. When I first encountered Vivid Image I was therefore wondering which of these categories this company would fall into. However, I quickly discovered that the man behind this company, Mev, was not only talented, intelligent and articulate, but also refreshingly straightforward. It later transpired that this is how he was, and still is, regarded by the industry as a whole. Not only was Mev an early pioneer in game development, but I am sure that his tutelage and example is in no small measure part of the reason why Turkey has grown to become a leading centre of innovation in game development and design."

Masahiro Ishii (Kemko, Japan):

"My friend Mev. I met Mev on Facebook again after a long silence.

A long time ago I met Mev and collaborated to develop Entertainment software between the UK and Japan.

I often would come and visit Vivid Image for technical meetings. Mev's powerful product was "First Samurai" which gave me a good sense of Japanese character writing and design for the product, which I had never seen before.

We spoke a lot about Turkish culture and foods, and also Japanese history, Samurai, traditional Japanese food and so on. During our communication he always gave us time, I was comforted by Mev's warm heart.

Once we had very nice Turkish kebab and the best place for me was enjoying dinner and communication at IZNIK Turkish restaurant with Mev. After finishing development of entertainment software we made a promotional music CD. I still regard Mev as a best friend to me."

Shahid Kamal Ahmad (Sony PlayStation)

"I was blessed to be born when I was, because it meant that arcade games and home computers came into my life during my formative years, and drew me in completely. In the early 1980s, there was of course no Internet, but legends were being made, and a few names came to the fore in the magazines of the time as the leading voices in the exciting new medium. This was when I came across the work of "Mev Dinc". His work was of a consistently high quality and I admired him greatly. Everyone I spoke with said good things about him. In a quirk of fate, he and I both did games for Telecomsoft and Electric Dreams, but we didn't actually meet for the first time until a few years ago. Mevlut and I became friends very quickly, he is warm, generous, talented, and humble. It's unusual to meet one of your heroes from your formative years, let alone become friends with them. Mevlut is an inspiring man, and his journey has been amazing. "

Ulas Karademir (VP Productions Unity Technologies)

I heard Mevlut's name, his achievements, his story way too late in my life and it took me many years to meet with him in person. Once I met him, I was so happy.

His story is so amazing and so inspiring. He paved the way for lots of game developers like myself. Mevlut's humbleness and creativity constantly inspire you to build new games and ideas. He is warm, friendly, and listens to you with curiosity.

One thing really amazing about him is how connected he is, he knows many people, he has an incredible network, touches so many lives.

I had so many great conversations in the last couple of years with him, and enjoy his company every time. He is a true Turkish Game Developer Legend.

His work and his book will continue to inspire current and upcoming generations for many years to come.

Steve Merrett (Amiga Action, PlayStation Plus, Bethesda)

"I was a someone who grew up an avid fan of Zzap! and Crash magazines. Written by gamers for gamers, they also showcased not just the talents of people behind games, but their personalities, too. This lit a fire in me wherein I grew fascinated by the people who made the games I loved. The Tony Crowthers. The Stavros Fasoulas. The Andrew Braybrooks. And one name that grew in prominence as my interest grew was Mev Dinc.

Mev has seen it and done it all. He produced the stunning Spectrum version of Last Ninja. He was responsible for ports of Enduro Racer and also created Gerry the Germ. But Mev's rise to the prominence he deserved coincided with my own baby steps into the games writing career I craved. And Mev was a very patient man who gave this wet-behind-the-ears, wannabe Gary Penn, his time.

By this time Mev's star was in the ascendancy with Hammerfist and the hugely underrated Time Machine. I loved both these games, but the latter especially. And during its preview phase I got to speak to Mev for Amiga Action. And he was brilliant. He was patient with me as I raved about stuff, he was candid about the hoops he had to jump through to get where he was, but his enthusiasm was contagious. And it had to be as Mev has probably dealt with more industry nonsense than anybody should.

He has produced some fantastic games, but has also seen so much hard work go unused when a hardware launch, he was supporting, fell by the wayside. He has also been the victim of a (then) huge triple-A publisher going under, leaving his First Samurai game in limbo. Such a shame as First Samurai deserved so much more prominence than it eventually got.

But still he cracked on and the next time I saw Mev was when I was on the official Nintendo Magazine at EMAP and he was the man behind UbiSoft's Street Racer, a decent karting game with a varied ensemble of characters. Our paths crossed again at a trade show where there were people dressed as characters from the game and Mev, while as unassuming as ever, was quietly proud of the fanfare the game was getting. Nobody could begrudge his success for that and you could only be pleased that he was being supported with a proper marketing push.

Life got in the way then and I didn't see Mev for ages. His Vivid Image team went the way of so many others when he returned to his native Turkey, and he was an occasional figure you saw in articles about classic titles. Our paths then crossed at an event and we became in contact via Facebook. This is where Mev revealed his plans for a book about his life, which I hope covers every detail of a varied and fantastic career. Mev is a survivor. He has seen so much and emerged on the other side – and that tenacity is clearly a trait that harks back to his early years in Turkey. Bloody hell, who wouldn't want to read a story about a man who constantly faces down adversity…?"

Foreword

There is a real nostalgia now for the early days in the computer games industry in the 80s when everything was a blank canvas full of potential and ready to be explored by eager developers. We lived and breathed this new form of entertainment, from its earliest days with Pong and text adventures such as Colossal Cave, to the pinnacle of entertainment technology embodied at the time by arcade games. A whole generation grew up with these influences and of course for many of us our greatest dream was to work in computer games.

The event that turbo charged this new entertainment industry was the advent of home computers such as the Commodore Pet and Sinclair ZX80. But it was the second generation where things really started to take off, when the Sinclair Spectrum and Commodore 64 launched. Soon dedicated developers were working from their bedrooms and spare rooms to create those early computer games, pushing the computers so hard there was almost steam coming out of them.

It wasn't long before programming stars started to emerge from among these early pioneers and one of the greatest, someone who I had the absolute pleasure to work with, was none other than Mev Dinc.

I first came across Mev, a self-taught programmer, when I was creating 8-bit graphics for the Spectrum for Electric Dreams, a studio of Activision. By today's standards those art efforts may look crude, but at the time they were truly state of the art. It was Mev's brilliance that really made those games shine. His programming on Enduro Racer was a tour de force as he managed to squeeze every bit of performance possible to make the Amstrad CPC version really sing. To produce any form of 3D game on those 8 bit platforms was a major programming accomplishment and testimony to the skill of Mev. Of course he wasn't someone to stand still and as the computers and consoles continued to evolve, so did Mev. He honed his programming to an astonishing level as the years rolled by, constantly pushing the systems he worked on to deliver jaw dropping results.

We worked on a lot of titles together, but one of my favourite memories that really stands out from the others, was our time on Aliens together. We had an impossibly tight deadline to hit – produce the game in time for Christmas with only about five weeks left until the big day. We all worked flat out, living on takeaways and with very little sleep in the studio. I even remember at one point I was so exhausted trying to finish the animation frames for the queen alien that I actually ended up dreaming with my eyes open! However, throughout all of this I don't think I saw Mev once lose his legendary cool and his sense of humour. This is exactly who this man is, an endlessly kind guy, who kept smiling throughout it all, the person who kept his head when everyone else was beyond shattered. And somehow we did finish Aliens in time and then all probably slept for a week whilst the game charged to the top of the charts to hit the number one spot.

This book offers a fascinating insight into a dedicated man who always dreamed big, someone who's life culturally straddled both Turkey and the UK. If you want to learn about where success is first born you'll soon discover it in the early chapters where those foundations were created in his family life, and will leave you desperately wanting to try cornbread!

Mev enjoyed a meteoric rise in the game industry and later returned to his home country to help grow Turkey's own game industry to become the powerhouse that it is today. This book has it all, the story of a man's life evolving and changing to meet the challenges of the game industry that transformed itself into a world leading form of entertainment.

Although I worked in the games industry to 2006, I can honestly say that my time working with Mev was one of my favourite periods of my entire career. And that had everything to do with the great man himself, a real talent and wonderful kind guy who is very much one in a million, and someone I am lucky enough to call a friend.

Nick Cook (former Art Director of Pivotal Games and
Author of Cloud Riders, Fractured Light and Earth Song series)

Preface

I spent my childhood as an only child with my mother and our relatives in the village where I was born. My father left us, and the village, behind for Istanbul when I was only 6 months old.

I owe my mother a lot. She did so much for me, as all mothers do for their children. I was her whole existence and reason for living, as if she held onto life just to bring me up. Despite our hardship and the absence of my father, she raised me very well. Perhaps the most important thing being that she enabled me to study in high school, despite everyone else's objections.

I saw my father for the first time when I was about 10 or 11 years old. I started to see him a lot more just before my high school years; when he was working in the city of Samsun (the Black Sea) for the Ulusoy Coach Company.

Although I had never intended or planned for it, I started studying at the Ankara Academy of Economics and Commercial Sciences in 1974, after obtaining satisfactory results in my university exams and with the financial support of my father. My university years were filled with political unrest, student uprisings and military clashes, making it almost impossible to study and receive any academic education.

As I grew up and continued with my university studies, my father started to develop a greater interest in me. Unfortunately, I lost my father in 1975; just as we were really getting close. My dad's sudden passing completely changed my life, and I began to spend more time in Istanbul with my uncle, where my dad had been living. I only went to Ankara once in a while, but most of the time we were either too scared or not allowed to attend classes. The 70s in Turkey were very difficult and dangerous times indeed.

During in-depth discussions with friends, I was someone who always believed that getting married before the age of 30 would be very stupid. However, in a twist of fate, while only 19 and still a university student, I married an English girl I met in Istanbul in 1976. I didn't speak a word of English, and she not a word of Turkish! After living and facing a lot of hardship together in Turkey for about two years, we eventually moved and started living in Southampton, England in 1979.

Now that I was in England, I initially thought I could study for a master's degree, but instead I found myself working at a factory. For 5 years I was making communication cables that connected continents. After much insistence from a work colleague, I ended up buying my first computer, a Sinclair ZX Spectrum, in 1983, at a time when I had zero knowledge of computers and no interest in video games. I taught myself programming and game design within two years. All while still working at the factory and learning the English language.

Once again my life was about to change completely. In the fantastic gaming sector, which I entered completely by chance, I have managed to reach and touch millions of people in England, Turkey and the rest of the World, during a gaming career which has lasted for over 33 years.

I consider myself one of the luckiest people in the world. What can be better than doing a job that you love and making a successful living out of it? So how did it all start, how did I get tricked into gaming?

I was someone who had never played or had an interest in games. I had no training, inclination towards or prior knowledge in computing. However, within 2 years, I became a professional games programmer, and soon after managed to make a name for myself.

How did I achieve it? What was the secret of it all? I really don't know the full answer. That is why I wanted to write this book and maybe you will find some clues while reading it.

I believe in natural talent. Ability and talent combined with enough enthusiasm and effort can bring about success. Of course, you also need the appropriate environment and conditions. Being in the right place at the right time is also very important. My being in England during the early 1980s, right at the beginning of the golden age of computer gaming, allowed me to discover a hidden talent in game programming and design.

Believing that it would provide hope and inspiration to many young people, I wanted to tell my life story, and also share some insights and details of my work. I have tried to write about my life and experiences honestly, openly and sincerely without any exaggeration. In fact, I may have even tried to tone some of it down, so that you wouldn't think *'surely, that can't be true'* or *'no way, that doesn't even happen in the movies!'*

I shared all my memories to the best of my recollection, and as accurately as possible. I meant no offence to anyone mentioned in the book; please accept my sincere apologies in advance, if inadvertently anything I have shared upsets anyone.

I wrote the Turkish version of the book between January 2016 and October 2018. I started writing it in Barcelona, continued in London, and finished it in Istanbul. I wrote the English version in the months of April and May 2020, during the Covid 19 lockdown. I managed to complete the first draft, first reading and correction in less than two months. As the saying goes; there's good in every evil.

I am very grateful to my friend Jamieson Lee Hill, who kindly read and helped me edit the first draft of my book to make it more elegant and flowing.

My heartfelt appreciation goes to my English nephew Michael J. Holley (Author of Plaster Scene and The Dead Man's Curse, who generously proofread the final draft of the book.

I must extend my thanks to Gary Arnott, who kindly created the wonderful doodles/icons for my games used in the headings. I am most grateful to Richard Langford, Andy Green and Oncu Ozgonul for the book cover design.

Many thanks to my good friends Rod Cousens, Jon Dean, Nick Cook, Charles Cecil, Jon Hare, Paul Gardner, Shahid Kamal Ahmad, Masahiro Ishii, Steve Merrett and Ulas Karademir for their wonderful and generous words.

And I would like to thank, from the bottom of my heart, all my colleagues who have contributed to my work; those who helped me achieve my dreams, my family, and most of all, the gamers who have played and enjoyed my games.

Let The Game Begin!

AND THE GAME BEGINS!
Childhood and The English Years

My Village, Cihadiye (the Black Sea city of Ordu)

My birthday

I was born in Cihadiye village, which is 1300M above sea level and in the city of Ordu, in the Black Sea region. I have a life story to tell, but I don't even know my real age. Whenever I asked when my birthday was, my late mother would always say, "You were born in March, you are 9 months younger than your cousin Ilhan, and the same age as your friend Orhan."

Then when I would ask her when Ilhan and Orhan were born, she would always brush me off and say, "How should I know, son?" In actual fact, I have lived all these years and I still do not know exactly when I was born or how old I really am. And I no longer have my mum (RIP) to ask either!

Nowadays people share videos and photos of even their unborn babies! The earliest photo of me that I remember being taken is when I was about ten years old. I wanted to put it in the book, but I couldn't find it anywhere. I don't think I knew anything about birthday celebrations during my childhood and don't even remember celebrating my own until maybe the university years.

Even to this day, I always avoid celebrating my birthday, since never growing up with the tradition and also never knowing my date of birth. How can I celebrate it when I don't even know which year, month or even day I was born, let alone the exact time of birth? I never really bothered with my birthday, and unfortunately, didn't allow my family and friends to enjoy it either.

Earliest photo (13 years)

1

It's not really that important is it, to know how old one really is? What really matters is how long we have left to live. Everyday could be our last day. If only we could pretend to be born on each new day, and enter a new age at the end of it. This way we could embrace and celebrate each day. Maybe this is how I console myself for not having a proper birthday like everyone else. We say life is too short, and yet we live and behave as if we will live forever, but when the time comes, it's too late.

Although it's almost impossible to remember our first 3 or 4 years, I clearly remember most things even today about my childhood and how I grew up in the village.

I don't know the exact details, but I know for sure that I was registered 2 years older on my birth certificate. In those days, most babies weren't registered straight away anyway, especially if you were born in the winter months like I was. In truth, there was no way of even going to the registry office in town due to the heavy snowfall.

Just like the others I was registered much later. And my uncle (mum's elder brother) registered my age 2 years older than I actually was, so that I could start school at the same time as the other kids! Not just the day, but also the month and the year were made up. My official birthday is the 17th May, but according to my mother and other elderly relatives my actual birthdate is something like the 9th March. I say this because they were never sure. However, the month of March seems fairly certain! At least now you can see why I can't be bothered with my birthday celebrations.

Our primary school education lasted for 5 years followed by a further 3 years of middle school. I think I started school when I was around 5. And now imagine a school with just one classroom, and all the pupils from 1st to 5th grade all studying together in one room and with one teacher. So, we all listened to each other's lessons!

Our (First and Only) Village House...

This is where my village house was, 2018

My great uncle built our first, and only house, when I was around 6 or 7 years old. Until then my mother and I would visit our many relatives one by one. Staying for about a week at each, until we'd exhausted the entire village.

Stays were not in any particular order and the duration would vary too. I just followed my mum and wherever she stayed, that's where my temporary home would be too.

Sometimes we would travel very far to the neighbouring village to visit one of my aunts. Just after starting school, we were bought a small piece of land near my great aunt in the district of Saricicek (it means yellow flower in Turkish). This is where our two-bed timber house was built. The plot of land was around 300 square metres in a triangular shape; the house was built at the widest end, and nearest to the road.

The little house had one small living room and one bedroom, but I don't remember ever sleeping in it. Basically, because it was freezing cold in the winter and we always slept in the living room. I can't recall whether we had a fireplace or a stove, but at least the living room was a little warmer.

We had a toilet outside, just by the main door. I dreaded going to the toilet, especially in the cold winter nights. I hated it so much! The expression 'it froze my ass off!' was really apt.

The outside walls of the house weren't protected from the cold at all, and they weren't plastered or anything, just bare timber boards. In time, the timber would dry and shrink in size resulting in massive gaps in the walls. I still remember vividly how poor mum would try and patch all those gaps and holes with pieces of cloth, so that we would be protected from the dreadfully cold winter winds.

I'm writing these lines while in Barcelona in our lovely flat. It's heated and has air conditioning too, although we try to use it as little as possible to avoid allergic reaction. The temperatures only go as low as 7-8 degrees celsius in the winter and when that happens we still have to cover ourselves with extra blankets to keep warm.

I really cannot remember how we managed to sleep and stay warm in those freezing winter days in Turkey with snowfall sometimes reaching as high as 2 metres. No matter how well my mother patched those gaps and holes, the thin timber walls did very little to keep the cold out. We must have worn several layers of clothes and a couple of woollen quilts over us just to get us through the night.

As human beings, we seem to be able to adapt to and learn to cope with even the most difficult circumstances and conditions. I find it interesting how we can be both fragile and strong at the same time.

I remember my mum always scratching my back to sleep. Looking back in hindsight, I must have had some kind of eczema. My son Nejati never had it, but my daughter Sila had really bad eczema when she was two. The poor soul couldn't sleep with the horrible itching and I would try and scratch her to sleep too. It was really tough to put her to sleep, and very exhausting too. My strokes would inevitably slow down as I got sleepier and then Sila would immediately prompt me and guide my hand; "Daddy, do it like this, do it like this!"

Mum grew potatoes and some other vegetables in our garden. She would plough the land by hand with the help of Ayse, the daughter of my great uncle

Pehlul. Pehlul was a close relative from my father's side and he lived nearby. I would just play by myself in front of the house while they worked.

We wore black rubber shoes all year round, right until high school. We used to go to Golkoy on Saturdays, our little town a few miles from the village. We always walked to it and it took about one and a half hours. We would walk downhill most of the way on a winding rocky footpath. It was harder on the way back and would always take a bit longer, as we had to climb uphill.

During a summer, I once saw someone with a pair of sandals while in town, nothing as fancy as we have nowadays, just simple plastic ones. They looked so much nicer than my rubber shoes for sure. It was certainly something new and I don't think many people had them either. I really fancied a pair myself.

I started pestering my mum, "Please mum, buy me a pair." She couldn't afford them and naturally kept saying no.

One day while mum and Ayse were working the land, I started it again, "Please mum, please buy me a pair!" She kept telling me off, trying to quieten me, but I just kept at it. She had probably had enough, and picked up a hard piece of earth and threw it at me. It just whistled past my head, but I dropped like a sack of potatoes! First making a big sound as if I was badly hurt, then laying there still. When mum saw me like that laying there in silence, she rushed over in a panic. She was making sure I was okay, trying to make me feel better; cuddling me and landing kisses all over my face. She must have been terrified because I was her everything... "My dearest, please don't die, I promise I will buy you two pairs!"

I remember singing sometimes in the house; some traditional folk songs that I heard and learnt on my aunt's radio. My mum would tell me proudly how my singing would impress all those people who passed by our house.

I recall how I could pick up and learn some things very easily and quickly. For instance, learning all the different styles of Turkish songs from traditional to classical. I still remember most of the melodies and still perform some of them from time to time, mostly to myself! However, I have a bad memory; I've forgotten most of the lyrics, and I'm very bad at remembering the names, but I never forget the melodies.

Manastir Primary School, Cihadiye, 1962

The primary school age was seven, but I ended up starting school when I was only five because of my uncle registering me as two years older.

I had already learnt to count and was very good at it. It was my cousin Melek who had taught me to count. She would be very proud of me and pat me on the shoulder every time I successfully completed my counting. I was so chuffed and full of myself too and I made some meaningless funny noises every time

Melek said "Bravo!" Even now, I remember her laughing so loudly at my proud silly look and posture.

The Black Sea villages are spread over very wide areas. Within our village, even the distance between different districts was several miles, meaning that families within the same village could still be far apart. There was a lovely winding river running right through the village dividing

Primary school, still burning logs to keep warm
School was one room and adjacent to the Mosque

it into two distinct sections. Both sides of the village were on very big hills surrounded by massive forests and open lands. We had many relatives from both mum's and dad's side in each section of the village. As a result, I used to end up travelling around the entire village, as we moved from relative to relative, and crossing the river several times. There was another village, Yuvapinar, several miles away from ours where my aunt lived and I remember visiting her once or twice a year.

Despite the large spread of the districts and miles of distance between them, there were only two schools in the entire village. One on either side of the valley. Some of us had to walk miles to school, one and a half hours of walking each way. It used to be really difficult to walk the distance in those cold winter days. In fact, it was terrifying, especially on the way back home after school, because in those short winter days it would get both darker and colder very quickly.

Sometimes snowfall would reach two meters high, forcing us to remain inside the house. My school was in the district of Manastir, where my mum's family home was. I spent some of my early childhood there with my cousins until our house was built in Saricicek. There was quite a distance between Saricicek and Manastir. We would walk for ages on our little feet to and from school. There was another district even beyond mine called Elmalan where we had more relatives, mostly from mum's side. Elmalan was about half an hour walking distance from our house. Every morning I would wait for Sener, one of my relatives and childhood friends, to walk to me from Elmalan, so we could walk to school together. During the very difficult winter conditions coupled with the fear of dogs along the way, I was always pleased to have Sener with me.

Sener sadly died a few years ago, still very young (RIP). In truth, he really didn't like going to school in the winter, and more often than not after walking all that way to me, sometimes he would refuse to walk the rest of the way. I'd say "C'mon Sener, why are you turning back after having walked all this way?" He would simply repeat the same excuse, "I have a bad stomach!" I would be so angry with him, but I would find the courage to go to school by myself.

Our school was adjacent to the village mosque and was the only school on my side with just one classroom and one teacher. So, it was one special school! Just imagine, all the years in one room, studying and learning at the same time.

When the teacher was focussing on the fourth and fifth year pupils, the rest of us were required to be extra silent. The teacher would give us special exercises to complete such as writing the same sentence as many times as possible on the same page repeatedly, in the smallest, but still legible size. The concentration was amazing. We were so focused on trying to achieve the most number of sentences we could fit on the page, that we didn't even notice that the time had passed. There was absolute silence on our part. I'm sure the fear of getting a big telling off from the teacher also played its part. Although I don't ever remember the teacher losing their temper, instead the methods used to keep us quiet were quite ingenious.

I have a high level of focus and concentration when I put my mind to something. Maybe I gained some of this in my village school. Even now I can work for hours on end until I reach my target.

Generally speaking, I was quite competent with my studies and always achieved high marks. However, I never liked reading and memorising things, finding it daunting and boring. And in my entire education, I never really liked homework and preparation for exams. Just passing with average grades was good enough. In short, I am quite lazy and tend to get bored very quickly if I'm forced to do something that I don't like much.

Anecdotes From Primary School Years

We used to get a lot of snow in the winter. We had a stove in the middle of the classroom, and to keep the room warm we would burn lots of logs. The school didn't have any firewood, so we were all expected to bring some with us each day. Thus, we walked to school with a chunk of wood in one hand, and our school bag in the other. Mind you, when I say school bag please don't get the wrong impression. It was nothing fancy, just a cloth bag that would literally freeze. In fact, it felt like carrying a bag of ice!

I think it was after my 2nd year that we continued to carry wood to school even during the warm weather. At that time, America was providing powdered milk to many countries as part of the Marshall Plan Aid programme. Many European countries had accepted this aid including Britain. At school we would make milk with the powder, heating it to drink in the mornings and sometimes making yogurt as well. I remember hating the stuff; it tasted nothing like the natural milk and yogurt we grew up with. In a village, in the middle of nature, we were made to drink this awful tasteless milk. As if having to consume it wasn't bad enough, we had to actually make it ourselves. The whole experience nearly put me off yogurt for good, which is crazy as it's probably my favourite food of all time!

Actually, I nearly forgot to tell you that my breakfast was almost always yogurt with cornbread (maize bread). We didn't have any animals, so I don't ever remember us having milk in the house or mum making any yogurt. Most mornings on the way to school I would first stop at my aunt's to have my yogurt/ cornbread breakfast. Unfortunately, my aunt would always give me a piece of bread left over from the day before, which had become rock solid overnight. Having this hard bread with the cold yogurt wasn't fun, but for some reason I always loved having it and was never fed up.

My aunt would also cook fresh cornbread every morning as well. It would smell wonderful, but she would always give me the old stuff. Sometimes though we would wait for my aunt to see to the animals and, as soon as she left the house, my cousin Hatice, my aunt's daughter, would give me a fresh piece. I would quickly try and eat it before my aunt returned. In actual fact, Hatice probably tell had my aunt that she had eaten the fresh bread herself.

I must say, the combination of freshly baked cornbread and yogurt is still my favourite dish. I make my own organic yogurt and cornbread regularly, and yes, I still have it for breakfast too!

My daughter Sila also loves yogurt. She has it with almost every meal, so much so that she even adds yogurt to yogurt soup! My son Nej doesn't eat it that much, but he likes yoghurt juice; maybe it's in our DNA. Everyone loves my yogurt. Sometimes I get carried away and start thinking maybe I could produce it on a large scale and make a global success of it. Another Chobani perhaps! Chobani is the number one American producer of Greek yogurt, founded by an immigrant Turk.

Let's get back to our logs. So most pupils had plenty of logs at home, so they could bring one to school. Forests surrounded us, and the villagers were allowed to chop down dry trees to make wood. But my mother and I had no way of chopping wood and bringing it home and we only ever had enough to burn for ourselves. In actual fact, I think my elder cousin Burhan (my aunt's son) used to even give us that. So, unfortunately, I never had any spare logs to take to school. But I had to find a way…

My great uncle Kamil (mum's elder brother) was the Village Imam (priest) and he was also a very good carpenter. He built our house. Uncle Kamil was also very temperamental with a very short fuse. Actually, he and mum were terribly similar in character.

Uncle's house was situated somewhere between our house and the school, so I used to walk past their house on my way to school. My uncle had quite a bit of land which was protected by hedges and a wire fence to keep out other animals.

On my way to school, I would remove one wooden post at a time, randomly from the wire fence so my uncle wouldn't easily notice. Of course, after a number of days of doing this he would eventually notice the gaps! He would then start moaning and swearing while repairing the fence.

Once he became so angry and he started swearing like mad at whoever the person was who was doing it, "I pray to Allah to punish him!" etc. My cousin Kadriye (youngest daughter in his family) tried to calm him down, but when she realised there was no stopping him she said; "Dad, please stop swearing and cursing like that. I think it's our Mevlut who is doing it. He's taking the posts to school for burning." Apparently, he went absolutely berserk!

"How dare he steal from me, shame on him, if he wants to steal, surely he should steal from someone else's fence instead of his own uncle's!"

I was so scared of my uncle, so much so that when Kadriye told me, I avoided him for ages. In our village the relationship between the young and the old was very strict. We were mostly scared of our elders and even the elder brothers and sisters would rule over the younger siblings too.

Years later, when I started to live in the UK, I was completely shocked to see how much more relaxed and friendlier relationships were within a family. I couldn't believe it when I heard kids calling their parents and elders by their first name. It's unheard of in Turkey, even today.

We were mountain people, used to living in harsh conditions. To be honest, I think this enables the development of a stronger character and maybe affects one's attitude to life as well. Our people also had a remarkably interesting sense of humour; we had many quirky characters with fascinating stories. Here are a couple of them to give you a flavour of mountain life.

Coruh Huseyin

Coruh Huseyin was a very short man. He and his family lived next door to my aunt. I spent a lot of time with his two sons, and the younger one was my age.

It was a village tradition to visit the sick with a hot bowl of soup. In those days, we had no electricity in the village. On one early evening, in the moonlight, Coruh and the Village Muhtar (Governor) were on their way to visit a sick neighbour, about fifteen minutes' walk away.

The Muhtar was in front, followed by Coruh holding the soup container trying very hard not to spill it. They were walking along the rocky pathway. Unfortunately, Coruh suddenly tripped and dropped the soup container. Muhtar, sensing what had just happened behind him exclaimed,

"Please be careful Uncle Coruh, don't trip and fall over!" said the Muhtar without looking back to see what had occurred.

"I'm fine Muhtar, just getting up!" said Coruh.

"Please be careful with that soup, don't spill it!" replied Muhtar.

Coruh responded, "I'm looking for the container."

By saying 'getting up' and 'looking for the container' without actually admitting to 'falling over' and 'spilling the soup' our Coruh was being cheeky and also thinking he could save himself from the embarrassment of actually having spilt the soup!

Half Lord (Yarım Aga) Huseyin

I have never been that sure why Huseyin couldn't quite make it to acquire full status as a Lord. It could have been because he was always starting a new business, making a success of it and then losing it all, before repeating the cycle all over again. Sometimes, he would do several things at once, never quite fulfilling his potential in any of them. But he was an amazing character, well respected and loved by everyone. A truly colourful personality. His youngest son told me the following incident many years ago.

Huseyin and his son were sitting in their office in the village. This was in the mid or late nineties. He needed to make an urgent call to his bank manager, but all the phone lines were down. Whenever the son dialled the number he was greeted with a recorded message of a lady; *"All the lines are currently very busy, please try again in 15 minutes."* And each time the son informed Huseyin that the lines were busy, and would then try again in fifteen minutes.

Huseyin was getting very frustrated by not being able to speak to the manager. He kept asking his son to ring back almost every five minutes, still without success.

In the end he exploded and picked up the receiver and dialled the number himself. Just like the son, he was also greeted with the same message, '…please try again in fifteen minutes.' Not even realising that it was a recorded voice message, he started to beg the lady to connect him to the manager!

"My dear lady, it's very urgent, I promise I will only use the phone for a couple of minutes!" but the recorded message just repeated itself and then clicked off. Huseyin was getting angrier and angrier each time. Dialling the number again, it was the same lady with the same message. "Please try again…"

Huseyin exploded; "You f'ing lady, I'm begging you, just two minutes I'm saying, why are you not connecting me, I will come and f'ing kill you". Sadly, Huseyin passed away at the end of 2020, RIP.

The Effect of Talent, Education and Environment on Success

I very much believe in the importance of natural talent. One can learn almost anything by hard work; some better than others, but unless one has the natural ability it's almost impossible to excel. I mean, you could not reach the level that would make you stand out from the crowd, and make you successful.

Like I mentioned before, I had really enjoyed singing many traditional Turkish folk songs since I was very little. I managed to learn the songs and imitate the singer very quickly, and all the different styles too. I don't have a powerful voice, but my song rendering is quite good, if I say so myself.

I always loved the sound of saz (similar to Indian sitar), a traditional Turkish instrument, and I always wanted to learn to play it. We had some great traditional folk singers and songwriters such as Ruhi Su and Neset Ertas. Their singing and playing are just beautiful and I always imagined myself on stage, playing just like them! When I moved to England I got into rock music, and then I started imagining myself playing the guitar like Tony Iommi and David Gilmour. Unfortunately, for the life of me I could play neither the saz nor the guitar, zero, zilch, absolutely useless. Oh well, maybe next time!

At university I stayed at the Sivas student dormitory, named after one of the big cities in central Turkey. It's known for traditional folk singing and saz playing. I shared a room with 7 other people; we had four bunk beds, which made the room look a bit like a prison cell.

One of my cellmates… sorry roommates, was from Sivas and he played amazing saz. I used to listen to him play so many times, and sometimes I would join in with my singing. One day I thought to myself, here's a great opportunity for me to learn to play the saz from this guy. Well, I can't remember how long we were at it, probably well over a year, but I was hardly making any progress. I just wasn't getting it! It was so frustrating for both of us.

One day my friend approached me in a most friendly way, as if to avoid hurting my feelings; "Can we talk, let me treat you to some nice beans too?" Frankly, he couldn't really treat me to anything else, beans were what we almost always had at the dormitory canteen! It was our staple diet. I said, 'Sure, why not' because I fancied some beans myself!

As we started tucking in, as if we hadn't eaten for days, in a hesitant voice he muttered, "I'm going to say something to you, but please promise me you won't get angry!" I replied, "Well, since I don't have a clue as to what you're going to say and how mad it might make me, I'm not sure if I can guarantee anything upfront." With a very soft and comforting voice, as if to make sure not to upset me or rather anger me, he declared; "Look mate, we've been trying this saz thing with you for over a year now, I'm truly sorry to say this to you, but you're absolutely crap at it! You can sing great and imitate great singers, but please give up on the saz, so we can both be saved from anymore suffering!"

It was such a huge disappointment to hear him say it so bluntly, but I knew what he had said was true! Upset yes, but not angry with him, just frustrated at my lack of ability to grasp the concept of musical instruments.

I thanked him for his genuine effort and patience in trying for months. I said to him that he was absolutely right, I was rather crap at it. The reality was that I couldn't even play the bloody simple wooden flute in the village when I was a little kid.

My point about talent will become much clearer when you read how I taught myself programming in just two years, and carved a name for myself in gaming. As you can see it's not all a lost cause regarding instruments; I am rather good at blowing my own trumpet!

My Sporty Side; Football, Table Tennis, Swimming...

I can't really remember when I first kicked a football, but I think it was in the early years of primary school. In fact, I remember how quickly I got the hang of controlling the ball and running around with it. I was really pleased with myself; our teacher was even more so. It was him who spotted my enjoyment, command, and control of the ball. He told me that I displayed a lot of potential. That in itself gave me a lot of confidence. I've always enjoyed playing football though, right through my university years straight through to when I lived in England. I played for the cable factory team when I worked at the Standard Telephones and Cables Company (Southampton). I even played football with my good friend Jon Hare, the man behind Sensible Soccer and Cannon Fodder!

I first experienced table tennis in middle school. Our music teacher was very good at it and he taught us how to play. I learnt it too and became really good at it after only a couple of weeks. At first, I was giving the teacher a really hard time, even in the early days, and a few weeks later I was giving him no chance whatsoever. Even now, I still play table tennis whenever I get a chance. Such a great game; so fast, plus it requires quick reflexes and you get a great workout too.

Years later when I started working at the cable factory, a work colleague (I think his name was Ken, in case he reads the book!) introduced me to squash. It's very similar to table tennis in terms of style and technique. In all honesty, I'd already told him that I was quite good at table tennis, but I'd never held a squash racquet before. To cut a long story short, I learnt the game very quickly, giving my friend a real challenge after half a dozen sessions. What's more, I was thoroughly enjoying it too, even more than table tennis. After a short while, I became really good and started beating him. He couldn't believe how quickly I had become so good. However, I tried tennis a few times in England,

Kazangolu (Pot Lake)

and I just couldn't do it. I never felt confident enough with the game. It was technically different from table tennis and squash and somehow it just didn't suit me.

It was obvious that I was very sporty, I could learn how to play most things quite well in a short space of time.

Back in my childhood, I learnt how to swim in our village river with the other kids.

There was a small pool in the rocks which we would always use. It was about two metres deep at most, surrounded by trees and big rocks. The water was always cold, but we got used to it.

I felt extremely comfortable in the water, swimming like a little fish, and trying to show off too, holding my breath under water, jumping off trees. All of this would really impress my cousins and the other kids, and this made me feel great and encouraged me to do even more. This all added to the confidence I had in myself at such an early age.

Present From The Town Governor, A School Uniform

We used to have lovely weddings in our village lasting for 3 days. It was like a carnival for us kids with wonderful food and lots of sweets. The best cooks in the village would get together and prepare all the favourite dishes with lots of special puddings and sweets. My younger uncle's wife Duriye (RIP) did most of the cooking; she was so amazing and I loved it. I grew up eating her wonderful food and I eventually learnt to cook most of it myself. I still continue to cook quite a bit of it at home.

The Georgians living in Turkey managed to keep most of their local traditions such as singing, dancing, food and wedding ceremonies. Until now, I haven't told you that I'm a Georgian, how did I miss that out? Yes, both my parents are Georgian, in fact, our whole village was. In the early 1900s, our ancestors came and settled first in Artvin (Eastern Black Sea) and then in Ordu (Central Black Sea), both seaside towns. I am such a proud Georgian and I really like our traditions and culture.

When they first arrived in Ordu, the Georgians settled quite close to the main city in the surrounding villages. The biggest local produce of Ordu is hazelnut, in fact one of the biggest producers in the world. Unfortunately, our people left Ordu and went way inland, about fifty miles away from Ordu, and high up into the mountains! Apparently, they ran away from the mosquitoes and malaria. We used to tease our elders by saying "Okay, we understand why you decided to run away, but for God's sake, leaving all those hazelnut fields behind and settling in this God forsaken, good for nothing mountain village, why?"

In our village it was difficult to grow most vegetables, and the only major crop we grew were potatoes and corn. Of course, hazelnut has always been such a valuable product. In recent years our villagers also decided to plant hazelnuts, but the climate isn't quite right for it.

As I already mentioned, the village weddings were wonderful. Young and old, male and female would dance and feast together for ages. The Black Sea region is mostly known for Horon, a traditional dance. Our villagers adopted some of the Horon dances and mixed them slightly with the original dance routines from Georgia. It was quite different to the traditional Black Sea Horon and to the Georgian dance. It was almost as if they had created their own set of Horon dances, a fusion of both cultures. We grew up with these fast Horons and used to dance our hearts out at weddings.

The Horons were accompanied by a Davul (drum) and a Zurna (Shawm), a woodwind pipe instrument. We were lucky to have a Zurna master, Kemik Huseyin, from a neighbouring village. Huseyin was the best of the best. I could dance to his zurna playing for hours and that's exactly what we did at weddings. Some of our elders were extremely good at the Horon and we would try to imitate them. I loved performing the Horon at every opportunity we would get.

Like me there were two other kids who were rather good at Horon; Horoz (Roaster) Mehmet and Koreli (Korean) Selahattin (so called because his father had gone to the Korean War in 1950). We became the famous trio. Every now and then, several village schools would get together for a big event; all day we would run, play football, dance etc.

On one occasion we had the Town Governor attending the event and our teacher asked us three kids to perform the dance… and dance we did! The Governor was extremely impressed, and he decided to give us school uniforms as presents. We were absolutely chuffed; I was so happy. We used to wear a black top with a white neck collar for our uniform. Of course, the ones our parents bought or made for us were from the cheapest cloth you could get, but the uniforms given to us were unbelievable, beautiful, silky smooth cloth. I didn't want to wear it for fear of damaging it. In fact, I finished my primary school with it still intact!

This simple present impacted my life in a such an important and profound way. In my early years I started seeing that I was a bit better at some things than other kids around me. Our teacher would always say lots of encouraging things to me about my class performance, as well as my achievements at sporting events. Being awarded a gift or honour by the Governor was the seal of approval, which boosted my confidence to another level. I was levelling up, just like in games.

I believe confidence is just as important as talent, knowledge, and experience, if not more. I benefited from my confidence throughout my life.

After relocating to Turkey in 2000, I had a few chances to dance the Horon with my cousins and relatives. It was so nice to relive some of the old memories. The young ones were especially impressed by my performance, but it was nothing like the good old days… it never is. It's such a shame to lose some of the old ways and traditions. I guess the younger generation doesn't even know what they're missing!

Natural Skiing

Whenever we kids did something together I was the one who generally organized it. I don't like taking risks, but I enjoy being at the forefront of things, especially if I'm good at them. I get a lot of joy out of my own success, but I never deliberately show off or take it to the point of being arrogant.

But at the same time, when I feel really proud of my achievement, I wouldn't be too modest, and wait for others' praise or acknowledgement. As I said before I couldn't learn to play the saz or the guitar, but I do know how to blow my own trumpet! I believe I do this in acceptable and balanced measures.

Despite all of the success I have had, people still consider me a down-to-earth, modest and very approachable person. In all sincerity, I hope you will think the same by the end of the book. Indeed, I respond to every message I ever get from young developers seeking my advice or gamers who have played my games.

Behind our school there was a very steep hill, and in the winter we used it as our skiing slope. You will remember that we only wore simple black rubber shoes; no boots, no wellingtons, no nothing. And we wore these rubber shoes all year round too. I can tell you they are not very comfortable in the summer, so it's a good job it never got too hot in the highlands! Also, because of the constant wear, our shoes would become smooth underneath, just like the F1 tyres after 15 laps or so!

Imagine us in the icy winter conditions; we couldn't walk straight without skidding and sliding. Not that we wanted to walk straight. We turned the whole thing into a lot of fun. We would walk to and from school ski walking and, when we skied down a hill, believe me it was probably as fast as using skis.

There was a kid by the name of Tahsin in our class, chubbier than most of us and with a huge backside! We would take Tahsin to the top of the hill behind the school, sit him down, two of us either side and holding his legs, carefully drag him right down to the bottom, thus creating a long straight ski slope! We did this after school before we went home, so that the next day we would have a fantastically fast ski slope all ready and prepared. If it snowed a little overnight, then that was even better, as it covered the icy slope and sprayed snow all over the place when we went down it.

Full of excitement, we couldn't wait for the morning and to try out our new slope. As usual, I was expected to try it first. In truth, I didn't need much encouragement, but all the kids would start cheering me on, daring me to break a new record. I really cannot remember if any of us had a watch, I certainly didn't. I bought my first watch just after middle school I think. They probably counted, but I had no idea really if I was faster or slower! I couldn't count with all that excitement and adrenalin, but even if I could have, the other kids probably wouldn't have said it was fair!

So, I went to the top and all the others crowded at the bottom, watching and waiting in anticipation. It had snowed a little more than expected, so I could only just make out the path, but what could go wrong? It was just straight down the hill!

My ski pole was a single one-meter long, strong stick and I held it with both hands, slightly at an angle to balance myself and control the speed. Suddenly, I started the descent! I was only a few meters into the slope, and instantly I felt scared. It was as if I was going faster than ever before, in fact, way too fast. I thought I was literally flying! My wooden ski pole wasn't much use against the combination of tremendous velocity and soft snow.

I could hear the kids shouting and screaming with excitement, cheering, and clapping. I could even hear some saying, 'he's too fast, definitely a new record!' I was more than halfway when my foot caught a bump! No kidding, I literally took off head first, completely out of control rolling like a big snow ball hurtling towards the wall of the mosque at the bottom of the slope. The other kids, not realising the severity of what was happening, continued with their cheering and screaming. Bam! Crash! I suddenly hit the wall with a tremendous wallop! It was a horrible impact. Apparently, I was lying very still with blood pouring out of my nose and skull!

I was so lucky to have survived. I wouldn't have been so fortunate, if it weren't for our wonderful teacher. Our teacher, in effect, was also the village chemist and doctor. Maybe they purposely sent teachers with extra knowledge and skills, or maybe most teachers were like that in those days because most villages were remote and miles away from the towns and hospitals. In the heavy winter conditions, and without electricity or transport, we couldn't go anywhere and the roads could be closed for days even weeks.

I was saved by my teacher's immediate action and first-aid treatment. Only when I came round did I realise what had happened; I felt great pain, very sore and aching all over my body. I remained bandaged for some while, my teacher dressing my wound and replacing the bandage a few times.

As an Only Child Living With Many Kids in Other Homes

Until we had our little house built, my mum and I lived with our relatives a few days or weeks at a time. We had relatives in almost every corner of the village and we would randomly visit them one after the other. We were like nomads, always on the move. We did this all year round, and for years. Although we were welcomed and loved by everybody, it was really tough for me. I never felt comfortable or happy with moving around like that.

And I was happier at some relatives more than others. This was largely because some treated me with more affection and compassion, and also some had kids of my age with whom I could play with and have more fun.

Because my dad had abandoned us when I was still a baby, my mum would only stay with her own relatives. It wasn't until much later that I would also go and stay with my dad's.

There were a few favourite relatives who I always looked forward to spending time with. One such family was Moda Mehmet's place (moda as in trendy, because he always dressed immaculately). Turgut, their elder son, and I were almost the same age, and we were like brothers. We really enjoyed spending time together, and, Moda Mehmet and his wonderful wife Gulayse were very generous and welcoming too.

Moda Mehmet's father was Mehmet Ali; one of the well-respected elders of the village, who lived on the other side of the river. I also enjoyed staying with them because they loved us so much and always made us feel at home. Uncle Mehmet Ali was the one who always gave me pocket money on Saturdays, so I could go to the cinema with the other kids. Almost the entire village would be in Golkoy on Saturdays. Villagers would come to sell their produce, such as potatoes, eggs or even animals, and at the same time do their town shopping.

Saturdays for us kids was a very important occasion, as we would go and hang out in town and go to the pictures. Also, we would swim in the famous Skylake (Gokgolu).

Although Moda Mehmet was a nice man, both Turgut and I would receive quite a few hidings from him, and these would always be encouraged by mother! In the winter months we did a lot of skiing with Turgut. Their house was surrounded by lovely woods and lots of hills, which was perfect for skiing and playing in the snow. Frequently, we would ski but sometimes we would just roll down the long hills like a snowball for miles. It was amazing fun. We would get soaking wet at the end of it, which my mother really hated. The poor thing would complain that I was ruining my trousers and she couldn't afford new ones! Seeing that my mother was really cross and upset, Moda would give us quite a bit of a telling off, followed by a couple of slaps. But it was so obvious he had no intention of hurting us, he just did it to please mum! I used to see her look content, as if that had taught us not to do it again. But we always did it again and again, as that was the only fun we could have in the winter months and we loved every bit of it. We weren't going to give it up just because of a telling off.

Most families had plenty of land, and quite a few animals too. I would be with many of the kids who shepherded their animals all day long. We were supposed to keep a close eye on the animals to prevent them from entering neighbouring lands and also crops. But most of the time, we would be immersed in playing and completely forget about them. We would receive a lot of telling offs of course, and I used to feel very bad and guilty about this as I always felt it was my fault. Things like this made me feel really uncomfortable about staying at other people's homes. Afterwards, I would always be more careful than the kids of the household about watching out for the animals, just so that the parents wouldn't scold us.

No matter how much I was liked or welcomed, there were always small things, which would remind me that I was at someone else's house. For instance, sometimes the kids would go and take something out of the cupboard to eat, nothing special, just a piece of bread or a biscuit or something. They just didn't think of offering it to me, perhaps they simply thought I should help myself too. They probably saw me as part of the family but I just couldn't find the courage or feel comfortable about helping myself, I felt so uneasy about it. Even nowadays when I go to my cousins or close relatives, I tend to decline their offer of staying the night. I still feel the discomfort and unease.

'There's no place like home!' as Dorothy in the Wizard of Oz rightly puts it!

Visiting My Aunt in The Neighbouring Village Yuvapinar

My mother was the youngest of five siblings with two brothers and two sisters. We became neighbours with my eldest aunt when our little house was built. The other aunt married someone from Yuvapinar; another Georgian village about three hours walk from ours. We would go there once or twice a year and stay for a few weeks. I really enjoyed my time there; it was a bit like a holiday further up in the mountains. Certainly, it was always good to see them. Everyone there liked me a lot, especially the kids, who for some reason were always happy to see me. Perhaps, I was bringing fresh ideas into their games? They really enjoyed spending time with me, which of course made me feel very happy to be there too.

But I would always dread the terrible walk to get there; I just hated that long trek. It seemed to take forever with my little feet, as I was only five or six years old. Plus, I was already tired of walking to and from school, as well as travelling the length and breadth of the village all year round.

Forty-five minutes into our walk, I would start moaning and continually ask mum for a break. I would really give my poor mum a hard time for the duration of the trip. In the end, she would just lift me onto her shoulders, and carry me for ten minutes just to shut me up! That shoulder ride was amazing; I must have really enjoyed it. Luckily for mum, doing it once would do the trick and I would walk the rest of the way. Maybe I knew she wouldn't do it more than once and if I tried my luck, I may have not got it at all. It was a good compromise. I can never repay my mum! I hope she's happy wherever she is because she deserves it as much as anyone. (RIP)

Middle School – Golkoy

I consider the middle school years the most important in developing one's personality; it's the first important step into maturity; shaping personality and character and making us distinctive as individuals.

This is when we start to understand and learn better too. Through interaction with new people and environments, we gain new experiences that help with character formation. This is also when we discover more of our inner talent and natural inclination towards things. Aptitude, you could say.

Middle School, 2018   Gokgolu (Skylake), 2018

Here we go again, it was more walking to school; no school bus or any sort of bus back then. This time from village to town, and the walk was even longer and much tougher. We had to walk the rocky paths up and down massive hills. It was a bit easier going to school, as it was mostly downhill, but coming back home was exhausting, especially after a long, tough school day.

I used to pay a lot attention to what the village elders would say about life in general. There were so many proverbs, most of which I still clearly remember, and use. I find it fascinating that after having lived in the UK for over twenty years, I had nearly completely forgotten my native Turkish when I returned to Turkey, and yet I still remembered many of the proverbs.

I must have been very young when I first heard from a village elder, 'never to tread on a piece of bread, as it was blessed food, and it should be picked up and placed by the side of the road.' After some thought I came to the conclusion that this must make it easier for the birds to eat the breadcrumbs.

As a result, I was always looking in front of me while walking, to avoid stepping on any breadcrumbs. Whenever I saw any, I would pick them up immediately and place them on the side of the road. It felt so good to be able to do my little bit to help the birds; I always get a lot of positive energy from performing good deeds. Even now, I get so much satisfaction and joy out of helping young people whenever they come to me for advice.

Walking so attentively also made me very sensitive about ants and other creatures on the ground. I could easily say; 'I wouldn't harm an ant', which is an important saying in Turkish culture indicating good heart, similar to 'I wouldn't hurt a fly'. I'm not a religious man, but I do believe in something special. Indeed, I very much respect nature and all its glorious colours and creatures, including us humans.

Ever since I had started noticing the wonderful ants, and other creatures, I always believed that we ought to be equal. I don't believe for one second that humans are superior. Our intelligence gives us an advantage, but it shouldn't give us the right to dominate other living beings. If we were to treat the natural world as equals, then I am sure we wouldn't have all the inequalities that exist in our societies throughout the world. Inequality between colour, gender, race and religion – without it the world would be a much better place.

I can't remember what subjects I liked the most during my middle school years, but I hardly did any studying. Usually I would only do enough homework to satisfy the teacher, rather than try and achieve top marks. I must have mentioned that we had no electricity at home in those days and I remember having just a simple oil lamp, which hardly gave any light. Truly, it was so difficult to study with it, but I wasn't exactly dying to complete my homework.

I remember being utterly and completely useless at art; I still cannot draw a stick man. It's really weird that I failed at art in the same way that I did with guitar and saz. I cannot fully comprehend 3D modelling, and the complex and intricate looking buildings always amaze me. Some of them are just pure works of art.

I first discovered my failure at art in middle school when our art teacher sat us all in front of the lovely big tree in our schoolyard, and asked us to draw it. Some of the drawings from other kids were just brilliant, some looked like exact copies, which was very impressive. Tragically, mine looked nothing like it; in fact, it didn't even look like a tree. Well, my art teacher made it very clear that I had a long way to go and I would have to work really hard to improve my art skills. Most people think he put me off, he didn't help for sure, but I don't think he was the reason. I'm just not good at drawing, just like I'm not good at some other things. My orientation is awfully bad; I'm a lousy navigator and can get lost very easily. Also, I'm unbelievably bad at playing computer games, which is quite pathetic considering I've been making games for over thirty years!

Lucky To Be Alive!

This is something I will never forget as long as I live. Near our house was Uncle Pehlul, my dad's uncle. Both my mum and I spent a lot of time there, as both Pehlul and his wife were close relatives. Pehlul's wife was my mum's aunt and he was my dad's uncle. Like I said, most Georgian villagers were related to each other.

Uncle Pehlul had two daughters and four sons; the eldest son was always away working in big cities. I spent a lot of time with the brothers Ali and Bekir. When I started middle school, I also started spending more time with people much older than me, rather than my peers, as I seemed to enjoy their company more. In some ways, I felt like I had matured too quickly. I still went swimming and did other things with my friends, but I spent a lot more quality time with the elders. But it was Bekir that I spent most of my time with. He was such an intelligent and witty man and always very nice to me. In the past he had also worked in some big cities, did some coal mining too, but after a while he stopped completely. He wasn't contributing to the household at all, but just lazing around the house. As you can probably appreciate, Uncle Pehlul wasn't very happy about it, but Bekir just didn't care. I cannot remember the exact details, but I did once hear a rumour that he fell in love with a girl in the village. However, the parents didn't approve of the marriage. This made Bekir very rebellious against life in general, refusing to do any work and take any responsibility for anything. Eventually, he did get married later in life and had a couple of sons. The eldest, Muhammed studied computer science and successfully graduated from one of the top universities in Turkey, Istanbul Technical University. He was inspired by my success in computer games.

Uncle Bekir and I did have a lot of fun together in their beautiful old two-storey timber house. They mainly lived on the first floor with the living room, kitchen and a couple bedrooms. Almost every day, we played football in the house. I cannot begin to tell you how much fun we had. We had one of those highly bouncy, dense, tiny rubber balls, about the size of a squash ball. They were so bouncy and very difficult to control in the house with furniture everywhere. It was just crazy how the ball bounced around like mad, falling into pots, going under shelves, beds, all over the place. There was also live commentary from us. "Wow, this is unbelievable, another great pass by Mevlut, as the ball goes right into the big pot by the goal, the ball bounces back out of the pot, and towards Mevlut's head, what a fantastic pass by the big pot; and, yes, beautifully headed by Mevlut! I must say that was another spectacular goal! Excellent play by Mevlut and the Pot, it's driving the opposition absolutely potty!"

I stated earlier that walking back home from middle school was a lot harder, especially in the winter. Sometimes the snowfall would completely obscure the pathway and it would be so difficult to follow the route on a very rocky terrain. It was very dangerous and at times we would get heavy snowstorms and we couldn't see each other. Heavy snow, hard wind and thick fog made it so difficult to walk at a decent pace. We weren't exactly protected with winter clothing either. I really cannot remember what we wore in those dreadful conditions. I certainly don't remember having a winter coat; we probably just wore layers of jumpers and a thick jacket with a woollen scarf and gloves, probably knitted by our mums.

One afternoon, a bad snowstorm started after school, so everybody decided not to risk walking back to the village in those difficult conditions and instead would stay the night at their relatives. My Imam uncle's family stayed in their town house in the winter instead of the village. I could have stayed the night at my uncle's, but as I grew older I wanted to stay less and less at other people's homes, no matter how closely related. I told the other kids that I was going to walk back to the village. They all said I was crazy, and one of them even offered to go with him to stay the night at his relatives, but I declined. It was a bit insane, and I was taking a huge risk by going to the village all on my own in a big storm like that.

First of all, I started walking at a brisk pace to get home as soon as I could. As I climbed up the hill, the fog became denser and the snowfall heavier, as did my feet. I was slowly walking through the deep snow. I started to feel the cold, and became worried for the first time. I was just moving forward on instinct, hoping that I could make it home somehow. All the while, it was getting harder to make out the path. I must have been about halfway before I started feeling very tired, I thought about walking back to town rather than continuing, but I still moved forward. Suddenly, I felt someone coming up behind me. Before I could turn, there was a hand on my shoulder. I couldn't believe it, it was Bekir, the last person I expected to see. I was so relieved; he most probably saved my life. For the rest of the trail, he led from the front and I followed with a newfound energy.

Bekir would sometimes go to town to gamble and stay the night, and would then come back to the village in the morning. Gambling was such a big problem in our village. Bekir's father gambled a lot too. In fact, my uncle Ahmet, mum's younger of the two brothers, was one of the wealthiest and most respected people in town, but he tragically lost everything to gambling and afterwards he left town, and his family, for good!

As a general rule, Bekir would normally spend the night in town, especially in a storm like that. But on that occasion he decided to go home and so early too. Maybe he wanted to get home before the weather worsened or he had lost all his money. I'll never know why, but what I do know is that Bekir (RIP) probably saved my life!

Uncle Bekir

My cousins Gulderen (far right) and Ali and friend Ates (who helped with the first edit of the Turkish book)

This photo was taken in 2018 on the very path where Bekir came to my rescue.

My Sporty Side Develops Even More During Middle School

Soon after learning table tennis from my music teacher, I was beating everyone, including the music teacher. In fact, some of the teachers would play me for

Friends from Middle School (Me at the back), 1970

soda and simit (a traditional crunchy-sesame bagel). Since I was always winning, it meant I had a free lunch, which would allow me to save my daily pocket money of 25 kurus for a rainy day!

You could just buy a quarter loaf of bread with 25 kurus, so saving up would mean that I could treat myself to my favourite tahini halva (traditional Turkish sweet). A favourite of mine still is a fresh quarter bread, halva and some cold water to wash it down. I try not to buy a lot of halva these days as I cannot resist it and once I've started it goes too quickly. Not the healthiest of foods, especially at my age!

We all loved going to the pictures on Saturdays, it was probably the most exciting entertainment for us kids, but it cost 1 Turkish

Lira (TL), which was like 4 days' worth of pocket money. But, thanks to my teachers I could save up enough money to treat myself to the cinema too.

The only time we could go to the cinema was after school on Wednesdays or Saturdays because they were both half days of classes. We also had teachers patrolling after school hours to make sure we weren't out in the evenings, so, we could never go to the evening shows in the week either. So it was Saturdays when we would often go. Fortunately, the latest movies would always premiere on Saturdays, as that's when all the villagers would flock to town. Us kids would really look forward to the Saturday matinees to see our favourite stars.

A Couple of Stories About the Cinema...

My cousin Ilhan was the eldest son of my younger uncle Ahmet, the one who lost everything gambling. They lived in town when we were about three years old, and my mum and I stayed with them quite a bit. After losing everything and my uncle abandoning them, my cousins then had to go and live in the village.

I really can't remember when I first went to the pictures, but I loved it. I already had several favourite actors and couldn't wait to see their new movies. One Saturday, there was this action movie starring one my favourite actors, Orhan Gunsiray. It didn't matter what rating the movie was, as there was no age restriction as such. My cousin Ilhan and I were going to the cinema together for the first time. He told me he'd never been before, we were probably seven at the time and it was going to be his first movie experience. I was really excited as it was my favourite actor, but Ilhan was even more excited, continuously asking me what it was like and what sort of film it would be. I said that it would be a lot of fun with some action, our hero beating up lots of baddies and there might be guns too. We were used to guns, some of the village elders would show off their guns at weddings! They would have firing competitions on swinging eggs hanging from the tree branches. The champion was a one-eyed guy, which presumably made it easier for him to aim. He would win every time!

Anyway, the cinema was full, and the movie started straightaway with ten minutes of action, fighting, fists and bullets flying. I could sense that Ilhan was tense and worried, especially after the guns started firing. I tried to comfort him by whispering that it wasn't real, it was a movie and it was going to be okay. Well, the action really intensified, and our hero had a gun in his hand with what seemed like unlimited ammunition firing away like mad, suddenly chasing the big boss. He was running towards the screen as if he was firing at us and the bullets were flying over our heads. Ilhan suddenly disappeared under his seat, hiding from the oncoming bullets while holding his head down. He was so scared, even though I tried to reassure him that it wasn't real! Realising everyone was okay, he sat back in his chair and watched the rest of the film without any other problems. We laughed so much afterwards. Ilhan still loves telling this story.

As I've said, Saturday was the most important day for both the villagers and the town people. The villagers would come to town to sell their produce and animals, and then they would shop for things they didn't have in the village like sugar or salt.

Some of the kids would go early in the morning before school with their families to help carry the goods to town. They would ask the teacher for special leave and the teacher would always grant it.

It would be like a festival for us as we mixed with the town kids, playing football, going for a swim in our lovely lake, Gokgolu (Named 'Skylake' because of the lovely blue colour) or just going to the cinema. Some kids would not only help carry the produce to town, but also help sell it in the market. I was very poor, but I never had to do this since we didn't have any produce of our own. In a way, this made me feel quite privileged, which probably helped me appreciate things even in those days.

I didn't always manage to save up enough pocket money to go to the cinema. As I mentioned, I would be given pocket money mostly by uncle Mehmet Ali, but also other older relatives would give me some if they saw me in town. Once I had enough pocket money I could then go to the pictures with my friends. Generally, I would hang around at the cattle market, where most of the elders would be, buying or selling animals.

On one Saturday I was just wandering around the market as usual, looking for my cinema angel (the person kind enough to give me money to go to the pictures), greeting my elders to make sure they had seen me; a gentle nudge here and there as I would I never ever have asked for any directly. I forgot how many times I went around, up and down the market, but no luck at all that day. For some reason nobody was paying me any attention. Maybe everyone was having a bad day. The situation was worsened by the absence of my biggest cinema angel, uncle Mehmet Ali, who would usually come to the rescue at the last minute.

My friends were getting impatient as the matinee approached, trying to hurry me as if there was anything I could do. I was gently nudging into people but nothing, not a sausage. I was extra especially sad because they were showing a Yilmaz Guney film, my all-time favourite actor. My friends didn't want to wait much longer, they didn't want to miss the beginning, nor did I, but what could I do?

I was so upset, crying inside, so I decided to do one more round of bumping, nudging and greeting everyone. Most of them just greeted me back; "How are you Mevlut?" But nothing more, nobody was digging into their pockets!

I gave up and started walking back towards the cinema. As I was leaving the market someone tapped me on the shoulder, I turned to see one of our relatives, Pepel Mehmet. I don't remember him ever giving me money before, but he just handed me a one lira coin!

Oh my God, I cannot put into words how happy I was. With the money clenched in my fist, I ran like mad to catch the beginning of the film.

I went straight to the ticket office, handed over my money and waited impatiently for my ticket. I was completely out of breath, and I was going to miss the start of the film. The guy behind the counter was double-checking the coin I gave him before handing me the ticket. His face suddenly changed though, looking like a raging bull, and I didn't know what had happened to make him so angry! He started shouting and swearing with all the expletives under the sun, "How dare you, you little cheating bastard? You think you can fool me with your little brain?" He kept swearing and throwing insults at me for a bit, and then tried to throw the coin back at me through the little window!

"You little bastard, trying to cheat me with an outdated coin, eh? Get out of here, you fucking so and so, before I kill you!"

I started running like mad again, but this time away from the cinema. I was so scared, and upset. I just couldn't understand what had happened. I was the happiest kid in the world a few minutes before, and now this. Such conflicting feelings, I was absolutely gobsmacked and must have cried for ages. My relative had, inadvertently, given me an outdated coin that was no longer valid. What upset me the most was the fact that the guy called me a cheat! Of course, he didn't know whether I had tried it on or not, but he had always liked me before, and so his reaction was just too much.

After the incident, I avoided going to the cinema for a few weeks to avoid him. In the end I told my friends what had happened, and one of my friend's fathers explained everything to the man and all was okay again. I could then go to the cinema again, but I didn't forget that incident for a very long time. And I always double-checked my coins from then on to make sure, especially for the cinema!

My Own Film Making Attempts...

I remember having quite a few vaccinations in the middle school years. Of course, we never knew the importance of it, but we had no choice about having them. As I write these lines the world is trying to find the vaccine that will save us all from the deadly Covid-19!

Health officers would visit the school to carry out the vaccinations. Injections are still one of the most terrifying things that can happen to me. I am not kidding, even today I'm still very reluctant to give blood samples, even the thought of it terrifies me. My daughter Sila is just like me, she tries to avoid them at all costs! I don't remember my son Nej being that scared when he was little, but he had all his vaccinations done in the UK.

As a side note, the fear of snakes is another big phobia of mine; it's the fact that you cannot see where they are, and no chance of knowing when they are about to sneak up on you. I always avoided walking in overgrown grass.

One of the health officers was Cemal, a relative from the village. I really didn't have to have it done and I can't remember how it was carried out in those days. Maybe it wasn't even via injection, possibly with just a razor blade, so no wonder I was scared shitless. Excuse my French! So, I made a run for it, jumped out of the window and tried to wait it out in the yard until Cemal went away. I thought he would overlook my absence as we were related. Plus, he really loved me, as we would spend so much time together in the village.

Nevertheless, he sent one of the boys after me with a message; "I promise not to vaccinate him, he can come back." I really liked Cemal, and fully trusted him. In fact, I thought he would let me get away with it, and so I went back like the gullible fool I am. Of course, he did vaccinate me, while trying to convince me of how important it was. If I were to catch a virus or something I may not able to make films with him ever again!

While Bekir and I played a lot of football, Cemal and I made a lot of pretend films. We would mimic our favourite actors! There were several very famous and popular actors and actresses at the time to choose from. My first favourite was Orhan Gunsiray opposite Ayhan Isik and as I grew older Yilmaz Guney, an internationally well-known and award-winning talented actor/director became the favourite, at this time alongside Cuneyt Arkin, who was another very famous Turkish actor. Cemal would spend most weekends at their second home opposite our little house. They had a beautiful place with lots of green hills and open fields. It was perfect for grazing cattle. God, we used to roll around on those hills and fields for hours acting out our action movies. Cemal was a tall and well-built, handsome guy, he could have easily been a real actor. We used our imagination to come up with lots of pretend scenes, but it was mostly action with fighting! We had

Yilmaz Guney   Orhan Gunsiray   Ayhan Isik   Golkoy Cinema

the perfect setting and location for jumping and rolling about at will. I would be the hero most of the time, and always win.

Sometimes we would get so carried away with our acting that I would feel as if I could become a real actor, and make my own movies too. However, I never had a chance to make a real movie, but I did end up making and working on quite a number of action adventure games with both ninjas and samurais!

Who knows, perhaps in all of the fancy scripts and acting in those lovely fields, the seeds for my future gaming career were sown?

Languages and Pronunciation

I never had to retake any of my subjects in middle school, although I hardly studied or did much homework. However, I always managed to achieve high enough grades to pass. But I was rather good at some subjects, I remember getting top marks in Science and French. I was, in fact, the best in the class at French. I managed to learn the grammar quickly and easily, but never worked enough to develop my vocabulary. My French continued to be strong at high school too; I was also the top student there.

While talking on the subject of French, I remember an incident with one of my childhood friends from the village, Bocuk Ali (Insect Ali - almost everyone had a nickname in our village, although I don't actually remember having one myself!). We were in the same class with Bocuk and during one French lesson, the teacher, for a quick test called him to the blackboard. Georgians have a real problem with the pronunciation of certain letters. For instance, instead of 'F' we use 'P', which sounds completely different! In Turkish we have two different usages for the letter 'I', one with the cedilla on top 'i' and one without 'ı' (lower case 'i' but without a cedilla), which doesn't exists in English. Both sound very different from one another; 'i' sounds as in the word 'bring' whereas the 'ı' sounds more as in the word 'milk'.

So, the French word 'rouge' in Turkish is 'kırmızı', but our Bocuk always pronounced it as 'kirmizi', which sounds very different and also very wrong in Turkish. The funny thing is that the French teacher himself was from our village and a Georgian too, so he should have known better. But whenever the teacher said 'rouge' our poor Bocuk would say 'kirmizi', so unsatisfied, the teacher would repeat the French word hoping or expecting Bocuk to correct himself. But Bocuk was unable to correct himself, and he paused, thinking to himself "I'm one hundred per cent sure it is red (kirmizi). In fact, he uttered the word 'kirmizi' each time getting more and more confused, and less sure! On the 4th attempt, the teacher gave Bocuk a clip round the ear, continually repeating the correct pronunciation "it's kırmızı, my son, kırmızı!"

Poor Bocuk was already having enough difficulty with the French lessons, and the last thing he wanted was to worry about his Turkish pronunciation!

Another Anecdote With Bocuk

As you may remember we only did half-days at school on Saturdays. To help their parents, some kids asked for leave in the morning, so they could go to town with their parents and set up the market and manage the stalls. More often than not, the teacher would grant this but sometimes the teacher would decline; either when everyone asked for leave or he wasn't exactly convinced that the kids were really needed for help.

On one occasion almost everyone had asked for the day off including me! The teacher was just saying no to everyone. Nevertheless, our Bocuk left it too late to ask, but with great determination, kept raising his hand to try his luck. The teacher simply said "No, that's it; no more, let your parents manage without you tomorrow!" More determined than ever, Bocuk kept his hand up and was continually waving it to catch the teacher's attention. The teacher had just about enough and said; "I said no, Ali, just no, your parents will manage, come to school tomorrow, and that's that!" Bocuk said, "But Sir, I don't want the day off to help my parents." The teacher puzzled, said, "what then?" and Bocuk replied, "Sir, I'm going to be very ill tomorrow!" The teacher and the entire school, yes, all five classes, couldn't stop laughing!

High School Years, ORDU...

Ordu is a lovely seaside town in the central Black Sea region and was a three-hour drive back then from our town Golkoy. Nowadays with improved and shortened roads it only takes around one and a half hours.

I had never been to Ordu town centre before starting high school, although we had come to the surrounding villages for hazelnut picking a few times. If it weren't for my mum, I wouldn't have started high school at all because everyone was advising against it. Even though everybody thought I was very clever, and good with my studies, nobody wanted me to continue with my education. They simply told mum that I should just start working somewhere as an apprentice, and become a professional tailor or something. Obviously we were very poor, and back then mum couldn't even afford to send me to high school, let alone university. I never imagined myself going to university anyway, but at least high school would be good I thought.

But mum took me to Ordu and she started working at a hazelnut factory. She rented a room from a family she knew, and we started living in Ordu. My father also started paying me more attention and getting closer to me at around this time. He worked at Ulusoy Coach and Travel Company in the city of Samsun, a major Black Sea city, a hundred miles west of Ordu and during school holidays I started staying with him there. Dad also started supporting me, giving me some spending money, buying my schoolbooks and more importantly clothes. All of this made my high school years much more manageable.

Everything was very unplanned though, without any real goals or aspirations on my part. I first went to the general high school, but after a month I decided to register with the commercial high school thinking that after graduation I would be able find a job at a bank, since I had no chance or wish of going to university.

As in middle school, I was doing well in my studies; I was the top student in French and typing. The French teacher would sit me at his desk during exams to prevent me from helping others. But I would write the answers on small pieces of paper, roll them up and throw the paper back when the teacher couldn't see. I still can't believe how I was never caught but it's very possible that the teacher did see me and simply ignored it. He was really fond of me, he thought I had great potential and promised he would help me go to France to study at university! I had no idea how I was supposed to do that, but it still felt good. I'm sure he was just encouraging me to improve my French even more.

Isn't life amazing? I never did go to France after high school, but I did go to the UK instead, and without speaking a word of English! But eventually, I would also go to France in the 90s, to produce a couple of games with Ubisoft, a major French publisher.

University Years - Ankara, Istanbul

My father started paying me more attention, and embracing me as a son. He first saw me when I was around ten, and now I had finished high school and become a young man ready to go to university. Although I had no intention initially, I was encouraged by dad's support and attention and I entered the university exams.

There were three commercial science academies; in Ankara, Istanbul and Eskisehir, which the commercial high school students could apply for. I achieved surprisingly high results, which allowed me to choose from all three. The Ankara one was the best of the three, and also the nearest to Samsun where my father was, so I registered at the Ankara Economic and Commercial Science Academy with my dad. He bought me all the schoolbooks and some clothes as well. Ankara is the capital city and that was the first time I had ever seen it.

I was now a university student, and my dad was getting more and more involved with me. Although he was able to help financially, it wasn't enough, so we also applied for a student loan.

The university years in the mid to late 70's were the most difficult times that Turkey had ever faced, and I still hope Turkey never has to face such trying times ever again. I have no idea how we managed to survive, let alone study. At some point the student riots and uprisings got completely out of hand, with political fractions fighting each other. The division wasn't just with students, it was widespread everywhere, the teachers unions, the police force, and even the army.

Frankly, I just used all my common sense, reasoning and intellect to survive it. We were staying at a private student dormitory, Sivas, named after a major city in Anatolia. It was a new dormitory and so were the students staying there, so they had no political affiliation or direction. Therefore, we were a good target to influence and recruit by both the left and the right-wing groups. Moreover, universities and dormitories were under the influence and the control of these two main groups.

Horrifyingly, our dormitory was attacked a couple of times; on one occasion we were shot at from the dormitory opposite during the night. Unbelievably, one of the other students was actually shot in the knee while they were asleep. Luckily that was the only casualty, but we were so scared and we couldn't recover from the shock for months. The police came the next day to investigate, but they did nothing more than ask a few questions, and then promptly leaving as though nothing had ever happened.

In that terrible period in history, there were to be many incidents of heavy fighting and bloodshed between the student groups, to either gain or keep control of universities. Tragically, many students died, all very young and probably with a great future ahead of them. Their precious lives were wasted, all for the sake of politics. It was a shocking tragedy. You may find it hard to relate to that level of violence. It was indeed a horror to endure and a dark time in Turkish history.

Lucky to Overcome The Troubled Times...

Our university was under the political influence and control of a strong right-wing group. A group of police would be present to prevent any possible trouble or fighting. Of course, the strange thing was that the police force itself was divided too, and if the left-wing police group was present, then the left-wing students could come to school and at least take some lessons!

We only ever turned up if there were important classes or exams, otherwise we stayed well away. Although, we had some great lecturers, unfortunately we couldn't really benefit from them. I was also hanging out with a small group of friends, one of whom was the daughter of the Governor of Ankara, which did help to make our lives so much easier. We were almost untouchable because of her; she was, after all, the daughter of the most powerful official in town. As such, we were still able to go to school but it didn't help with our studies much because some of the lecturers, depending on their political affiliation, wouldn't always be able to come either due to the threats from the student groups. Crazy times, indeed!

Political Polarisation; The Biggest Enemy of Society

In truth, the main political polarisation was amongst the students and the workers. It also spread like wild fire across teachers, police and the army, which in the end resulted in the September coup of 1980, by the Army. Turkey is still paying the price and facing the consequences of that era. The bloodshed that wasted so many bright young people and stained the country forever!

Unfortunately, the polarisation Turkey has been experiencing in the last decade or so seems to have divided the country right down the middle, which I find to be even more dangerous. Before the eighties, most of the fighting and power struggle was amongst the students and workers. With the whole country divided in two, God forbid, if something similar was to happen today, it could turn into a civil conflict that involved the majority of the nation. I do hope I'm wrong.

University - The Maturity Years

Despite the difficult and troubling times, I managed to make some great friends both at the dormitory and the university. Eight of us were staying in one room with four bunk beds. It was a rich and diverse mixture of people. We had many students from many different universities, all studying different subjects and all coming from different cities and backgrounds. It really was a great mix; rich, poor, rural, urban, Kurdish, Georgian and more. At the dorms, we had law and medical students from high profile universities, and they were always studying, non-stop. I had heard before that especially the medical students were, in particular, the real grafters in terms of studying… In fact, my roommate in the opposite bed was studying at Hacettepe, one the top medical schools in the country. He was at it all the time; reading, researching, preparing notes and pinning them to the wall above his pillow just, so he could continue reading them as he was falling asleep!

We always stayed up late, well into the early hours of the morning, I don't remember going to sleep before three. About five hours of sleep is still enough for me, I still go to bed late. In those days, we would mostly discuss the topic of the day, which was almost always about politics, of course. We would also discuss important life matters such as marriage and kids too. I always maintained a position that one should never get married before the age of thirty. I affirmed that you must live your life to the full; gain enough experience, status and economic means before even thinking about marriage. The irony of this statement will be seen a little later!

We also played card games, and although forbidden, we would also sometimes cook food, and consume wine or raki (Turkish Ouzo).

I went to university together with Resat, a friend from my hometown, in fact, from a village next to mine. We spent a lot of time together. One other student who I became great friends with, and enjoyed spending time with, was Ugur. He was a law student and the son of a high profile political and religious figure. Although his family lived in Ankara, he decided to stay at our dormitory, so he could be independent. He also worked part-time at the headquarters of Sekerbank, a big state bank. Therefore, he always had plenty of money and knew how to spend it too. He was very smart and always well dressed; we used to eat out quite often at nice restaurants thanks to him. Great credit to Ugur as he was very generous and treated me to nice food and traditional Turkish sweet baklava. We used to eat it by the kilo, as there was a popular place, Haci Baba, and it was the best. Years later when I went to Ankara, Haci Baba was one of the first places I visited. I just love baklava and kadayif (another very popular Turkish sweet).

Mentioning kadayif reminded me of a lovely story with my cousin Abdullah (RIP). Abdullah and I were studying at the high school at the same time, and at some point we even shared a room. His father and mine were cousins, so we were closely related but also great friends, like brothers. Furthermore, his father, Mahmut Dinc, was a well-respected teacher and also a very good businessman, so, they were reasonably well off.

Well, Abdullah was allowed to eat at Kervansaray, a popular local restaurant in Ordu city centre, twice a week. This restaurant is still going today, and even more popular now. Quality is timeless.

Abdullah would take me with him whenever he went to eat there. He was allowed to have a three-course meal, and he would let me have the dessert - how sweet of him! He knew my love of kadayif so it was a very generous, and thoughtful treat for me. And I would always have kadayif without exception and order it at the same time as he had his main meal.

Because I liked it so much I would eat it really slowly, taking tiny bites with my fork. Yes, I would really try to make it last! Anyway, he would watch me eat my kadayif with tea. Then, he would always finish well before me but there I was still

With Abdullah (left), 1974

at it. The bottom of the sweet was the best bit, soaked in syrup, lovely and soft. That would be my last bite! I just didn't want to finish my precious sweet. Abdullah would wait patiently but moaning to me, 'C'mon, get on with the bloody thing, we're late!'

On one occasion I must have really over done it, he was so pissed off that he exploded,

"For fuck's sakes man, why can't you just eat the bloody thing properly? You are torturing both the kadayif, and me, please just get on with it and finish it, I promise I will buy you another one!"

Seker Bank headquarters, where my friend Ugur worked, was in the city centre, an impressively high building. They had a really big and posh staff restaurant on the top floor, which had the appearance of a 5-star hotel. Ugur would always inform me whenever they had my favourite dishes on the menu; lamb leg broth, aubergine kebab, and of course, my favourite kadayif or baklava!

Generally, I would go there twice a week for lunch, sign in at the reception as Ugur's guest, and stuff myself with a great three-course meal. All free, of course. I only had enough money to just get by let alone eat out, so thanks to Ugur I was being treated to wonderful food all the time.

During one lunchtime, I was there at the reception waiting for my favourite food, about to sign in and go up. Meanwhile, some smartly dressed men in suits were leaving, presumably the top executives from the company were going out for a business lunch.

As I was signing the guest book, someone leaned over my shoulder and said, "How are you, son? I hope our food is to your liking and you are enjoying it!" I thought maybe it was someone who knew Ugur, and saw me signing as his guest. I casually replied, "Thank you Sir, I'm certainly enjoying your food, it's so delicious." He simply said, "Afiyet Olsun oglum," (Turkish for 'Bon Appetite, son') and left. I suddenly saw the panic on the receptionist's face, subtly trying to warn me with his expressions and gestures.

After the executives left, the receptionist said to me in a very relieved voice, "Kid, you're so lucky, I thought you

With my friend Ugur. At the Dormatory, 1975

were going to get a good telling off for coming here all the time to eat! Do you know who he was?" I replied that I had no idea, and he exclaimed, "He was the CEO!"

"Wow," I thought, "that was a close call." I laid low for a couple of weeks after that, for things to cool off, but Ugur said it was no problem at all. In fact, the CEO had noticed my absence and asked Ugur if there was something wrong with me! A bit of a rarity maybe, but it just goes to show that there are still some nice people in this world. Now with the blessing of the CEO, I was back to my free lunches in no time, and with increased frequency too!

It was also at university that I was introduced to some incredible music and musicians, great Anatolian rock and traditional folk; Cem Karaca, Ruhi Su, Zulfi Livaneli, Neset Ertas... Everyone was reading all the time, political and philosophical books in particular; it was a very intellectual environment. I'm afraid I hardly read any books; I was very lazy in that regard just like with my studies. But I still enjoyed participating in the discussions, using my own logical thinking and approaches to argue my case.

Some of our friends would get really annoyed with some of my remarks and tell me to read some books before making big statements. I would annoy them even more with my reply, "You guys read too much, you are all very confused!"

Despite the difficult and dangerous environment, I can honestly say that the university years were very productive. Not so much as in academic terms, as we could hardly attend any classes, but I learnt so much from all the socialising and discussions with such a diverse group of highly educated and intelligent young people. The knock-on effect was that I started maturing into a responsible and decent person, I think. That's why I always advise young people to complete their university education, if possible. My early maturity was probably also aided by spending a lot of time with my elderly relatives.

I had already mentioned that I was firmly against marrying too young, not before thirty at least. I was quite adamant and determined about this, and whenever I met a girl and started going out with her, I would make sure she got that exact message before things became too serious.

But I did have to learn very quickly about not making such huge sweeping statements about life or setting concrete rules; in short, never say never!

Losing My Dad So Soon After Finding Him; 1975 – My Life Changes Completely!

In my second year at university, the passing of my dad completely destroyed me; especially since I had just found him again and we were beginning to get closer. It was such a devastating blow, and the pain of losing him lived with me for a long time! Dad's death would start a chain of events that changed my life completely. All the events following dad's loss seemed utterly out of my control; I had no direction, no goals, I was simply trying to cope with it all, by using my intellectual capacity, logical thinking, patience and whatever strength I could muster in my limited arsenal.

Dad

My dad had left us for Istanbul when I was only six months old. He then worked and lived in Samsun with one of his cousins, Ekrem, for years. He was there while I was at high school and I spent a lot my summer days there. But then he suddenly decided to move to Istanbul along with his cousin's family. He visited me at the end of 1974 in Ankara, with Ekrem's wife, to get my blessing about the move. He knew it would make life a lot harder for me as Ankara was right in the middle between Istanbul and Ordu, with a twelve-hour coach ride each way.

Ankara-Samsun-Ordu was perfect as I could visit my dad first and then my mother and repeat it all the way back to Ankara. But dad's moving to Istanbul changed my coach rides for the worse. Now going to Istanbul from Ankara first, and then from Istanbul all the way to Ordu to see my mum, and then back to Ankara was going to be a real pain to say the least.

I knew the decision was already made, and I had no way of influencing it, so I reluctantly gave my approval, but I also tried to show how disappointed I was.

I always visited my father first during school breaks and holidays, but in the summer break of 1975 I decided to go to my mum first instead. It was a protest about dad's move to Istanbul and a way I could show him my resentment.

Whilst walking through my hometown, Golkoy, the manager of the local post office suddenly appeared and gave me the devastating news in person: My dad had left this world! It was unbelievable the way he did it, just like he was delivering mail, matter-of-factly. I'm sure he didn't mean to be so insen-

sitive, but the way I learnt of dad's death was just so cruel and soul destroying. Shocked to the core, I didn't know what to do. Struggling with the utter pain and shock, I felt absolutely numb standing on the spot for a good fifteen minutes. Many thoughts raced through my mind; how stupid of me it was not visit him first, it was all my fault, I bet he was really sad and

Dad (left), his cousin Ekrem, his family and me (far right)

upset with me, I wish I had seen him before his death… I felt just awful. I was broken inside, tears streaming down my face the whole time.

I thought about how my life was now unfolding in a such an unpredictable manner. I didn't know what to do or how to find a way out of it. I felt so lost.

Istanbul, Here I Come!

The heavy impact of my father's sudden death badly clouded my judgement, I felt empty; I had no appetite for anything; life, school, Ankara. Lost inside, I just did not know what to do; I was utterly clueless. Luckily, we didn't have to attend uni every day, so I decided to go to Istanbul and spend some time with uncle Ekrem and the family. I thought it might do me some good being there with them. Ekrem's son, Sadan, was my age and we were like brothers, and we always enjoyed each other's company.

I didn't know Istanbul at all, in fact, I think that was my first trip! Good job I spent a lot of time with Sadan, as he knew Istanbul very well. Actually, he had moved to Istanbul well before his parents and my dad. Often he would take me to different places, meeting lots of people, mostly relatives. Of course, Ekrem's relatives were also related to me so it was nice spending some time with them. I was also visiting different parts of such an amazing city.

Being in Istanbul and spending time with my cousin and meeting lots of new people did me the world of good. I started coping with life better, still very sad inside, but at least I was keeping myself active and occupied, and enjoying this amazing city. Good old Sadan also introduced me to some of Dad's very close friends; I got to learn so much more about dad, through listening to their stories. I thought what an interesting and powerful character my father had been because his friends had so much admiration for him.

Apparently, he became a fisherman when he first came to Istanbul from the village. He made a name for himself as a fisherman too. All these wonderful stories and memories made me really proud to be his son.

Knowing so much more about him filled me with joy, but also saddened me at the same time. Facing the fact that I would never see him ever again was one of the hardest moments of my entire life.

Uncle Ekrem rented a tea shop/café; it's a traditional place where Turks drink tea, coffee and play cards, backgammon and so forth. Until then I had never done any proper work other than hazelnut picking a few times, but even then I always found ways to skive off most of the time, and didn't do much picking. I would make good friends with the landlord's kids, and they would insist on playing with me. So, in actual fact, the landlord overlooked my absence, but I always got paid, so my mum didn't mind at all. Come to think of it, she seemed quite pleased about it. Amazingly, I once became friends almost immediately with the only daughter of the landlord on the second day of our arrival and I didn't do any work for the remaining four weeks! We would do the shopping and help carry the lunch to the workers in the field every day, which was all I did. What a cushy job! My cousins were teasing me all the time, saying I should get married to her and that I would be set for life with all those hazelnut fields. No chance, she wouldn't wait until I was thirty! Incidentally, I have never forgotten the wonderful taste of that bread, and hazelnut. I still have it occasionally. Some memories stay with us a lifetime! I recommend you try it, but please make sure it's the raw hazelnut instead of the roasted one and always with sourdough bread.

Every day, Sadan and I had to get up early in the morning, almost at dawn to open the café, and get things ready. God it was tough doing it morning after morning but we had no choice. I learnt to brew tea in big pots, that's the most consumed item in Turkish cafes. Many people would come in for an early fresh cup of tea; some of them would also start playing cards or 'Okay'. Okay is a game, which is generally played by four people, and sometimes as there were only three of them, and they would have to wait for the fourth, Sadan would sit in to start the game. That was the done thing by the cafe owner to get the game going, but our Sadan loved the game so much that he would never stop. Unfortunately, they also played for money and he always lost more than he could win, and so our hard earned money would go back to the customers. We didn't have a clue as to how to run the cafe at all and we quickly ran out of our tea, coffee and sugar stocks. In the end uncle sold it off to save himself money!

When Mev Met Janet...

Sadan also introduced me to another close friend of my dad's, a man from Trabzon, a big city in the Black Sea region, to the east of Ordu. He had just returned from Germany after working and living there for many years. In the 60s and 70s a lot of Turks from the rural areas went to Germany as workers. There were hundreds of thousands of Turks who went to Germany to work at the factories in the industrial complexes. Furthermore, there were workers from other countries too such as Greece, Poland etc. Germany had a serious labour shortage at that time and this is how they overcame it. There's still a huge community of Turks living in Germany, most of them second or third generation now, feeling more Germans than Turks. A few of them are successful football players playing for top clubs in Europe such as the international football star, Mesut Ozil (Arsenal).

I cannot even recall dad's friend's name now, but I started spending a lot of time with him. He had bought a small corner shop in Aksaray, one of the suburbs of Istanbul near the historical quarters. We used to spend hours in that shop drinking tea and listening to him telling us many stories about their adventures with my dad. Apparently, they went fishing together for a couple years. He told me all the minute details, where they worked and how tough it was to establish a stronghold there and how brave my dad was. My dad had once become very ill from all that fishing in the freezing waters.

Such a shame, I hardly knew anything about my dad's life. We never ever spoke about it; he never uttered a word about my mother and why he left us. I couldn't ask him either. From what I was told in the village, my mum and dad were really in love with each other, they married despite all the opposition from my mother's family. She was the youngest, and her family wanted her to marry someone other than dad who was very poor and with no future. But love knows no bounds, and my mum decided to run away with dad, which was absolutely unheard of in our village.

To this day, it still remains a mystery to me as to why my dad left mum and I so soon. Neither of them ever married again for the rest of their lives. They certainly vowed to remain married 'until death do us part', but not together! It is such a sad story, and so very close to my heart. Mum never really told me what actually happened between them. It still pains me that I couldn't even ask dad! And I will never know either. Now that they are both gone, it will remain one of life's mysteries.

Back to Sadan and the tales of my adventure. One day, Sadan and I went to the shop as usual, but dad's friend seemed unusually excited. He told us that his girlfriend was coming from Germany, and that she was also bringing a young English girl with her as a guest. He was so happy, in high spirits like a little kid. Sadan and I looked at each other thinking the same thing for sure; what the hell, what girlfriend, and wasn't he married already to his wife and two kids in Trabzon?

He asked us to man the shop while he went to the airport to pick them up. We just waited in the shop.

My Life's Taking Shape - First Steps To First Marriage, 1976!

Sometime later, Dad's friend came back to the shop with his girlfriend and a young English girl. Of course, neither Sadan nor I could speak a word of German or English. We exchanged some simple greetings in Turkish and German, but we didn't know whether the English girl could speak German or the Turkish lady knew English. To be honest, I didn't have a clue as to which language was being spoken, as it was all Greek to me.

Anyway after some tea and short introductions dad's friend closed the shop and said he was taking his guests home. He also told us to come tomorrow before lunch as if he had already made some plans. In response, we just said okay. All I knew was that he lived somewhere in Besiktas, another major district in Istanbul by the Bosphorus. So, we all said our goodbyes and left. The lady was from Sivas; remember the name of my university dormitory? My destiny had already determined my path through life; I just had to play along as best as I could, just like a game.

Our series of get-togethers started the next day, and we would meet every day before lunch, have some tea and freshly made home sandwiches. Sadan and I would take the ladies for walks and sightseeing. Everyone seemed very happy, just walking around, having coffee, sweets and quite a bit of fun. We couldn't have any real conversation with Janet, apart from a few exchanges with the help of the Turkish lady. Janet seemed to be having a good time. With limited conversation via Turkish-German-Turkish we continued with our sightseeing for a few weeks, as we had nothing better to do anyway.

Sadan told me that he fancied Janet; I wasn't surprised to hear it, as she was a lovely young girl with blue eyes and long blondish hair. And Sadan was trying to stick close to Janet and hold her hand to help with crossing the road and in that manner, he was making small moves, trying his luck. But, Janet didn't want to know at all, in fact, she seemed quite uneasy with Sadan's gentle advances.

Instead, Janet started to stay closer to me, and was always walking with me, avoiding Sadan's advances. In fact, a few times she even held hands when crossing the road or put her arm in mine while walking together. Although Janet getting all close and cosy with me felt rather great, I didn't think much of it to be honest. I was still very upset about my dad's death, so, getting involved with someone was the last thing on my mind at the time. Plus, I was about to go back to Ankara for a week or so for some exams. In any case, I simply thought Janet felt safer with me, nothing more.

Meeting Cuneyt Arkin, The Top Movie Star!

This is another funny story. If you remember I made my own little action movies when I was really little, pretending to be Yilmaz Guney and beating the hell out of Cuneyt Arkin, one of the top actors in Turkey. Just like Tarik Akan, Cuneyt was such a handsome man, and he easily could have become another Alain Delon if he were from Europe. Cuneyt and Tarik would mainly star in soppy love films, which we hated. We were perhaps jealous of their handsome looks!

Cuneyt Arkin

One day, Ekrem's wife took me with her to see Cuneyt Arkin's father. I really cannot recall the details or reason for the visit but I was quite happy to see the man in the flesh. He really looked the business on the big screen and I was curious to meet him in person. We arrived, and they shoved us into the living room of this beautiful detached house in the district of Levent, quite an upmarket area of Istanbul. After a little while someone came and took Ekrem's wife to Cuneyt's father. Then, she simply told me to wait there.

I was sitting in Cuneyt Arkin's living room. 'How amazing is this?' I thought to myself. Next, I started remembering how in my childhood I used to beat up Cuneyt, and whether I could I tell him about it if he came into the room? Or should I lie instead and tell him how I beat up Yilmaz Guney playing him? There was no sign of him at all, and I couldn't even hear any male voices. I think it was around lunchtime, and I thought how silly of me to think that he would be home, as he was probably at a film set shooting his latest film.

But then suddenly Cuneyt walks into the room. 'Oh my God, what shall I do, get up and wait for him to greet me first?' I thought. My heart was beating like mad. Then, he said hello in a very soft and welcoming voice. I said hello back and just stared at him absolutely fixated by his beautiful face. I thought to myself that this guy was even more handsome in the flesh! Then he just poured himself a drink and left.

I remained in absolute awe for a while, but then became quite angry with myself, 'How stupid of you Mev, why didn't you tell him about your childhood memories, especially if you said you played him and beat up Yilmaz Guney?' He would have been so impressed that he may have even offered me a small cameo role in one his movies!'

All of a sudden, Ekrem's wife came back and told me we were leaving! Damn, I blew it! What an opportunity missed, if only I could have found the courage to tell him. Who knows, instead of making games I may have made films, I could've been a contender...

Back to School and Ankara

I went to Ankara for a few days for an exam, I think. God I had missed the dormitory and my friends. It was so good to see them all again, and they were very pleased to see me too. I told them of all that had happened in Istanbul, especially about the last couple of weeks, with the German lady and the English girl. They all started teasing me, classic boy talk. 'You lucky so and so, an English girl too.' I kept telling them I wasn't at all interested in her, I was still mourning my dad and what would I do with an English girl anyway? And I also explained the reality of the situation, 'She doesn't speak a word of Turkish and I don't speak a word of English, besides I'm still a student and don't have any money, I couldn't even afford to buy her a meal.'

We had a law student whose English was very good. He said he would teach me a few cool English phrases and also write them down on paper so that I could practise them for when I got back. This way, at least I could say a few words in English, and impress Janet and her friend. Not thinking much about it, I just said sure, that's not a bad idea.

Unfortunately, Ankara and the universities were very active with student disturbances but there was not much going on in terms of education. I can't even remember whether I sat my exam or not. After a few days, I caught an Ulusoy coach (because of my dad's job trips were free for me) and I was on my way back to Istanbul, armed with a couple of English phrases to try out on Janet. 'That should surprise them all', I thought to myself!

The real funny thing is that it never crossed my mind to ask my friend what they actually meant. He just said Janet would be really impressed with me. I've always been so trusting of people, or too gullible to be precise; I never thought for a second that the sentences would contain swear words or could embarrass me. Sadly, I am still suffering from my instant trust in people. I never even think about it twice, I always assume the best in people. What's even sadder is the fact that I never seem to learn from bad experiences.

I'm Going to Show Off

Before I went to the shop the next morning I remember practising the English sentences time and time again, to make sure I didn't mess up and embarrass myself. I had asked my friend to write the pronunciation in Turkish, so I could practice and learn them easily.

I was back in the shop the next day, at our usual meeting time, having tea and our sandwiches. They wanted to know how Ankara was. I told them it was the same, probably even worse, and that I couldn't even take my exam etc. Istanbul was no different, but we were staying well away from the universities where most of the trouble was occurring.

Here we were again, trying to have a conversation in the silly German-Turkish-German lingo, and it was really tiring. I said wouldn't it be nice if we could all speak the same language. It didn't matter which language, but just one we could all speak. Dad's friend said it was a shame that as a university student I didn't know any English at all. I said, you are right, I only learnt a little French, and that's it.

Thinking I could perhaps seize the opportunity now and use my newly learnt English, I jokingly said that I had learned some English while I was in Ankara. He was so surprised and happy to hear it. He responded, "Please go on then, let us hear it, I'm sure Janet would like it and probably teach you some more" He was really trying to encourage me as if I needed any! He had no idea that I was already to deliver my English.

Really, I had put a lot of hard work into this and I was determined to put it to good use. I replied, 'I'll try, please tell Janet.' Immediately, he told Janet and his girlfriend that I had learnt a couple of English sentences, and I was going to try them. Oh my, everyone was so excited about it, even more than me, I thought to myself, 'I hope it goes well and I don't mess up.'

The big moment had arrived and I took out one of the two pieces of paper at random, not knowing at all what they meant, so they were both the same to me. We were all sitting on stools in a circle around a small round table. They were waiting with excitement; I could see Janet's smiling face wondering what I was going to say. I must have resembled a baby about to say their very first word!

So with a momentary pause, I double-checked, and repeated the phrase in my head a few times for the very last time.

Then, I made myself a little more comfortable, and very carefully and slowly started reading it; "Nobody can love you more than me".

There was no reaction from dad's friend or his girlfriend! In actual fact, they didn't have a clue what I had just said, and more importantly, nor did I! In trepidation, we were all waiting for Janet's reaction. I was expecting a big laugh or some other silly remark about my lousy accent.

But instead, Janet jumped up in the air shouting and saying things none of us could understand! Next, I was so shocked because she literally launched herself at me, holding me and hugging me! My mind was awash with thoughts, 'What in the hell did I say, what did that bastard friend of mine write?' In all honesty, we were completely puzzled. Janet started talking to them in German, presumably explaining what I had just said and why she reacted like that. As usual I didn't understand anything they were talking about, but they were laughing, exchanging gestures, and all seemed very joyous. I just sat there puzzled, and waiting for someone to explain what the hell was going on.

Dad's friend then explained to me what had just happened in full detail. Apparently, declaring my love to Janet in English had made her so happy! She was over the moon, and they were also very chuffed for her too! But I said to him that I didn't even know what it meant, and that I had asked my friend but he wouldn't tell me. Also, I thought it was just some English sentence that would impress Janet because that was what my friend said to me. He turned and said a few things back to them, but I couldn't see any change in Janet whatsoever. If anything she was even happier than before!

He said to us, 'Go on, off you go for your walks!' I don't think he told them what I said at all; the clever man didn't want to spoil Janet's excitement and happiness. In reality, I guessed that and decided to play along with it, thinking I would tell her somehow later. Maybe I could ask my friend for a new sentence to undo everything, but how could I trust that bastard friend of mine ever again? We went for a long walk, and Janet was so happy, walking with me holding hands the whole time.

With roommates in Sivas Dormitory. Me on the far right, next to my friend who gave me the English sentences!

After a few days of close encounters, and with such warm feelings pouring out of Janet, some serious feelings started in me towards Janet too. I think we had literally fallen in love. A 'love story' that was triggered in a very unusual and unique way, and it certainly wouldn't look out of place in a classic romantic movie.

Ironically, we were very close to Yesilcam too, the Hollywood of Turkey, near Taksim Square in Istanbul.

As the time went on, Janet and I started spending even more time together. I started going to their house in Besiktas too, and staying with them sometimes.

Ready to Get Married, 1976

No money, no plans and no goals for the future, and here I was seriously contemplating marrying Janet after twenty days or so. Only nineteen, and nowhere near thirty! Actually, the marriage was the only way Janet could stay in Turkey without incurring visa problems. Not that I was thinking on that level; I was just going through the motions and wondering where life was leading me.

My dad's friend thought the marriage was a good idea too. But his girlfriend thought it was perfect, as she really wanted Janet to stay in Istanbul longer term. Indeed, she had her own plans for Janet; opening a small boutique shop. And as she really loved Janet like a younger sister, the marriage seemed to be the best way of keeping her in Turkey. All in all, the planned marriage seemed to suit everybody else's plans too. Luckily, I didn't have a plan, so what could go wrong? So, we gathered all the paperwork and obtained the required documents from the police headquarters.

There was a little bit of insurance money to come from my dad; it was about five thousand Turkish Lira, not much, but we could live on it for a couple of months. Better than nothing, but I was told it could take months before I would receive it. Still, it was a guaranteed payment and I would receive it sooner or later. Basically, it was some money I could bank on. This in turn meant that I could borrow the money I would need for the wedding.

Before we could move on, there was one very important matter that I needed to sort out urgently. It was not going to be easy, but I had to get mum's permission and blessing for the marriage. She had devoted her entire life to me, so the least I could do was to make sure she was happy about my decision. Thus, I decided to go home to see mum, and also try and borrow some money. After which I would then come back as soon as possible to finish the marriage formalities. Now I had a plan too like everyone else. Things were getting really serious, and now I needed to behave responsibly and take the correct steps.

Going Home to Mum For Her Blessing and For Some Money

It was around February 1976. When I arrived in my small town of Golkoy, the weather was really cold and lots of snow on the ground. I had a military parka coat, which was immensely popular at the time, especially amongst us left-wing students. Almost everyone was wearing one. Armed with my winter coat and a lot of determination, I started my rounds to find some money from someone. I also had to convince my mum about this completely untimely and unrealistic marriage. I knew it would be hard, but I had to find a way and get my mum's blessing. So, I had my work cut out.

My mum's shock soon gave way to a determined out of the question stance. She said nothing but NO! I hoped she would break eventually and couldn't resist my pleas. The truth was that she really loved me and therefore I hoped she would cave in sooner or later. But I think all my elders; uncles, aunts and the rest of the village were against the marriage too. All in all, everyone must have thought I had gone completely potty; with no money, still at university, and if that was not enough a foreign girl to boot. Not even Turkish or Muslim! 'It cannot and shall not be allowed' was all they were saying. They were mostly right too; I didn't have any money, or a place to live, plus I was still a student with hardly any prospects for the future.

Janet wasn't exactly loaded either. I didn't know much about her financial situation, but from what little I gathered from conversations with dad's friend and her girlfriend, she worked as a social worker at an old peoples' homes. She didn't appear to have much money with her. At least she didn't have to get the okay and the blessing of her parents. She probably just wrote and told them she was getting married to a Turk. To be honest, I am sure they wouldn't have approved of the marriage either.

At the same time, I started exploring one of two options about finding the three thousand Turkish Lira (TL) I needed. I spoke with my dad's elder brother Husnu, as apparently he wanted to talk to me anyway about this marriage thing. I only stayed at my uncle's a few times when I was little, and we never really had a very close relationship, since I mostly stayed at mum's relatives. His apparent desire to help me both surprised me and also made me feel good. Maybe he was trying to make up for the past, and help his nephew, the son of his recently departed brother. He said he would help with the money and he assured me that he would give it to me in Golkoy in a week's time.

Money sorted, well at least promised, I now had to convince mum and get back to Istanbul as quickly as possible. She was still adamant and wouldn't move an inch from her initial position. In the meantime, days were passing with no communication with Janet, and she was just waiting for me to return without knowing what was going on. All things considered, I felt miserable and looked really dreadful with my parka and unshaven, tired face; which made me look even more desperate. I had to find a way to deal with mum and get her out of my way.

Out of the blue, it suddenly dawned on me that there was a way forward: why didn't I take my mum to see my great uncle, my namesake and revered Sufi Dervish, Mevlut? A holy and learned man, very well respected by all, he could really swing things around in my favour, and easily convince mum too, should he approve of my marriage. It was definitely worth a shot.

I suggested this to mum, and she jumped at the idea, presumably thinking that the holy man would object to my marriage to an English and non-Muslim girl even more than she did. Dervish Mevlut was a highly regarded old man; many people would visit him from afar to consult him and learn from his wisdom. Dervish and my granddad were cousins, and the Dervish's wife was my mum's aunt. We were very closely related from both sides of the family, and my mum and I spent a lot of time there in my childhood. In truth, I always felt very content and happy there, one of the very few houses I would be spoilt at. They always made me feel at home and I really felt part of the family. Also, Dervish had two sons much older than me, and they both loved me, always spending a lot of quality time with me.

We arrived at the Dervish's, this was a make or break situation. Mum and I agreed we would gracefully accept whatever the Dervish advised. My mum looked quite relaxed and for some reason I did too. The old man loved me and so I was sure he would do the right thing and approve the marriage.

Anyway, the Dervish sat us both down on the floor in front him. Mum started unloading, 'My dear Dervish, it's unbelievable, he wants to marry a foreign girl. And, she is not even Muslim either can you believe that? We have no money, he's still at university, what's the rush, it's as if no girls are left in Turkey!' Poor mum was desperately trying to win the case and convince the Dervish from the off!

Dervish with that beautifully white long beard and face turned to me, and simply asked; 'My dearest son, do you really love this girl?' I firmly replied, 'Yes, I really love her, Uncle Dervish'. By the way, remember I said that everyone in the village had a nickname? My mum's was 'Gogi' which means 'cute girl' in Georgian and everyone called my mum by this name. Actually thinking back, I think Dervish may have given it to her.

After my determined answer, Dervish immediately turned to my mum, and in a very comforting and soft voice, said, 'Gogi, Gogi, we shouldn't separate two determined young people who are in love with each other, we would commit a sin!' My poor mum was so shocked, she must have gone numb, her face turned blue with disappointment and probably anger! She wasn't expecting this from Dervish at all! Noticing my mum's utter disappointment with his decision, Dervish continued with an even more comforting, but also assuring voice, 'Gogi, Gogi, this young girl is God's guest who came from foreign lands, and fell in love with our son. Let them marry, we may even be rewarded by God for our good deed.' Raising his voice for the final comforting blow, he said, 'I don't know if it will happen, but imagine if she decides to become a Muslim too? You know what that would mean if it were to happen? Not just you and me, but all our families would go to heaven!' It was unbelievable; as if my mum's blue face were lit with some heavenly light, her face literally glowing with happiness!

Our Dervish was such a wise man, he had a way with words and he delivered them in the most effective manner. No wonder many people came to see him from many miles away. Now that the biggest and most important obstacle was out of the way, I could now just sort out the money and head back to Istanbul!

Money Money Money...

I had five thousand TL coming from dad's insurance and I think I had to pay two thousand TL towards my dad's funeral expenses. Which meant I could borrow three thousand TL and then be able to pay it back when I received the insurance money. Finding the money was becoming even harder than convincing mum. I was facing one obstacle after another, as if I was being tested.

I was so determined, and no way was I going to give up, I was getting married one way or another. My Imam uncle was absolutely against it, and very angry with mum for letting me do it. I was avoiding him at all cost, but he was also influencing others not to help. While I was avoiding my Imam uncle, my other uncle who promised me the money was avoiding me now! Honestly, I have absolutely no idea why he had changed his mind. The money thing was really getting difficult and requiring desperate measures. Realising that there was no help coming from my close elders, I turned my attention to moneylenders, but this was the last resort. We always heard stories about how these moneylenders would make life very difficult to say the least, if you failed to pay back the loan. I was really scared about the possible risks and dangers of borrowing from such people. My cousin Abdullah and his friends were helping me find a lender with more compassion.

No idea what they were thinking back in Istanbul, maybe they were slowly assuming that I had changed my mind and I wasn't coming back.

I don't remember how I found out, but I learnt that the government had just started giving the villagers credit loans via the state bank, Ziraat (agricultural) Bank. I thought I should be entitled too as I was from the village. Besides, I only needed three thousand TL and surely that was not a lot. I had no idea, as I had never borrowed money before. First of all, I had to find a way to convince the bank manager. If I qualified, I would pay it back from my insurance money.

One my of relatives from mum's side Masar worked at Ziraat Bank, he had graduated from the same Commercial College some 8 years before me. I thought I could be in luck, with the help of Masar we could get the Manager to approve the loan. Masar was an interesting character; he was such a clever and nice person. Yet a few drinks of raki (ouzo) would turn him into a nasty piece of work. Everyone in town would avoid him when he had had a few drinks; he was so fearless and frightening. He really liked me, so I went to him and explained the whole thing; about Janet, mum's consent the insurance money and now the final piece of the puzzle, all that I needed was this three thousand TL. Happily, he said we would go and talk to the manager together and he said, the manager was a good man and he would surely approve the loan. Moreover, Masar also assured me that he would be a guarantor for the loan if needed. 'Great, this should do it', I thought to myself.'

On the day of the meeting, Masar and I explained everything to the manager; he was such an understanding man, in fact, he was convinced very quickly, my down and out condition must have contributed to his positive response, as I really looked miserable.

The manager simply said that it wasn't a problem and that they could help with a credit loan, 'Mevlut is entitled to it, just fill in the forms and sign it but you must also obtain the signature of the Muhtar, the village governor'. So, we got the forms ready, all we had to do was bring the Muhtar to the bank to sign the forms, that's it. Almost there, I was so relieved. Eventually, we found the Muhtar, and asked him to go to the bank with me, as I said the manager was waiting for him. We were at the bank in no time at all.

The Manager told Muhtar that the credit loan was for me, and we just needed his signature to complete the application. But he said he didn't want to sign and he simply refused. Masar said, 'Why the hell not?' In response, Muhtar said he was given strict instructions by my uncle Imam not to help me in anyway. 'If I signed, he would find out', he nervously declared. We couldn't believe it. It was like a nightmare. Masar was begging the Muhtar, 'Please just sign it, you're not doing anything wrong, besides it's your duty and uncle Imam would not even know'.

Masar said to Muhtar, 'Imam is my uncle too and I would never do anything against his wishes, but on this occasion I'm with Mevlut and I'll do whatever's required to obtain your signature". Muhtar meekly replied, 'If I sign and the Imam finds out I really don't know how I would face him.'

All of a sudden, Masar, by now very much fed up with Muhtar's refusal to sign, said in a very angry voice, 'Muhtar if you don't sign it, I will smash your face in so badly that you wouldn't want to face anybody!' I think with Masar's threat and the manager's insistence, we finally convinced the Muhtar to sign.

Yes, finally! So now I was ready go back to Istanbul and start the formalities…

I Must Return to Istanbul at Once...

With mum's blessing and the three thousand TL in the bank, I was ready to start my journey back to Istanbul, and onto the next level in my adventure. The weather was really dreadful in Golkoy, but even worse in the highlands towards Ordu. This road was very dangerous even in good weather and no one was willing to drive us to Ordu. There was this section in the mountains called 'Nine Bend', which literally had nine insanely tight bends, one after the other going uphill with a massive drop on one side!

My cousin Abdullah and I decided that we would go by whatever means necessary. We knew this very young, but capable taxi driver, who we thought would take us and not surprisingly he agreed. He had an old, clapped out taxi, he quickly chained up his tyres and we were off. It was late afternoon.

We managed reasonably well, until we arrived at the bottom of the dreadful Nine Bend. The snow was falling heavier, we could hardly see ahead and the road was almost completely covered in snow. The driver made a few attempts but it was no good, we couldn't move an inch. The tyres were not holding the road at all, and the taxi was skidding and sliding like mad. We just stopped there and decided to walk to the famous pitstop about half a mile up the hill. It was owned by Asim, a man famous for making traditional menemen (a dish made with eggs, tomatoes and green peppers). He was always open, as his house was just around the corner. Clearly we couldn't stay in the car, as we would probably freeze to death. Subsequently, we started walking and it was getting harder, as we climbed the winding road. Thankfully, we finally made it to Asim's little cafe.

There was a Land Rover parked outside which we recognised. Abdullah and I looked at each other very pleased. It was the jeep of the local independent MP Kemal Gonul, he had left Golkoy way before us, but decided to stay the night at Asim's when the conditions became severe. We were inside and so relieved. They sat us a little further back from the heat, suggesting we should gradually warm up to the room temperature.

We started chatting with the MP and I was sharing my story, meanwhile Asim was making us his delicious menemen. The MP was good friends with my dad, and I had stayed at his hotel in Ankara for three months until I moved to the Sivas Dormitory. The MP's wife was Abdullah's aunt, and frankly the MP was a godsend in my troubled times. He promised to help me with dad's insurance, he said I should get the money in a couple of months, but suggested I went to Ankara to see him first in a few weeks. We stayed at Asim's until the morning and then all went to Ordu in the MP's jeep.

Abdullah and I had a nice meal at the Kervansaray where we used to eat occasionally during high school days. Abdullah teased me by saying he would treat me to a kadayif if I promised to eat it properly!

These photos were taken late 2018

With Asim by the famous Fountain   At Asim's cafe with my nephew Huseyin and friends Ates and Erkan

Finally, Back in Istanbul After Two Weeks

I was finally back in Istanbul, very tired and worn out, but triumphant and happy at the same time. With mum's blessing and the money sorted, everything was set to put things back in motion. I stayed the night at my uncle's and couldn't wait to go to dad's friend's shop. I went there the next day, much earlier than our normal meeting time. After a brief greeting, we chatted about this and that, but he was dodging my questions about Janet. Saying things like 'they may come later, they don't come to the shop anymore since you've been gone.' In short, he was behaving most strangely, as if he was keeping something from me. This went on for a couple of days; I can't even remember why I didn't attempt to go to their Besiktas house. He may have said something like they had gone to her hometown Sivas and would be back in a few days.

I think it was on the third or fourth day, sitting in the shop drinking tea and I was patiently waiting and hoping he would tell me something to relieve my pain and misery. Obviously, he could see I was in a mess and really down. Likewise, I could see from his face that whatever he was hiding from me was eating away at him inside. After all, he was dad's best friend, and there I was suffering in front of his very eyes, not knowing what was going on. He suddenly stood up and said, 'C'mon, we are going home!'

He told me everything on the way; how his girlfriend panicked about Janet marrying me and then leaving Istanbul with me. Which would mean all her plans for Janet would go out of the window. With my much-delayed return, she told Janet that I wasn't to be trusted and that I was never coming back. In truth, it had been about twelve days and there had been no sign, so she thought it was best for Janet to forget about me.

Heartbroken, Janet didn't believe her at first; in fact, she wouldn't even speak with her for days. However, after twelve days doubts had started creeping into Janet's head.

Dad's friend warned me how bad Janet was; she was utterly devastated and feeling awful… We arrived at the house, and as soon as we went inside, he started shouting and screaming at the top of his voice in German. To be perfectly, honest, I had no idea what he was saying, but he sounded very angry and pissed off, that's for sure. And then finally he said to his girlfriend in Turkish, 'That's it, no more lies about anything, Janet and Mevlut should decide what they want to do!'

I was stood slightly behind him, just waiting in anticipation. He then turned to Janet and explained some things to her in German, probably telling her about all my troubles back home and why I had been delayed. Suddenly Janet got up and rushed towards me, crying her eyes out, but seemingly very joyous too. Reunited, we finally held each other. What an emotional journey for us both! We were exhausted and had been through a lot of hardship without knowing the other's suffering. In fact, Janet's face had broken out in spots through worry. I couldn't believe it; the poor thing must have really suffered a lot, she really looked poorly.

After the emotions had settled down, I told them what had happened back home in detail, my mum, the money, and the scary journey, all of it. They couldn't believe it. In all honesty, Dad's friend's girlfriend felt very bad for what she had done, and kept apologising to us both. Thankfully, everything seemed to be back to normal. Subsequently we started the marriage process and managed to obtain from the police headquarters all the necessary paperwork and the approvals needed for our matrimony.

But things were to take another turn when my cousin, Hilmi came to see me out of the blue. Hilmi was the son of my aunt who lived in Izmit, a major industrial city sixty-five miles from Istanbul. My aunt was the elder sister of my dad, and she sent Hilmi to tell me to bring Janet to Izmit and move in with them. She said we could get married in Izmit and she would look after us. I told my dad's friend. He knew I didn't have enough money, nor a job and that it would be hard for us to survive in Istanbul. He was a very nice man and very understanding too. Immediately he supported the idea and he said it was for the best as it was difficult to build a future in Istanbul with little money. Janet agreed too, neither of us knowing what would be in store for us in Izmit.

We didn't know anything; we were just blowing in the wind. But dad's friend's girlfriend was right about her concerns for me leaving Istanbul with Janet! It happened much sooner than any of us anticipated, but she also gracefully accepted it. In hindsight, I hope she didn't feel too bad and curse us for leaving.

The Marriage and The Izmit Years, August 1976

My aunt lived in Alikahya, a settlement just outside the industrial city of Izmit. It had originally been a huge farm covering acres of open lands. My aunt's husband, Casim, had bought it in the early 60s. I don't know how the idea came about, but he bought the entire farmland with the money he collected from our villagers, who fancied the idea of eventually moving and living there. I guess the village people must have seen it as a way of getting out of the poor village life and to make a better living in the big city. So, many families chipped in as much as they could afford, some selling their animals or bits of their land to raise the money. You were allocated land in proportion to the amount you paid.

The project grew and grew and there was quite a big settlement by the mid-70s, as a lot of families had moved to Alikahya from the village. Most of my relatives were there too. My cousins and my school friends as well, so it was like returning to my home village. Equally, there were some major factories near the settlement and most of the people worked there. I guess that must have been one of the major reasons for settling there, so they could all find decent jobs.

Janet and I started living with my aunts. It was amazing the way the local people embraced Janet. Generally, the Turkish people are very hospitable anyway, especially towards foreigners, but my relatives were fascinated by the fact that Janet was my wife. They made an extra effort to make her feel welcome and at home. My aunt's house was always full of women from the neighbourhood but Janet was the main attraction! Janet couldn't believe what all the fuss was about. I tried to explain the fascination towards her in Turkish of course, not sure how much she really understood. Basically, I told her that they really loved me, as I was closely related to most of them and I had spent a lot of time with them during my childhood. Although she found all the fuss and attention irritating

From our marriage, 1976
Checkout the 32cm flares!

at times, she mostly enjoyed it, as she was really spoilt.

By the way, trying to communicate was really tough, but she was making very good progress with her Turkish, as she was studying all the time and she was picking it up rather quickly. Every day she had plenty of opportunity to practise with all those women! I was also developing skills to make our communication easier, inventing a new language almost; Tarzan+! In the meantime, some of my relatives were making things more complicated by trying to teach Janet Georgian too!

Here we were in a completely new place and with new surroundings, never knowing how it would all pan out; just taking things as they came.

Janet and I officially got married in August 1976 in Izmit with the simplest of marriage ceremonies one could get. There wasn't even a bridesmaid for Janet, just my cousin Hilmi as both the witness and the best man; just the three of us. For some reason I never liked wearing suits, I still don't, and presumably I never had a chance to wear one until I was at university and then I just couldn't be bothered. However, I think Hilmi convinced me and we got a tailor to make me a nice suit, my first ever, with a large collar and even larger flares. Remember it was the 70's and flares were actually in fashion!

The only other time I wore a suit was when I was the founding president of the Turkish Digital Games Federation in 2011. Then the Prime Minister, Erdogan had invited me to a very big banquet held in Ankara. Everybody told me that I should wear a suit. I bowed to the pressure, and bought a suit even though I've never worn it since. What a waste of a good suit, also I didn't even need it as several people there were only dressed smart casual including the president of the tennis federation.

Without knowing what was waiting for us, and in a completely carefree manner, we got married and started a new life together. We didn't even have a home of our own. It suddenly dawned on me, I thought this is ridiculous; I'm back living with my relatives again just like when I was a little kid. But this time not with my mum, but with my newlywed wife and at the age of nineteen!

We were so naive and unprepared, but trying to take things in our stride. It felt like life had given us these roles to play, and we were just doing our best. Well, we hardly had any money, I mean Janet didn't have any and three thousand TL wasn't going to last long, that was for sure. And, surely we couldn't stay at my aunt's forever as it would drive us both mad.

Sometimes there would even be religious gatherings at my aunt's house organised by her Hadji husband; quite a handful of people would come from neighbouring towns and cities. No idea what it was all about, I'm assuming it was some sort of religious communion or a congregation. They would ask us to leave the house before they arrived. We never asked why, but it suited us fine, as we didn't want to hang around anyway. The last thing I wanted was a grilling from some religious people about Janet and my marriage to a non-Muslim woman. Probably my aunt and her husband didn't want to face similar questions either. I had to do something about staying there, and do it quickly before it became unbearable for Janet and I.

What could I do though as I didn't have many options really? I thought maybe I could get a job at a bank; after all I had already graduated from a commercial college and was studying commerce and economics at university, well sort of, when I was able to attend.

I told my aunt that I was going to look for a job and we would get a place of our own in the city. She said it would be good to find a job, but we could stay with them as long as we wanted. She also said we should do something about Janet's name. I said, 'what do you mean?' She said, 'She's your wife and now living in Turkey, it would be proper if she had a Turkish name. Let's find her nice name.' We explained this to Janet and surprisingly she didn't mind at all. In fact, from what I can remember she liked the idea. Many women suggested many names and in the end we settled for Ayla!

Janet was reading the Quran for some reason, presumably wanting to know more about the Muslim religion, I really cannot recall the details and we were still unable to communicate in any detail. While looking for names, my aunt also suggested that Janet became a Muslim to complete the process. She was now a Turkish citizen and she should be a Muslim too.

Again, I don't remember all the details, but Janet decided to become Muslim; probably to please my aunt or she just fancied the idea anyway. I think she had to recite 'the kalima shahadah', effectively swearing allegiance to the prophet Mohammed.

So, suddenly my English wife became Ayla and a Muslim too. I thought our great uncle Dervish was right; maybe he did foresee, and knew all along that Janet would become Muslim. If you remember he had reassured my mum with the prospect of Janet becoming a Muslim. Great, I thought, my entire family were now destined for Heaven thanks to Janet! I do hope my mum is there; she deserves it more than anyone.

Looking For a Job to Become a Breadwinner

I started looking for a job preferably at a bank, otherwise whatever I could get. To be honest, I just wanted to start earning a little bit of money, so we could rent a flat. I always had long hair, even when we weren't allowed in middle school and at college. I thought if I were to stand a chance of getting a bank job, I had better look presentable, so I had my haircut and a shave. I then put on a shirt and literally started knocking on the doors of all the banks in the city. Most dismissed me immediately upon learning of my student status, and the rest said they would get back to me but never did. So, no bank job then! What else could I try? Not much really, my cousins were also trying to help me, but nothing was forthcoming.

I decided I would take whatever I could find, so I started wandering around the city, checking out shop windows for anything going. There was a fish market right in the heart of the city. Running parallel to it was the very busy main road with all sorts of shops. Right in the corner of the fish market there was a small shop that was selling dairy products; grilled chicken, chicken pieces, eggs, cheese and the like. There was a small sign on the door; the owner was looking for a shop assistant. I thought why not, anything would do, I went in and enquired about the job. A young guy behind the counter said the owner wasn't around, and he didn't know when he'd be back as he wasn't coming to the shop very often. I said I would pop back later and left. I then continued looking for other jobs but would keep going back to the dairy shop to see if I could catch the owner.

The young guy in the shop eventually told me a bit more about the owner. I learnt that he had graduated from my university, which I thought must increase my chances and so I asked him to mention it to the owner.

The next day I decided to go a bit later with the hope of catching him, as he must have to collect the cash from the till at some point, I thought. And there he was, sat behind his desk doing some paperwork. We greeted each other; he sat me down and ordered me a tea from the cafe next door.

We started chatting; I told him my whole story. He couldn't believe what I had gone through, and despite all the difficulties how I managed to marry an English girl, and still while I was a student. When I told him where I was studying he said, 'What a nice coincidence, that's where I graduated from many years ago'. It felt really nice; like schoolmates meeting after many years. He made me feel very comfortable too and seemed very keen to help.

Work in Exchange For Chicken and Eggs

He told me everything about his shop and how he started his business. It was just amazing listening to him. He was the man who first introduced the concept of selling chicken pieces in Turkey, before then you could only buy whole chickens. Apparently, he hired many farms in the surrounding cities and villages and set up chicken farms with the village people. He was supplying everything, the villagers were just looking after the farms. His business grew so rapidly and he had several of these chicken farms. He would buy all the chickens back from the villagers, even though they were his anyway, but that was how he paid the farmers for their service. Because he was paying for everything, he was buying back the chickens at a symbolic cost. Everyone was happy; he was getting his poultry and the farmers were earning quite a bit of money without taking any risks. He literally turned the whole thing into a small industry; but some powerful people with money also wanted a piece of the action.

This is so crazy; a couple of the new businessmen managed to convince nearly half the farmers to sell the chickens to them at four times the price, since they didn't invest anything in the first place. The farmers couldn't refuse such an offer. In the end, the farmers sold the owners' chickens to someone else!

That was the end of his business; he went bankrupt and lost all his investment in one swoop. All that was left were lots of loans to pay, and this little corner shop. He didn't spend much time there because he was avoiding all the debt collectors. Lots of pending court cases too. God, I really felt sorry for him and felt bad asking him for a job!

After telling me all his troubles, he said, he couldn't offer me a job with pay, but I could take home whatever I wanted from the shop every day; chicken, eggs and cheese, butter and other dairy products.

I don't think I thought about it much, it was better than nothing and at least it was a start. We would have fresh and healthy food to eat, which could amount to quite a bit of money. In the meantime I could continue to look out for other jobs too. I said sure, that would be fine. Also, I added that if I could bring some luck and a lot more sales to the shop, then perhaps he could make a bonus payment every now and then. Without committing to it, he said, 'That's a good idea; let's see how you get on.'

I had a job without pay, but lots of food to take home every day, what's not to like I thought. I told Janet, she just said to take it, and that we would manage somehow. Yes, we would have to manage, I thought, as we had no other choice.

Our Home in Izmit

Now that I had a job, well sort of, I could rent a flat. We found this two-bed basement flat just on the outskirts of the city. It was very grotty, but unbelievably cheap. That's all we could afford, so we had to start somewhere. I don't ever remember Janet objecting to anything, she was very supportive and we were mostly acting on instincts. There was a family related to my aunt in the neighbourhood, and my cousin was married to their eldest son. They would bring us lovely home cooked food sometimes or invite us to eat with them. In time, we made a few other friends too. Janet was okay. She was reading and also writing all the time. She always wanted to be a writer; she was working on some children's books with illustrations, and her drawings were really nice.

I was working away in the shop; grilling chicken, cutting up chickens into different pieces. Also, I made a few friends with the neighbouring shopkeepers. There was a big food retailer opposite our shop. There was this young man running it and the shop belonged to his rich uncle. We became really good friends, they were also newly married, and we started visiting them at weekends. It was wonderful and they would cook food for us. These meals were much needed breaks from eating chicken every night! After all, I was taking home chicken, eggs and cheese and nothing much else. After a while, we would get really fed up with eating chicken and eggs all the time, who wouldn't? I had turned the whole thing into a little game: 'What shall I bring tomorrow, can you remember what we had the other day, was it chicken breast or drumsticks?' We were afraid of turning into chickens at this rate!

One lunchtime, I was chatting to my friend from the retail shop and complaining about how we were really getting fed up with eating chicken all the time. Maybe we should fast and eat every other day; at least it may make it more bearable.

We couldn't decide which part of the chicken to eat next, just mucking about and joking about the situation. He suddenly said, 'Why don't we swap? You give me chicken, eggs and cheese, and I give you rice, pasta or whatever you fancy.' I said, 'Are you sure, wouldn't your uncle notice, I wouldn't want you to get into trouble for me?' 'No,' he said, 'No trouble, I also have my own allowance to take home whatever I want from the shop, similar to you.' 'Wow, that's brilliant, let's do it and start today,' I replied, and thought this would surprise Janet! That night I took home, rice, pasta and some other tinned food. Chicken was still the main ingredient in our diet, but at least now we added a couple more options; chicken with rice, chicken with pasta...

Saving a Kitten

Every morning Janet would see me off to work. The house opposite us had a wire fence. One day I heard a cat crying, obviously in some sort of trouble. It was a little black kitten all tangled up in the wire fence unable to release itself from it. I wanted to rescue the poor thing. Janet was watching me from the doorway, and warned me to be careful. Presumably asking me not to hurt the cat. She told me how she loved cats and that she had a big cat called Mog, I think, back home. I was really trying to be careful not to hurt the cat, and also not to get scratched myself; it was a horrible old barbed wire fence, looking very rusty. As I managed to release the cat, still holding it and pulling it out of the fence, the poor thing was naturally terrified. Then as quick as a flash, it suddenly released itself from my hand, while scratching me very badly out of fear. Immediately, I screamed and let out a yell. It really hurt and I was bleeding with a few scratches on my arms. Subsequently, I gave Janet the thumbs up, indicating that all was okay; the cat was free and I was on my way to work.

But she had heard me scream, and came running towards me, seeing me badly scratched and bleeding, she panicked. She insisted that we must go to hospital straight away. However, I assured her that I would be alright, 'We don't need to go to hospital for a cat scratch' was my response. Nevertheless, she was really panicky, 'Mevlut, it's really dangerous, it's a stray cat, and you also cut your hand on the rusted barbed wire. We must go to hospital and probably get you vaccinated.' I couldn't quite catch what she was going on about, but after a few gestures I could see what she meant. She was talking about getting an injection. Suddenly, I was absolutely terrified and tried to refuse, but she insisted.

Upon reflection, I thought she was probably right and it could have been very risky not to do anything about it. I could have easily been infected with rabies or something, which terrified me too!

Actually, I am not sure which one was more terrifying. You have to remember that needles scare me to death and from what I remember the rabies vaccination involved very long needles. Just the thought of them nearly made me faint. However, I had no choice and we went to the main hospital's emergency service. They didn't even hesitate and told me they would have to give me a set of nine injections in nine days, and into the stomach. It was just awful; for the last few injections, they could hardly insert the bloody needle into my stomach, as it had turned rock hard! No doubt, Janet's insistence probably saved me.

Rising Damp!

Looking back, our basement flat was tiny, very old and in poor condition. There was so much damp that the walls were wet from it, in fact, in parts there was running water. I still don't know how we survived it; maybe eating all that wonderful wholesome dairy food saved us.

My mother came and lived there with us for a few months. It was really nice that mum lived with her daughter-in-law and even though they couldn't communicate much, my mum was very happy. She also spent a lot of time in Alikahya with her relatives too while she was with us. In fact, she ended up spending the remaining years of her life there.

I worked at that little shop for nearly one a half years, all that time we lived in that grotty little flat, managing to survive and getting by somehow. In the meantime, I was going to school in Ankara for exams and attended a few classes whenever conditions would allow. It was 1978 and I was in my last year, hoping to graduate soon. But the political uprisings and riots were getting worse, making things very difficult to say the least. If I remember rightly, I think the troubles peaked around then.

In addition to this, I also managed to get my dad's insurance money after waiting for months, and so I immediately paid the bank loan. In response, I then received a lovely encouraging letter from the bank manager stating that he never doubted my intention of paying it back and that he was convinced I would do well in life. I thought that was very nice of him and it did give me a lot of encouragement.

I have always appreciated the acknowledgements and compliments from other people; I believe they instil that extra bit of confidence in us.

Decisions, Decisions...

Towards the end of the school term in 1978, realising that there was no prospect of my finishing university for a while, I suggested to Janet that she should go back to England as soon as possible. Until then we were just dealing with things as they came along without making plans of any sort. But, the conditions were starting to get out of hand and very dangerous, we were also finding it harder to manage too. This was the first time that I made a concerted effort to improve our life and help us build a better future. No long term thinking here, but at least we had to improve the current situation.

Janet going back to England seemed a sound decision, as things could have become much worse. I was going to try and stay out of trouble while preparing for my exams, and then take them when I could, and then eventually re-join Janet in England. By then hopefully, Janet would have a job and build some foundations for us to live in England, where we would be safer and better off too. It made sense, and reluctantly Janet agreed to go, perhaps she was fearing that we may never see each other again.

I remember seeing her off from the historical Sirkeci Gari (Sirkeci Train Station, the home of the famous Orient Express). It was a very difficult parting; 'God knows what may happen, we may not even see each other again' was the thought in my mind, but, we thought life was just taking us where we should go. What had happened so far was quite different to our plans and perhaps this parting was the start of a new beginning. We were trying our best under the circumstances to improve our chances for a better future.

As a side note, it's quite amazing when I think that decades later, I would produce Turkey's first and biggest MMORGP game featuring Sirkeci Station.

There were so many memories for me while I was taking pictures of the beautiful building for the 3D modelling work.

It was very tough for a few months after Janet's departure. I went back to Ankara, living in the dormitory with my friends again. They couldn't believe all that had happened to me in the last couple of years, nor could I come to think of it! I remember spending quite a bit of time with my cousin Abdullah; he was so good to me. Frequently, he would try to comfort me; he could see the suffering I was going through. I had sent my wife home and I may never see her again. How was I going to even get to England with no passport and no money? I remember writing a few letters to Janet while I was with Abdullah.

We were trying to write to each other as often as possible, the letters were helping us both cope. The post must have been a lot slower in those days and it took maybe two weeks to receive them from Southampton. I think I only managed to take some of the exams, and I still had two left, but there was no way of retaking them any time soon. We could only try again the following academic year, 1979, conditions permitting of course. Finally, it was time for me to go to England for a few months and come back to take the remaining exams.

England, Here I Come - The First Step to New Beginnings, 1978!

The big adventure of life continued to provide me with all sorts of unexpected surprises. Now at the age of twenty one, married but still at university, I was about to embark on yet another journey, full of excitement.

Firstly, I had to get a passport and it wasn't easy, as at the time there were travel restrictions; possibly because of the economic and political turbulence. It seemed like I was always facing obstacles, and I had to find ways to get around them. It was almost as if I had to crack the problems and solve the puzzles, just like in games.

I somehow learnt that I could get a passport by benefiting from a special permission which was given to the Ulusoy Coach drivers. Ulusoy was one of the big travel companies taking people to the holy land of Mecca for pilgrimage. My dad's long career at Ulusoy had earned him a lot of respect from both the company executives and his work colleagues alike. Therefore, I went to Samsun and with the help of my dad's friends and Ulusoy management, I got my passport within a week. Where there's a will there's a way, as they say.

I also needed some foreign currency, but this was also proving difficult. Frankly, I can't remember the details, but I probably called for the help of my good friend Ugur, who had connections with the right people at the right places. If I remember correctly, I could only get three hundred dollars from the

Central Bank; either that's what I was allowed to have or that was all I could afford. Considering the circumstances both could be true.

Now, all I needed was a ticket for my London flight. I don't recall the details, but it was my first flight ever; how exciting, my first flight and it was Istanbul-London. I can't remember how it felt as it was probably a relatively small detail in the bigger picture at the time. I was going to England, a country much discussed in our political discussions at the dormitory; many things were said, good and bad – the industrial revolution, the centre of democracy, developed, great and powerful history - one of the true symbols of colonialism, capitalism and imperialism.

During the flight I didn't care about any of it, I was so excited to be going there and not knowing what to expect. To be honest, I didn't know much about England at all. In fact, I didn't know much about any other country. All I knew about Britain was through the student discussions and reading a few political articles.

I don't ever remember reading a book of any kind, political or otherwise; if you remember I didn't even read my textbooks properly due to the fear of wear and tear, as I wanted to sell them to the new students to get my money back at a premium.

The only thing I read when I was little was a few comic books, my favourite being Texas, I loved it! The young sidekick to the main hero, Rodi, was my hero. The good Americans were fighting against the bad English for their independence, which sort of confirmed some of the imperialist accusations discussed amongst the students.

I thought I would discover and make my own judgment about England when I lived there. Surely, living in a country is way better than any book; 'live and learn' as someone said.

Landing at London Heathrow

With a head full of fear and excitement, I arrived at Heathrow Airport. What a tremendous feeling - I was now in England, which would end up being my home for the next twenty-one years. Utterly unbelievable! Who would have guessed at the time that this was my destiny?

If I remember correctly, Janet had come to pick me up with her elder sister Carol. I think I had some paper work with me for the immigration formalities; not able to speak a word of English they brought in a translator. After some questioning they let me through, I can't remember how I found my way to the exit or even how they allowed Janet to come and pick me up.

Wow, I was officially in the UK and with Janet, and I remember Janet's face was like a huge laughing emoji. My face too was a picture of happiness, so relieved and ecstatic to be with Janet again.

Logic Versus Emotion

I'm not good at showing my emotions at the best of times, and I have had so much grief over it down the years from the people very close to me, and rightly so. I really can't comprehend what makes people emotional or introverted. Everybody tells me people can change, but I am not sure if we are able to change certain characteristics we are born with or develop growing up.

Being unable to express my true feelings has always made me uncomfortable and angry with myself, but I just couldn't see a way out of it, even to this day. While I was a little kid growing up in other peoples' homes, and possibly not receiving enough love and affection, it had a lasting effect on me. I have always envied those who can easily display their emotions to loved ones, and in public. It may be my strong logical side which prevents me from displaying my true emotions. I am just too serious about things in general. In that respect, I guess it's not surprising that I would go on to become a games programmer.

Oh well, maybe I will have a more balanced character, the next time around…

First and Lasting Impressions

It was such a great relief to be back together with Janet again after a few months. I felt so safe, and so very happy. Janet was from Southampton, and living there with her parents. We went across London to Waterloo station on the underground to take the train to Southampton. My first impressions of what I saw and experienced was very positive.

They were talking the whole time during the journey, no idea what about, but they were talking quite a bit, and of course I didn't understand a word. I spent a lot of time looking out of the window trying to enjoy the scenery, and making mental notes of it all. It was a lovely day and the countryside was so beautiful, all green and so neat. I thought how impressive it was. Lovely little farms and houses along the way and such open countryside; flat fields with grazing cattle, sheep and horses. Of course, where I grew up it was all very green and beautiful, but it was also very hilly and full of mountains. I was surprised to see how flat England was, so different in comparison.

Meeting My New English Family, Mr and Mrs Hewes

We arrived in Southampton at Janet's parents. I met the in-laws, with some sort of sign language greeting. It felt so strange; they were all talking and feeling jolly, and I wasn't understanding a word, just wondering what might be in store for me. Janet's father George was a retired dockworker who was over sixty, and

In-laws house in Sholing

her mother Doris was a bit younger. They were genuinely nice and friendly to me; I could see they were trying to make me feel at home.

They lived in a rented three bed detached house with a nice garden, in a lovely part of Southampton, Sholing. Janet told me they were just about managing financially, which apparently most retired people did. Janet was working at an old people's home, not earning that much and she also had to work night shifts sometimes. Nevertheless, Janet was contributing to the rent and the food. My new in-laws were an average working class family; not a lot of money to spare maybe, but they seemed to have a reasonably nice and comfortable life. I was impressed, and I could see that England was a very developed country. I think they were able to rent this lovely house for less than normal because they had lived there for such a long time and also the property belonged to a trust or a foundation.

It was the start of a new adventure; a completely new environment, a different culture, different food, different weather, well not so much the weather as it was very similar to the Black Sea region, as in it rained a lot! However, I found it very difficult to get used to the food though, it was so different to what I was familiar with.

Janet wasn't earning enough for us to have our own place yet, so I was in England, at the age of twenty-one, and I was still living at someone else's house. Just like I did as a little boy, still poor and still a nomad!

Living in With The In-Laws

George spent most of his time in the garden where he had a nice shed and a small workshop with lots of tools. He was such a good handyman, always keeping busy. I was really impressed by this; in Turkey most retired old men just spend their time in the teashops, drinking tea and playing cards. George was always making things, looking after the chickens, growing vegetables too. What a contrast between the countries, I thought.

Our English neighbours seemed quite curious by my arrival, just as the Turks had been about Janet. But it was different from Turkey, nobody came to our house bringing food or inviting me to their homes. Again two very different cultures, one very forward and overly friendly, while the other more reserved and almost cold.

Good job Janet had learnt some Turkish, at least we could talk occasionally, otherwise I would have gone mad. It was tough not knowing any English at all, no conversation with the in-laws or the neighbours; nothing more than morning, hello, bye! The days were passing very slowly, not much to do other than look at some English language books. Spending time in the garden, collecting eggs and talking to the chickens. Actually, I used to think that animals understood all the languages of the world! So I used to tell the chickens all about our chicken diet in Turkey!

The in-laws had a routine life; they used to enjoy watching cowboy movies in the afternoons just before teatime. I would watch the movies with them, yes, just watch them; nowadays we would have multiple subtitles. I did enjoy the 'tea at five' though, what a lovely tradition I thought. It took me quite a bit of time to get used to the English tea with milk! Turks are also heavy tea drinkers, even more than the English, but never with milk. My mother-in-law, Doris, would make lovely, delicious tasting cakes, and I always looked forward to our teatimes. She was such a good cook.

Sunday Roast, Yorkshire Pudding and Custard

Janet's sister, Carol, and her husband Roy lived nearby with their kids Jennifer and Michael. I was spending most of my time at home, but Carol would sometimes come and rescue me and take me shopping with her. I'm not sure, but it was probably a big Tesco store. I had never seen such a supermarket before, and I was very impressed by it.

She would shop from a carefully prepared shopping list, and she'd also buy things for her parents, and those items were on the list too, marked as 'Mum'. I used to watch the way she shopped, she would be checking the prices carefully, sometimes changing her mind and swapping some items. I assumed she was trying to keep the cost to a certain amount, it was well planned and executed shopping. I guess I was quite good at observing the small details; this probably helped me quite a bit in my game design and development work.

Carol would drop me off along with her mum's shopping. She would tell Doris the cost of her shopping, and then Doris would pay Carol there and then. Carol would sometimes give Doris a small amount of change back. I'm sharing these details because, to me, it was so new and different; weekly or fortnightly shopping for some items, accurate and careful spending, charging mum the exact amount. Some of it I found odd, as it was so different to the Turkish culture. For instance, there's no way children would take money from their parents for food shopping, let alone take the small change back.

In fact, I started doing a little shopping myself from the local corner shop, as I was smoking in those days, I was mostly buying cigarettes. I was shocked to discover that the shopkeeper would give you such a small amount of change from, say, a ten-pound note. In Turkey, if you didn't have the right amount of change then every shopkeeper without exception would either say 'don't worry forget it, or pay later'.

Careful planning and having a set shopping budget were signs of progress and efficiency I thought. So, a lot of learning and adjustment was needed on my part.

We would mostly have the Sunday roasts at the in-laws but sometimes at Carol and Roy's. This type of family gathering would happen more often in Turkey, but I did love the Sunday roast, what a great tradition. Everyone would have a chance to eat meat at least once a week. Really, I adored the roast; in fact it was the only dish that I truly enjoyed having. As I said, Doris was a very good cook and her roast was second to none along with the yummy Yorkshire pudding and desserts with custard.

Getting a Taste of England

We would always have some vegetables with the roast, such as carrots, peas sprouts or greens; but they were just plain boiled vegetables, no spices or anything. I could never get used to the taste, as we always had very elaborate and tasty vegetable dishes back home. In Turkey, even as a side dish, vegetables were always cooked with a few ingredients. Even though I could never get used to the taste of plain boiled vegetables, much later I could see the benefit of consuming vegetables like that. It was probably healthier. Nowadays, I have steamed vegetables to preserve all the goodness in the food. Admittedly, adding some butter, black pepper and crushed red pepper does add a bit to the taste.

I was slowly settling in, becoming a part of the family, feeling a bit more comfortable, as the days and weeks passed. There were so many new customs to learn and adjust to. I was just taking it all in and moving along the path set before me.

Roy worked at the Standard Telephones and Cables Company (STC), which was situated at the Southampton docks. It was probably the biggest cable factory in the world, manufacturing analogue communication cables that connected the continents. I had no idea I would be working there soon, which would be the start of yet another major turn of events.

One evening Roy took me to his local pub. I had only been in the UK for a few weeks. A couple of his other friends joined us too. Roy bought me a pint of beer, I can't remember the type but it was quite tasty nonetheless, different to what I had been used to in Turkey. They were chatting away, laughing out loud, and I was just sat there listening without understanding a word. I began wondering if they were laughing at me'. God, it felt awful not understanding, and not being able to join in the conversation. I was like a little child, helpless; I suddenly realised the importance of language, can you imagine not understanding anything anyone says to you? I remember promising myself there and then, that I would learn to speak English as well as the English! That was probably the first time I had ever set myself a clear target.

They began playing darts, which was something I had never seen before. After a few throws Roy gave me a dart and suggested I try. Of course, I tried to tell him that I didn't have a clue about the game, but he didn't know what I was saying either. Anyway, I tried a few times, judging the weight of the dart and getting a sense for it. At the same time, Roy was showing me a few things on the board, probably where to throw, but most of the time I was even missing the board, darts were falling on the floor.

Everyone was laughing and having fun at my expense, or this was what I was thinking anyway. They probably didn't mean to be horrible towards me; they just found it funny that some Turk was trying something new and failing miserably at it. After a few lousy throws, I managed a couple of decent shots, almost hitting the bulls-eye. This time I received the thumbs up from Roy and his friends. Trying to keep my composure, I had a few more throws and I began to get better at it. In fact, I was almost hitting the targets Roy was pointing at.

Well, I was good at sports and I managed to get the hang of darts too but I never really felt good enough at it. And, although I didn't play it much, I did enjoy watching it on TV, there were some great players in that era such as John Lowe and Eric Bristow.

Of course, I loved football and I watched it on the telly whenever I could. Match of the Day was great (anyone remember Jimmy Hill?) I became a Liverpool fan very early on, but I can't remember why, apart from the fact they were brilliant. It was most likely Kenny Dalglish. I loved the skill he had and his intelligence, such a capable and clever player. Of course, later he also became a very good manager and won several cups with Liverpool.

I watched cricket a few times, but it was not for me, it was just too long and too slow for my liking. The other British sport I loved watching was snooker, although I could never learn to play it well enough. I just loved the game and admired watching the gifted players like Alex Higgins and Jimmy White. I remember that Steve Davis was a great player too, but I never liked him. He was so boring, and he nearly always used to beat my hero, Higgins!

Three-Day Train Journey to Istanbul, and No It Wasn't The Orient Express

During my first few months in England I had to return to Turkey in order to take my remaining exams. The political situation was even worse, more riots and fighting, many more young people dying, it was so sad. It didn't look like ending soon either, and I still had one more exam to take. It was so expensive flying to and from Turkey, and we didn't have much money.

This journey to take my last remaining exam was in 1979. Janet said it would be much cheaper by train and it was. But she never warned me that it would take forever and would be so boring. It took nearly three days! It qualifies as my worst journey of all time! She said it might be difficult to get food on the train, besides it would be expensive too, so she made me a nice food bag and put in lots of meat balls, cheese, bread and other snacks to last me the journey.

I can't remember how I managed the whole thing, how many stations and changes, I can't remember any of it, best forgotten maybe, I hated it! But I do remember that it took me ages to find a seat. I eventually found a carriage with an empty seat where I remained as long as I could. There was a young guy sitting opposite me, and with what little we could say to each other, I worked out he was from Iran, and like me was going home. We tried to make attempts from time to time to exchange a few words; his English wasn't very good either, maybe even worse than mine. It was nice though to at least say a few words and smile at each other. I had lost all sense of time; it was so difficult to remain in the same place for days; falling asleep a little but then always being woken up by something. I've never been a good sleeper during travel, and I could never sleep during those long coach trips in Turkey either. My neck, my legs, my whole body was becoming very stiff. I started trying to loosen my joints by walking up and down, but never straying too far from the seat!

I remember having a little bit to eat; I thought I should make it last the whole way, so I was rationing it. I made a sandwich with some meatballs and cheese, and offered half of it to my Iranian companion. He declined, and made a few signs and left his seat. He probably said he'd go and buy something to eat from one of the carriages. He probably had enough money. Anyway, he came back about half an hour later, empty handed and with an empty stomach. From what he could tell me, he couldn't find anything to eat. Just as Janet had warned me, there was no food on board the train. I said no problem, and insisted that he take some of mine. We shared my food, and together managed to arrive in Istanbul in one piece, I was glad it was over. Such a dreadfully long and boring journey, if only I had some music to listen to. I think the Walkman was launched in 1979, but I didn't have one and I didn't know anything about it yet, and probably couldn't afford it either.

Anyway, it was over thank God, and I promised myself never to board a train again, and I think I managed to keep my word until Eurostar!

Settling in England, 1979

After taking my final exam I returned to England, this time for good.

I would end up living in England for twenty-one years, right until October 2000 when I returned to my native Turkey to kick-start the professional gaming sector.

Janet's grandparents (Mother in-law's parents) also lived not too far from us, and they would visit each other quite often. Sometimes the grandparents would join us for Sunday dinner. The grandmother was a very big lady, she had such an imposing character and personality. The grandfather, on the contrary, was a very small man, much older and fragile looking. I think he had some health issues and he had to be careful with his diet. And, the grandma was very strict with him, she treated him like a little boy and was always telling him off, 'Take your hands off that, you know you shouldn't have it!' or 'Have you smoked again?' She was trying to protect him, but I thought she overdid it. The poor thing seemed terrified of her.

Such a shame my English wasn't good enough yet; I wish I could have spoken with him properly. He really liked me though. Janet told me that he had actually fought in the First and the Second World War. He was even in Gallipoli (Turkey) fighting the Turks, maybe that was one of the reasons why he liked me. He said the Turks were very brave people. He wasn't allowed, but he did love his smokes. I was allowed to smoke indoors by the fireplace and so that was where we sat. I would light a cigarette and share it with him. God, he was so happy puffing away, but his eyes were fixed on the door to see if his wife was coming. Poor thing, he couldn't even properly enjoy his last few cigarettes. Life can be so beautiful, and yet so cruel at the same time!

Sadly, he died a few months later, and we were all very upset. It was amazing to see how quickly Grandma deteriorated after his death. She was such a fearsome woman but suddenly lost a lot weight and turned into a fragile thing in a matter of weeks. Despite how strict she was towards her husband, she must have really loved him. After all, he was her lifelong companion, someone whom she had shared her whole life with. His passing must have created a massive void in her life.

I have heard of this a number of times since the grandparents' passing; when one of an old couple dies and the other follows not long after, as if they hold each other to life. I wonder if we appreciate our loved ones' love and companionship enough when they are with us?

I'm quite good at adapting to new surroundings, environments, people and cultures. I did, after all, spend all of my childhood with different families. I had to learn to adjust to different characters and expectations, and I suppose all this made me as resilient as I am. As a result, I was adapting to England, and to the English people, reasonably well.

Must Do Something About The Lingo and Do It Pronto

I must learn English well and do it quickly, that was my first main target. There was a technical college near the city centre; St. Mary's, which gave free English lessons to foreign students. We didn't have enough money to take a fulltime course and I was getting really frustrated not being able to speak with anyone. I had to wait for Janet to get home, so I could talk to her a little, but even that wasn't exactly a flowing conversation.

As far as I was concerned, I simply had to learn English as soon as possible. I started going to the college regularly for a couple of hours, a few times a week. I was very good with my French back in middle and high school, and I thought I could learn English quickly too. I was really enjoying the lessons. There were lots of young people from different countries; Spain, Italy, Brazil and so on. It was great mixing with lots of different students. I was picking it up rather quickly and doing a lot of reading at home too.

Janet found another place where they gave free lessons, so I went there too. I think it was an English teacher giving free lessons at a community centre. She was a very good teacher, and seemed very pleased with my efforts and progress. She decided to help me even more after I told her about my intentions to do a master's degree. We became very good friends; Janet and I even spent time at their holiday home in Bournemouth a few times.

I was making very good progress and quickly developed a good grasp of the grammar. I could see that I had to work more on the pronunciation, but I knew that at my age and with a Turkish and Georgian background, it would never be perfect. Therefore, I decided to concentrate more on expanding my vocabulary and improving the use of the language. All foreigners spoke with funny accents anyway, the main thing was to be able to understand the spoken and written word easily, and then be able to reply. Later on, I also found another course at the Southampton University, which was specifically designed for commercial and economics studies. I wanted to do a Master's Degree in Economic Planning, so this course was perfect. It helped me a lot; it provided a more advanced foundation to improve my English. Thus, I was now learning big words and forming more sophisticated and complex sentences.

All in all, I was incredibly pleased with the progress I was making, and so was Janet and her family. My teachers were also acknowledging my progress and giving me additional support to help even more. All of this gave me much more confidence to get better.

I met a Turkish student at the Southampton University; at first it was brilliant speaking in Turkish, almost nonstop trying to make up for the last few months, but then I realised it was slowing down my progress in English, so I stopped. I also decided to avoid any other Turks for some years to come to avoid any distraction. I was going full steam ahead and nothing could slow down my progress.

The First Test of My English

At the college, we were able to obtain English language certificates, and the Cambridge First Certificate exam was coming soon. Our teacher said I was ready for this, as I asked if I was competent enough to get decent results. He said yes, definitely. Really, I wanted to make sure that I achieved top marks; I didn't want to just pass, as I had throughout my education. I wanted to speak English properly and become proficient in it, and back it up with my certificates. A good command of English would help me with any future endeavours in England.

Overall, I thought I did quite well with the exam, but wasn't sure as to how well. It was so exciting waiting for the results. I was so pleased when the results finally came and I had the top result in my class. The result read something like 'passed with credit' and I also had B+. Anyway, the teacher said well done and that it was a very good result for such a short period of time.

Afterwards, I took it home and I was so happy with myself, showing it to Janet and her family, who were also very impressed with the result. However, I was quite surprised when nobody said anything about the 'with credit' part. I had a quick look and I knew credit had something to do with money. I just thought I'd performed so well that I was to be awarded with a small monetary prize! My poor interpretation of 'with credit' probably came from the fact I studied economics at university!

A Taste of The English Language

I wasn't sure about it, so I didn't ask anyone to tell me what this 'with credit' thing was all about. I thought there was only one way to find out and I had nothing to lose. The next day, I arrived at the college and went straight to the lady at the reception showing her my certificate and pointing to the 'with credit'. I asked, 'how do I get this credit?' She looked at the certificate and then looked back at me, rather puzzled and said, 'Do you mean this credit thing on your certificate? You're asking me if you will be paid for it?' I replied yes eagerly. She then started laughing so loudly that she scared me, she said, 'Sorry love, you won't get paid any money for that, with credit means you did very well with your exam, that's all'. After hearing this and understanding why she was laughing so much, I laughed with her! It was a shame at the time that I couldn't say, 'Sorry love, I was just pulling your leg!'

I told everyone back home what had happened, and we all had a jolly good laugh about it. And, that was my first understanding of the depth of the English language, and the fact that there was more than one meaning to most words. It's that word play which is so important in the excellent British humour. In fact, I think that British comedy is the best in the world. I've enjoyed some amazing TV classics over the years such as Not The Nine O'clock News, Have I Got News For You, Fawlty Towers, Young Ones, Blackadder, Only Fools and Horses just to name a few.

A few months later there was the JMB (Joint Metropolitan Board) certificate exam, which foreign students needed to obtain before they could study at UK universities, and I passed this too. All I had to do now to expand my knowledge of the grammar and vocabulary was start reading newspapers, watching TV and of course, talking with English people.

George, my father in-law was also teaching me some slang and local dialect; 'All right nipper', 'all right mush', 'get out of it...' All apparently used in Southampton or in the South. George had retired from the Southampton Docks and slang was probably used there a lot. I also used these words myself when I started working at the STC cable factory.

The Arrival of The Iron Lady

In just a few of years, I had lost my dad, become married at nineteen, and started a new life in a new country. If that wasn't enough, I was now about to witness a massive change in the UK. At that time, Thatcher was making big changes and offering big hopes too. Generally, big changes always bring misery and hardship to the less well off. The rich and the powerful always benefit from social and economic crises. A series of privatisations of important public companies and utilities coupled with the mine closures and later the unfair poll tax created social chaos in the country over the next few years.

One of the early policies put in place by Thatcher's government was the increase of the overseas student fees. I think it was around £900 per annum before, and now the fees shot up to £3,000. That was effectively Janet's full salary! Since I was not yet eligible for home student status and our financial means wouldn't stretch that far, suddenly my hope of doing a master's degree went out of the window. I was so disappointed; the only option left for me was to start looking for a job.

I think Janet suggested that I should apply for assistant manager jobs with training since I was a university graduate. I can't remember how many jobs I applied for, but some promptly replied by saying I wasn't suitable and some never even bothered. Presumably my Turkish degree didn't hold much value or maybe me being a foreigner didn't give me much of a chance. Anyway, after a while I gave up applying for those jobs and told Janet that I was prepared to do any job, odd jobs, day jobs, whatever. Ultimately, it would be better than doing nothing. Just as I had done in Izmit, I could start with any job I could find and then try and look for something better. She helped me go to Manpower (a recruitment agency), as they had lots of temporary day jobs, from unloading lorries to pushing wheelbarrows and stacking shelves.

I did this for a few months, having never done a proper day's work in my life before I found it very hard. Especially a three-day stint at a construction site pushing those wheelbarrows, that was truly awful. I wasn't used to it and I had so many blisters on my hands. The only job that I enjoyed was unpacking broken or damaged chocolate boxes and repacking them. We were allowed to eat as much as we wanted, at least that's what we were told. At first, I thought it was silly as people would eat chocolate all day, but, of course, you can only eat so much and they knew that! We were also allowed to take some home too. I enjoyed being able to sample so many and establish my favourite ones over the few days I worked there. My favourite three were Cadbury's Caramel, After Eight and Terry's Chocolate Orange, and in fact, still are.

Now that I was at least doing some odd jobs and making a little bit of money, we decided to rent a council flat near the town centre. It was close to St. Mary's College. There were some high-rise council blocks in the area; our one was a four-storey building, a flat on the top floor. It wasn't brilliant but much better than our flat in Izmit. At least we had heating, hot water and thank God, no damp!

Gizza Job - I Can Do That!

Since I was doing all these difficult and heavy jobs, I decided that maybe I should look for a permanent job at a factory or something. I was desperate and prepared to do any job I could get. I felt like Yosser, who became an icon in the Thatcherite Britain of the 80s, in the TV series "Boys From The Blackstuff". Since Roy was working as an accountant at the STC cable factory, maybe he could help me get a job there.

One evening we were having dinner at Carol's and we started chatting about this and that, how I was getting on, my English, jobs I was doing. I asked Roy if he could help me get a job at his factory. Roy said there was no way I could do that job as they had day and night 12-hour shifts; 4 days on 4 day off, but with 25% compulsory overtime. So sometimes you worked for 6 days solid. He also added that it was a closed shop and they never advertised their jobs; they always tried to employ the relatives or close friends of the existing workers. That's how they could make sure that the new workers would stay on for a long time, rather than leave after a few months. It was hard work and really boring apparently. Roy did his best to put me off; he painted such a bad picture. He genuinely thought that I wouldn't last more than a few months which I guess would undermine his reputation with the management.

But I said, 'Roy, I really need this job, I can do it, and I'll stay there as long as necessary'. Surely, it couldn't be worse than the horrible day jobs I had been doing. He finally agreed to speak with the manager.

Roy managed to arrange a job interview for me. God, I was so nervous, this was my very first serious job interview and it was in English! The manager also repeated what Roy had already told me about the hard conditions and that I was a university graduate and I wouldn't really last there for long etc. But I did all I could to assure him that I really needed this job and that I would stay and work there as long as I was allowed to.

Seeing both my desperation and honesty in my appeal he said, 'OK, we'll give you a chance and see how you get on. You can start next week'. Wow, I got a job, I was so happy. I thanked the manager and assured him that I wouldn't disappoint him. I then popped in to thank Roy and left the factory where I would then work for the next five years. The factory was at the Southampton Docks, a big complex with many facilities and production lines.

Power to The Working Class

On the way home, I was thinking about the last few months. Here I was in the UK, the country we had so many discussions about at university; stating how its system was unjust for the workers and the less fortunate, and that the capitalist system should be changed for the better. We were the young revolutionaries with compassion and aspirations for a better world.

Well I thought, laughing to myself, I have now become a worker myself and in the very core of the capitalist system too. Would I need to help myself or be able to liberate the workers from within? This wasn't a good time to be joining the working class as Thatcher was hell-bent on reducing the power and the influence of the unions. But, here I was, a member of the British working class; maybe I could become a working class hero, who knows? I couldn't wait to tell Janet, I was so happy to get a proper job and, from what Roy told me, with decent pay too.

Making Cables - The Cable Guy

I was to make cables for the next five years and become very good at it too. It was indeed a boring and hard job; the twelve-hour shifts were awful, changing from day to night, back to day was so tough. My sleeping pattern and eating habits all went haywire; I didn't know whether I was coming or going. To be honest, I was really disappointed about the prospect of working here for years, and possibly even retiring from here! Oh my God, even the thought of it scared me. Some of the older workers had already been here for twenty years, and although they were only forty or so they looked sixty! Some of them did warn me that this job could wear me down. Frankly, I could see it myself; the evidence was there before me. I could really see how some people looked a lot older than they were, really tired and worn out.

Nevertheless, I really needed the job and had to find a way to cope and stay with it. Besides, it really paid well; in fact, it was one of the best-paid jobs in the country. At least we would live comfortably without worrying about money, which was the main thing, as anything could happen with the government's harsh new economic policies.

To begin with they put me on a production line with an experienced worker who was effectively in charge of the line. He lived in one of the high-rise buildings near our flat. He was a black guy of Jamaican origin, probably in his fifties, and was very friendly towards me. I was told to learn the job well, so that I could start running and manning the whole production line myself. That meant a rise in position with a pay rise too. There were two people working on it, so they could take it in turns; you had one hour on and one hour off.

The core of the cable was made there, with so many steel reels in a turning metal cage that created the wire strand. This was then covered by a copper metal sheet and welded on the seam automatically. It was quite an impressive production line; it could make sixty feet of cable per minute. However, it was so noisy; all those steel reels turning like mad inside the rotating cage resulted in a deafening noise. We couldn't even hear each other speak. They provided us with headsets to keep the noise out, but it was more uncomfortable wearing them than the constant, horrible humming and whooshing sound we would be subjected to. Faced with the risk of losing our hearing, we had to wear them, but sometimes it would become unbearable. Even now I have a slight loss of hearing and I'm sure the wall of sound at the factory must have caused most of it.

No matter what, I was determined to persevere, learn the job as quickly as possible and run the line myself. We were paid weekly and I was already earning more than three times what Janet was. I would moan and complain all the time, but I also put up with it. Besides, complaining was like medicine to me, it kept me going, fired up and more resolute.

I think we were producing the TAT-6 and TAT-7 (transatlantic telephone line) coaxial cables connecting USA and Britain. These cables were approximately 6,000-7,000 km long respectively. TAT-7 was the last analogue cable produced. I was involved with the initial production and testing of the first ever fibre optic TAT-8 before I left the factory in 1985.

After a few weeks I became the assistant line driver (controller), I was an able man and operated the production line by myself. We had three men working on the line: the driver, the cable guide (guiding the steel cable onto the big drums that was wound on for storage and the next line of operation

– covering of the cable with polyphone plastic), and the third guy downstairs keeping an eye on the copper sheet reel. In addition to this, he informed the driver to slow the line down to the required speed, so he could replace the empty copper reel. This would be done while the line was still running. The line would only be stopped for replacing wire bobbins or when a steel wire broke, otherwise it was a 24-hour non-stop operation.

Now that I was a fully-fledged and qualified cable worker, I had to start doing overtime too, which meant working six days. Whenever I did overtime I would always get the most boring and unwanted jobs; the laying of the cable into big tanks at the end of the production line, where the cable was covered with the protective polythene layer. My line was noisy and ran at sixty feet per minute, but generally you would walk up and down the line double checking things for smooth operation and replacing empty bobbins. At least the time used to pass relatively quickly.

While the polythene line ran at ten feet per minute, it was so slow. Basically, you would hold the cable the whole time guiding and laying it down in the tank, making sure there were no big gaps in the layers. Equally, to make sure all the layers were level again and the cable didn't get damaged or tangled up. It was so slow that on several occasions, especially during night shifts, when I came to relieve the worker before me, I would find him fast asleep with cable all over the place and some of it over him. Luckily the line was too slow to cover the person completely and cause any real danger. The cables in these tanks would be subsequently loaded into massive tanks inside huge cable ships. These ships were used to actually lay the cable in the sea.

The polythene line was a non-stop 24-hour operation too; first the cable was covered with polythene granules and melted onto the cable. Then the polythene cable would be cooled down and put through a shaver to get rid of any excess and reduce the diameter to the exact size. There were two bins in the line to be manned from time to time (perhaps a couple of times in the hour); one bin held the polythene granules, which had to be refilled, and the other bin collecting all the shaved polythene dust. Refilling wasn't too bad, but emptying the dustbins was just awful. I think we put a mask on, but polythene dust would go everywhere; into our eyes, hair, clothes even through the overalls we wore. It would take fifteen minutes to air hose all the dust down, and we would have to do this every time. This is the job you were mostly likely to get during overtime. And everyone hated it. In actual fact, I didn't want to do overtime, but we all had to do it, there was no choice.

The third major production line was for the part of the cable that would be laid on the shore (buried underground). To protect the cable further, it was first covered with a layer of thick aluminium wires and then with tar. If you thought the polythene line was bad, the tar line was twice as bad. There was an absolutely awful tar smell, no matter what we did, it always absorbed into our hair, and we would wash our hair with a special heavy shampoo which I'm sure damaged our hair. The cable would become so heavy with the layers of thick wire and all that tar, and you needed several people to pick up just a few feet of the thing. And, it was absolute murder when it came to loading it onto the cable ships!

Cable being loaded into a massive tank

The final cable would be loaded into massive tanks inside the big cable ships. There was an elaborate and quite a complex line that allowed the cable to travel from the factory all the way to the cable ships, and sometimes we would have to do this job too. This was another job I hated; it was really tough. Everyone else loved it, as we were paid so much more; sometimes even double if you were lucky enough to catch the weekend session. It was piecework too, so we had to load so much capable on the day and the quicker we finished the sooner we would go home. I couldn't understand the mentality behind it; they would work like mad to finish half an hour earlier. The polythene cable was much lighter and there would be more of it to load; to finish early they would run the loading line faster and faster. God, we would sweat like pigs! About fifteen people in the tank, for thirty minutes or so at a time in our overalls, taking turns to have a breather, and back in again. This would go on for hours!

The cable with tar was so much heavier and of course so dirty. We would wear overalls, steel cap boots (it could easily smash your toes if it fell on your foot, that's how heavy it was), and helmets to protect our heads. We had a couple of Indian Sikhs and they always refused to take their turbans off and wear a helmet. However, it was absolutely compulsory and necessary to wear helmets for protection. They would argue for ages and I can't remember how they would resolve it, but it happened on every load. There's this inevitable clash between religious beliefs and life's realities, both of which must be respected and somehow co-exist.

Again, about fifteen men would take turns guiding the tarred cable and laying it in the tank, and it was so tough. They would always push the speed to the max, but it was heavy and difficult to hold and pass to the next person. Sometimes some would drop it, and then they would slow down to recover the cable, correct the layer, pack the gaps and carry on.

If you were the union representative or a friend of them, then you would spend more time on the speed controller. Truly, it was the best job to have during loading; just adjust the speed as requested; down a half, up a half. The union people always got the cushy jobs. They and their friends would also get easier jobs on overtime too. A real injustice!

While doing all these difficult, tiring and risky jobs I would remember all the endless discussions we would have in the dormitory; about workers, unions and all the injustices, and I was now witnessing most of it myself first-hand. Clearly, I could see how people used power and position to their own advantage at every level. Such a shame really, that humans can be so selfish, greedy and also quite brutal to maintain their advantage.

Despite all the difficulties I wasn't going to give up, I did my best to carry out my work to the best of my ability. Very quickly I moved up to be the fully qualified line driver, and now I had an assistant. As I moved up to the line driver position, my normal shit work became more bearable. In addition, my English was getting better and better, enriching it with the localised slang words and expressions. But I just hated the overtime and the cable loading. I didn't want all that extra money; I'd rather not do it at all.

Subsequently, I decided to go and see my GP and see if I could obtain a Doctor's report stating that my back wasn't suitable for cable loading and also heavy lifting. As it turned out my GP had a friend with him, some sort of expert on back pain or something. He examined me as well and discovered that apparently my left side was a quarter of an inch shorter from the waist down, which could cause problems with heavy work in the long run. I wasn't sure whether to be pleased that I was going to get away with not doing the dreaded boat loading or worried to hear that I may have a serious problem! The Doctor assured me it wasn't anything too serious but he could give me a medical report. That was easy!

I went to the union guys with the report and told them that I couldn't do cable loading. They said it was fine as there would be others who'd be more than happy to take my place for the extra money. That's what I thought, and so I was mightily relieved that I was off the boat loading work. Furthermore, I also said I didn't want to do the overtime either. They joked by saying why didn't I quit all together while I was at it. Eventually, they said they wouldn't mind if I didn't do overtime, as long as the management sanctioned it. For a while I didn't do overtime either, but for some reason I was asked to do it a few weeks later. I thought as long as there was no boat loading I could manage the overtime. Plus, it was quite a bit more money, which meant we could save up and use it later if we needed it.

Most of my work colleagues couldn't understand how I could refuse all that money for a little bit of hardship with the cable loading. They were right of course, it was a lot of money, with just a few boat loading work shifts, they would earn enough for their next holiday. But I'd rather earn a little less and also have a little less hardship. Overall, to me life was always about establishing the right balance between things.

Getting Close and Personal With The British Working Class

I was now getting used to the working conditions and fully adapting to the new environment. My communication skills were improving, which enabled me to have more conversations during my off time, which was every other hour. We worked one hour on, one hour off. If you were on the dreaded polythene line, then you had to go and empty the plastic dustbin and refill the polythene granular bin during your time off. So in effect, you never really had a full hour's break.

There were all sorts of people working on the shop floor; English, Scottish, Irish, Indian, Pakistani and we had one Italian and one guy from Australia. It's a real shame that I can only remember one or two of the names. On second thoughts, it's best not to name any names at all! During our time off, we all sat in the canteen where we also had breakfast, lunch, tea and coffee.

Talking about breakfast reminded me of my yogurt plus cornbread combo I used to have as a kid in the village. In my early years in England I really missed my yogurt and cornbread. We used to have Danone yogurt, but it was never the same. And no cornbread until much later when I discovered I could buy corn flour from many of the Pakistani shops, and so I started making my own bread. But first I discovered cornflakes in the UK and I used it as a cornbread substitute. It tasted very similar to me, and I would have my cornflakes with yogurt as well as milk, and instead of adding sugar I would add a little salt instead, which made the cornflakes taste more like cornbread!

I used to have cornflakes and milk in the factory canteen for my breakfast just like most others did. When they saw me add salt to mine they couldn't believe it, they thought I was so weird! However, I tried to explain how I ate yogurt with cornbread and the bread was salty, so by adding salt I was making my cornflakes taste like cornbread. Well, they still thought it was disgusting; at least I had learnt a new word, 'disgusting'.

At work, there was a small lounge area with a few comfy sofas and armchairs. This is where most of the tea drinking and conversation took place. Others used to sit at the tables either playing cards, or reading. I didn't have any books to read, but there were always books and magazines lying around. Generally, I just browsed through some magazines.

My English was improving, but I still had a long way to go. I was misspelling or misusing words sometimes really badly, and the reaction of the English workers would be rude, almost brutal. Actually, they would ridicule me to death. They were mostly unforgiving and always taking the mickey (piss). Yet there were a couple of nice guys who would intervene and give the others a good telling off, or 'bollocking' as was commonly used! But that didn't stop the barrage of insults. I became very good friends with the Australian guy, who would always stick up for me.

But, they were even more brutal with the Pakistanis. It was non-stop. Recalling that time, I remember that there was a young Pakistani guy and every time he walked into the canteen several of them would call out; "Oi Paki, get the fucking teas in!" This would be the mildest of insults and they would constantly throw insults at him. Eventually, the poor guy would break down and cry. Nevertheless, I would try and stick up for him with my limited language, but to no avail. The Australian guy would help if he were also in the lounge. They would simply dismiss our objections with, "Fuck's sake, we're only kidding around, no harm meant. Just passing the time." They would sort of apologise. They probably thought it was okay to muck about a bit and laugh at someone else's expense. The fact of the matter is that they were simply being racist, no doubt about it. I don't believe they even tried to empathise or imagine what it felt like to be at the receiving end of such racial harassment.

As they knew me more, my English was improving and they also started behaving more friendly towards me. After all, I was married to an English girl, and I didn't look like a classic foreigner I guess; I could be Spanish or French. Come to think about it, the English probably hated the French more, so it was just as well perhaps I wasn't French!

Coming Up With Ideas For The Suggestion Box

While I was on the production line, I was constantly thinking of ideas about how to make improvements. I had so much time to think while walking up and down checking the line for possible faults and problems to prevent major shutdowns. It was quite a complex line, and we used to get a few serious problems and considerable downtime. We would often get wire breaks, those bobbins were turning at some speed and there was high tension on the line enough to break slightly tangled wire.

They had already implemented some sensors to catch the broken wire; it would beep and a light would flash on the control panel. But if you were away from the panel, checking either the bobbins or the rest of the line, then by the time you came to the panel to stop the line most of the time the broken wire would already have gone through the strand mills. The broken end of the wire would go through the copper welding stage and on its way towards the winding drum!

This would mean a huge downtime and considerable amount of scrap cable. Repairing the broken wire, resetting all the mills that made the wire strand, cutting and scrapping the cable to the broken wire end would take a lot of effort and also downtime costing tens of thousands of pounds, plus, quite a bit of scrapped cable; I can't remember the cost of a one-foot cable, but I recall that the amount of scrapped cable every year would amount to hundreds of thousands of pounds in value. So, wire break was a major problem.

Anyhow, I came up with the idea of automatically slowing the line down to twenty five feet per minute; no matter where the driver was, the line would slow down enough to prevent the broken end from going through the mills. This in turn, gave the driver the time to stop the line and catch the broken end before the crucial stage. Then he could weld the ends of the wire and just start the line again within quarter of an hour, just like changing an empty bobbin. What's more I also suggested moving the positions of the bobbins, so that even if the wire break occurred on the bobbin closest to the mills, the driver would still have a good chance of catching it in time.

We had a suggestion box by the canteen. I wrote it all up as best as I could and put it in the box. After a few weeks I got a reply saying that it was a great idea. However, the engineers had already thought of something similar, but it wasn't considered practical. Nevertheless, with my new approach they would review it again and see if it was feasible. The amazing outcome was that they paid me twenty pounds for the idea!

Brilliantly, they did successfully implement my idea in just a few weeks, and it saved lots of downtime and a lot of cable and therefore money. In addition to this, I came up with a couple of other ideas, for which I was paid fifty pounds each. But then I remember getting paid five pounds for some other idea at which point I stopped thinking and wasting my brainpower! Just as well, as instead of spending time thinking of ideas for them, I would be busy thinking of ideas for myself!

Learning The Game

I started to get on well with everyone, making friends, playing football and squash and really becoming one of them. Of course, once I started socialising and participating in the activities, my standing improved and I earned their respect as a person. Also, I was constantly learning new words, some fancy and some slang. Truly, I was arming myself should I need to exchange insults with them because I was keen to give them back as much as they threw at me. They really enjoyed it too. If you can't beat them join them! I was one of the lads now, alright mate, alright mush, alright nipper; these were my go-to greetings.

My Australian friend and I were in the lounge having our break. He told me how impressed he was with me that I had managed to make friends with everyone and at the same time giving them a hard time too when called upon. So I said to him that I needed one strong insult to give them a big shock, 'I want to use it when they tease our Pakistani friend. Surely you Australians must have one or two insults for them since they don't think much of you either.' He said, 'You are right, the English don't like us, but it's alright as we don't like them either!' He said, 'You can try calling them 'pommy bastard!' That should surprise them.' I repeated it myself a few times to double-check. I was trying to add a hint of an Australian accent too.

The usual suspects walked in and sat around giving the usual greetings. And then in comes our young Pakistani friend, the easy and constant target. They went off on him as ever; 'Oi Paki, get the fucking teas in, and make mine two sugars, mine one sugar and be fucking quick about it.' I thought what better time to use my newly acquired fresh insult, 'Let's try it and see how it goes'. I got up looked around making sure if everyone was paying enough attention to me. I then said in a raised and firm voice, 'That's fucking enough, alright?' They looked amused by my unexpected outburst, almost shocked. I continued while I had everyone's undivided attention. 'Just stop this shit, you pommy bastards!' and then I sat down. I'm not kidding, there was complete silence, not a word for a good few seconds, except for my Australian friend, who was trying to contain his laughter. The reaction was amazing, 'Fucking hell mate, where did you learn that, nice one Turk, that told us'. Everyone was laughing, even our Pakistani friend.

This funny incident cemented my friendship with everybody for good, it was as if I was now accepted into the English club.

Welcome Baby Nejati, November 1980!

Now that we had our own place, both working and earning enough money to live comfortably it seemed the right time to grow our family. Janet gave

birth to our son Nejati in November 1980. Really unbelievable, now I was a father too! Nej was born as a very healthy baby, almost 8 pounds.

Before Nej was born I was imagining if he would have two different coloured eyes: maybe blue and green? Can you imagine that, wouldn't that be amazing? I did have a wild imagination. Of course, his eyes weren't different colours, but they were beautifully blue. Incidentally, my father had blue eyes too as did Janet.

Years later when I learnt that David Bowie (RIP) had two different coloured eyes I thought my idea wasn't that wild. Well, that was until I discovered that actually his eye was discoloured because of a punch he had received from his friend when he was young.

Nej was turning into a lovely baby; he brought us so much joy and happiness. Janet stopped working and I was earning enough money anyway. I remember Janet entering Nej into the local Kodak baby contest; he won the 'bonny baby of the year' prize! He grew up to be a handsome young man. Well, I had better move on now before I embarrass him further.

If I had a son, I had decided that I would give him my dad's name, and with Janet's consent that's what we did. For starters, my dad's name was registered wrong, as it should have been either Nejat or Necati. But it was recorded as Nejati. Completely wrong yet that's what his official name was. I was registered on the wrong date with the wrong age, my dad with the wrong name. What's wrong with my family?

In hindsight, I wish Janet hadn't agreed or at least suggested for him to have an English name too. Poor Nej got so much stick from his peers for his name. Kids can be so cruel and unforgiving; Nej had light brown hair, blue eyes and was perfectly English looking apart from the name. Poor thing, he must have suffered so much from the teasing from the other kids. Just because of his name he was treated like a foreigner. Damn you racism!

Janet Sees My Cousin's Death in Her Dream

I cannot remember the exact date, but on this particular day I had come home from the night shift and had gone to bed straight away. Janet woke me up late afternoon to get ready for work. Our twelve-hour shifts started at 7AM or 7PM.

With Janet and Nej, 1982

Before I was out of bed Janet wanted to tell me something but there was sadness on her face, which worried me. She looked at me and then said she wanted to share something that would upset me, but it was best I should know. I said okay, but I was really worried. Trying to be very careful with her words, she told me that she had seen my cousin Ercan die in her dream last night!

Janet was into Tarot cards and also claimed to be a capable medium. Of course, I never believed in that sort of thing in the slightest, but she would surprise me with some of the things she would say. So, I really was curious to hear what her dream was all about. She described it in such detail that one would think she actually saw it in real life. She told me how Ercan was chased by gunmen in the middle of a street, and shot down from behind while running. Apparently, he tried to get away, but couldn't. She said he lay there for a while and then died. Ercan and I were like brothers and Janet had spent some time with him when we were in Istanbul. I was so upset but, of course, I didn't believe it. Well, I didn't want to believe it, as it was a dream, after all.

But years later, in 1991, when I went to Turkey to do my army service, I learnt that Ercan did die in 1980. My cousin Ali (Ercan's uncle) told me all the details, and the similarity to how Janet had described it to me was unbelievable. I told Ali that Janet had seen the whole thing in her dream. He was as bewildered as I was.

Ercan was such a bright and clever young man with a very bright future. He was about to graduate from one of the best medical schools in Turkey, but was gunned down by the right wing rivals in May 1980. This happened a few months before the military coup that put a stop to the killings. Unfortunately, the coup also put a massive dent in the democratic and social progress of Turkey and the country still hasn't fully recovered from it.

Being Henry The 7ᵗʰ in My Past Life

When I was back living in the UK again in 2016, Janet and I were talking about life. Janet said, 'I know you don't believe in these things, but I can tell you who you were in your previous life'. I told her that I had reservations about a lot of things; I'm a programmer and mainly based my thinking on logical grounds. 'But, do please tell me, I would like to know,' I replied. She said, 'Don't laugh, but you were Henry the Seventh!' Trying to contain my laughter, I suddenly realised that it all made sense. I was in England centuries before, and I was simply returning home in 1979. I said I'd rather be Henry the Eighth though! Shame on my bad luck, maybe next time. We had a good laugh about it!

For the first time this made me seriously think about it all. I thought, why would a Turkish kid, from a remote village in Turkey, marry an English girl, and then go and live in England? Just a twist of fate, just a simple coincidence, preordained 'kismet' (fate) or simply our destiny taking over? Maybe all of these and more, I really don't know. Every part of our life seems to be like a piece of a big jigsaw puzzle, our bigger life. Maybe everything or nothing in life is an accident. Here's what I would love to have asked one of my favourite fictional heroes, 'I'm all ears Mr. Spock, what's the logic behind it all?'.

And Mum Joins Us in The UK

My mum had already lived with us for a while in Izmit. While I was in England building a new life and a future, my mind was back home with my mum. 'She must be really missing us, and longing to be with us, especially now that she has a grandson too', I thought to myself. She was living with our relatives in Izmit, so at least I knew she wasn't lonely. I was fully supporting  and providing for her, and my cousins were taking care of her. It would be tough for her to live in England; no language, no friends or relatives, but I thought at least she will have us, especially Nej. She will manage. Finally, I convinced her and she came to England to live with us at least for a while.

Janet was able to speak with her in Turkish enough to get by, taking her out, showing her around and generally trying to make her comfortable and happy. She was very good with mum. And, mum was very happy to see me and spend lots of time with Nej too. She seemed okay for a time, but gradually it was really getting to her. She was missing Turkey, her comfort zone, the food, her friends, everything. I had made just one Turkish friend in Southampton who we would see occasionally. He was also married to an English girl. Luckily, her mother had also come to England, and it was nice while it lasted. Both mums spent quite a bit time together, but his mum returned to Turkey after a few weeks.

After a couple of years she found it too difficult to cope. Being with Nej or me simply wasn't enough and she was really sad about not being in Turkey. It gradually became apparent that she patiently lived with us all this time, almost three years, just hoping that we would all go back to Turkey with her after a while. When she realised it was not going to happen, she became very agitated, angry and started behaving irrationally. It was as if she was trying to force me into going back with her.

We had a very difficult few months; it was getting unbearable for everyone. I was trying to explain to her how I had absolutely nothing in Turkey, and what a struggle it would be to live there and start from scratch and raise a three year old. And the outlook in Turkey was still very bad and it would be way too risky to start a new life there. She accepted my reasoning, but the poor thing just couldn't bear the idea of living without us, and not knowing if she would ever see us again. In the end though, we decided that it was best for mum to go back. Of course she was very sad to leave us behind, but also quite relieved that she would get out of this unhappy situation. She went back to Izmit. I made sure she was well looked after by our relatives. I was hoping to bring her back again sometime in the future and, we could go and visit her in Turkey too.

Getting into The Game: Kluki – The Card Game!

During our breaks some of the workers played cards in the canteen. Now that my English was much better and my relationship with all my colleagues was more friendly, I began integrating with them more and more. One day I decided to check out what card game they were playing. I watched them a little, and very quickly realised that what they were playing was a very traditional game from Turkey. In actual fact, I played it from high school days, and it was also one of our pastimes at university.

I asked them if I could join in and play with them. They dismissed me with an immediate insult, 'Fuck off Turk, you couldn't play this, besides we are playing for money and you wouldn't be up for that!' I said, 'Well, you can teach me, how hard can it be, I'm a bright man, I can learn it in a few days, besides I have money too?' One of them replied, 'OK, why not, let's take some of his money.' And another said to take his place because he'd had enough for now anyway.

I joined the table. We decided that we would play a few hands, so that they could show me the general rules and how it was played. I could get the gist of it as it were. It was a game I knew, and I knew it bloody well, but I couldn't let them in on it. We call it '51 (Ellibir)' in Turkey. I think they called it Kluki or something; it probably came from Greece, as with most things which are common between our two countries; yogurt, a lot of traditional sweets and dishes. In fact, The Greeks and the Turks are more like cousins than enemies. Unfortunately, because of the horrid politics and international powers we are encouraged to remain enemies and hate each other throughout history. This is a real shame!

They agreed to my proposition saying, 'Okay, let's teach this Turk the game, and a lesson and take all his money'. Naturally, I was pretending to have never played it before, but it wasn't easy to keep my cover. I couldn't give them any signals. We played a few hands and decided that I had grasped it enough to start for real. Then, I said I would learn more as we played, although it would cost me a little. But no problem I said, it's only twenty pence a hand, no big deal, and I will have some fun for a couple of pounds.

We were now playing for real, the cards were dealt, there were a few people watching too, probably wondering how I would fair. I was just mucking about a bit, showing my hand to them, asking if I was doing it correctly and so on. Their reaction was typical of course, 'You stupid so and so, you're not supposed to show us your hand, and we did tell you that you couldn't play!' I said, 'It's OK, I want to learn it properly so I will enjoy it better later, I know I'm not going to win for a few hands'. We had about forty minutes of the break left, we played a few hands and, of course, I lost them all. 'Thanks Turk, that's our cigarette money sorted'. I used to smoke then too, was it Raffles or something?

I went into the canteen on my next break and there they were already waiting for their Turkish prey. We had a full hour of play this time and there were even more people watching, obviously they had told the others about me. They continued with their usual teasing, as if trying to wear me down psychologically; this stupid Turk thinks he can beat us at our own game, and take our money too. You'll see we'll take you to the cleaners.

We had a couple of games and I lost again. But I was dealt a very good third hand and everyone was watching too. Now was my chance! I thought I should try and win this, such a good hand, shouldn't be difficult as I only needed 2 cards or something. And, I won the hand in no time! They all looked very surprised because I finished my hand so quickly; I just said, it was beginner's luck and that I had had a very good run of cards. Besides I had lost more than six straight hands, winning one should be fine, surely. They said, sure, there's a lot of luck involved in the game and even I could win every now and then.

I started playing with full concentration, and I was also getting a reasonably good run of cards. I was winning about three out of every five games, sometimes I was finishing four times in succession. They couldn't believe it, completely shocked, I couldn't believe my luck either. I wish you could have seen their faces; they were absolutely gobsmacked. The insults were flying around, 'Fucking Turk, you come over, marry our daughter, come and work at our factory, and if that's not enough, now you're taking our fucking money at cards! This is ridiculous, it's beyond luck, in fact, it is outright robbery..."

I said I didn't remember ever being this lucky in my entire life. I couldn't believe it. I joyfully declared, 'I have enough money to buy several packs of cigarettes, thanks to you guys. Don't worry, we will play again, and I'm sure you'll take it all back and more". They were shaking their heads in disbelief...

Hello Sinclair ZX Spectrum, My First Computer, Late 1982

My Life Was Destined to Change Again

Sinclair ZX Spectrum

Veno Dos Santos and I had become very good friends. He was a young man and I am not sure, but I think he was of Jamaican origin, perhaps a few years older than me. He was the quality inspection officer. It was such a great job; he would inspect all of the production lines every hour or so and spend the rest of his time in his office. He never mixed with the other crowd in the canteen. After becoming friends, he would spend a lot of time with me when I was on the line. Chatting about all sorts of things.

Thinking he could appreciate my situation better than others, I used to moan to him quite bit about things. How my life had turned out for me, marrying and coming to England was great, but for fuck's sake, what's this with making cables and all that! I could probably end up retiring here... We became very close, even our families started spending time with each other.

He had a ZX81 computer, one of the early gaming machines manufactured by the legendary Sir Clive Sinclair. He used to play games on it, he would tell me many things about it, but I knew nothing about computers and had no interest in games either. He said he was trying to make his own games and had begun experimenting with programming. Once he brought his ZX81 in to work when we were on nights. Excitedly, he set it all up; he had a small TV connected to it, and a cassette player/recorder. Next, he did a few things and started playing a game with some moving black white images, and that was the first time I saw a computer game. Overall, he seemed to be quite good at it, and enjoying it too, but for some reason it didn't grab my attention at all. In fact, I didn't think anything of it.

One day he came to me very excitedly, showing pictures of a computer in a magazine. Mev, he said, 'Look at this thing, this is the new version of my computer, much more powerful and it has colours too, it's called ZX Spectrum.'

I could see his excitement, but I didn't understand why. He said he was going to put his name down for one, and I should join him. He said, 'Go on, what have you got to lose, you will enjoy it believe me, besides it'll help you to take your mind off things by playing games, and stop you bloody moaning and complaining all the time!'

Veno managed to convince me, and I said yes, OK as if to stop him from pestering me about it. What the heck, I thought, I could just sell it if I didn't like it. It must be something quite valuable and important if we are putting our names down months in advance. It was sometime in 1982, and it cost around £150. Well, I could easily afford it too, if anything my little Nej can have it, and probably enjoy it when he is older.

After some wait, Veno came rushing to the line exclaiming, 'Mev, our machines are ready'. Instead of waiting for them to be posted, he said we would drive in his car to the Sinclair offices and pick them up. We arranged to drive to Camberley, near London, at the end of our next shift.

God, he was so happy and excited, like a little kid getting the best birthday present ever, I had never seen anyone happier!

How I Became Mev

It was such a surprise when I realised that English people seemed to be very lazy with foreign names. They had so much trouble with my full name Mevlut. 'Sorry, say that again, how do you spell that, fucking hell, that's an unusual name'. To which I would say, 'Yes, it is unusual, it's a bloody foreign name. And, as it happens, I actually find your names quite unusual myself too.'

In the end, I decided to make it easy for myself, and for everyone else. I simply suggested for people to call me Mev; nice and simple, easy to spell and pronounce too. Every now and then Mev would be confused with Merv, but that I could live with. So, Mev stuck, and I now had a new name too, Mev Dinc, which turned out to be my pen name as it were.

What Am I to Do With My ZX Spectrum?

My computer stayed unboxed for a week or so. Veno kept asking me, 'Have you checked it out, isn't it cool? I brought you a copy of this game for you to try', handing me a cassette. I said, 'I hadn't even opened the box yet'. He was so annoyed with my indifference to the whole thing.

I'm not sure how long after, but he came to me while I was on the line, rather excited,. 'Mev, there's a new version of the machine, we bought the 16K, but they've now brought out the 48K version, 3 times more memory!'

Not that it meant anything to me, so I just asked him, 'Is that good?' He said, 'Of course, it means bigger and better games. We can probably just pay a small difference and get the new ones.'

So, off we went to the Sinclair offices (in Camberley) again, in his Ford Granada to swap our machines; mine was still boxed and untouched! We went to the reception, and I said to the girl working there; we wanted 48K, but we got 16K instead. 'We came all the way from Southampton', I said, as if it was Sinclair's fault. She looked so busy and tired. There were stacks of 48K machines all over the place. She just said, 'Please leave yours here and just take the 48K ones'. And that's what we did. I can't even remember paying the difference, she just said goodbye, and we said thank you and left. Maybe she felt sorry for us coming all the way from Southampton. Veno was well pleased, he even promised to give me a few good games to raise my interest and excitement level.

Warming Up To Gaming, 1983

We were into the New Year now, and I still hadn't even set up my computer. Veno became really cross with me, 'C'mon man, at least open the bloody box and have a play around with it'. He was right, I should at least look at it and see what all the fuss was about. Who knows, I may even enjoy it, and get some relaxation.

I opened the box, a little black thing that looked like a keyboard, power supply, and quite a thick book that said Spectrum Basic, or something like that, on the cover. I had a quick browse through the book, but just couldn't make out what it was about. It was in English alright, but lots of new words that I couldn't understand. There were some Basic programs in it to try out.

While trying to set it all up, I discovered that I needed more things to go with it; a TV as well. 'OK, I can hook it up to our TV set', I thought. Next, I connected everything as per the instructions, powered it up and that came up was a white screen with a message. 'That's it, what do I do now?' was my reaction. Looking at the instructions again, I also discovered that I needed a cassette recorder. What the heck, I thought? Apparently, that was how you load the games into the machine. It wasn't worth buying a tape recorder for the one game that I had. Veno had promised me more so I would buy it when I had more games. I typed a few things on the keyboard, tried a couple of things from the book. Nothing overly, or even remotely exciting. And I then unplugged the whole thing and put it away. It didn't impress me much, but then again I had no clue as to what to expect either.

Meeting With Brian Marshall

I told Veno about the cassette recorder. He suggested I should just go to a shop and buy one, 'It shouldn't cost much.' He said he would give me a couple more games to encourage me.

There was a local TV/HiFi shop in the city centre where I had bought my first music system, one of those all-in-one Toshiba ghetto blasters. In fact, I had chosen the model with detachable speakers, it was quite a fancy thing at the time. By detaching and putting the speakers further apart it would give me a better stereo sound. My music listening hobby had started with my 'Tosh'. I Probably bought my Tosh before the popular Toshiba TV campaign slogan 'Ello Tosh, Gotta Toshiba' in the 80s!

In due course, I asked the young man behind the counter if they had any cassette players for computers to play games. Obviously, I can't remember if it was the same guy who sold me the music system. In response, he showed me a few, and I bought one of the cheaper ones. Suddenly realising that I also needed a TV set, I asked him if they had any 14inch colour TV sets at reasonable prices. No idea why, but most monitors and TV sets used with computers were 14 inch for some reason. Maybe 14 inch was a good match for the resolution the machines were capable of?

He said, he actually repaired TVs at the back of the shop, and they had some second-hand sets that I could look at. As it happened, there was a 14-inch second-hand set in a good condition, and at a reasonable price. In the end, I bought the TV as well.

The guy in the shop said his name was Brian, and that if I had any problems with the TV I could always bring it to him to check and repair if needed. I thanked him and told him I was Mev, and left.

Life moves in mysterious ways. In fact, I had just met Brian Marshall, the person with whom I would become very close friends. And, more importantly he would end up doing the music for most of my games. The games which I would start developing in a couple of years! Neither of us had a clue at the time, not yet anyway! It was as if I was gradually gathering all the pieces for the jigsaw puzzle of my life.

Subsequently, I went home to set up my computer with all the bits needed in place. All ready now, and all I had to do was to load up and start the game! I popped the game cassette into the cassette player and hit play; it started making some weird sounds, and lots of coloured stripes began moving up and down the screen.

After a while it said, 'Loading error, please try again'. I can't remember how many times I tried again and again; sometimes I would forget to rewind the bloody tape! After a good few attempts I gave up, nearly giving the whole thing a good kick in the butt.

I called Veno a few times and complained as if it was his fault it didn't work. Well, I guess it was his fault, introducing me to the whole thing in the first place! I told him that I just couldn't load the game no matter what I tried. And that it kept giving me error messages. He said I needed to adjust the tape head with a screwdriver! I shouted, 'Screw this, this is just too much hassle!' It seemed everything was getting in the way and I was making such slow progress. Frustration started to set in. However, I kept on and slowly but surely I was also getting rid of the obstacles one by one.

I'm not sure now whether it was at work or home, but Veno brought one of those small, flat-head, watchmaker screwdrivers, and showed me how to adjust the tape head. I managed to load the games by adjusting the head whenever needed. I became quite good at it too, and I could tell almost immediately by the tone of the sound if it was right or not, like tuning a guitar by ear. It was really satisfying to solve the tape head problem before losing my head. Such small problems could become so annoying and easily drive you mad. Everything seems such a big problem when you don't have a clue.

What started with Vino's insistence was turning into another major turning point. And with it, my own life was turning into a big game too. And, I was just trying to play it as well as I could.

Let The Excitement and Curiosity Take Over!

Now I had everything setup to try and enjoy this thing. In due course, I started playing a few games, but to be honest I just didn't find them that enjoyable. Admittedly, I noticed very quickly that I was not very good, and wasn't improving much either! Interesting I thought, I was good at sports, but not at computer games. Perhaps it was a bit like playing instruments, which could mean that I would never become adept at it.

I started to delve more into the Basic book to understand what it was about. I even tried out a few sample program listings to see what they did. 'Who knows, this maybe more fun than playing?' I thought to myself. At least, I was keeping myself occupied by trying to explore things further, which was the main thing at the time. I was typing lines of code into the computer and then executing them as instructed. Sometimes it worked, sometimes it didn't. I would carefully double check, and find some typing errors, correct them and try again, and bingo. It worked, 'Wow, this could be fun', I thought.

After a while, the experimenting with program listings was going reasonably well. Overall, I was enjoying it. Especially when changing things and seeing different results, which felt great as I was making things happen.

Gradually, I was finding myself getting more and more into the idea. Thus, finding the whole thing more fascinating. Also, Veno had told me about computer magazines, so I went into the local WH Smith, and started browsing through magazines as well. To be honest, I never read books, but I was reading these magazines like crazy, every line, and some pages more than once to make better sense of things.

There was this Popular Computing Weekly magazine with lots of program listings, and articles on programming. I thought to myself 'This looks more interesting and it's weekly too, so I won't have to wait long for the new issues'. I could be lazy about things, but if I put my mind to something then I could become so impatient. If it's something I really want, then I would do everything to have it as soon as possible. Therefore, I couldn't wait to get home with the magazine, and to start typing those new listings. The curiosity was taking over, almost killing me. Behaving like a little kid who cannot wait to open his presents.

This magazine was excellent, so many different things to try out and learn. But some listings just wouldn't work, no matter how many times I retyped them. Generally, I'm very stubborn too, not one to give up easily. But I would discover it the hard way that some of the listings had typos in them. And the typos were causing the problem (bugs). Unfortunately, without enough knowledge I couldn't spot the typos/errors myself, not yet anyway. You had to wait for the next issue with the corrections. They were really simple, and silly errors. God, I cannot tell you the amount of swearing, cursing and laughing, all at the same time, as I was typing and retyping the error ridden lines into the night. Only to discover a week later that there were listing errors!

Despite hours of typing/retyping, I was really enjoying this programming thing a lot, and wanted to learn more. It was turning into a major fascination, and I was becoming so curious to understand how it all worked. With no education in computing or programming and with my still limited English, I had to work harder. But, I really wanted to learn it and more importantly become very good at it. However, the more I played around with the sample programs the more I was getting into it.

Programming Becomes a Passion!

By now, I was really going for it. Buying and reading more magazines; trying out all the stuff that came with the cover tape. The magazines would come with a cassette full of free games and samples. I was consuming it all like crazy. But listings weren't enough, they all looked similar and very simple as time went by. So I started trying out little programs of my own, and after a good few weeks I even wrote a small guide to 'Spectrum Peeks and Pokes'. These were simple

Spectrum specific instructions to make the machine perform simple tasks, such as change the screen colours etc.

Some magazines were publishing third party sample programs sent to them. I remember sending my Peek/Poke guide to a magazine for publication, but they declined. Probably found it too simple, but they did wish me better luck next time. That wasn't going to deter me! A few months later, I wrote a little game and sent it to another magazine. 'Invasion of Donkeys From Mars', or something like that, was my first fully functioning and playable simple game. The Martian donkeys had eyesight problems and apparently eating lots of carrots was the cure. And discovering that Earth had enough stock of the stuff they decide to invade us. Not so fast Donkeys! Our hero would fire carrots at them to stop the invasion. Donkeys would eat the carrots and seeing that they could see instantly, they would return home without landing. Thus, saving us humans from the possible invasion! I thought it was quite original and nothing much like other games, although I had only seen a few other games. Unfortunately, my game was rejected too as was my guide. Nevertheless, I must say that I was very impressed with my progress, and I wanted to try even harder and improve my programming skills more.

Fascination was slowly turning into a passion now, as I wanted to learn more and more. Those simple listings were simply not cutting it. The first game I played that impressed me was Arcadia by Imagine Software. I thought it was beautiful, which was a kind of arcade shoot'em up, similar to those early space invaders type games. It was very colourful with beautiful and multiple enemies, coming down at you in lovely moving patterns and sequences. It was so much more impressive than all the listings I was trying out. Inspired by this, I thought that I had to check out professional games and learn how they make them so much better. Arcadia was very fast, and everything was moving very smoothly too. Thus, I set myself a standard now, it was my early benchmark as it were.

Because I found Arcadia so impressive, I was also eager to play and discover it more. But I just wasn't good enough, no matter how much I played or how hard I tried I kept dying and losing all my lives very quickly. 'Game Over', I started seeing this so much that I also started thinking my programming was going to be over before it started. Getting better and better, but never good enough to advance far enough into the game. I just wasn't a competent gamer. Perhaps just as well, instead of playing games I was concentrating on making them instead.

Welcome My Son, Welcome to The Machine... Code!

With my limited knowledge and ability I was making slower progress than I wanted. And I was getting stuck along the way quite often too. My maths wasn't that good either, as I had studied economics and commerce with limited maths education. Now I was reading things like Binary (base-2 numeral system, which uses only zero and one) and Hexadecimal numbers (base 16, or hex, it uses sixteen distinct symbols, "0"–"9" to represent values zero to nine, and "A"–"F" to represent values ten to fifteen). Hex is a more human friendly representation of the decimal-coded values. Of course, I was a complete stranger to both and couldn't see anything friendly about the Hexadecimal system.

Yet, I didn't know anything about HEX or Binary numbers. Thus, I thought I needed more material; the Spectrum Basic book, and magazines obviously weren't enough.

In one issue of Popular Computing, there was a small article on machine code. It basically said that if you wanted to become a good programmer and write games then you had to forget Basic and you had to learn machine code. Apparently, it was much better and faster! Without knowing the difference I said to myself, 'That's it, I will learn machine code'. Subsequently, I typed in the sample program and it worked straight away. But, it was completely different from Basic, a completely new language and instruction set. A bit like switching from English to Latin. It's a bit like Decimal and Hex comparison; Basic programming is more human friendly than Machine Code. So, without realising one bit, I was, in fact, getting myself much deeper into the programming world!

Therefore, I had to learn something entirely new, most probably much harder too. 'Oh well', I thought, 'if it is the best programming language, then I had better learn it'. From now on, I was only interested in machine code examples that came with the Popular Computing magazine. There weren't many samples, so I was able to quickly try them all out. And then, I would spend time understanding how it all worked by constantly changing things in the actual code and checking the results. It was purely trial and error, using a little of what I knew and a lot of just logical thinking. I was doing it over and over again until I was satisfied that I fully understood what the code did and how it did it. As far as I am concerned, there isn't a better way to learn things. Well, in terms of programming anyway.

By now, I was working on my programming at work too, during my breaks. All my colleagues were going mad at me, 'C'mon you Turk, you can't learn that thing, stop wasting your time, let's play cards'. But, I simply ignored them, and got on with it. Without the computer I was just reading and writing little bits of machine code on paper, so I could test it all when I arrived home. Now I was spending all my spare time on programming. Janet was encouraging me too from what I can remember, seeing that I was really into it, and also enjoying it.

Passion Turning into Addiction

No matter how tired I was, after arriving home from my night shifts, I would spend at least a couple of hours trying things out before going to bed. I was practising and improving my coding nonstop, at work and at home.

While I was making nice steady progress, I suddenly got stuck big time. There was this problem which I just couldn't get my head around. Spectrum was a Z80 processor based machine (Zilog Z80 was conceived in 1974, it's a software compatible extension of Intel 8080). It was an 8bit machine meaning you can only store values between 0-255 in one memory address or slot. Any values bigger than 255 needed 2 memory slots; I was looking (or peeking) at the values stored in the two addresses, but I just couldn't work out how they represented the actual number. I added the two values, multiplied them or tried many things, but it didn't add up. It just didn't compute as it were. Thus, I was at a complete loss, and it was driving me mad. Obviously, I was missing something very fundamental and simple. But, I just didn't have a clue as to what it could be. No information in any of the magazines that I could find. No Google or anyone else to ask either!

Maybe I should try the Southampton University, surely they would have a course in machine code programming, or a computer science lecturer who could give me some pointers, I thought to myself. Looking back, I can't even remember who it was or how I found him; I told this young lecturer that I wanted to learn machine code programming and asked him if they had any courses I could take. He said there wasn't anything for machine code or assembly language. But, he said that there were maybe Fortran or Cobol courses, I can't recall which. Incidentally, Fortran (mainly used for scientific computing) and Cobal (used for business) are similar to Basic programming, meaning more human friendly and easier to use. I said they wouldn't do, without even knowing what they were. Then, I told him that I needed to learn machine code or Assembly language, as I wanted to make games. He simply said, in that case I had to learn it myself. I told him that that was exactly what I had been trying to do, but I was stumbling into many problems all the time. He suggested my best bet would be to buy and read some suitable books on the subject.

I Discovered The Magic of Coding, So I Thought!

One day, I went to a bookshop and found the computer section. There were quite a few books; basic and machine code programming for BBC Micro, Spectrum and Commodore 64. Wow, I couldn't believe the number of books on programming. Obviously, it was such a new, but very popular thing, that everyone was bringing out books on games programming. There were a few books for programming on the Spectrum and as I was sifting through them I saw it.

There it was, I thought this should do it, the title said it all; 'Spectrum Machine Language For The Absolute Beginner'. I thought, 'This is unreal, someone wrote a book just for me; Machine Code, Spectrum, the absolute beginner, that's me!'

I bought the book and went straight home as fast as I could. In fact, I was so eager to read and check out the contents that I couldn't wait to get home. I had never read and completed a book before, but I thought, I would certainly be reading this book inside out and several times too!

It was such a well-written book, very easy to follow and understand. How the computers functioned in the simplest form, how the memory was organised and worked, and how the numbers were stored, all very nicely explained. It had many clear and simple examples; like using matchboxes as memory addresses. But I was quickly browsing through it to find the bit that I had got stuck on. I found it, the thing that had been bugging me for days; storing large numbers like 32768 in memory.

The book explained it with a simple formula; in the Z80 values are stored in memory as low byte first followed by high byte. And the formula to find the value of the number is = high byte × 256 + low byte. And to find the high and low bytes, you simply divide the original number by 256; 32768/256 = 128 (high byte) and the remainder being, in this case, 0 (low byte). And we apply the magical formula we get 128 (or 80Hex) × 256 + 0 = 32768.

Now I don't want to lose you non-technical types, but I couldn't workout the logic behind how large numbers were stored in memory. Obviously, there was some logic or formula or representation behind it, but I had absolutely no idea yet. I was swimming in deep and very muddy waters. So, with the help of the book, I learnt how numbers bigger than 8bit (0-255) were stored in memory.

Hey presto, that was it, I suddenly got unstuck from my bugging problem. It felt like I had just solved a magical mystery, the hardest problem that I had faced in programming up to that point. I was over the moon, so relieved and happy. It is quite amazing when you don't have a clue about things. The relief and excitement of discovering this simple formula had given me so much encouragement and confidence. Without realising that I was still right at the very beginning and still had so much to learn. The good thing was that I was very eager and ready to do so.

Now that I had managed to remove a big stumbling block, I could move forward and make much quicker progress. And that was exactly what I did.

I was working away like crazy, using all my spare time and at times, I couldn't even sleep from excitement. It was nonstop, just trying things out, and if things went wrong and my computer crashed or stopped working, I would simply unplug and restart it again. I wasn't afraid at all, I never thought I could damage the computer, just like a little kid touching all the buttons without any fear.

And as such, I would try all the examples in the book, experiment and change codes. Experimenting nonstop, so much so that after a certain point the whole code would become my own. As if I had created the whole thing from scratch myself. I knew exactly how the code worked, what each instruction did. This wasn't like reading a textbook and memorising things, it was like being in the kitchen and actually making the food from a recipe, but always adding and changing ingredients, so that I could almost call it my own recipe. In time and with every step forward I was increasing both my knowledge and experience, becoming more competent and daring. It was a great way to learn things and get better. As I progressed I was trying out more complex things. Now, I started feeling very comfortable with programming on the Spectrum. Trying things out at will, and feeling in full control of things too.

To be honest, at times I was a bit shocked at how fast I was progressing. I couldn't believe it, I was learning the Spectrum inside out, and also becoming a decent programmer at the same time. Veno couldn't believe my progress either, he was shocked too, but was giving me a lot of encouragement. Although there was no way to measure my knowledge, I was now meddling with other people's games. All my work colleagues were thinking I was going completely potty with this programming thing. That was all I was doing.

By now, I was breaking into other games and learning new things from them. I could find out how they did certain things and play around with some of their code to see if I could improve things. To impress Veno, I even started poking around with some of Veno's games. Changing bits in the actual code and giving the modified games back to him. Things like infinite lives or energy or whatever helped Veno to play the games and complete them.

Ready For My First Professional Assignment, Late 1984

Veno left the UK by the end of 1984 for the USA for a better future for himself and his family. He was a clever man and didn't want to spend the rest of his life at the factory. Amazing to think how it was him who really wanted to become a programmer and make his own games. But instead, he made me buy a ZX Spectrum, encouraged and led me into becoming a programmer myself!

I continued at full speed developing my coding skills, and learning the Spectrum inside out, so I could create games. My first attempt at doing a fully-fledged game involved coding a board game, which I played as a kid in my village, and knew well. It is called Nine Man's Morris (Turkish version called Dokuz Taş – Nine Stones/Pieces). No idea how I came across it or what initiated it in the first place. But I managed to code a fully functional 2-player version with all the rules successfully implemented. It played and looked quite slick, and I was very pleased with the result.

This was my first complete game, a finished product as such. And, I designed and coded it all myself, and all in machine code too from start to finish. This really instilled a lot of confidence in me.

My next project was to write a fully functional and usable graphics editor and animator. This was quite an ambitious project at this stage, but I thought if I were to make games I needed graphics, and an editor to create them with. I couldn't draw a matchstick man myself, but I knew someone who could, Janet. If she could use it with ease, and produce some graphics easily, then a game artist would certainly be able to.

By the time I finished the fully functioning version, I was really proud of my editor. It looked nice and slick with a very easy to use user interface and a number of useful functions. You could edit at pixel level, have different zoom levels, and it had a nice frame animator too. You could save and reload your work to and from tape. Janet was very good at drawing and she easily created lots of nice graphics with the editor. She really enjoyed using it. In fact, it wasn't much later that Janet would actually create the main character of my first game, Gerry the Germ.

I used my editor as a show reel, and to showcase material to demonstrate my programming knowledge and ability. I attended my first games show in 1984 in London's Earls Court. One of the people who had seen and liked my editor was none other than Tony Rainbird of Rainbird Software and Firebird (British Telecom). He was really impressed with my editor and made very encouraging and positive remarks on the presentation and coding aspects. He told me to contact him as and when I decided to make a game. In fact, that was exactly what I did a few months later!

Time to Leave Cable Production For Game Production

I was getting ready to quit my job and leave the factory. I had taught myself programming in two years, and I was ready to start my professional game development career. Janet was fully supportive. As luck would have it, towards the end of 1984, the management announced 'voluntary redundancy'. The idea was to optimise the workforce by encouraging the older workers to leave early with a cash incentive. Depending on the number of years of service (minimum 5 years to qualify) you could take around £8,000 - £20,000, which was a lot of money. What great timing for me, as I was planning to leave anyway, but now I could leave with some money.

Not bad I thought, this makes a change, the luck seems to be on my side. I was about to complete my five years, which meant that I would also be just in time to benefit from the voluntary redundancy. So, I applied.

There were too many applications, a lot more than the management expected. But what made matters even worse was the fact that the majority of the applications came from the younger workers, the exact opposite of the intended goal. Shortly after, the management updated the requirements accordingly to make it more difficult for the younger workers to leave. The most important new requirement was that you had to have another job lined up, and prove it with an official job offer. That made it much more difficult for most of the younger workers. But I didn't care as I was going to leave anyway. However, it would be nice to leave with £8,000 especially as I was going to start a new career. A new career in a new industry which was full of unknowns and uncertainties.

Everyone was also warning me against leaving and starting something completely new. By the way, I had no chance of coming back to the factory should I fail. And they were right of course, I was taking a huge risk. They really couldn't see how I could succeed with limited knowledge and experience, which I had gained by just reading magazines and books with no formal education or training. On paper, it did look quite crazy.

Time to Come Clean!

I said, 'Look guys, thanks for your concern and I really appreciate it, but I know what I'm doing. Trust me, I am cleverer and brighter than you think, I know I can do this'.

I added, 'Don't you remember how quickly I learnt that Kluki game and started taking your money? Just after a few hands I was taking you to the cleaners, were you not surprised by my ability? Did you ever wonder how I managed to do that?'

They all looked a little puzzled and were waiting in anticipation. 'Go on then', said one of them, 'Let's hear it, how did you do it?'

I started carefully explaining everything… The game you call Kluki is actually called '51' in Turkey. And it's one of the most played traditional card games. In fact, there's hardly anyone who wouldn't know how to play it. They all said, 'Fuck off; you're pulling our leg', 'it's called fucking Kluki.' I replied, 'Yes, it's called Kluki here, and I'm telling you it is called 51 in Turkey. Believe me, I am telling you the truth. Besides, I had a reputation for being one of the best 51 players during my high school and university years. How do you think I could learn the game so quickly, and beat you all just after a few hands? Yes, I am very clever, but surely not that clever.'

After a few friendly insults, they were convinced that I did learn it far too quickly for a beginner. And, that I played it like a pro. They really appreciated my telling them the truth in the end. It probably made them feel a bit better to know that they lost to someone who was very good at the game. We had a good laugh about it, quite a few of them tapped me on the shoulder, and uttered a few nice complements; 'nice one mate', 'well done nipps (nipper)'.

Working My Way to Becoming a Games Programmer, 1985

It was quite unbelievable that in just two years, whilst working at the factory as a cable worker, I was seriously making a massive transition to becoming a programmer and game developer.

I was definitely leaving, but I also wanted to take some cash for sure. My application was already in, now all I had to do was to find a job with a letter of confirmation. Honestly, I had no idea, if there were any programming jobs going in Southampton. I already knew about Quicksilva, a very impressive local developer of Spectrum games, but would I be good enough, would they even be looking for a new programmer? I started looking in the local papers for job postings for computer programmer positions. Games programming specifically. Frankly, it felt a bit weird, almost surreal. Just a few years ago I was prepared to do any kind of work, but now I was looking for a games programming job.

It seemed like the path was already set, and I was just walking along it without quite realising. I saw a small job posting: 'A Commodore 64 (C64) programmer is looking for a capable Spectrum programmer to help with a game conversion'. Unbelievable, I thought this man was looking specifically for me; surely, I was the man for the job, as if there were no other Spectrum programmers available! Who knows, maybe there weren't any?

What a Start; The Prospect of Working on 3D Ant Attack!

The guy's name was Surjit Dosanj, and the game project in question was the Commodore 64 (C64) conversion of the classic Spectrum game 3D Ant Attack! Perfect I thought, I could get to know a little bit about the C64 too. Spectrum and C64 were the two pioneering machines of the early days of the gaming sector. Both had strengths and weaknesses but they both equally contributed to the formation of the industry. Some truly great early games were developed on both machines, and the UK did play a fantastic part.

I called Surjit and had a quick chat on the phone. He seemed quite impressed with what he had heard, so we decided to meet up. He probably invited me to his house. All freelancers were working from home back in the day, which is what I was going to do myself.

We met and discussed the project. I was going to help him understand the Spectrum version of 3D Ant Attack, so he could do a better job putting it onto C64. Easy enough, I told him I could help him, as I knew Spectrum inside out. And also added that I fully coded using machine code. So did he as it turned out. He seemed quite impressed with my knowledge of the machine, and even more with the fact that I had taught myself machine code in such a short time. He couldn't believe that I was actually learning programming while working at a factory. Anyway, he offered me the job on the spot. I said I needed an official letter of a job offer to give to my factory management. He said no problem; he'd do the letter on a letter headed paper, sign it and send it to me.

Great, I now had an official job offer, so I could certainly leave with a lump sum payment. I handed my letter to the management, but a few days later I was informed in writing that I couldn't leave yet as I was needed at the factory. What? How was I needed at the factory more than anyone else? Crazy I thought, I felt both important and pissed off at the same time. I went straight to the union rep to appeal the decision; surely, they couldn't refuse my application? I had a right to apply and leave just like anyone else, and I had provided everything that was required. The union rep said I was right, but they were desperate to have me for a few more months. Since I was the only worker involved in the new 'fibre optics cable' tests!

Hearing the explanation made me even more pissed off, because I had only warned them a few weeks ago about this. The fact that I was the only worker doing the tests, and that I would be leaving soon, meant that they had to train a few more workers to take my place. STC and GEC had setup the first computer-based automated fibre optics production line in the mid-80s at our factory, using the latest technology of the time. We had started the fibre optic cable tests a few months before, and the production line was very impressive. The cable was so much lighter yet with much bigger capacity than its analogue counterpart.

Because of my interest in and knowledge of computers, they decided to put me on the fibre optics line. Basically, I took part in and helped the engineers with all the tests. It was great as I was doing this newer, cleaner and more fun job, even during my overtime. It was great working with the engineers closely and suggesting ideas. In fact, it made me feel really inspired. The engineers knew of my intentions about leaving and starting a gaming career. And several times I had suggested that we trained a few other guys as I was planning to leave soon. Obviously, the engineers didn't believe that I would or could leave, and did nothing, nor did the foremen or the union people. No one took my intentions seriously other than myself.

And, now I was being told that I couldn't leave because I was needed for fibre optics tests! How unfair I thought.

Finally we reached an agreement whereby I would stay on for another couple of months to help train a few others, and then leave with my redundancy money. They also decided to compensate me for having to leave later than I intended by paying me two thousand pounds extra cash. That was fair enough, as it was only a couple more months, and I would still be able to help Surjit with the 3D Ant Attack conversion during my time off work.

Game On: Gaming Career Starts in Earnest, March 1985

Wow! What a journey and adventure so far! In about eight years, I had been through more major twists and turns than most people probably face in a lifetime. I lost my father, met and married an English girl while still at university and with zero English. Moved to England, worked on the shop floor at a cable factory for five years. While working at the factory and learning English, I also learnt to become a games programmer, and all by myself with zero knowledge or interest either in games or computers. Amazingly it happened, and now the game could truly begin. Game on...

And so it began! I started working on my first professional game project, meeting and helping Surjit on the development. First, I disassembled the 3D Ant Attack code; it was hundreds of pages of code. Sandy White, the original author of the game, had also provided all the source and graphics from the Spectrum version. Quicksilva was the publisher of the game; a very successful Southampton based Spectrum game developer. Rod Cousens was heading the business and Mark Eyels was also there helping with game design I believe. Little did I know that I would eventually end up working on many games and becoming lifelong friends with Rod.

It was a superb start; I did learn a lot working on this project, improved my knowledge of the Spectrum and programming, as well as getting to know a bit about the C64 as I had hoped. Of course, working with another programmer also benefited me with his experience and insights.

Leaving My Overalls Behind For a New Career

The months went by quick enough, and I left my working class overalls and cable career behind to start a completely new journey full of challenges. Though without a clue as to what was in store for me, I was so excited and determined to give it my best shot. After I left the factory, I continued to work with Surjit for a while longer.

First Encounter With The MSX Game Machines

 As far as I can remember, at the time there was an effort by Microsoft and ASCII to create a unified standard gaming machine under the MSX brand. All the major Japanese companies were involved such as Sony, Pioneer and Panasonic. It was quite big in Japan, but it didn't find great success in the rest of the World. It was an attempt to rival the success of the Spectrum and C64 and also create a standard in the hardware side of things. The hardware was based on the Z80 processor just like Spectrum and Amstrad, which made sense for programmers like me to take some early interest in it. But I remember having lots of compatibility problems between different brands. What worked perfectly on Toshiba MSX, didn't necessarily work on say the JVC one. In many ways, I guess it is very similar to the PC (personal computer) problems we still experience today. It didn't do very well in the USA and Europe as Spectrum and Commodore 64 were already dominating the market and Amstrad was also doing well in France and Spain.

Surjit was also trying to do projects on the Amstrad, and told me that he had special contacts. However, I am not sure exactly how long I tried things on MSX and Amstrad with Surjit. But since I really wanted to do my own games, I eventually parted company with Surjit, and started working on my first game.

While working on 3D Ant Attack, I saw that Sandy White had written the game part in Basic and part in machine code. All the bits that required extra performance were written in machine code. Apparently he had written the machine code sections manually, i.e. without using an editor and compiler. He had entered all the HEX values of the instructions of the code by hand. Without getting too technical, it is so hard to find errors and debug the code in this raw format. It is quite a task to even write the whole thing like that, and I still find it hard to believe. That's what I heard at the time, so I cannot vouch for it.

Anyway, full kudos to Sandy for producing 3D Ant Attack, such a great game and a landmark product. Certainly, it was one of the early classics of the 80s, for sure.

Incidentally, I became good friends with Surjit, who once invited me to his house to taste home cooked Indian food. It was all very delicious but my God, too hot to handle; tasting many different dishes trying to find one mildly bearable. Alas, every spoonful was way too spicy! However, it did give me a taste for the wonderful Indian food, which I have been eating at every opportunity ever since. In fact, I have recently invented my own Chicken Korma no less!

My First Game, Gerry The Germ, 1985! (Firebird – Telecomsoft)

I was now stepping into a completely new world, an adventure full of unknowns and excitement. Beforehand, I had already made some preliminary preparations for my first game. Although I wasn't playing many games and admittedly never very good at them, I did think of some interesting ideas. This way I could create extra attention, and interest as my coding ability and cute graphics alone might not be enough. Just as in cinema and TV, in games too, the player always seemed to be playing the hero and fighting baddies. Why not do the opposite, I thought? It could be risky perhaps, but it could also surprise some people and make a quick impression.

By now, I was quite confident with my coding ability, and my ideas were interesting enough too. If the concept was compelling enough and coupled with the anti-hero element, it should create enough stir. That was my intention.

In terms of gaming environment what could be better than human anatomy, I couldn't come up with anything better? Indeed, the human body and its various organs would form the game environment and all the different levels needed. And what better than a germ as the main character, trying to destroy the body? The player was actually helping the germ to achieve this. What's not to like I thought?

In due course, Janet, using my graphics editor, came up with a really cute germ character. Generally, I have always been quite good at coming up with names and enjoyed playing with words. In fact, the English language is perfect for wordplay. Well, the title of the game was simply 'Gerry the Germ'. Janet also came up with a simple background story; Gerry had graduated from a medical school. I decided on which body parts to use and with the help of Janet we gave them some silly names; Stonemac, Kiddin'em, Heartist, Lungaroo, Blundder. I did say silly!

Janet had done some sketches for different level layouts based around my general ideas. She also did some lovely sketches of Gerry. It was great that Janet did all the preliminary art, as I couldn't draw a straight line. She was an aspiring writer; working on children's stories with very nice illustrations as well as novels.

I had a simple game design document of a few pages with the main character and most of the level ideas worked out. In addition to this, I had already shown my graphics editor and some other demos to a couple of companies at ECTS (Earls Court) in London, ca. 1984. Actually, I remember receiving very good feedback for my work, which had instilled a lot of confidence in me. In fact, this was when I finally decided that I should leave my cable job and make games professionally! I took the compliments as a stamp of approval for my knowledge and ability to become a professional games developer.

Close Encounter of The First Kind With Publishers

The first publisher I went to was Mirrorsoft, a Mirror Group Newspapers company. It was part of the Maxwell Group, owned by the late Robert Maxwell, founded circa. 1983. In actual fact, I probably got the contact information at the computer show I had attended in London. Quite a few new companies were starting to get into games too in the mid-80s, so the timing seemed to be on my side.

Another major company with an interest in games was British Telecom, then not as yet privatised. They had two labels; Rainbird (mainly publishing adventure games) and Firebird.

As an aside, while talking about Telecom, it's quite a contrast between Turkey and the UK as a comparison. When I relocated to my native Turkey to kick-start the gaming sector at the end of 2000, there were no such big companies showing any interest in games. My initial efforts towards the establishment of a professional gaming sector raised a lot of interest, and I had many meetings with many major companies and groups over the years, but none really showed serious interest. Not until Turkish Telekom bought my Sobee Studios with the vision of the then CEO Paul Doany. Suffice to say that you will read all the juicy details about this part of my adventure later in the book.

Back to 1985; I believe Jim Mackonochie was the first CEO of Mirrorsoft. I cannot recall exactly who it was that I presented my idea to, but I cannot begin to tell you the excitement I had beforehand! There I was, showing my first game idea to a publisher trying to get their interest; the germ, human body, anti-hero, and all. But my excitement very quickly turned into a big disappointment when they simply told me that the idea was too risky for a reputable group company to even consider, let alone publish it. Eek! The brakes were put on my dream! They simply stated that no way could they possibly publish such a game, and wished me luck elsewhere. And that was that! Gutted! What a disastrous start to a career or even an early stop, before it had even started. I was literally shown the door by the first publisher!

What a shock, the reaction of the publisher shook me so badly that I almost lost all desire. It took me a couple of days to recover from it. I lifted myself and reassured myself with the thought that surely another company or person may like it, as there were other publishers to try. 'Too soon to give up on the first hurdle, I must get over it somehow, and be positive', was my train of thought.

One of the other companies that I had shown my demos to, was the British Telecom company Telecomsoft (Rainbird and Firebird). Tony Rainbird, who was heading the publishing, was really impressed with my work, and had suggested seeing him when I was ready to make my first game. And ready I was. Obviously my confidence was dented a little from the Mirrorsoft rejection, but I made an appointment to see Tony. Nothing to lose from trying, but all to gain. This time, I decided to be a little more careful with my idea to avoid receiving a similar negative reaction.

Trying to hide my nerves and excitement, I explained what sort of game I wanted to make, and how I intended to make it different enough to create interest. Incredibly, Tony's reaction was the complete opposite of Mirrorsoft! He said that he loved the idea, and that it was very unique. Also, Tony loved the Germ and anti-hero aspect! Result! He even went on to say that they would like to publish it. OMG! I could hardly contain my excitement, but I am sure Tony must have seen the light of the smile exploding on my face.

'Wow, he is probably going to ask me how much I want', I thought, in a panic. 'But, I don't have a clue, how much should I ask for, how much can I ask for? What is reasonable, what about terms, agreement, not a clue, nowt, I know nothing. Probably in a worse situation than poor Manuel, in Fawlty Towers!'

No knowledge, no experience and worst of all, no one to ask, and no bloody uncle Google either! To be frank, I really cannot remember the exact details, well it was thirty-five years ago! However, we started negotiating, sort of!

Negotiating Life's Problems to Business Negotiation

And, Tony asked me how much I wanted. I simply said, 'I really don't know to be honest, this is my first game, but I can tell you how much I would need to develop it'. I gave him all the details. It would take me around eight months, I needed a graphics artist, I had to pay for music too. Plus, the fact that I was married with a five-year-old boy and also had mortgage payments. None of it was Tony's problem, but I guess I was merely explaining my situation and trying to justify my needs. In a way, I wasn't trying to get as much as I could of course, but didn't want to give him the impression that I just came up with a random number. And, I finally told him that I needed around £1,000 per month.

Tony was looking a bit puzzled with all that detail and possibly with the monthly cost too, but he appreciated my honest stance at the same time. He simply said, 'that means you want around £8,000, right?' I didn't want to say 'want', instead, I said, that's what I need. Obviously, I had never negotiated with anyone before, not like this anyway. Turkish people like to haggle and bargain when they shop, but I never remember doing it much myself. Maybe once or twice when I bought shoes during my university years.

I was just trying to strike a balance between keeping Tony's interest alive, and also making sure I had enough money to live on for eight months or so.

Responding to my request, Tony said he fully understood my situation, but £8,000 was way more than they normally pay for a game. Apparently they normally paid around £2,000 - 3,000. He also added that they paid good royalties too unlike other publishers. Royalties? I didn't even know what it was or would mean in terms of revenue. I could guess that sixteen-year-old kids developed most games. At that sort of age, £3,000 must have been a lot of money for them. I said I was expecting quite a bit more than that, as there could be a little delay. And I had no idea how I could manage with that sort of money. I also told him that I was thinking of paying £2,000 towards graphics and music. It seemed I was quite generous to pay this much considering that was how much they paid for whole game normally. To be honest, I have always tried to be fair towards people who have worked with me.

Tony said, 'I really like your idea and also believe you will do a good job, but let's think about it for a few days.' Noticing my disappointment, he quickly added, 'I will call you and make you an offer.'

That at least kept my hopes up and I thought he would offer me something around £4,000 - £5,000, and I could manage with that since I had money in the bank. Finally, I thanked him and said I would look forward to hearing from him and left.

On the way back home, I thought I should wait for a few days and then I would call him. To be honest, I didn't want to call him too quickly to make him think I was desperate.

Actually, I felt I was being quite reasonable with my expectations. 'Let's see what happens, we could agree a halfway point or something. It would be a start', I thought. In any case, successfully completing my first game would increase my chances of getting more for my next game.

The Waiting Game!

I returned to Southampton without a deal, and rather disappointed. But it was nowhere near as bad as the Mirrorsoft experience. At least Tony liked my idea and he was going to make me an offer. And the worst-case scenario would be to just accept whatever he offered me. Surely, that wouldn't be bad for my first project? After all, I would have a publisher to release my game.

While waiting, I started working on the game, doing lots of bits and pieces in design, and also coding some elements. Improving my music and sound fx editor. Oh yes, I was also writing a music editor to compose the music for the game. When one thinks about it, it was quite amazing in the early years. In actual fact, we weren't just programming games, we were also developing game engines with all the tools needed; graphics editor, level editor, music editor and any other tools that we would need along the way depending on the game. There weren't many available in terms of third party tools, as far as I was aware of anyway.

A week or so passed, but still no news from Tony. I didn't want to call him either so as not to weaken my position, so I decided to wait. Working away but hoping every day that he'd call; one ear on the phone. Janet was trying to comfort me, 'He will call, he liked your idea, he's probably busy with other things...'

In the meantime, I was working nonstop, but also looking for an artist to work with me. Not sure how, but I found Tim Boone. Actually, maybe I put an ad in the local paper?

Anyway, he came to my house to meet me. Then, I told him all about the game, and also informed him about Telecom's interest. If they make me an offer then I could, in turn, offer him the graphics position. He was probably in his late teens, just like most of the other whizz kids. In fact, the UK gaming industry was started with these amazingly talented whizz kids, many coders, and doodlers. Gerry The Germ would be the only game I worked on with Tim, but we remained friends. He went onto become the editor of legendary gaming magazine, C&VG. Tim also contributed to the Game Master TV show on Channel 4, hosted by Dominik Diamond and later by Dave Perry and others. The show also featured Sir Patrick Moore.

And, Tony Makes The Call!

It was thirty-five years ago, but I remember it like it were yesterday. It was one of the most important phone calls of my life. I think it was a Wednesday and as usual I was waiting for the call while working away on the game. Every now and then, I would make a move for the telephone, but stopping myself at the last moment. It definitely wasn't a pride thing or anything like that but I really wanted Tony to call me instead of me calling him. Maybe I wanted to show strength of character, perhaps to myself more than anyone else? I could wait, I was patient and quite resilient too. Another few days of waiting wouldn't hurt, I kept repeating to myself.

But I was also getting fed up with all the waiting, and not knowing Tony's intentions. I was maybe losing valuable time by waiting in case he was no longer interested. In all honesty, I was going back and forth in my mind, not being able to decide one way or the other. In fact, this is one of my main characteristics, continually evaluating, thinking about even small details. By and large, it makes it very difficult for me to get on with things, as I cannot relax. It doesn't make me less efficient or productive, but it sure makes me agitated and frustrated with myself.

This is silly I thought and I finally made a real attempt to make the call myself. 'Just simply ask and find out if he's interested, that's all. No rush, he could take his time as long as he was still seriously interested in making an offer' was the internal dialogue in my mind.

But, half way to the phone, and I wimped out! Obviously, constantly thinking and evaluating can also make you a little indecisive too.

By around early afternoon the same day, I got up from my chair, but this time I was really determined to make that bloody call. Before I took a step, the phone rang, no exaggeration! Wow! I sat back down and waited for Janet to pick it up. Janet called out in a rather excited voice, 'Mev, it's Tony on the phone for you!'

Adrenalin pumping, I literally ran to the phone, and there it was, the call I had been waiting ages for finally came. Tony said, 'Sorry to keep you waiting, I have been very busy, but I had a good think about your game, and we want to publish it.'

'No problems about waiting Tony, as I have been working on the game.', I eagerly replied.

Tony continued, 'I like the idea and I think you will do a good job with it too. And, we have decided to pay you what you need to make the game, £8,000."

OMG, internally it was like I was flying! Immediately, I gave a thumbs up to Janet, who was waiting in anticipation. She could clearly see my excitement.

Trying to contain my excitement and maintain composure, I responded in a reassuring way, "Thank you so much for your offer Tony. I will do my best to deliver a good product, and make sure you are not disappointed."

Tony also added, "Please keep the deal amount to yourself, and don't share it with anyone." Well, I thought to myself, that's easy enough as I don't know anyone to share it with.

I said, "Don't worry Tony, I promise, I won't tell anyone, even my wife!" He said his people would send me an agreement to sign, wished me luck and we said our goodbyes...

Nobody Can Stop Me Now!

Soon after leaving the factory I had bought my first house. It was a lovely three-bed semi with two receptions, very close to the in-laws too, in Sholing. I was using one of the receptions as my office. It was quite a good size room and my father-in-law George made me a long work desk, big enough to accommodate three people. He did such a great job with it, and I developed quite a few projects on that desk.

Tim Boone also joined me and we started working together really well. Likewise, Tim was very excited too, as it was probably his first game project.

Now, I also needed to sort out my sound stuff. It is important to make it clear that Spectrum had only a beep sound, and you could only have very simple sound effects in the game. But you could try and have something sounding a bit better on the title screen for each different level. To achieve interesting sounds from a beep, we needed to use and apply some very clever programming tricks. To be able to do this we had to use all of the computer's capacity and capability to generate these fancy sounds. So, while the music was playing there wasn't much else we could do, hence we were stuck playing the tunes on the title screens before the actual game started.

Our First House

Do you remember Brian Marshall? He was the guy at the electronics shop, where I bought the cassette recorder, TV, and the Toshiba music system. I really cannot remember the early days of how our friendship developed, but we had become very close friends with Brian by then. Also, I may have visited the shop a few times about music systems; I was also just getting into listening to music. What is more, Brian came to our council flat a few times when I was still at the factory and learning to program.

My Biggest Hobby: Listening to Music

My biggest enjoyment in life has been the actual making of games, but as you know by now, I have hardly played any games. Basically, I could never enjoy them, as I was never good enough. I had also miserably failed at learning to play saz or guitar, but I always enjoyed singing and listening to music.

After living in the UK, I had the opportunity to listen to a lot of music. Especially in the factory, during working all those boring hours, listening to music was my biggest joy. I remember using my first Sony Walkman to death, every day I would listen to hours of music. It very quickly became a favourite hobby of mine. Likewise, I also started getting interested in Hi-Fi equipment too, very quickly realising that I could enjoy music more on a better system. As well as listening to music, I also spent a lot of time reading hi-fi magazines. This was how I relaxed during and between long and tiring coding sessions.

The first ever LP I listened to was Janet's Moon Dance by Van Morrison. And, the first couple of albums I bought were The Wall by Pink Floyd and Animal Magnetism by Scorpions. Because I didn't have a lot of money to spare, I paid a lot of attention to the notion of 'value for money', which forced me to search for the best bargains, thus increasing my knowledge about equipment too.

I soon built myself a decent music system, which consisted of a classic Sansui SR-232 Record Player, a Sansui amplifier, and another classic, Acoustic Research AR 18s speakers. These speakers were brilliant; even though they were small, they could really rock, I bought two pairs as a backup. Then I gradually upgraded my system as I got more into system building, and of course, had more cash to spare.

I currently have a high-end special edition British ATC active speaker system (EL 150A), signed by the designer. In fact, I visited their manufacturing facilities in Stroud, Gloucestershire twice, and met Bill Woodman, the founder, and the designer of these great speakers.

Years ago, I used to mainly listen to rock but now I listen to all sorts of music. Of course, paying special attention to well recorded albums with good production value and performances. Listening to live music is another experience altogether. And, I was lucky enough to see some of the best bands and artists in the world, including Pink Floyd, Queen, Black Sabbath, Thin Lizzy, Neil Young, Scorpions and Metallica and a few jazz bands. Well, I did say I liked rock!

With Bill Woodman and my ATC speakers, 2016

In fact, I love listening to music for hours on end, day after day. It is food for my soul.

Back to Lo-Fi!

Back to lo-fi computer music! Brian used to come around to my house, and see all the work I was doing. He found it all very fascinating. He just couldn't understand how I managed to learn the whole thing, and now I was actually making a game.

Really Brian was a very talented musician, he played drums in a local band. I used to go and watch them wherever they played. It was really great for me, as Brian would take me to all the wonderful country pubs where they performed. And sometimes Brian would drive me to lovely pubs in neighbouring villages to taste local beers. In fact, Brian also taught me how to drive. I took all my initial lessons from him, and he was a brilliant instructor. We spent a lot of time with Brian, he was a great photographer too, and took so many wonderful pictures of Nej.

My first car was a clapped out old Ford GTI MK II. I loved that car with its lovely wheels. I forget the number of repairs I had done to it. It was once stolen too and we found it dumped somewhere minus the cassette player!

While I was writing the music editor, I would ask Brian to have a go and test it for me. Basically, I wanted to see what he could do with it, and how easy it was to use. In truth, I didn't even know who would do the music at this point. Although Brian played the drums in the band, he was a very talented all round musician. He had a superb electronic keyboard with which he would compose so many lovely tunes.

It was easy enough for Brian to play around with my Music Editor and he was soon having lots of fun with it. He couldn't believe the amazing sounds he could produce by touching different keys on the little rubber Spectrum keyboard. I was also impressed with the little jingles he was creating. Some of the sounds were really impressive and interesting. I was well pleased with my achievement. We could both see the potential of creating some fancy tunes with this. Each keystroke was generating lots of interesting sounds, or samples of instruments at different frequencies. And depending on how long the key was held down would also affect the sound. I was tweaking some of them to see if I could make them sound more interesting and different as per Brian's suggestions too.

Brian was creating many small tunes on the fly. I would store them in memory and play them back. We would look at each other with amazement. However, there was no way of editing what Brian composed. So, he kept trying different versions. Actually, he would have several takes of the same melody that he was trying to create. And then he would decide which one to keep. Truly, we were both enjoying the process. Suddenly, I realised that Brian was perfect for the job - he could do all my music. And, that's exactly what he did for most of my initial games!

Brian composed some brilliantly crazy tunes, and my favourite is the title tune of my second game Prodigy. I think it's absolutely amazing considering the limitations of my editor and the lack of any real sound on the Spectrum! I have included a QR code under the Prodigy section, so you can listen to it while reading the book.

I was also very lucky to have legendary 8bit musician Rob Hubbard doing the music of the Commodore 64 (C64) version of Gerry the Germ. It is one of Rob's best works, for sure. C64 had a proper sound chip (SID), which allowed for better music. And there were some other great C64 musicians around from the early days such as Ben Dalglish (RIP) and Matt Grey.

Here's a sample of the Gerry The Germ C64 music by Rob Hubbard. You can access the YouTube link by reading the QR code with your mobile device. Most modern phones have this function built into the camera app. If not you will need to install a QR code reader app.

Had a Great Development System, But Wasn't Aware of It

The Spectrum version of Gerry was going well. There was another computer, Amstrad CPC (by Sir Alan Sugar) that was competing in a market dominated by Commodore 64 and the Spectrum. Amstrad was also based on the Z80 processor, as was the Spectrum, which meant I could program both. Therefore, I decided to develop the Amstrad version of Gerry as well. In fact, I ended up coding the Spectrum and Amstrad versions of all my games.

I decided to buy the Amstrad CPC 6128, higher spec machine with 128K memory and a 3inch disk drive. Eventually, I was using the Amstrad CPC 128 to write and create all my code on. And then, I would send/download the finished code to Spectrum via a board/card that connected the two machines via the RS232 ports. Also, I had a very good editor and a compiler developed by a company out of Oxford, the land of clever people.

If I am not mistaken, I had seen an ad for the RS232 card in a magazine. Subsequently, I actually drove to Fareham near Southampton to purchase it. Then, I obtained a bit more info on it at the shop and it just made sense to have it. And what a good purchase it turned out to be, making my development process so much more efficient and easy. If the Spectrum crashed and things went belly up, I would just simply reset the Spectrum, fix the bugs on the Amstrad and try again. It was fast too; I could compile the whole game in about 2 minutes. But waiting for two minutes seemed too slow, of course, as I had nothing to compare mine with! I actually learnt much later that I had, in fact, built myself a very fast and efficient development system, without realising it.

A few months into the development of the game, I decided that I should also do the C64 version. It was just as popular as the Spectrum, and it would be brilliant to develop all three versions in parallel. So, I started looking for a C64 programmer in Southampton. Honestly, I can't remember how, but I probably put an ad in the local paper. Just a few days after, I found Edwin Rayner, an amazingly talented young C64 programmer. He agreed to join the team almost immediately. Now we were a 4-member crew doing three versions. Edwin wrote the C64 versions of all my games I was developing for the Spectrum and Amstrad. We were such a great little team and really enjoyed working together. We were really capable, ambitious and productive too. With doing the C64 versions, I also learnt to program in 6502 (C64 processor), again in machine code, but with a completely different instruction set and syntax. Once you learn to program in one well enough, you tend to learn the others reasonably quickly. Later I also learnt to program in Motorola 68000 processor (used in the Amiga, Atari St and Sega Mega Drive) and Intel x86 (MS-DOS – PC).

Going Multiplatform With The First Game

I visited Tony in London, to report on our progress and also talk to him about doing Amstrad and C64 versions of the game. In reality, I had taken a risk by already starting development, but his reaction was very positive, and he loved the idea. 'The more platforms the better,' he said, which pleased me a great deal. This should make it easier to ask for more money, I thought. And it did, I think I got another £2,000 or £3,000 for the Amstrad and C64 versions.

Everything was going well, suddenly I was developing three versions of my first game. We worked long and hard, and completed the game within the timeframe I had set. It was my first attempt, although technically very good on all machines the content was limited, and it was a small game. But my God, it was bloody hard to play and complete, and it was probably going to be one of the toughest and most unfair games ever!

It received mixed reactions from the press, but almost all were impressed with the technical and visual aspects. Even getting ten out of ten for technical achievement. But they all found it too small, and too difficult. And some found the idea of the player helping a germ destroy the human body to be in bad taste, as Mirrorsoft had feared. In the retro gaming community world, some people still talk about it being such a tough game.

All in all, it wasn't commercially successful, but it helped me to establish myself as a capable developer who could successfully complete three versions at the same time. Not sure, but probably only a handful of developers were able or chose to do this. Releasing three versions of the same game was an important business aspect for the publishers.

Firebird released a special C64 disk version in the States. For some reason, the game did quite well over there, which really surprised us all, almost reaching a cult status. Americans normally don't like tough games, at all, maybe we made the disk version a bit easier, I can't recall. It was amazing to receive royalty payments from that version for a while. It wasn't big money, but it was an important thing to experience with the first game. I had learnt the importance of royalties and made sure to have a royalty clause in all my subsequent agreements.

This was a good start, and I got paid well with a taste of royalty payments too. Also, I met some nice people from the industry, Tony Rainbird, Herbert Right, Colin Fuidge, and Angela Sutherland to name but a few. I also met some other developers who also had their games published by Firebird and Rainbird.

My first game experience gave me enough confidence and determination for creating better and even more ambitious original games.

Prodigy, My Second Game, 1986 (The Activision Years)

While still working on Gerry The Germ, I was racking my brains about the next game. Although I didn't play or own many games, I was constantly checking out what was making good impressions and having an impact. Generally, I'm very observant too, and I could easily spot unique and interesting stuff for inspiration. One of the best developers of the 8bit era was Ultimate Play the Game, and they had some fantastic games under their belt in the early years, and some more in the latter years too.

After their highly successful Alien 8 isometric game, they had just released Knightlore, which looked even more impressive both technically and visually. In fact, both were great games and perfectly suited to the Spectrum. An isometric viewpoint is a method for visually representing 3D objects in 2D dimensions. Or to put it simpler in gaming terms, it's a technique to make a 2D game look more 3D. Isometric games were very popular in the early years. The legendary Last Ninja series used a slight variation on the technique, which made it visually even more impressive. It's quite interesting, to say the least, that I would actually end up coding Last Ninja 2 soon after my Prodigy game!

Since I seemed to be technically adept, I thought of having a go at the isometric genre myself. But I wanted to add something technically even more stunning to make a better impact. This is something I would always try and do in my future games too. All of the existing isometric games used static flipped screens i.e. you played on a static screen, and you moved your character around in it to do things. When you completed all the tasks, then the player would be presented with the next screen (level). There was no scrolling or movement of the actual backgrounds (playing area, only the player character and/or some computer controlled objects or characters moved.

The Prodigy game idea was based on isometric 3D, but it allowed the playing area to move (scroll in the direction the player wanted to move. That meant that the player would be presented with much bigger levels, instead of one screen, the levels would be several screens wide. And the player would move around in a bigger area trying to perform many tasks while avoiding many obstacles and enemies.

The game would look just as visually stunning as Knightlore, but would be technically more impressive because of the scrolling aspect. This would in fact make it the first 3D isometric scrolling game, and that would be cool I thought. Edwin was technically very capable, and together we pulled it off. Again we would develop it on all three formats. The C64 wasn't very suitable for this sort of 3D-esque game, but Edwin did a great job. What was great was that I had a nice concept for the game too, with lots of interesting gameplay elements and ideas. This time, another young local graphic artist, Gary Thornton, joined us to do all the visual stuff. Gary did a good job with the graphics, considering Prodigy may have been his first game.

Firebird was very keen to publish Prodigy too, but Rod Cousens and Jon Dean were also interested in signing up my next game. Feeling very content, I thought what a great position to be in. I really can't remember how the talks started, but I had a brief encounter with Rod when I worked on the C64 conversion of 3D Ant Attack. Also, Rod was now running Electric Dreams, an Activision subsidiary. Jon Dean had joined Activision and had setup their internal software development studio.

Electric Dreams was based in Southampton, which was an advantage, plus they offered me so much more money. Clearly, it seemed they really wanted to sign me up as the local developer. I really enjoyed working with Firebird, but the Electric Dreams offer was very enticing. It was much better, and was an offer I simply couldn't refuse, and so I didn't.

Working With Rod Cousens and Jon Dean

This was the start of a long business relationship and friendship with both Rod and Jon, which has lasted to this day. I never forget the amount of fun we all had deciding on the title of the game. I was using the code name Nejo, after my son Nejati, and in fact, the little baby in the game was called Nejo! We were coming up with all sorts of silly names like Perambulator (one of Rod's!), but in the end we settled for Prodigy. Through my second game, I met two other industry veterans; Mark Eyles, who wrote the box cover story, and David Rowe, who did the box art.

Again, both technically and visually, Prodigy was very impressive, but unforgivingly difficult. It was quite tough to make progress while negotiating with all sorts of obstacles and enemies. But as soon as you died you would be sent back to the beginning of the level. And to add insult to injury, I was sending the player back to base with a fancy retrace of the path they had covered! It looked visually and technically impressive, but it was very annoying to the player!

Another fancy feature that I added was to process all the moving objects and enemies off camera. The things that the player couldn't see were processed to make the game more realistic. Since the player couldn't really see and appreciate what was happening off screen and off camera, it merely caused an unnecessary performance hit. Meaning I was wasting some of the computer's processor power for something that the player was not able to fully appreciate. It was a waste of resources that could be used for something else. I realised this after the game was released, but it was an important lesson learnt. Never do anything unless the player can visually see and appreciate it.

Our enemy characters were intelligent in that they could cleverly patrol complex 3D mazes and find their way around. They didn't follow a set path, they could randomly change direction and sometimes, if within range, they could follow and try and catch the player. In addition, they could find doors, and wait for moving doorways and openings and then go through. All this was very impressive, but I'm not sure the player could even notice it. There was quite a bit of primitive AI going as it were, but wasted really. A mini map, similar to those in racing games, showing the moving enemies may have helped and impressed the gamer. Non-player characters could even decide when to enter certain rooms and areas. Oh well, maybe next time!

Despite a few important mistakes I did learn a lot from my first two games:

1) Don't make games too hard. And always use dynamically adjusted difficulty levels depending on the player ability. All players have different skill levels and it would be great if the game could automatically adjust the difficulty on the fly according to the individual player.

2) And, don't waste resources by doing fancy stuff unless the player can clearly and visually see and fully appreciate it.

Overall, the Prodigy game was received well by the press, both for its visual and technical achievement. But it was very tough to play, unforgiving and frustrating! Such a shame! But, onwards and upwards I thought. No additional royalties, but the development fee was good enough. More importantly, it cemented my reputation as a good programmer, and I had already become an important coder for Activision to call upon.

Here's an example of the great music Brian Marshall composed on the Spectrum. The Prodigy title music is truly a classic. I think even the band Prodigy would appreciate it! Remember, all this from a beep.

Enduro Racer, 1986 (Approaching Star Programmer Status)

After only two games under my belt, I was fast becoming a reliable and capable professional programmer delivering products on all platforms, and on time too, which was a crucial attribute to have.

Just as when I was readying myself for my third game, both Rod and Jon asked for help. This would be the first of a few occasions that I would be called upon for rescue projects. They asked me to convert the excellent Enduro Racer game from Spectrum to Amstrad. The original was such a brilliant conversion from Sega arcade to home computer, one of the best ever.

For whatever reason the original developer, Giga Games, just didn't want to do the Amstrad version. Like I said, I was probably one of the very few that did multiple platforms. It was such a big and important license for Activision, and they were absolutely desperate to get it done quickly. I can't remember the exact release date, but they only had two months or so at the most. They were literally begging me, but I really wasn't interested, as I wanted to do my own games. Besides there was so little time, and I wasn't sure if I could do it. But, I agreed to meet the programmers, and have a look at it at least.

They came down from Scotland to meet me in the Electric Dreams offices. They were very bright and clever guys; they had done such a fantastic job adapting the big arcade game to the Spectrum. It was an impressive looking 3D motorbike racing game. They went through all the important details of how they had created, and coded the 3D racing tracks, the bike handling and riding model. I couldn't understand any of it, not one bit, and I was supposed to be a decent programmer myself. All the technical stuff was just going in one ear and coming out the other. I was just nodding my head hoping they wouldn't ask me anything technical! It really was a great feat of programming on their part. They left all the source files with me and went. I thanked them, and said that I would take a look and get back to them for any help.

I told Rod and Jon that the game was technically very hard and demanding. And that it would be almost impossible for me to convert it to Amstrad, let alone doing it in a couple of months. But I promised them that I would have a closer look at it and let them know my final decision. But they both kept saying I was the only programmer who could pull it off, please give it a try. They were really trying to convince me. They were making very good offers to entice me as well, a decent development fee plus royalties. In response, I just repeated that I would take a look and get back to them, with no promises. To be honest, I was very good at not committing myself to anything upfront without being 100% sure. This served me well, and established my reputation as a true professional.

Should I, Could I?

To start with, I had a brief look at the code here and there to see if I could undertake such a big project. It was a big title, and was getting great reviews and ratings in the magazines, and regarded as one of the best games on the Spectrum. It was very tempting of course, if I could pull it off then it would really help my career. But I was scared, I just couldn't see myself managing it, it seemed beyond my technical knowledge and ability. The graphics were excellent and it would be very easy for me to convert them to Amstrad. But, I could only attempt to do it in the monochrome mode as it would be impossible to do in full colour mode. That would be like rewriting the whole game. However, I could use the graphics as they were, more or less, and I could get help from Nick Cook, who did the Spectrum graphics.

All in all, I was trying really hard to get my head around the whole project. I needed to find a quick and dirty way to do it, and that was the only way. More importantly, I only had a few weeks. The first thing to do was to get their source code on my system, and get the original Spectrum version working within my development environment, so I could get closer to the project this way. Once my version of the code worked on the Spectrum, then I could have a closer look at ways to come up with some ideas and methods to try out.

Emulating The Spectrum on The Amstrad

Incidentally, I knew the Amstrad machine very well too, having already developed two games on it. With my own games, I just did a straight port of the Spectrum version to Amstrad. I wasn't doing a dedicated Amstrad version, as it would take so much longer and it wouldn't be commercially viable. It was a real shame for the Amstrad users, but unfortunately that was the norm and what almost all companies did. Basically, just a quick conversion for extra revenue.

The first thing that crossed my mind was to try the same thing with Enduro Racer, i.e. get it working on my system for the Spectrum and then do a straight conversion. As usual, I could use all the clever techniques I had already developed, and probably come up with some new tricks too. This way I could leave most of the original Spectrum code untouched, especially all the clever bits I couldn't understand! Surely, this could work, it would be like emulating the Spectrum on the Amstrad.

In fact, it would be possible to have the entire Spectrum code working on the Amstrad, all the racing bits, track creation, and handling. In a nutshell, all the difficult bits. I didn't even need to know or understand how any of it worked. If I did a racing game of my own in the future, I would cross that bridge then.

All I had to do was to just replace the Amstrad specific codes such as joystick, keyboard control, sound and any other hardware specific stuff. All of which I had already coded before for my games anyway, so I may just have to modify some of the original code or do some additional coding, that was it.

The hardest thing turned out to be getting the Spectrum source code working on my development system. There was incompatibility between the editors and compilers Giga Games and I were using. I had to go through hundreds of lines of code to change all the labels, which took a week alone! Anyway, what a relief, in the end, I got the original code working on the Spectrum. Now I could start playing around with it.

First of all, I started to look at some important routines where I could make improvements if possible, as I needed all the performance I could get on the original code. Basically, I needed the extra performance to make room for the rather complex and involved conversion code I had to write and use. The conversion code would have a performance hit on the game, but no problem as long as the end result was acceptable and the game wasn't too slow.

Without getting too technical, in game development we always use a screen buffer. This means instead of creating and writing everything the player sees directly onto the computer's screen, we create it in a buffer/shadow screen in memory (RAM).

If you write to the screen directly (and we write many things one after the other in milliseconds; background graphics, player character, enemies etc.) you would get a lot of flickering, which isn't pleasant and it renders games almost unplayable.

Flicker is caused by the fact that the TV refreshes its screen every so often and when you try to write to it during refresh it causes flicker. That's why we create the screen in the background somewhere in memory, and then copy it over in one swoop and as fast as possible to the actual screen. For zero judder and flicker you must do this in 60th of a second (60 frames per second) and during non-refresh. On most 8bit machines such as Spectrum, Amstrad and C64 the best we could achieve would be around 20-30 frames per second. I hope I haven't lost you non-technical readers completely, I better move on.

I left the original Spectrum code to do all its magic and create the Spectrum screen in an allocated buffer somewhere in the Amstrad memory. Then all I had to do was to copy this screen to the actual Amstrad screen that the TV displayed, but doing it as fast as possible. This was because I wasn't just copying the Spectrum screen, but also converting it to the Amstrad format at the same time since the screen formats are completely different.

And hey presto it worked, I couldn't believe it, and the speed wasn't too bad either. I could optimise and make improvements here and there, even reduce the number of trees drawn on the edges of the tracks etc. However, I didn't want to fiddle with it too much causing possible bugs and other problems.

Because of the method I used I had the whole game finished, with maybe a few bits of touching up and tidying up here and there for any small bugs that may have crept in. I thought, 'Wow, I did it, it worked, and the whole game is ready. Wait till I show it to Jon and Rod.'

In the meantime, Jon was calling me every now then checking my progress, but I was not giving anything away. Instead, I was just saying I was still examining the whole code to see how I could do it, if at all. Believe me, I was working so hard, through the night, only sleeping a few hours then back on it again. Normally they were not allowed to call me before midday, but sometimes they were so desperate and would call me around ten o'clock, but Janet would simply tell them I was asleep. Well, I was becoming a star programmer and you can't just call stars willy-nilly.

It's Show Time!

After about 3 weeks or so, I had the whole thing working just bar the few glitches here and there. Goodness me, I was so satisfied with my achievement, but also absolutely knackered, having hardly slept for three weeks or so! Jubilantly, I called Jon and said I was ready to go in with a demo. They were so excited that I had already started the project and even managed to create a demo.

I arrived at their office and they were all waiting in anticipation, Rod, Jon and the others. I had the game on a floppy disk, I popped it in and loaded it up. Jon sat down with excitement. The main menu screen came up, all looking nice and complete, all the functions were there. He went through them to check they were functional, and they were, even all the settings worked. Then giving me a nice smile as if to say 'I knew you could do it Mev baby'. He always called me that.

And then Jon hit 'Start' to play. The track loaded, and he started riding around. Doing all the fancy stuff like jumping over the obstacles and he seemed to be having a lot of fun. Jon and everyone else started commenting, 'Bloody hell, this looks really nice, well done Mev, we knew you could do it'. After that, Jon loaded the next track, and again it all seemed fine. Jon was playing, but he was completely shocked and very pleased at the same time. He was constantly praising me, 'You are a real star, I knew you could do it Mev baby!' Suddenly, it occurred to everyone that Jon was actually playing a finished game.

They were all so happy and pleased. And so was I. Jon and Rod gave me a big hug, reaffirming that they knew I could pull it off. Rod then told everyone as he always did at every opportunity, 'I taught Mev everything he knows.' In fact, this was a running joke between Rod and I throughout the years. He would always say that he taught me how to code. Of course, he never taught me any coding, but he did give me the opportunity, and also provided support whenever I needed it in later years in my career, as did Jon.

Amazingly, I was now truly a star programmer for Activision. By the way, Amstrad wasn't as big in the UK as it could have been, due to the dominance of the Spectrum, but it was very successful in France, Germany and Spain. With Enduro Racer, I was now a well-known programmer in Europe too. In the end, it turned out to be a good opportunity and also a good decision to develop it.

Aliens & Big Trouble in Little China, 1987

The successful development of Enduro Racer elevated my status to one of the most important programmers in the eyes of Rod and Jon. But this also made me the first port of call whenever they were in trouble. They convinced me to help them out with the Aliens conversion from the Amstrad to the C64. The Amstrad version was very different from the US version and so much better too. In fact, it was a great game, and Activision wanted it converted to other machines. We basically helped with the C64 conversion. Again, I was helping with the original code on the Amstrad, and my C64 programmer Edwin Rayner was helping with the all-important sprite routines.

Jon Dean also told me that they had had another big movie tie-in (The movie 'Big Trouble in Little China') in development for months. However, there were major problems with it and they needed my help. I said to Jon 'Not again, I really want to do my own games rather than rescue projects'. He said it was nearly finished, and he would get me all the source files, and I could probably finish the whole thing in a couple of months or so. I replied that I would take a look at the source.

We were all working at the Electric Dreams offices to very tight deadlines with a number of projects on the go. That was when I met my fellow coder and friend Nick Pelling, a great C64 programmer. Actually, I think he was working on his C64 Firetrak game. Nick always had a hand towel around his neck; I found him many a time sleeping with his head on the keyboard and many letters imprinted on his forehead! Apart from going home a few times for a good sleep, shower and clean clothes, we mostly lived in the bloody offices for weeks.

Jon eventually handed me a cassette with the source files and a supposed demo. In truth, I spent ages trying to load the demo, but every time it would get stuck on the title screen, and no amount of tape head adjustment was helping. Obviously, there wasn't much more than the title screen, which was why it was giving errors. Cut a long story short, I ended up coding the whole thing from scratch from the existing design, which was done by Jon and his team. Also, Nick Cook was doing the graphics for both Aliens and Big Trouble, which was great since we had already worked on Enduro Racer together. In fact, we worked very closely with Nick and I really enjoyed teaming up with him. We got on well, as he was such a nice person and one of the great graphics artists too. Nowadays, Nick is a successful novelist.

I really loved the film, Big Trouble In Little China. I wish I had had more time to develop it, and had got involved with the design too. We just had to code it as quickly as possible, and finish all three versions (Spectrum, Amstrad and C64) in about three months max. As always, I just did my best to make the best of the situation.

Would You Like Chilli Sauce With That?

During Aliens and Big Trouble there were other projects that were also on tight deadlines. There were so many of us working together, day and night and under a lot of pressure. We would sleep in the office, work and eat there too. I remember Jon and I buying lots of doner kebabs and burgers from the local Turkish takeaway in Southampton!

One particular incident that springs to mind is when a programmer or Activision employee joined us and stayed with us for a few days. He loved his burger with plenty of chilli sauce. In fact, he would brag about how much he loved his chilli sauce, and that the Turkish sauce just wasn't hot enough. Well, Jon and I happened to go out and get some food, and I told the owner that his chilli wasn't hot enough, and that one of our guys thought his chilli was rubbish. He just said, 'is that so? OK, I'll give him something extra hot then.'

I warned the guy that this time he should be pleased as the owner had put something special on his burger. He simply said, we'll see about that and took a big bite. His immediate reaction was 'Well, it's a bit better I suppose, but still not that different'. Another big bite, and a few seconds later he didn't know what had hit him. He looked like he was on fire, and drinking his coke like mad as if to put the fire out. Fortunately, he recovered after a while, but I am sure he stopped having chilli sauce for some time after that!

Another funny story involving my programmer Edwin Rayner. Like I mentioned previously, Edwin was an excellent programmer, but a bit of a perfectionist. Routinely, he would keep changing and improving things, thus he would take his time with things always running behind schedule. Working to such a tight deadline wasn't Edwin's thing.

We would have weekly product meetings, assessing how things were going with various projects. I think the project manager was newly employed Dan Marchant who stayed with us more than Jon did. Anyway, Dan would ask everyone how they were getting on with their tasks. Edwin was helping with the all-important sprite routines on the Aliens, and helping me with the C64 version of Big Trouble.

By now, we were towards the end of development and were all quoting a few days or so on the remaining things. Getting close to completion, but also getting very close to the deadline. Overall, some projects looked risky, and there was a lot of pressure on everyone, and also a lot of tension in the air. In actual fact, Dan was feeling the pressure more than most, and trying to keep things tight to get things finished, and delivered on time. The main C64 programmer kept saying he was almost done, but was still waiting for the sprites. Dan would ask Edwin, 'How long will it take you to finish the bloody thing?' Because he was really pissed off after several weeks of Edwin's repeated reply, 'I think I can finish it soon, probably it will take me one and a half hours!' Actually, this probably happened a few times.

On the all-important last meeting, after everyone said their bits, Dan turned to Edwin last, as he always did, and said in a very calm, but firm voice, 'Edwin please tell me how long before you give those sprite routines to the programmer. And, I'm begging you please don't you fucking say one and a half hours!' Edwin paused a bit, scratching his chin, and taking his time and composing himself and his answer. Trying very hard to make sure he didn't piss Dan off any more than he already had. With a slight smirk on his face, Edwin said, 'I think about one hour and three quarters!'

No exaggeration, we all fell off our chairs, laughing our heads off for ages, we just couldn't stop!

It was really tiring, but in the end, we successfully completed all our projects. Although Big Trouble wasn't as good as it could have been, once more I managed to successfully rescue another project for Activision. And, I also helped with the Aliens game. Of course, in the process I made a decent amount of money too, in a reasonably short amount of time.

From what I remember, Big Trouble in Little China wasn't a big success in the movie box office either. Yet I always thought it was a great movie and thoroughly enjoyed watching it, and more than once too. However, the Aliens game became a number one Xmas hit.

Knightmare, 1987

Jon Dean somehow convinced me, yet again, to help with another big license, the Knightmare TV show. Activision had acquired the gaming rights. This wasn't a rescue project at all and he wanted me to program it for all three machines from scratch (Spectrum, Amstrad and C64). Although I wasn't involved with the original design, I was going to develop the entire game myself, so it shouldn't be too much of a problem. Besides it was a great project, and I was going to get paid quite well again. The game was going to be based on the ground-breaking Knightmare TV show.

Jon and his wife Elaine had already completed the game design. Although I had helped out quite a bit during developing it with the user interface, and had come up with some nice original way of entering commands to play some parts of the game. It was a room-based arcade and text adventure. You moved your character around and executed a set of commands, as you needed. I made the accessing of the commands very intuitive and had to do a lot of compression to squeeze all the commands and the text based answers into the limited memory. Again we would work with Nick Cook, who did all the graphics, which were great as usual.

The TV show was a huge success, but we were limited to how much we could do on the 8bit machines. Still, it was a good project to have under my belt. David Rowe did the excellent digital illustrations used in the TV show as backgrounds.

After only a couple of years in the industry, I had done two original games and had also been involved in the development of some big name titles such as Enduro Racer, Aliens, Big Trouble In Little China, Knightmare and Super Hang On. Not bad at all I guess, but I really wanted to develop my own original games.

Finally Back to Making My Own Games?

After successfully completing Knightmare, I thought 'Thank God, now I can get back to what I set out to do; making my own original games'. I was thinking about what I should do next, experimenting with things. I had an interesting looking and horizontally scrolling game environment with a fancy looking viewpoint. Unfortunately, when I moved to Turkey I lost everything, including all my old source code for my experiments, and early games too!

Oh no mummy, it's Jon Dean again! I was presented with yet another rescue project, but this one was even bigger than Enduro Racer. It was 'Last Ninja 1 (LN1)' for Spectrum and Amstrad!

'C'mon Jon, just let me be, give me a break mate. Enduro, Aliens, Big Trouble, Knightmare and now Last Ninja'. This was turning into a nightmare, I thought I was becoming a conversion man! I had hoped Knightmare really would be the last time! In fact, there were some development companies, which did just that, convert games from one platform to another.

In later years, Probe became the biggest company that provided development services for big publishers, which was founded by the late Fergus McGovern (RIP). Sadly, Fergus died in 2016, such an early and terrible loss.

Reaching Stardom With Last Ninja 2, 1988

Last Ninja was really a special game on the C64, technically amazing, the best graphics you could get anywhere. And a very unique take on the isometric games, which made it look even more 3D. It was really gorgeous. Strangely, it was quite hard to play; you had to be pixel perfect to pick up objects and weapons, and during interactions with the backgrounds. When I had a quick go at it, I didn't get very far. Me being crap at playing games probably didn't help either! It was a great job by System 3 and the development team; namely John Twiddy (coding) and Hugh Riley (graphics), and Mark Cale (CEO) and Tim Best (RIP) helping with the main design. The game was published by Activision, hence the reason why Jon knocked on my door again.

Apparently, the Spectrum version had been in development for nearly eight months, but the final game was still way off. Therefore, they really were desperate to finish it ASAP as the Spectrum owners had been waiting for ages, and it was beginning to affect System 3's reputation. Equally, the rumours of it being cancelled were going around too.

Eventually, I agreed to see the Spectrum version as it was. As far as I can recall, it was Mark (who conceived the original idea) and Jon together who showed me the demo. What I saw looked unfinished, and also compared to the C64 version, the screens didn't look as impressive, nowhere near as detailed or 3D. What is more, it was very slow to move around. In fact, I was surprised, as the screens looked very sparse and there was not much going on. Obviously, there were performance problems. Maybe it was an earlier demo, but after 8 months I was expecting something more finished and polished.

They asked me if I could help with it, and try and make improvements, so that it would be good enough to publish. It was obvious that Mark wasn't satisfied with the results, and to be honest, I wasn't surprised. In terms of colourful graphics, Spectrum had no chance against the C64 version, but as far as the details and 3D look were concerned, it could and should be identical if not better. To me, the game was very suitable for the Spectrum, like Alien 8, Knightlore and my own Prodigy.

It was so tempting, such a huge title and surely if I succeeded then my career would catapult. Afterwards, I would certainly become one of the top coders in Europe. But there wasn't much I could do with the existing code, and it would take me too long to even get to grips with it. All in all, it had to be done from scratch, and no chance of doing it in less than six or seven months. In actual fact, they said it had to be done in two or three months. I just told them no way!

Anyway, they said that they were about to start Last Ninja 2, and they couldn't delay the start of development much longer. Subsequently, I suggested that they should simply can the first one altogether. Also, that they should state that they had worked very hard on the development, but the results weren't satisfactory enough for System 3 to publish the Spectrum version. In addition, I recommended that they announce that Last Ninja 2 would be developed on the Spectrum and Amstrad alongside the C64 version. They would be releasing all three versions together. They agreed to the idea and also very quickly we agreed on the commercial terms. In a matter of days, I decided to join the Last Ninja team.

This was another major step in my career, and an important change to my life too.

Joining The Last Ninja Team

My career was moving at an amazing pace, and bringing with it some major and inevitable changes to my life. By now, I had been in England for nine years, and already carving a name for myself in one of the most fun, and fastest growing industries. I was witnessing all the exciting developments and changes that were taking place, and I was playing a small part in it myself. Probably not fully realising or taking it all in, it was all happening way too fast. Nevertheless, I was very pleased with my progress and success, considering only a few years ago I couldn't even speak a word of English. On top of that, I didn't know anything about games or computers or have any interest in either of them. But now I was working on some great games and quickly becoming a reputable name.

My Success Creating Cracks in My Marriage

While my career was skyrocketing my relationship with Janet was under a lot of stress. Because I was so involved and immersed in my work, I probably didn't quite realise it. Janet always supported me, which may have prevented me from seeing any problems in our relationship. Also, Janet's lifelong passion and ambition was to become an author. In fact, she had written several books including a couple of children's books too. Unfortunately, none of them were published, so she never had the break she longed for, but she never gave up trying.

Back then, I remember Janet asking me a few times if I would help her to get her books published. Since I was very good at getting my games published, she probably thought I could help in getting her books out there too. In addition, she had sometimes asked me to read her books and give her feedback. Unfortunately, I didn't know anything about books or book publishing, so how would I be able to convince a publisher to publish someone else's book? In truth, she really needed a literary agent. My English was getting so much better, but nowhere near good enough to read her books, and give her meaningful feedback.

Sadly, I remember even having little fights about it, but I never thought of it as a major thing. But she was getting more and more frustrated and feeling the disappointment. In the meantime, I was rapidly moving up the ladder with my career, and I don't know if this fuelled her disappointment even more. It was as if I was knowingly refusing to help her, which wasn't at all true. Frankly, I just wasn't the right person to provide the help she needed.

At one stage, she went to Germany with Nej for a short break, visiting her best friend Lilian. Lilian was from Brazil, and they were really close like sisters. They were working together in Germany before Janet came to Istanbul in 1975. We had also stayed with Lilian and her German boyfriend for a week, a few years before and we'd had a great time.

Janet had returned from Germany, and I was just finishing some projects with Activision, as always very busy and tired. To be honest, I could almost sense something unusual about Janet's general attitude, and the way she was behaving. Actually, I really can't remember how long it went on like this, but one day Janet said she wanted to talk. It was one of those moments where time stood still as she spoke. With great difficulty she simply told me that she didn't love me anymore. She went onto explain that there wasn't anyone, and that nothing had happened other than

a chance meeting with someone on the train on the way to Germany. She said they didn't even speak with each other, but that had been enough for her to realise.

And that was that. Of course, I was shocked, but somehow I wasn't really surprised that much. Maybe I was blinded by workload, success, and all the excitement of developing games. And perhaps, I wasn't giving Janet enough time and attention. Added to this equation was Janet's frustration about not getting her books published, and possibly thinking that I was not helping her. Maybe it was all of this, or something totally different, I still don't know. But, these things happen to the best of marriages. Certainly we weren't the first couple to go our separate ways. But still, it broke my heart. It turned my life upside down and created a massive void. All of which took a while to recover from.

Truly, I wasn't expecting this, and it really badly affected me to say the least. Having to separate from Nej really broke my heart. In all honesty, I never thought I would leave my son as my dad had done, but we never know what surprises life holds for us until they happen. In actual fact, I had even promised myself never to leave Nej, but it seems I had forgotten about not making big promises.

Nej was 8 years old at the time of breakup, and apparently the worst age for separation. In truth, Nej initially may have blamed himself as apparently most kids at this age do. But possibly in later years he blamed Janet, or me, or both. Although I did my best to support and be close to Nej as much as possible, it may not have been enough for him. It must have been tough, and he still may not have fully recovered from it. Looking back to my younger years, I remember being angry with my dad for a long time, right until the high school years. Obviously, my dad wasn't even around, but my being around probably wasn't good enough for Nej. I guess it is never quite the same as being together.

After this bombshell, I was going to Watford, north of London to the System 3 offices to meet with the C64 team John Twiddy, Hugh Riley and Tim Best. I would stay there for a few days to discuss the game, and come back and work from home in Southampton. Also, Hugh was living in Manchester, and would come down periodically.

Moving to London

Though heart-breaking, Janet and I had decided to separate, as it was for the best. In due course, I moved to Watford and shared the office/house with John Twiddy. This is how my long collaboration and friendship started with John. As a rule, I would go down to Southampton at weekends and spend time with Nej, but it was really tough. Too many things were happening, and much too fast.

This made it very difficult to manage or to do the right things. Most of the time in life, we don't even know what is right or wrong anyway. Isn't that half the trouble, not knowing what the best course of action is? Plus everybody's rights and wrongs and priorities are different, as are the ways we all cope with life's difficulties. Genuinely, we are all so unique. Perhaps this is the fundamental reason for incompatibility in living and sharing a life together?

This was a poignant life change, which I found very challenging. It was really making me sad not being able to spend quality time with Nej, and only seeing him at weekends in Southampton. Much later, when I had my own place in London, Nej lived with me, and went to school in London. However hard these things are, life goes on, we try and learn to survive and manage somehow because there's no other choice. After I moved to Turkey in late 2000, Nej followed after a couple of years. From that time onwards, he has remained in Istanbul and has worked with me most of the time. Nowadays, he is still working in games as a Senior Lead Game Designer.

Working on such a big and important game as Last Ninja 2 kept me very busy and occupied. Which made it a little easier to cope with the pain of the breakup. Also, I got on very well with the whole team and became friends with John, Hugh and Tim. Furthermore, I also got on well with Mark Cale and had no problems with him at all. He had a reputation for being difficult, but we had a very good understanding between us. What's more, he appreciated the fact that I was doing an important job for him, and he probably made sure not to upset me or annoy me in anyway. It is complete speculation on my behalf, but Jon Dean may have even warned him that I could simply walk away from a project, if I weren't happy with things.

Overall, I was an important part of the team, and I was there to save System 3's reputation regarding the Spectrum version. Plus, I was working alongside the C64 team, helping with the design and ideas, and developing both the Spectrum and Amstrad versions. Phil Harrison may have just started working there too, helping out with design. At that time, he was probably in his late teens and had such a great network of programmers and artists. Amazingly, he knew all the top developers in the industry and at such a young age.

All of us were very aware that we were working on a big title, and wanted to make Last Ninja 2 even better than the first one. This was no mean feat. John and I were together all the time since we were sharing the same house. We were working very closely, and constantly exchanging ideas. I don't ever remember having an argument or disagreement about anything. In fact, John and I got along famously. We were really a great team, and when Hugh came down he also stayed with us in the same house. I remember how we would spend a few days working as a team, and enjoy each other's company too. This chemistry probably had a lot to do with Last Ninja 2 becoming the best of the series, as we really were a good team. Also, Jon and I spent a lot of time with the late Tim Best too, all of us socialising together.

I had made it absolutely clear from day one to everyone including Mark, that I would leave after I finished Last Ninja 2. As I have said before, I always wanted to set up my own company and make my own games. In truth, Rod Cousens and Jon Dean also knew this, although they convinced me to do some of their games. In the end, these games earned me quite a bit of money and, more importantly a solid reputation too. But my ultimate desire and ambition was to develop and produce original games with my own signature.

Therefore, this subject came up several times while working on the project. Mark would tell us how we could all work together on other projects and talked about his big plans. Almost trying to prevent me, and the others from leaving. But, every time I would remind him that I had my own plans.

It was going very well, all three versions were being developed in parallel, John coding the C64 and me doing the Spectrum and Amstrad versions. I had Gary Thornton helping with the graphics; as we had to do a little bit of extra work converting Hugh's C64 graphics. John had a level editor that both he and Hugh used to create all the different screens and levels. Following suit, I did the

same and wrote my own editor for the Spectrum. Both Gary and I used it to make up the same levels on the Spectrum once all the graphics were converted.

As usual my friend Brian Marshall did all the music for the Last Ninja 2 game. Here's the title music for Level 2. Please remember folks that this was 32 years ago, and on the Spectrum with a beep.

From Last to Next

We had a couple months left to finish Last Ninja 2. In my mind, I was making my own plans, and this time I was determined to make my own games! Absolutely no more rescues or third-party games no matter how big. I was adamant that it was time to be my own boss, working at my own pace and place. And I loved the idea of owning the whole thing, the company, copyright, intellectual property, the lot. Actually, I had had a good taste of this with my first game Gerry The Germ, thanks to Telecomsoft's very fair and generous agreement.

But this time things would be different; I wanted to set up a company rather than work freelance. We had been working very closely with John and Hugh for months. And it was inevitable that some discussions would take place about setting up a company, developing original games, doing our own things. Not necessarily together, but it seemed they also had a desire to do their own things. At the end of the day, most successful individuals would like to have creative control and produce their own work. John had already done the C64 conversions of Tau Ceti and Ikai Warriors, both of which were excellent games.

We were very pleased with the progress of Last Ninja 2 and the fact that we were nearing completion. And it was becoming clear that we all fancied the idea of launching our own project. Since we had been working so well together, it just made sense to seriously consider setting up a company together too. So far, we had gelled and worked well together, and we could do so even better if we had our own company making our own games. It was such an obvious and inevitable direction to take. In the end, I don't think there was any hesitation about it. Bob's your uncle, we decided to go ahead with it.

We were individually reputable developers and together we would form a formidable and desired team. All the major publishers would want to work with us. Also, I already had very good relationships with Activision and Telecomsoft, both big companies, so we should be able to get a decent deal from them too.

Looking back, we were really excited at the prospect of having our own company and making our own games. We were determined to finish Last Ninja 2 as soon as possible, and make a great job of it too. We wanted to make sure that our excitement didn't cloud our work towards the project on hand. Furthermore, we also had to keep it quiet from Mark, as he was still making plans for us, and also making promises to entice us and sign an agreement soon.

However, I did keep reminding Mark that I was going to go my own way after I had finished the game. Diplomatically, John and Hugh were just saying, let's finish the game and we'll see. All this vagueness probably agitated and worried Mark even more. In all honesty, it was quite a difficult and awkward situation for everybody, but it couldn't be helped.

On one occasion, I told Rod that I was going to set up a company after Last Ninja 2. Also, that John and Hugh also wanted to join me. Naturally, Rod panicked, 'please keep it quiet, and make sure Mark doesn't hear about it. We don't want Last Ninja to be affected adversely in any way!' Obviously, it was such an important title for Activision. And for us too, for that matter.

Of course, I assured him that we would do our best to deliver Last Ninja 2 on time, and make sure it was as good as we could make it. In return, Rod knew he could rely on my professionalism. Also, he asked me to promise him that I would talk to him first before anyone else, and that I wouldn't sign up with any other publisher before letting him know. Naturally, he didn't want to lose the opportunity of signing us up before anyone else. He knew me so well, as we had worked together for so long. With John and Hugh also on board, we would be such a great team to sign up.

At that point, John, Hugh and I were discussing the potential publishers; Activision was the first and obvious choice, and the other was Telecomsoft.

First of all, I wanted to see how keen and interested Telecomsoft would be. It was Angela Sunderland whom I contacted if I am not mistaken, simply telling her our intentions. On balance, she seemed very keen, and said, 'We should talk, we would definitely like to sign you up.' We had two very big companies interested in us. So, I told her that Activision was also interested and that we would evaluate both offers, and decide accordingly. Throughout my life, I have always tried to be open and straight with my dealings.

Top Secret Meeting at a Service Station!

Next of all, I called Rod and informed him that Telecomsoft were also interested in us. He wasn't surprised. Also, I said it would be nice to decide which publisher to go with before finishing Ninja. Subsequently, Rod suggested meeting up and discussing things. Secretly, we decided to meet up somewhere nobody would know or guess, well away from Watford. Hugh was down from Manchester as well. So I arranged with Rod to meet up on the M3 (London-Southampton motorway) at one of the service stations near the London end! Really, it was like a scene from a film, a top secret meeting at a service station. I cannot tell you how exciting it felt!

The night before the meeting we were discussing what we could get, and how much we should ask for. We didn't have a clue, and it was so funny when you considered our situation and circumstances. Up until that point, we had been paid well for our work and generally getting as much as we could. Also, it transpired that I managed to negotiate better fees for myself than John and Hugh. Having a great start with Telecomsoft helped me too.

Using my own experience, I was trying to convince them to ask for as much as possible. But they both seemed hesitant, and kept saying nobody would pay us that much money. They were almost afraid of not getting a deal at all if we were too aggressive with our demands. In the end, I asked them to leave me to do the talking.

'Let me try, I have a very close and friendly relationship with Rod. Besides, he could only say no to my offer, he wasn't going to throw us out of the meeting, nothing to lose.'

It made sense. Anyway, we agreed that I would be the spokesperson, do the negotiation, and they would just back me up.

In hindsight, I cannot remember if Mark noticed all three of us disappearing like that. Nor can I remember the time of the meeting, but it may have been late afternoon, early evening. We normally worked all hours under the sun anyway, so it wasn't as if we were skiving off work. Nevertheless, we were worried that Mark would suspect something. The meeting probably lasted for an hour or so. Rod is a very clever businessman, and here we were with considerable talent and reputation, but with no real business experience. I had signed a few deals in the past, but they didn't amount to more than £30,000 each at the most. Well I thought, we were now in the big league and I should set my target accordingly. This could and should be a considerably big deal. Prior to that, I had worked with Rod many times and always felt very close and comfortable with him. Plus, I was quite good at staying firm and maintaining my position if I believed I was reasonable with my demands. And Rod knew that.

When he realised that I was chosen as the spokesperson he said jokingly, 'I see, Mev is going to try and shaft me again. Come on guys, don't let him do that.' He was trying to get John and Hugh involved and possibly trying to weaken my stance. However, John and Hugh remained firm and underlined the fact that I was representing the team.

As always, Rod didn't miss the opportunity to tell John and Hugh that he taught me everything I knew! We had already decided on what I would ask for and I was trying to get as close a deal to it as possible. To be honest, I cannot recall the exact details, but in the end I said to Rod that if we were to agree there and then I would call Telecomsoft the next day, and tell them that we had already signed up. Rod really wanted to work with us, and didn't want us to go anywhere else. We reached an agreement and shook hands. It was something like five years or five games, whichever happened earlier, with a deal amount in the region of several hundred thousand pounds. It was certainly a lot more than both John and Hugh expected.

Rod was really pleased, but we were even more so. With a great deal under our belt, we left the service station, and couldn't wait to get back to finish Ninja as soon as possible.

Both John and Hugh were impressed with my performance and were happy that they had let me do the negotiating. The deal earned me their complete trust and respect, and from then on, I would be dealing with the business side of things such as agreements and negotiations with their consultation. Truly, we had a fantastic deal with Activision for our new company, which we hadn't even set up yet.

Finally, we successfully completed Last Ninja 2 on all three versions. It was regarded as the best of the series. Obviously, I don't know the exact numbers, but I am sure it sold a lot of copies. We got great reviews from all the magazines. As usual, I personally presented the game to the press. I remember once going to Ludlow (Newsfield Publishing) to see Crash and Zzap! magazines in Mark's Ferrari. Mark had a real thing about Ferraris. However, I never forget the unbearable noise I had to suffer during the round trip to Ludlow - great car to drive, but not all that comfortable on a long ride. Incidentally, I actually helped System 3 produce Last Ninja 3 a couple years after we left.

The Beginning of The Vivid Years, 1988

From left Mev, Hugh, John and Phil just behind   From a magazine interview, with a full
me hiding as a Ninja   head of hair.

We formed our company Vivid Image Developments Limited in September 1988, and rented our first office in Watford. It created quite a buzz in the industry and received a lot of attention from the press, thus setting high expectations. We did several interviews, and placed an ad in a couple of magazines: 'A new beginning from the developers of Last Ninja 1 & 2'.

Now we were entering new waters; without knowing how deep or muddy, but nevertheless extremely excited. From the outset, we decided that I would concentrate more on the business, design, production and management. I was not going to do fulltime coding, as it would distract me too much from the day to day running of the business. John would continue to program on the C64, and we would find programmers to help with Spectrum, Amstrad and Amiga. At that time, Commodore Amiga was fast becoming the leading machine for some developers and publishers alike, and companies such as Psygnosis were fast setting new standards. Hugh was going to create the main graphics on the lead machine Amiga, and oversee the visual aspects of all the other versions.

Phil Harrison was our first employee and would be helping with design, documentation and also finding suitable people to join us. Remarkably, he had such a great network of young programmers and artists, and besides, who wouldn't want to work with us? Overall, we didn't have much trouble finding good programmers for 8bit formats.

Since deciding Amiga should be the lead version, we needed a good Amiga programmer who could also do the Atari ST version, a rival machine to Amiga with the same processor. Interestingly, this rivalry started with Spectrum and C64 and then continued with Amiga-Atari ST, Nintendo-Sega and PlayStation-Xbox... All in all, this sort of rivalry is a healthy thing to have, as it creates competition for better products on each platform.

We would be developing on five platforms now, which meant a lot of skews and people to manage, not an easy task to say the least. The game was really becoming a serious business, indeed!

So we started working on our first game, discussing ideas, Phil coming up with lots more and documenting all things discussed. Thus, creating a design document that everyone would work from. In fact, it was Phil who designed the initial concept for our first game Hammerfist.

At this juncture, I must mention here how Phil went onto become one of the important names in the industry. After we parted company with him, years later he held very high positions at Sony PlayStation, Atari, and Microsoft Xbox. And now, at the time of writing the book, he is heading Google Stadia. Well done to him!

Amiga 500, Legendary Game Machine

Amiga first came out in 1985 and it was called the Amiga 1000. Commodore probably marketed it as more of a business machine, aimed at businesses such as magazine and book publishers amongst others. To be honest, I don't think they had the game industry in their focus or on their radar at all. Well, at  least not until 1987 when they released the A500. It was the gaming industry that turned Amiga into being one of the all-time great gaming machines.

One of the first major efforts has to be Shadow of the Beast by Psygnosis, a visually very impressive game, which set graphical standards for others to compete with. Incredibly, Amiga created a completely new excitement and opportunity for us developers to demonstrate our skills and ability to produce great games. This, of course, set a doubly important target for us to achieve! It was of paramount importance that our first game was really good. With a precedent set, it had to take full advantage of the Amiga hardware, showing what we were capable of both technically and visually.

Our First Game Hammerfist, 1990

We had two main characters to control and choose from, male Hammerfist and female Metalisis. Each character would have different strengths and agilities giving the player the opportunity to decide which one to use to overcome obstacles, opponents and situations presented to them. It was decided that the

game would be played on static screens, with no scrolling or movement of the gaming area. Frankly, I didn't like this idea, as I thought scrolling would give us more flexibility to come up with more ideas and a variety of levels. However, the others said that if we had static screens, then we could go to town with each screen having a lot more detail. Hence, lots of animation, lots of opponents and lots to do for the player.

To be honest, I wasn't hundred per cent convinced, but went along with the majority decision. Fabulously, Hugh really went to town with the graphics, making use of the lovely extra colours from the Amiga and its additional graphical capabilities. It really was looking like an Arcade game, really mind-blowing visually. Although it did look impressive, I personally still wanted something to rival, and even better, Last Ninja. After all, that's what people would expect from us. Undeterred, John, Hugh and Phil really believed that we could still achieve what I wanted with Hammerfist.

During that period, we did spend a lot of time to really make it visually stunning. It also took us time to find the right developer for the Amiga. In the end, we decided to work with a very talented, but relatively inexperienced developer from Newcastle. In actual fact, I think John knew him somehow, as he was himself from Newcastle. To be fair, it was really tough to manage the Amiga version remotely as the developer worked from home. Therefore, John and I had to visit him a couple times to provide support. Eventually, he did finish the game, and technically managed to make a good job of it. But it turned out to be a lot of hard work and so much to deal with too. All of which put a dent in the overall quality of the game. Eventually, we released the game in 1990 under the joint publishing label Activision/Vivid Image. Having a joint label was part of the Agreement, which I had requested from Rod, and which I also used subsequently with other publishers.

The game was received quite well from all the major press publications with good reviews and average ratings of 90% on all formats. Unfortunately, it wasn't a commercially successful product and didn't bring any more revenue than the advances we received from Activision as per our agreement.

At this point in the story, it would be amiss of me not to mention my good friends Charles Cecil and Norin Carmody, with whom I met at Activision in our early days. Charles left just before Hammerfist was released and went on to form Revolution Software (Broken Sword fame). They are one of the most successful British game developers. Although our interaction, during the Activision days was limited, and relatively short lived, we have remained lifelong friends with both Charles and Norin, and try to see each other whenever we can.

Ultimately, I find it interesting how we can connect and bond better with some people on the journey of life. There must be some special attributes that draw certain people together to form that special chemistry.

Konix Multisystem, European Console Initiative, 1989

In the meantime, there was more excitement brewing in the UK - namely, the emergence of a new game console, which could become the European console to rival Japan. Conceived by a Welsh entrepreneur and codenamed Slipstream, it was quite an ambitious piece of hardware with advanced features. It featured a moving chair with unique forced feedback, steering wheel, motorbike handles, the lot!

Wonderful Loading Screen by
Paul Docherty aka DOKK

Very exciting stuff indeed, and all the top publishers and developers were supporting it, and wanting to be a part of it from the start. In fact, my good mate Jon Dean was coordinating the whole project, and Vivid Image was also invited to contribute to it with Hammerfist. Although, I wasn't going to do any programming anymore, I just couldn't resist the temptation. The console was based on a more powerful version of the Z80 processor, which I was very familiar with from my ZX Spectrum programming, so it was right up my street as it were. Eventually, we decided that I would code the Konix version. 'Who knows, I may do such a great job with it that Konix would become the lead version and possibly help the Amiga version to be better too?' I thought. Konix was only slightly better than the Amiga, and it was really a lot of fun to be programming it. Truly, I really enjoyed working on it; I was also attending all the important industry meetings where the console and its features were discussed.

That was when I met with the legendary developer Jeff Minter (Llamasoft). Along with a couple of other developers, we together discussed how the console could be further improved.

Some of us developers felt that the proposed 128K RAM wasn't enough and it should be at least 256K, Amiga A500 had 512K! And I also remember personally suggesting hardware support for sprite mirroring and flipping, so that the same graphics could be used for both directions in X and Y coordinates without extra storage. This would help make better use of the limited memory. The final system came with 256K RAM, and hardware sprite flipping.

The Konix version of Hammerfist was coming along very well, and everyone was very pleased with my progress and achievement. It was a great feeling to see our game being featured as one of the showcase games at shows. It was also slated as one of the games that would be released with the console.

Unfortunately, the console never saw the light of day, as they couldn't find the required investment, or agree on commercial terms with the likes of IBM and Amstrad. That was that, and the dream of a European console died at birth, and with it my 8 months of hard work went down the drain! It was such a real shame as Konix could have been a real contender!

Konix Launch: From left Peter Stone, Peter Billota (me just behind two Peters!),
Jim Mackonochie, Rod Cousens in the middle, Jeff Minter, Jacqui Lyons and the last two are Gary Bracy and Mark Cale

Playing Hammerfist on Konix for Jon Dean making a demo video

Time For Time Travel With Time Machine, 1990

Our second game also featured a unique concept, and was based on time travel. It was conceived and initially designed by Hugh and his wife Lisa. It really was a fantastic idea, but because of the memory constraints and the slow loading times, the game could only become a great little game, rather than a great big game. What's more, it even won the most original game award in a magazine, but it never achieved the success it could and should have done. In today's world, it would make a great game on modern day devices with the current technology, and the capabilities offered even by mobile phones.

During this time, we had worked with some notable and legendary programmers of the era on Time Machine, such as Raffaele Cecco (Spectrum and Amstrad) and Jason Perkins (Amiga - nowadays the Managing Director of Curve Digital working alongside Stuart Dinsey, the legendary journalist and editor of CTW and MCV).

At the time, I shared a flat with the great graphics artist and friend Dokk (Paul Docherty) in Bushey, near Watford. In those days, I remember listening to a lot of Neil Young together on my hi-fi system (in particular the Freedom album). Jason also lived in Bushey where we would have weekly get-togethers; I remember having a lot of fun there. There were a few of us. Jason Perkins, John Twiddy, Duncan Meech and I would meet up once a week. Duncan was also working on a game for System 3 at the time, possibly Tusker.

We would have great times together with a few drinks and lots of laughs. But almost always towards the end of the night, there would be some silly challenge or competition, mostly between John and Duncan. The one that I can never forget is about eating dry Weetabix bites. They would try and outdo each other by eating the greatest number of dry Weetabix; no milk or water! It was crazy, I cannot remember who won or lost but several times I thought they were going to choke on the stuff!

From Last Ninja to First Samurai, 1991

And finally, we started on a game that I felt should have been our first game to launch the company with. Never mind I thought, it's better late than never.

Although both Hammerfist and Time Machine were received well and scoring around the 90% mark, they never achieved the level of success that met the expectations that Vivid Image had promised, and was capable of. Even so, we were regarded as one of the top developers in Europe at the time.

Third time lucky perhaps? And why not, we had all the ingredients. I got on very well with the legendary developer Raffaele Cecco during Time Machine, and we became good friends, and spent quite a bit of time together socially too. He later lived in the Turkish minority quarter of Manor House in North London. I even visited his home a few times. At the time, he agreed to continue to work with us and develop our third game together. Truly, Raff was not only a great programmer, but a great game designer too. And Raff and I always seemed to complement each other with our ideas. Overall, we exchanged many ideas and in the end, decided on a Samurai game. I really wanted to play with the Ninja thing. We had made a name for ourselves by developing the first two Ninja games and it would be fitting that we would do a martial arts game of some sort.

I always enjoyed coming up with interesting game titles, playing with words, and also creating some parody with well-known titles if possible. Back then, I thought of doing a Samurai game and calling it the First as opposed to Last Ninja. This could create an interesting discussion point amongst the journalists. We called the game First Samurai, and almost every magazine that interviewed me mentioned the name parody between First Samurai and Last Ninja. Some even made reference to the great Akira Kurosawa movie, 'The man started with the First, and will probably end it with 7 Samurai.'

Remarkably, it was going to be a huge game with about ten big levels. Raff was designing the original level layouts with some gameplay elements. John had written a plug-in for the Amiga Deluxe Paint, so that the artists could test the graphics they were creating with the touch of a button. In addition, John also wrote an excellent level editor for the Amiga too, which was combined with the Deluxe Paint plugin. This meant that the artist could test everything in the actual gaming environment, which was all very clever and advanced stuff. Bear in mind that this was well before the Photoshop and plug-in days.

It was going to be Raff's first Amiga programming, and it turned out to be one of his best achievements. He was so capable and very quick to adapt to the new hardware. He did the same thing on Sega Mega Drive when we did Second Samurai.

In the meantime, we were hearing some rumours that Activision were experiencing financial problems. It seemed very difficult to continue with our working relationship, and with the support and understanding of Rod we parted company without any problems. Time to look for a new publishing house.

Closer Encounter with Mirrorsoft!

If you remember, I was shown the door by Mirrorsoft with my Gerry the Germ game in 1985, some six years earlier!

So much had happened since then, I had become a very reputable programmer with a great development studio and partners to match. Mirrorsoft had also become one of the biggest publishers signing all the biggies such as Sensible Software (Sensible Soccer, Cannon Fodder) and Bitmap Brothers (Speed Ball, Gods). Now I had to find a new publisher for Vivid Image and for First Samurai, which was promising to be a major title on the Amiga.

Both Mirrorsoft and I had moved on from my first encounter with them back in 1985. This time, I was in a much stronger position, and also had a much better proposition.

Also, this is the period when I became friends with Jon Hare, Eric Mathews and Mike Montgomery amongst others. Together we appeared in a few magazine interviews and features. I actually invited Jon and Mike to a gaming event in Turkey, in the mid-2000s. It was great to see and spend time with them in Ankara and Istanbul after many years.

Ultimately, we signed up with Mirrorsoft (a Robert Maxell Group company). I managed to strike a similar deal to Activision where our games would be jointly published under Image Works and Vivid Image labels.

Another twist of fate? Ironically, I was now working with the company that refused to take on my first game in 1985. And six years later they were absolutely delighted to sign me up! In actual fact so was I. They had a great team of people, and I had a brilliant working relationship with all of them. Looking back, some of the names that come to mind are Peter Bilotta (CEO, and former CTO of Activision, so I knew him from Activision days), Sean Brennan, Cathy Campos, Alison Beasly and Jon Norledge.

At that time, we were making great progress. Great programming coupled with great graphics and sonics made the game so popular right at the start of development. One very positive thing was that I always enjoyed a special relationship with the press. In fact, I got on so well with everyone, I spent a lot of time with them, and they would come to our office or I would visit them myself. Likewise, they enjoyed receiving all the info and insights about our games directly from the developer rather than a PR person.

Our working progress interviews and articles appeared in all the major Amiga magazines mostly with front covers. In addition, Amiga Format did a special 6-page spread with front cover with a demo disk. Moreover, they also featured an in-depth interview with Raff, John, Teoman (Irmak) and myself. We shared all the clever tricks and techniques we used to create the impressive graphics and sound samples.

It was Paul Docherty (DOKK) who did the excellent original First Samurai character; it had lovely animation frames and a fancy blur effect on the sword animation. Although I cannot remember the details, Dokk didn't continue with the project. And we managed to find another great artist, Teoman Irmak, who did all the rest of the graphics. Interestingly, Teoman was also originally from Turkey like me, and we got on well and saw each other socially too. He is a great artist, very professional and reliable, so we worked well together. As a matter of fact, he did a great job with the visuals and complemented well with Raff's excellent programming.

When the time came to release the game, the Image Works marketing team did a very good job with the launch, and the marketing. Funnily enough, I remember doing my infamous Samurai pose with a fully naked torso by the Peace Pagoda in Battersea Park. Hilariously, it was so bloody cold, and I nearly froze my you know what off! Nevertheless, the pic was used in several magazine interviews and reviews. Much later, it even managed to find its way onto Computer Trade Weekly in a news piece by Stuart Dinsey himself.

Me with the Samurai pose in 1991, Battersea   Battersea Park, 2016
Park, London

Putting this into historical context, these were the early years of the rising stars of the game development community. Some game designers were now making reasonably good money, and some were getting pop star treatment in the press.

Overall, there were lots of notable achievements in Samurai including many clever programming techniques and tricks, coupled with great graphics, massive levels and a vast array of varying environments. Equally, there were a vast array of opponents, different styles of game modes, lots of fighting (both armed and unarmed), and not forgetting the amazingly refreshing and unique sound effects.

However, I was no longer doing much coding, but I was helping out with the sound system and various other special techniques we were experimenting with such as super colourful skylines. Basically, Amiga had 16 colours, each colour with as many shades. It was a very well thought out and designed piece of hardware, with very powerful and dedicated processors for different tasks such as graphics and sound. There was another special processor called Copper that was used for additional graphical tasks. What this meant was that it enabled us to do critical changes at the beginning of each frame or even mid-frame, and down the scan lines of the entire screen. Therefore, you could momentarily interfere with the colours by using certain tricks and techniques. This in turn would allow us to display more than the 16 colours which were normally available.

Without getting even more technical, basically with the use of the Copper we changed the colour on every raster/scan (pixel) line vertically, so that we could have loads of shades of colours down the skylines. Of course, almost all developers were applying this sort of technique to get extra shades of colour. But there was always a very sharp transition line between one set of 16 shades to the other. As a result, it didn't look smooth enough, and the colour change between different shades could be clearly seen with the naked eye, which ruined the otherwise impressive effect.

Pushing The Amiga to Its Limits

In due course, John wrote an editor for playing around with Copper and colours, so that I could experiment. I was trying to achieve some interesting and maybe better results for our game. My aim was to find a way to make the transition smoother, almost unnoticeable. Frankly, I cannot remember the number of hours I spent through the night, trying like mad, experimenting with all sorts of combinations.

This was characteristic of my undeterred dedication to find solutions to problems. So stubborn and determined to find a fix, I just could not leave it. Obsessed with solving it, I kept at it for hours and days and I was getting very nice colour bands and spreads, but always had this sharp line between the different colour shades. No matter how hard I tried and whatever I did, it was still bloody there. By now, it was driving me mad, and this sharp transition was ruining the overall effect. If only I could get rid of it, then our skylines would look amazing.

Never one to give up easily, I stayed in the office for many days and nights. One night I just kept at it, but decided to mess around with the order of colour shades. Basically, shading went from 0-15 for a colour, then it started again from 0-15 for the next colour. Instead of going 0,1,2...12,13,14,15 then 0,1...14,15 again, I tried something like 0,1,2...12,14,13,15,14 to finish the previous shade and started the next with 0,1 or 1, 0,1,2 or something like that. Thus, I slightly messed with the order of a few colours at the end and the beginning of the shading order.

Suddenly with certain colour combinations, the sharp line disappeared. Amazingly, I just couldn't see it! Finally, I had done it. As I said, it only worked on certain colour combinations; red, blue, pink etc, but it was more than enough to give me several lovely skylines.

After that victory, I spent a bit more time to discover all the combinations and values that worked, and then I made a note of the numbers and went home happy as Larry!

In fact, I was over the moon, and couldn't wait to share the results with the guys. It was just discovered by nonstop trial and error, but I guess a lot of great things are discovered in this way. The moral of this tale is that determination and hard work eventually yields fruit.

Of course, John and Raff loved the results, and our skylines looked absolutely brilliant, in fact, better than any other game before. For years afterwards, everyone including programmers would congratulate me on our achievement, and wondered how we pulled it off. It was just a simple trick that fooled the human eye. But please don't tell anyone, let them read it for themselves in the book!

Brilliant Title Music and Unique Sound Effects

In terms of sound, like most people we were using Portracker, a third party sound engine and tool for playing music and sound fx. What was superb was that Amiga had a very good sound chip providing four channels of stereo playback. Therefore, it was great to be able to have nice music playing in the background while playing the game.

But we had to do some clever tricks to mix the sound fx with the background music since there were only four channels. So, I worked quite hard to come up with interesting ways to maintain the main beat of the music playing and use two of the channels for the sound fx as and when needed. On top of this, we also alternated between left and right channels to make the sound fx more interesting, as it were, instead of always coming from the same channel or side.

It was Nicholas Jones who did the Amiga in-game music; Nick was Raff's close friend, who had done the C64 versions of Raff's Spectrum games. Basically, Raff was using some temporary samples ripped from his music CDs for testing purposes. In a way, they were a bit like placeholders, so that we could replace them with the proper sound fx after we had had them produced by a professional musician. I also used these test samples to test the integration of background music and sound fx, testing channel swapping etc.

Some of the samples were from classical music, some from rock groups such as Queen; Raff was just messing around and having a play around. Thinking that I was worried about him possibly keeping the test samples in the game, he kept assuring me, 'Don't worry Mev, I will replace these, I'm using them just for testing.'

But when I was doing my tests and playing around with things I thought some of the samples sounded just incredible. Maybe we should use these in the actual game was the thought in my mind. I certainly had never heard anything like it before! They could blow people's minds, they sounded so unique and impressive. And, we could find even more interesting samples and modify them slightly if needed. One day I told Raff that some of the samples sounded brilliant and we should use them in the actual game. Additionally, I requested him to bring some of his CDs, so I could rip some samples myself and experiment. Trying things out is always a fun thing to do, for me anyway.

Raff had even sampled his own voice for testing; 'Oh no, my sword!', and the brilliant 'Hallelujah' sample, which impressed the hell out of people in the final game! I said to Raff, 'We are keeping all the samples, as they all sound great and unique. This should really impress everyone.' And this is how the unique and interesting sound fx took shape for the final game.

Because of the brilliant early reaction, and the press interest in the game, we were getting a lot of music demos from young musicians. It was important to have great title/intro music for the game, and receiving all these demos was like a blessing. In due course, I carefully listened to all of them, but there was one tune that really stood out of the crowd. It was composed by one young Michael Davis; I think he was probably 16 years old. It was so perfect for the game, and it really captured the whole essence and the spirit of the concept including the Japanese setting and culture. To me, it is one of the all-time great tunes on the Amiga or any computer. Actually, I still listen to it, and use it as a demo tune in my game development talks and presentations to university students.

With all the technical, visual and sonic achievements, the game received great reviews in all magazines with ratings of 90%+, and appearing on the front cover of a few. The game also won the 'Game Of The Year' award at INDIN 1991, a special industry charity dinner event, which raised money and was started by none other than Rod Cousens.

Many fabulous reviews coupled with a great award, and excellent marketing and sales support from the Mirrorsoft team, and we were set to begin reaping the financial benefits. What could go wrong?

INDIN Award, 1991

Intro & Music

The Death of Robert Maxwell

Robert Maxell was one of the UK's biggest media tycoons, the owner of Mirror Group and also Mirrosoft. His sudden death while on his yacht caused a massive shockwave across the country, and, of course in our industry. What was going to happen to Mirrorsoft? What bad luck, First Samurai had only just shipped! Honestly, I cannot remember how many units went out in the first batch, but there's a figure of 80 thousand, which has stuck with me all these years. In truth, I'm sure we could have sold a lot more as Amiga was very popular at the time, and the game was regarded as one of the best Amiga games.

Around the same time the 090 help lines were becoming popular. And I remember receiving a call from one of those helplines that served the gaming community. He was probably the owner of the service as he wanted to know how many copies we had sold. The reason being that he was surprised by the number of calls they were getting on First Samurai! He said, 'Mev, you must have sold it by the bucket load, most calls are about your game!' I can't emphasise enough how absolutely gutted I was that there were so many people playing the game, but we were not benefiting from it. Clearly, they were probably copying it to death in the schoolyards, and calling the helpline because they couldn't pass the protection codes between levels. You needed the original manual for it!

With bated breath, we were just waiting to see what would happen, as there were so many rumours, from management buyout to other publishers purchasing it. Suddenly, we heard the terrible news that the whole group, including Mirrorsoft had gone into receivership. We were devastated to say the least; the game was not being duplicated anymore and no payments were made.

It took me ages to reach the receivers (Arthur Anderson and Co.) and after many phone calls I managed to get the final payment at least. But they categorically said that they didn't know if they would be doing anything with any of the games. In the grand scheme of things, I think they were dealing with much bigger issues in the group than games. So that was that. Subsequently, no more copies would be produced and thus no sales. Tragically, this meant no more money or royalties, no nothing.

Sadly, Bitmap Brothers, Sensible Software and Vivid Image were all badly affected by the unforeseen and sudden demise of Mirrorsoft. Luckily, I always had two important clauses in my agreements: keeping copyright and IP rights, and the all-important termination clause, in the event of receivership or bankruptcy. The first thing I did without wasting time was to issue a formal notice of termination to the receivers. At least once we got all the rights reverted back to us, then I could try and see how I could salvage First Samurai, and see if I could exploit it further.

First Encounter With Ubisoft, 1992

Overall, the situation was putting a lot of strain on our company and I couldn't see an easy way ahead. We had to find a strategy to recover, and generate revenue somehow. Actually, I cannot recall the exact details as to how the whole thing was initiated, but I managed to strike a deal with Ubisoft for the PC version of First Samurai. Although Ubisoft weren't a fully-fledged publisher yet, they were the biggest distributor in Europe. Looking back, I think I had met the CEO, Yves Guillemot at shows a few times. Also, maybe he showed an early interest in working with me or somehow got in touch and asked for the PC version after the demise of Mirrorsoft. They probably distributed the Amiga version in Europe.

Anyhow, this would be the start of a long working relationship with Yves and Ubisoft that would last until the end of 1998. Ultimately, I decided to code the PC version myself as quickly as possible, so that Ubisoft could publish it. As a result, this would bring in some cash that was needed desperately. This time I was doing a rescue job for my own company. To finish it quickly I literally converted Raff's machine code (68000to PC MS-DOS (8086line by line! Apart from a slight loss of performance, the PC version looked identical to the Amiga, only less the brilliant music and sound fx. However, I decided to manage with the PC speaker sound! But there were some especially talented people around in those days. Notably, Martin Walker, who was both a great programmer and a musician too, did an excellent job with the PC music for our game.

After hard graft, I managed to finish the PC version in about three months. Not sure how much I managed to get from Ubisoft, but every bit helps in difficult situations. The main priority was that I had to keep the boat afloat and the flag flying.

Rod Cousens to The Rescue

Even though the PC version gave us some breathing space, it wasn't enough. Therefore, I had to do better and bigger things with First Samurai to generate more revenue. Over the years, I always remained friends with Rod and asked him for advice from time to time, and he was always happy to help. In the past, I had rescued some of his important projects, and this time it was Rod's turn to come to the rescue.

At the time, he was at the helm of the American publisher Acclaim Europe. They were also in talks with the receivers to buy bits of Mirrorsoft or some of its important titles. Our ray of light in this tumultuous storm was that Rod helped me to license the First Samurai game to the Japanese publisher Kemco via

Acclaim. At that time, Kemco were licensing titles from the UK and developing them for Nintendo SNES; games such as Top Gear (Gremlin). In the end, this deal turned out to be a real saviour for Vivid Image because the license fee was quite substantial and more than enough to save our skins.

First Samurai Goes Home to Japan, 1993

In this period, I was just moving along or following the path, finding new openings, and initiatives. Now suddenly we were going to work with a Japanese publisher and having our game published on the legendary Nintendo SNES console. Truly, this was something quite remarkable because here you had a programmer of Turkish origin, making games in the UK, and involving Ninjas and Samurais! And now to top it all, I was about to go to Japan.

I hit it off with Kemco right from the word go. First of all, we were invited to Japan to meet the company management and the development team to brief them about the game. Then, they wanted to develop, and adapt the game to the Japanese market as they saw fit. We thought that made sense, as the Japanese market was different, and their gamers preferred tougher games. At the time, I thought they would have loved my challenging Gerry the Germ game. Furthermore, they also wanted to redo most of the graphics, probably reduce the size and the number of levels to fit the SNES cartridge. In the end, we decided to provide as much assistance and help as they wanted, but leave the rest to them. However, we always had the creative control if needed.

I remember how John Twiddy and I travelled to Japan together with Masahiro Ishii, the Managing Director of Kemco, on the same flight. I sat next to Ishii-san for some of the duration of the flight. We got to know each other a bit more, and exchanged info about our cultures and traditions. I could immediately see how proud they were of their culture, which I respected. We discovered many common things between the two countries, such as eating and sleeping on the floor, which I did when I was a child. The cumulative effect of these simple and small exchanges created a warm and sincere bond between us, and it quickly became obvious that we would get on well.

Filling me in, Ishii-san told me that a big group company in Japan owned Kemco. Also, that Okuhara-san was the chairman, who wanted to be in games for the fun. In addition, that the group was very big with many different companies including a steel factory and a chain of nursing homes and Korean restaurants.

In hindsight, I think it was Rod who had warned me about the Japanese people; their culture and ways of conducting business. Forewarning me that it would be difficult to get close and become friends with them. 'Even after many years you may never meet their families' he had said. I remember joking about it and saying that the problem probably lay with the English rather than the Japanese, as the English weren't exactly the warmest and the friendliest of people.

Joking aside, in my experience I did find that the English people always seemed to keep a distance. Besides, in our Turkish culture we hug and kiss with friends and families, much more than the French. Whereas, in comparison the English seemed quite reserved even when family members and friends would greet each other. Admittedly, I could clearly see that people were much warmer and friendlier as you went up North. People in the Midlands, Yorkshire and beyond appeared to be very welcoming and more receptive. In particular, I loved the Liverpudlians, my love of the Liverpool team must have helped a bit too.

Confidently, I told Rod that I would earn their friendship and respect in no time. Actually, I was quite good at adapting to a new culture and environment, as I had already managed it reasonably well in the UK.

During the entire flight to Tokyo Ishii-san and I became very close, he was very friendly and sincere towards me. In fact, on our first night in Tokyo, Ishii-san took us to a traditional Japanese restaurant with his wife and kids; where we sat and ate on the floor. We were really honoured by Ishii-san's gesture, and very warmly welcomed.

The next day we meet Okuhara-san and the Kemco team at their headquarters in Kure, Hiroshima. We were able to see that great city, and the terrible devastation it had suffered from the atomic bomb. It was so upsetting to see. Will we ever learn to live in peace?

Similarly, Okuhara-san was also very friendly towards us, and seemed to be fascinated by my being a Turk, living in the UK, and working on Ninja and Samurai games. Thus, we instantly fell into friendly exchanges with the help of Ishii-san, as Okuhara-san didn't speak any English. Equally, we didn't know any Japanese either. And I thought I could never learn it either after Ishii-san telling me about all the different dialects they had, and having real difficulty with understanding each other.

The Taste of Japan

All in all, we really had a wonderful ten-day stay, both Okuhara-san and Ishii-san spent a lot of time with us. They introduced us to lots of lovely Japanese food, and the inevitable karaoke bars, and plenty of Saki! Truly, they looked after us very well. What was extra special was that Okuhara-san once sent us very special octopus sushi while we were eating in one of his Korean restaurants. Apparently, it was a rare dish from the North and came from a special place. Ishii-san told me that it really was a magnificent treat from Okuhara-san.

Finally, we completed our lovely adventure in Japan, and returned home to the UK. Afterwards, we kept very close contact and communication between us, providing as much support us possible, but generally leaving it to them to make the final decisions about the game. At times, I felt the game was becoming too different, much smaller (partly caused by the game cartridge limitation) and perhaps a touch too difficult for the European market. Yet at the end of the day, it was really their call and I didn't want to intervene much.

Okuhara-san and Ishii-san were always traveling and visiting Switzerland and England. Halfway through development Okuhara-san and Ishii-san planned a trip to Europe and specifically, London. Ishii-san informed me in advance that Okuhara-san was also coming.

Initially, I panicked, as they had looked after us so well, and now it was my turn to return the favour. Really I didn't have a clue as to where to take them. Sure, there were a couple of really nice Chinese restaurants, but that was out of the question. An Indian perhaps? They were staying at the best hotels and probably ate at all the top restaurants in London too. No matter how hard I tried, I just couldn't think of anything interesting enough.

How About Some Delicious Turkish Food Instead?

In the end, I thought I should just take them to my little Turkish kebab place in Hackney, 'Mangal'. A very traditional place, and with great quality Turkish food, they would really appreciate it I thought. At least, it would be unusual and probably unexpected. You could even go so far as to say a unique experience for them! It would be a pleasant surprise and fitting too, since I had shared a lot of information about Turkish culture.

Immediately, I checked with Ishii-san to see if they had tasted Turkish food before. Luckily they hadn't, great I thought. But I was still a bit apprehensive about the Mangal kebab place. It was a place I went to quite a lot with my Turkish friends in Hackney. The restaurant had wonderful food, but it was a very simple and unassuming little place. In fact, I used to visit the Hackney and Manor House areas quite often when I started living in London. Plus, I could eat and buy Turkish food, which I had missed down the years. Also, I knew the owner of Mangal very well too. Knowing that he would certainly give us the best treatment possible.

The day came and I picked up Okuhara-san and Ishii-san from their hotel, and started our black cab ride to Mangal. At first, I told them that I was taking them to a small local Turkish place. As we got closer, driving along Stoke Newington Road, I did not know what they thought. On the face of it, Hackney looked a bit run down in those days compared to how it is today. Then, we arrived and went into this little kebab place with just 4 tables! But as usual, there was quite a long queue outside, some either waiting for a free table or to be served for takeaway. After a short greeting with the owner and the chef Mehmet Usta, we sat around by the fireplace where he cooked all the wonderful meat.

The Turkish Kebab Delight

They seemed reasonably intrigued by it all, sitting around the fire, and watching chef Mehmet doing his magic. He was also showing us extra attention, and trying to make us feel at home. I had already arranged to have my favourite, which was a special shish kebab dish, with yogurt and melted butter. It really was a delicious dish and better than what I had tasted even in Turkey. Also, Mehmet took extra care to make it even more special for my important guests.

Planning ahead, I had already warned Mehmet that my guests were from Japan and that they would be tasting Turkish food for the first time. So, Mehmet was really trying hard to make sure the food was delicious, but also putting on a show with his cooking skills. He made a special meze with very finely chopped tomatoes, onions, parsley, lemon juice and plenty of olive oil. He was really showing off as he was finely chopping away at all the ingredients in a lovely rhythmic tempo. Thankfully, my guests seemed suitably impressed, and I was pleased that it was going well so far.

Next, Mehmet served us our main dishes. I said, 'Bon appetit and I hope you enjoy your first experience of Turkish food'. A little nervous, I was waiting in anticipation, and after a spoonful or two they both told me that it was absolutely delicious. What a relief, I was so pleased. They kept thanking me, and complimenting Mehmet almost after each bite. They really loved it, and I was well pleased with my choice.

As you may know the Japanese don't have big portions, and they don't eat much either. Mehmet really went to town and gave us even more than usual, so our plates looked like mountaintops. Halfway through, I could see that they were struggling with it. And Ishii-san said in a very quiet voice almost with the fear of offending the chef, 'This is delicious, but we are really full, and unable to finish our plates. Would we offend the chef if we stopped?' I said, 'He may not be offended, but he may think you didn't like his food, which would upset him, I guess.' He replied, 'Oh', with a big disappointment and they both tried to continue with great difficulty. But I immediately told Ishii-san that it was absolutely alright for them to stop. You should have seen their relieved faces.

They loved the food and repeatedly thanked both the chef and me. Furthermore, we also had a little bit of baklava (a special Turkish sweet) to taste with Turkish coffee. Clearly, they were so delighted with my choice and the experience. They were really grateful and thankful. Happily I told them that I would take them to another Turkish restaurant in central London the following night. They were fine with my idea.

Okuhara-san, Ishii-san, John and Me in Tokyo, 1993

Revisited Mangal in 2016 with Sıla and Lancelot. Luckily, Mehmet Usta and the delicious food were still intact.

Now Some Raki (Turkish ouzo) and Belly-Dancing!

The next night I took them to Efes 2, another Turkish restaurant, but a more trendy, popular place attracting a lot of English customers too. It was situated right in the heart of London. This time John, Teoman and Raff joined us too. Both Okuhara-san and Ishii-san had so much fun, lots of food and raki (Turkish ouzo). What is more, they really did like their drink, and loved raki, which is quite a strong drink. Also, they danced like mad for ages with the Turkish belly dancers.

Although I was really concerned initially, later I was so relieved to see them both very happy with the whole experience. After that Ishii-san and I met several more times in London, and each time I would take him to my friend Adem's lovely Turkish restaurant, Iznik in Highbury. Where we always enjoyed our food, wine and conversation. We have remained friends ever since. A few years ago we reconnected on Facebook, often exchanging messages.

Overall, the Nintendo SNES version was quite good technically, but it didn't quite match the Amiga, and it was too tough for the European gamers. However, we had received a very good license fee, so it made a substantial contribution to our company's survival and continuation after the tragic demise of Mirrorsoft.

First Samurai C64 & Commodore 64GS, 1993

At that time, the Mirrorsoft incident had created a big dent in our company in the short term, and also in our confidence. This in turn put quite a bit of stress and uneasiness on the relationships between John, Hugh and I. It was quite understandable that everyone had different ideas and plans as to what would be best for the company, and for themselves. First of all, Hugh was mainly working from Manchester and only coming down as and when required. We were going through difficult times and Hugh was not able to contribute as much to our efforts because of this. Naturally, I cannot remember all the details, but we parted company with Hugh. In any case, it seemed that he wanted to have a break away from it all. From what I can recall, he went and lived in Greece for a while.

Back in those days, I got on very well with Hugh and his wife Lisa, and I went to Manchester spending a lot of time with them. After he left, I lost contact with Hugh for a long time, and years later our paths crossed on Facebook, as is the case for most people these days. Hugh had worked for different companies in the States and lastly at Ubisoft. I think his last assignment was a managerial position in one of Ubisoft's Indian studios. From what I can gather, he is now happily retired and living with Lisa on a Greek island. Lovely people, I hope we get a chance to spend time together again.

We continued with John for a while longer, renting an office in North Harrow. We had quite a close relationship with Commodore, and with our knowledge and capability with the C64 (mainly John's, of course), we were involved with the ill-fated C64GS console project from day one. To give it context, Sega and Nintendo's success convinced Commodore to create their own console. However, instead of starting with a new piece of hardware, they decided to turn their existing and successful C64 into a console. It was a sound idea on paper, and all the major publishers and developers decided to support it. The new console, C64GS (C64 Gaming System) would have a cartridge port just like Nintendo and Sega, making games load super-fast. Frankly, I can't remember if they added anything else.

Unfortunately, most people just wanted to take advantage of the new machine, and earn extra cash by just putting out their existing titles. Commodore also must have thought porting existing big games and providing fast loading would convince the gamers to buy into the console. Not surprisingly, it backfired; why would people pay a lot of money for the games they had already played with not much additional content or feature other than just faster loading? Inevitably, it failed. Such a shame really because I think if Commodore had invested money in new games that were specifically designed and developed for the new machine it could probably have succeeded.

Anyway before it flopped, we had created a development system for it. Also, we had helped their German partner who were designing and developing the cartridge. In actual fact, it may have been the same company who were involved with the Amiga CD32 project. Although Commodore did try with CDTV and CD32, they could never achieve the success of either C64 or Amiga.

In total, we sold around 15 development systems and provided support for many games that were put on the cartridge. Even though we made some money from it, in the end, it failed to fulfil expectations. Sadly, it was almost dead on arrival.

Equally, it was around this time that we had just finished the C64 version of First Samurai, almost two years after the original was released. It was a tremendous effort and achievement to be able to port the original Amiga version to C64. What is more, Jon Williams did a great job with programming and Matt Sneap with graphics, and of course, as always with the quality support by John Twiddy.

Stunningly, Commodore Format rated the C64 First Samurai as one of their all-time top five games!

C64 Game System

First Samurai C64, 1993

Spectrum Samurai artwork created by Andy Green, 2018

Mev Marches to The Turkish Army, 1991

When I settled in the UK I hadn't completed my compulsory service in the Turkish army. Having been away from Turkey for years, I technically had 'a draft dodger status', and thus couldn't go back to Turkey. The likelihood was that I would be picked up on arrival, and sent straight to an army base. It was 1991, more than 12 years since I had left Turkey. Where had all the time gone?

The years had flown by and so much had happened in the last 15 years too. When I thought about it all, it was like a filmstrip, everything just passing by in a blink. Unbelievable; the marriage, the son, cable factory, ZX Spectrum, programming, breakup, games...

Back to the story, I had heard that the Turkish parliament had just passed a law, which allowed Turkish citizens living abroad to pay for their army service, and only do two months, instead of the then usual 18 months. Certainly, it was an opportunity not to be missed. It would be perfect to complete my service and get it over and done with. This would allow me to freely travel to and from Turkey whenever I wanted. At the time I had an English girlfriend who worked at the BBC and wanted to go to Turkey, but with my draft dodger status we couldn't. She was also encouraging me to do the military service. Therefore, I applied to the Turkish consulate in London and paid the fee. A few months later my turn came, and I went to Turkey for my army service, in March 1991. There were thousands of us, mostly coming from Germany and only a handful from the UK.

As we were nearing the completion of the first month, we heard a rumour that the paid service time was about to be reduced to one month. This effectively meant that we could be released any day. Oh dear, it was like time had stopped, almost every day we would wake up with the hope of it being the last day of service, but it never came. It was annoying as we ended up finishing the bloody second month having waited in anticipation every day for an early release! To add insult to injury, they officially announced and confirmed the reduction of paid service to one month, on the actual day of our release! So cruel, but that's armies for you, there's no room for compassion or logic.

The army service was reasonably easy and comfortable as most of the officers were sent to the Iraqi border because of the Gulf War. While in the army, I was trying to help out with the business at the same time. With special permission I obtained from the commanding officer, I was able to receive and send faxes to and from John and my girlfriend too! At the time, the fax machine was the best thing since sliced bread, I would exchange several faxes every day.

Fortunately, I was getting fax letters from my girlfriend, several in a week sometimes, whereas the other soldiers had to wait for weeks for letters to arrive from their loved ones. Frankly, they were so jealous of me that I was scared they would complain to the officer, but luckily they didn't.

Vivid Image Becomes Mev Dinc, 1993

Sadly, the demise of Mirrorsoft and all that effort with the Commodore console (C64GS) coming to nothing added to the existing stress and also affected our relationship with John. Naturally, I always highly regarded and admired John as a programmer, but to me he was also a great friend. Without doubt, he is one of the best programmers I have ever known, alongside Raff, and although we had a long partnership we also had a great friendship.

Unfortunately, the strain of financial problems, and the continual effort and hard work to keep the company afloat were making things really difficult. All this coupled with future uncertainties was too much for him to bear, I guess. Actually, John always preferred the comfort and security of a permanent job with a decent salary. In the end, we agreed to part ways. I would continue with my efforts to move forward and see how I could improve the situation. Subsequently, John went back to System 3, which must have really pleased Mark Cale. To be honest, John is not only a great programmer, but also one of the most reliable people you can have on your team. Interestingly, I discovered years later, when we met in London in 2016, that he was still working there at System 3 and seemed to be quite happy about it.

Now I was my own man again, and had the sole responsibility and control of Vivid Image. On the other hand, it meant that I had the full burden and the weight of the company. But at the same time, I also felt relieved, as I could be more decisive about my future plans and direction. It is easier to make decisions when you know that only you will face the consequences.

Second Samurai – Psygnosis and Sony, 1993-94

Despite some setbacks, everything was moving at an incredible speed, so many things were happening with so many changes. Activision, Mirrorsoft, Ubisoft and now Psygnosis who were one of the great British developers and publishers. In fact, Psygnosis wanted the First Samurai game, but we had decided to go with Mirrorsoft. Who knows what may have happened should we have gone with Psygnosis? Upon reflection, we shall never know. But I can tell you what happened with Pygnosis after Second Samurai though.

Well, I put the word out that I was looking for a good home for Second Samurai, a follow up to the great First Samurai. Frankly, I was very ambitious and had set my target very high; 'a sequel to end all sequels' was my strapline!

Actually, I remember Stuart Dinsey doing a small piece on the front cover of Computer Trade Weekly using my infamous Samurai pose. That, and all the other news in game magazines attracted the interest of a few publishers, one of which was Psygnosis.

Ian Hethrington of Psygnosis was very keen to pick up Second Samurai, as he didn't want to lose out the second time round! Thus, Ian made me a very good offer, which I accepted almost immediately. At the time, Psygnosis was a good choice I thought, with their reputation on the Amiga coupled with a very good deal for the Sega Mega Drive version too. This meant that we would be developing on consoles too, an important step for the future.

Once I took on the sole responsibility of Vivid Image, I decided to rent a big house, and work from home for a while. During this period I had Nej living with me too. He went to school in London for a few years.

To be perfectly honest, I had to put all that had happened with Mirrorsoft and First Samurai behind me somehow and start over. Now that I had a new publishing deal, we could start developing Second Samurai. Thankfully, the same team was working on the game; Raff, Teoman and plus Brian Marshall doing the music too. Although Brian never became a fully-fledged games musician, he could do our music for the Amiga easily now. I remember how he could just use his own keyboard, compose, and record the music and give it to us. Next, we were able to convert Brian's work into the format we could use in the game. A lot of things were advancing and some things were becoming easier.

In truth, we wanted to surpass the technical and visual achievements of the first game, no easy feat of course. But we were always ambitious and managed to deliver. Plus, this was going to be our first sequel, and it had to be bloody good as far as we were concerned, and we had the necessary means to do it. The thinking was 'Let's start with two Samurais; one male character and one female character to choose from'. The concept of two characters would also complement the name Second Samurai. Every bit helps I thought.

Of course, there are no female samurais in Japanese samurai culture. Nevertheless, it was only a game and it was my samurai after all, as I had already told Okuhara-san when I was in Japan! When we were discussing First Samurai with Kemco in Japan, Okuhara-san had said to me jokingly, 'there are no dragons in our Samurai culture, and I am surprised to see them in your Samurai game.' I simply said half-jokingly, 'well, it is my Samurai game as you say, and I put whatever I want in it.' He loved my direct, but honest answer, and after a huge laugh he got up and gave me a big hug. He replied, 'you are right, it is your samurai!"

Once we had enough impressive aspects to showcase, I started my rounds with the magazines as usual, previewing the game and sharing our plans for it. As always, the initial reactions and reports were great, many excellent first look and 'working progress features' in many magazines and some featuring it on front covers. Generally, I would visit Pygnosis at their headquarters in Liverpool periodically to show the progress. Fortunately, we had a very good relationship with them and I loved visiting Liverpool too. To be honest, I was very lucky in that I always enjoyed good relationships with both publishers and the press alike.

Both Raff and Teoman were also working from home. But we would meet up at my place as often as needed with Raff, and Teoman coming down less frequently. However, I visited Teoman and his wife a few times in Birmingham, where they lived.

Finally, we completed the project! I cannot recall how long it took us, but we successfully completed the Amiga version, and delivered it to Psygnosis. In the meantime, the Mega Drive version was also coming along very nicely. It was looking very different to the Amiga version, but also much more impressive. Brilliantly, Raff had taken advantage of the console's extra power and features, and added extra touches. This was something I would be doing too when I was actively programming. That was one of the reasons why we enjoyed working together, as we had very similar approaches.

Me at HMV music store with DJ David Jensen

This was our first console game, and we wanted to make a real impression with it. Really, Raff was such a capable programmer and very quickly mastered the machine and made the most of it. Amazingly, the Mega Drive version looked and played like an arcade game. Even better, we were getting great feedback at shows, and special events. One thing I remember clearly was Psygnosis holding a launch event at the HMV record store in Oxford Street. Raff and I showcased our game there and visitors were really impressed with our achievement.

Me (left) with Raff and a gamer playing Second Samurai on MegaDrive co-op mode!
From the HMV launch

Gaming Becomes Cool With Sony PlayStation, 1994

Sony's first real attempt into the industry was with MSX computer back in the mid-80s. But this time Sony wanted to bring out a next generation console, and all the signs were there for a very exciting and impressive piece of hardware. And that's exactly what PlayStation turned out to be. Sony aimed big, and had big plans for its big console.

Photo by Evan-Amos

As we were about to launch Second Samurai on Mega Drive, Sony bought out Psygnosis! 'What's going on here, I cannot keep up with all this?' were my immediate thoughts. My life and career paths seemed to be full of excitement, surprises, and twists; there wasn't this much action even in movies! Suddenly, I found myself involved with Sony too in a way, as I had to also deal with their big plans. Would we even feature in their big plans?

Apparently not, I received a formal letter from Ian Hethrington explaining the new situation. Psygnosis was now becoming part of Sony, and all major decisions would now be made by Sony according to their strategic plans. In short, the bad news was that Sony didn't want Psygnosis to support any consoles other than PlayStation, and, wanted all existing console projects to be canned with immediate effect, including our own Second Samurai Mega Drive version!

Wait, there was more bad news. They had cancelled our project and also had no intention of paying any outstanding money owed to us!

What, c'mon Sony, that was no way to play the game? If anything, that was foul play. It was such a huge company, making up its own rules, and asking us to just play along. Of course, I was both shocked and devastated, we had a great game about to be launched, and it was now cancelled. And as if that wasn't bad enough, we would not be getting paid the substantial amount of money contractually due!

In response, I exchanged a few letters with Ian, strongly objecting to the decision. There wasn't much I could do about them not releasing the game, but I had every right to demand the money I was owed. This was a one-way termination with no default on our part. As a compromise, I told him that I wouldn't claim any additional losses from the termination, but I would fight to the end to get the payments contractually due.

Although Ian was trying to be helpful, obviously he wasn't going to go out of his way to create problems for himself with Sony, which they had just joined. In response, he sent me another letter with an offer of payment as a settlement, but it was not acceptable as it was way off the total amount they should be paying.

What could I do? Surely I couldn't fight Sony legally, a massive company, and take them to court? The only weapon I had was my reputation and standing in the industry, plus a strong case as they were contractually obliged to pay up.

Meeting With Paul Gardner

My first course of action was that I consulted a lawyer friend of my girlfriend, but he said he wouldn't be able to help much with the case. In turn, he suggested I had a word with Paul Gardner, a partner in a much bigger law firm, who could take the case.

Eventually, I met with Paul, briefed him about my career, and also about the case. Coincidentally, he was just getting really interested in the game sector himself. In the end, he said it was great to meet with me, as he would like to chat and get a lot of insights about the industry. Overall, Paul was especially interested in the all-important copyright, IP, and licensing side of things, which was very important, and still overlooked by most developers.

In summary, Paul and I felt that my best weapon was indeed my standing in the industry. Anything negative coming from me regarding what Sony had done would not serve them well as they were just making a big entry into the industry. He said he would try and get hold of the lawyer(s) that looked after the gaming side of things at Sony.

Next, Paul called me a few days later, and we met up in their offices in central London. As luck would have it, Sony's lawyer looking after the gaming matters turned out to be Paul's friend! Even better, he said he was confident that we would reach an amicable and acceptable settlement soon. I thought to myself 'Great! I could do with a bit of luck!'

And, indeed, that's exactly what happened. A few weeks later, I received a letter from Ian Hethrington with a formal settlement offer and an early payment date, which I duly accepted and signed. Before I knew it, they had paid the full amount not long after.

After that, we became friends with Paul, and exchanged info about gaming from time to time. Furthermore, Paul would go on to become one of the most respected lawyers in our industry. Unfortunately, I lost contact with him after I returned to Turkey, but we managed to hook up again when I returned to London in 2016.

Actually, I was disappointed that our game was cancelled, but well pleased to have received the monies owed as it really helped me to just move forward without major problems. There was no alternative, but to just keep going, trying for bigger and better things. After all, that's what makes the journey more exciting and all the effort worthwhile.

So, what was next? What was in store for me? After all these twists and turns, I was still going strong enough, and it could only get better. That's what I thought and believed anyway. On balance, despite a few problems, my achievements hadn't been overshadowed by the setbacks. And financially I was comfortable too.

Make Way For Street Racer; First Ever 4 Player Racing Game, 1994

While working on Second Samurai, Raff and I discussed that perhaps we should develop another game in parallel, maybe on Nintendo SNES. The console games were getting better attention and the successful games were bringing substantially more revenue. And we could overcome our Mega Drive disappointment by doing something even better with another publisher.

With PlayStation coming into existence the console market was offering bigger potential for the future, as Nintendo and Sega would follow suit with new gen consoles too. After considering a number of ideas, we ended up going for a racing game. Maybe influenced by Mario Kart, I really cannot remember, but it didn't matter anyway. We would make ours very different, and as usual try and add some ambitious and unique features to make it special.

First of all, Raff came up with some initial ideas and characters, and then together we discussed and expanded the scope. In addition, I also wanted to include this very famous Turkish folklore character, Nasreddin Hodja, who is believed to have lived some four centuries ago. Ideally, it could bring a fresh look and feel to the game. More importantly, it would make me feel good about including something from my own cultural heritage too.

Basically, Mario Kart had a battle mode and I thought we should go one better somehow. As well as adding an interesting last car standing Rumble mode (influenced from American wrestling!) I also decided to add a soccer mode! These fancy and unique features should make our game both impressive and very different to Mario Kart, as we knew the comparisons would be inevitable. Comparisons with Mario Kart would only help our game's publicity anyway. Even so I wanted to make sure that we had our own impressive and unique features, which would be nothing like Mario.

In fact, playing football with cars turned out to be a lot of fun, and loads of players really enjoyed it. It's possible that our soccer mode may very well have inspired the successful Rocket League game, which came out in 2015, some twenty one years after our game.

With all the important features, unique cars and really interesting characters from many different countries around the world, it looked like we were creating something quite special. We approached our great C64 programmer friend Nick Jones for the task, and he agreed.

All set, we felt the coding duties were in good hands. Now all we had to do was to find a good artist to match Nick's skills. But, Nick out of the blue, decided to go to America. Unfortunately for us, he was offered work with David Perry (Shiny Entertainment), who himself had moved to the US some time ago. We understood that for Nick it was a good opportunity to work in the States and to this day, Nick still lives and works in the US.

Anyway, Raff said he would ask the twin West brothers; Tony and Chris, whom he knew from the Domark days when he programed James Bond. After several rounds of talks, we finally managed to convince the brothers to take on the project. Wonderfully, they seemed to be perfect for the task, Tony a brilliant graphics artist and Chris, an equally great programmer. They were like a small dream team and perfect for the game.

If we were to work on two projects then, I felt, we should move into a proper office space. Therefore, I rented a nice little office in a modern building very close to Harrow town centre. At the same time, I thought it was also time I bought a place of my own too, as I was fed up with staying at rented places. Somehow, I always made sure that I lived reasonably close to my office, as I never liked travelling to and from work, wasting valuable time. Looking back, it may also have something to do with the fact that I walked to and from school for eight years when I was a little boy. By then, I may have had enough of travelling far. Plus, I didn't like driving in traffic either and there is always plenty of it in big cities.

So I went ahead and I bought a lovely little old two-bed semi-detached house in the historical Harrow on the Hill with a small garden. This is where the famous Harrow School is, and, with many beautiful historical buildings including the old church which is over 950 years old, the whole area is under conservation. The house looked like it was converted from a horse stable, as it had the original vertically opening double door. Truly, it was a beautiful area, very hilly with cobbled streets and lovely old houses of varying sizes and shapes. With special planning permission, I had a loft conversion done which I used as a guest room.

Just before my daughter Sila was born, I bought a detached grade II listed house in 1996, which was about 360 years old. It was in a really bad condition, but I had it fully renovated with planning permission, keeping all the original features intact. It really was a beautiful house and we had wonderful times there. In all honesty, I truly regret selling in 2001, after moving back to Turkey.

Grade II listed 380+ year old house, Crown St., Harrow On The Hill, 1996 (Pic was taken with Gulsun in 2017)

My first house, a small semi (right half) Middle Road, Harrow On The Hill, 1993

Street Racer and Ubisoft Years, 1994-98

As already stated, whether we liked it or not people were going to compare Street Racer to Mario Kart, which wasn't a bad thing, extra publicity if nothing else. Plus, we were confident and determined to add some special things to make ours different and more impressive in some areas. Confidently, I knew that with Tony's brilliant and better graphics, ours would certainly look more impressive. Couple that with Chris's great programming skills, our game would perform better and possibly run smoother too.

In addition to Soccer Mode, I wanted something even bigger to create a real stir. Most importantly, it had to have something Mario Kart didn't. 'How about a 4-player simultaneous play mode as opposed to just a 2-player mode? Could we do it? I was certainly going to try.' Well, the initial reaction of everyone was along the lines of 'you must be kidding', but I didn't let this deter me.

Of course, I wasn't kidding at all and deep down I believed that Chris could pull it off. True to form, Chris and Tony didn't disappoint, and one day they came in with an initial demo, showing some tracks, and a couple of sample characters, all looking very nice as we expected. Both visually and technically top notch! The game was taking full advantage of the SNES's special Mode 7 display mode. Wow, I thought, this is going to look really good.

During the demo, Chris was showing the two-player split screen, which already looked impressive, nice, and smooth, and showing a lot of promise. But then we had an even bigger surprise, we suddenly had four split windows on the screen! Cautiously, Chris said, I shouldn't get too excited as he had so much more to do yet. But I did get excited, very excited indeed, I had seen the light, and there was no going back! No stopping us now, we would have the 4-player multiplayer mode one-way or another. Yes, what a result! I thanked them both for their great effort and asked them to put together a nice simple demo to show a glimpse of things to come.

Looking back, I am not sure exactly at what stage we discovered it, but apparently Nintendo was using a special DSP chip in their cartridges to improve the performance of their games. Also, they had implemented it on Mario Kart too, probably to help the two-player mode. Although, the DSP chip was available for third party publishers as well, it would add $3 extra to the cost of manufacturing. Hence, also adding to the retail price of the game.

With Chris's exceptional coding we managed to implement our 4-player extravaganza without the DSP, thus saving the $3. With this super achievement and cost saving I thought I could easily ask the publisher to pay me a $3 royalty, which I thought was more than fair!

Triumphantly, armed with a great game idea, and with an even better demo, I started my rounds for the right publisher. What options did I have? At the time, Virgin Interactive were quite active (sorry for the corny pun) with lots of clout and money, being part of the Richard Branson Empire. Just like Mirrorsoft they had some top titles and developers under their wings, and looked a very attractive proposition; David Perry (Aladdin, Earthware Jim), Westwood Studios, Doom II and so on. It was tempting, but I thought my game could get lost amongst all those big titles, and might not receive enough attention and care.

Everyone was talking about the next gen consoles and SNES was nearing its final legs. Accordingly, I needed a more dedicated and determined publisher that would do everything to exploit the title fully.

Ubisoft looked like such a publisher albeit that they had only just announced that they would become a fully-fledged publishing company. What is more, they had such a great distribution and marketing experience in Europe, and had done some publishing too. So all in all, it made sense that they would enter the publishing business in a big way. And how right that turned out to be, they are still going strong and are one of the top three publishers in the world. Well done indeed! As you may remember, I had already worked with them before with the First Samurai PC version, and I had a reasonably good relationship with Yves, the CEO, too.

Ubisoft really liked the idea and my plans for Street Racer. They probably thought it would be a great game to launch their publishing business. Subsequently, they made me a great offer, in fact, it was such a good offer that I didn't even consider any other publishers, and I said a resolute yes. In addition, they assured me that they would give it their full attention, and provide and allocate enough marketing support and resources to make the game a success. It was going to be their first major title, so it was very much in their interest to.

Thus, began our long working relationship with Ubisoft, which started with the Nintendo SNES version. By the way, I also got my $3 royalty, which we saved from the cost of the cartridge! Since Ubisoft were incredibly happy with our progress, initially they added Sega Mega Drive, and later on other versions followed such as Sega Saturn, PC, PlayStation, Gameboy and Game Gear, even the Amiga version! Thus, we would be spending the next several years working on many versions of Street Racer.

Ubisoft formally announced our agreement as a major deal to the press, which it was.

Gearing Up For The Chicago Launch by Ubisoft, June 1994

In truth, we worked very hard to deliver what we had promised and a bit more. True to their word, Ubisoft did their part in terms of marketing, giving their full attention and care. This included lots of great early previews, and news articles, which got us ready for an initial launch of the game at the Chicago CES, 1994 (Consumer Electronics Show), which later became E3 just for games.

Tremendously, Ubisoft had spared no expense and they had built a great stand with a massive video wall showing the eye-catching 4-player split screen. Incredibly, Nintendo was right across from us with their flagship launch of Donkey Kong Country! Even better, Ubisoft had great prize giveaways for the visitors. They were nice Street Racer jackets drawn from a box with a key handed to the people waiting in the queue. This was very clever marketing. Also, people, while waiting in the queue, were commenting on the big video images of the 4-player racing game. Really it looked very impressive and seemed to wow everyone looking at it!

By the second day, Street Racer and Donkey Kong were already the most talked about games of the show. Also, the same visitors were checking out both games, so in effect we were sharing the big crowd with Nintendo. We even had perfectly dressed cosplayers representing some of the in-game characters.

Fabulously, we were getting visits from the press too, wanting to know more. Besides that, Nintendo was sending over people, asking technical questions about the 4-player split screen. And I could see them taking notes about the small 8Mbit cartridge size (Donkey Kong was 32Mbit), and asking about the DSP chip. Once they had realised that the all impressive 4-player was done with an 8Mbit cartridge, and no DPS, their reaction was of utter shock! Oh! What a moment to behold! The culmination of months of hard work and team co-operation!

How exciting, and what a start it was for both Ubisoft and Vivid Image. They were very pleased with the reaction, and the results and the benefits of the excellent work they had put in. As for me, I was very chuffed and proud on two counts. Firstly, we had successfully achieved our ambitions, and secondly, I had made the right decision with Ubisoft, they didn't disappoint me, in fact, they totally surpassed my expectations. Victoriously, Street Racer had a turbo start at launch!

Back in the UK from the Chicago show, our game was big news everywhere, appearing on magazine covers with extensive coverage. We couldn't be happier. And, we had the London ECTS to come in September, for the full launch with a release date slated for around November 1994.

We had a great show in London too; lots of interest from the public, the press and the industry people alike. Ubisoft spent even more money on the publicity and the show. We had even better cosplayers; this time we even had a famous Page 3 model from The Sun newspaper, Suzanne Mizzi, representing the Surf Sister character. I have included a photo of her with me from the show, so you can try and put the name to the face.

Finally, we finished the SNES version for the three major territories; America, Japan, and Europe, which were effectively three versions and three different submissions. After testing the game internally with Ubisoft, the game was submitted to Nintendo for approval in all three territories.

A Bugging Bug That Won't Bug Off!

Overall, I think after a few important bug fixes we received final approval from the US and Europe, but continued getting just the one level A bug from Nintendo Japan, and from the same tester too. This problem was driving us all around the bend! Frustratingly, we just couldn't find it for several weeks and as a result Nintendo wouldn't let it go as it was a level A bug (the highest level of technical error).

This one particular tester was finding it, but couldn't describe what was happening. Frankly, the bug was really bugging me (sorry!) There was no choice. We had to find it and the whole team were trying so hard. Also, the only thing we knew was that the bug was occurring at the start of a race, right at the start line.

In the end, we discovered that this tester was trying to get the turbo start to work, and he was pressing the acceleration button way before even the cars would line up! It was unbelievable! He was the only tester doing this in the entire world, and doing it consistently and causing the bug. Pressing the acceleration button before the actual start of the race, was causing the game to crash. Simply put, he was breaking something in the code before everything was initialised for the race!

Once we knew what it was, we fixed it quickly and resubmitted it. And, of course, we received the approval straight away, as Nintendo also wanted the game to be released. Lots of sales were expected. What a pain it was to go through this bug hunting and what a relief to knock it on the head eventually. In the end, I think it set us back by a couple of weeks, so it didn't cause major problems.

Finally, the game was released globally in November 1994 as planned. Fantastically, it did very well, and sold several hundred thousand units just in Europe. What is more, Street Racer remained in #2 position in the UK charts behind Donkey Kong Country for almost 10 weeks. Thus, Street Racer started a long and enjoyable relationship with Ubisoft. I had great times with Ubisoft, Yves Guillemot and his brothers, and all of the management people in France and the UK.

The Street Racer launch at London ECTS in 1994 was so much fun. Also, the UK marketing team, Vera Shah and Rozzen Leard did such a great job too. In addition, I would also like to mention Metro Mustafa and Imran Yusuf who helped with the play testing of the game.

Street Racer music
by Allistar Brimble

A letter from a 9 year old fan!

Reconnecting With Veno Years Later in USA, 1995

After developing my first few games, I tried to reconnect with Veno to share with him my progress. Do you remember him from my cable factory days? Truly, I thought he would like to know about my success, since he started me off with the whole thing. Somehow, I eventually managed to track him down. We exchanged a few emails and arranged to meet up during the E3 of 1995 in Los Angeles. This was the first ever E3, before then the computer games exhibition used to be part of CES (Computer Electronics Show).

It was an emotional meeting, we were so pleased to reconnect and see each other after some 10 years. Amazingly, Veno actually came to the show, and drove me to his house where I stayed a couple of nights. We did a lot of catching up, talking about the factory days, and gaming industry and of course, my own work. Apparently, he worked as a car dealer for a few years, but now had a successful computer repair service. He said he had given up on programming, but tried to stay in the computer business somehow.

He also told me how he tried to follow my progress in the games industry. He was really proud of my achievements, and very much appreciated the fact that I mentioned him in most of my magazine interviews. It was lovely to hook up again and we were both so glad to have seen each other after all those year.

Mingling With The Turks in London

The smooth completion and the commercial success of Street Racer made things nice and comfortable. Now, I could put the stressful times of the past behind me, and enjoy the moment. And also look forward to future developments.

Now that I was in London, I could start mingling with the Turkish people a little, and taste some of the lovely food I had longed for, for ages. So I did exactly that and I started frequenting the areas that were mostly occupied by the Turkish and Kurdish communities in Hackney and Manor House. Beautiful times! It was amazing, I could find anything I wanted food wise, it was like a little Istanbul, Turkey Town as it were. Even better, I became friends with a few people very quickly.

The most intriguing thing was to have found my Turkish friend, Erhun Cebi, from way back in our hometown Ordu! Erhun was a few years older than me. He used to own and run a teahouse in the town centre when I was at high school. This is where I used to hang out quite a lot after school to play table tennis. Erhun himself was a very good player, and most of the best players would come and play there. It was great to watch and learn from them. Later I made friends with a couple of them and we would play for hours on end. Great fun. We became very good friends with Erhun, and I continued going there during holidays and school breaks even when I was at university.

He was well read, politically conscious and very active. Because of all the student riots and political unrests, Turkey wasn't promising much of a future for many young people with high expectations. Somehow, Erhun managed to find a way to go to England for a better future. That was probably around 1975, well before I moved to the UK. At the time I had no clue that I would follow suit and go to England myself a few years later, though completely unplanned.

When I did my army service in 1991, I had briefly gone to Ordu to see my relatives, before spending some time with my mum in Izmit. When in Ordu, I went to see Erhun's uncle Kenan Cebi who was a lawyer to get some info on Erhun's whereabouts. My plan was to hook up with him upon my return to the UK. Unfortunately, Kenan didn't have much information, as they weren't in touch that much, but he gave me a few pointers. Years later I met Kenan in Barcelona and then after that in London. It was lovely to see him and spend time in Greenwich, we even went to a Joe Bonamassa concert there.

I cannot remember how, but I managed to track down and find Erhun in London some 20 odd years later! It was quite a reunion, so much to catch up and reminisce about. He was socially very active and well connected with the

Turkish community. In actual fact, he knew almost everybody. At the time, he was working as a train driver on the Piccadilly Line. It was so funny sometimes because whenever we would arrange to meet up, he would say something like 10 or 20 past the hour rather than 15 or 30. He was so influenced by the train scheduling. Sometimes, I would tease him about it, by saying how about 8:07, or 10:22 instead?

We used to see each other quite often and through Erhun I would meet many others, most of whom I also became friends with. All this mingling was helping me brush up on my rusty Turkish too. You know it is quite remarkable how one can forget their mother tongue over time. Actually, it took me a while to speak comfortably in Turkish, as I was apparently making some silly mistakes. What's more, I was doing a direct translation from English, and some of the expressions would come out totally wrong, but very funny at the same time! They would really take the mickey out of my Turkish, as did my coworkers with my English while at the cable factory. Luckily, I got better at Turkish in no time at all.

How I Met Gulsun (My Second Wife), December 1994

Another big chapter in my life was about to unfold, and bringing with it major changes. Again without any clue or indication of any sort.

Back then, going to Hackney (East London) from Harrow on the Hill (Northwest), where I lived, was almost impossible using public transport. Instead, I would drive there in my car, and mostly at weekends to hang out with Erhun and his friends. The Turkish community would have house parties with home cooked food and drinks. This was how they mostly got together to socialise. Honestly, I have never taken any chances and I have always been very careful about drink driving. Since I was driving, I would never consume more than a pint of beer or a couple of glasses of wine. To make doubly sure, I would have lots of coffee as well before driving back home.

Anyway, one day there was a big party Gulsun was putting on. It's very likely that we had seen each other before at another party or two, but I didn't know Gulsun at all. Frankly, I am not even sure if we had exchanged hellos.

First of all, Erhun was invited and asked me to tag along as usual. My life was about to radically change. A milestone was approaching! Anyway, I went along without knowing that I would be meeting with my future wife! As I keep saying, life works in mysterious ways! Also, I was going to Paris to see Ubisoft very early the next morning, which was going to be my first Eurostar trip. Therefore, I hadn't really planned to stay too late, as I had to get up really early the next day.

As the night went on it seemed that everybody was having a great time. As the host of the party, Gulsun was saying hello to everyone and checking they were enjoying themselves. Casting my mind back, I think we may have had a couple of exchanges of 'How are you, fine thanks, nice party', but that was about it. There I was chatting away with her friends, some of them Irish and English, actually from Gulsun's after school children's club work. And I also met with her niece Isil and her boyfriend Turgay with whom I was chatting away about my work and other things. Well, it was well after 1am with all the guests gone. After doing a little of bit of tidying up, Gulsun also joined us.

To be honest, I cannot even recall what all the conversation was about that kept me there all that time. Generally, I am very disciplined about my planned schedule, and I had planned to leave around midnight for my early trip. I had this grotty Street Racer t-shirt with washed out colours on, so I didn't look at all serious or overly impressive.

In reality, I normally wear similar clothes whether at work, socialising or attending meetings. I'm not known as a smart dresser. I just remembered how I wore an all creased up cotton jacket at the Indin Awards in 1991. This was a very important event for me as our First Samurai game was nominated for the Game of the Year Award. Being an industry dinner for charity with a special host everyone had turned up in their tuxedos. There I was standing out like a sore thumb! Even now I remember Rod Cousens teasing me for my lousy attempt to appear a bit smarter by at least wearing a jacket. He said, 'Oh, well done Mev for making a real effort for the occasion!' To which I replied, 'Well, I am the only one here who looks like a creative person, look at the rest of you; all dressed up in black as if you're attending a funeral!' Luckily, I still picked up the Game of the Year Award for First Samurai, and presented by Rod himself no less.

Back to the party! It must have been around 2am or something; I said to Gulsun and the others, 'I really must go as I am going to Paris early in the morning'. And added that I had to catch the 7am Eurostar train from Waterloo. To be perfectly honest, I am not sure how much of what I told them they believed, but anyway I told them all about my games and the Street Racer release with a French company, hence, my visit to France.

In truth, I wasn't trying to impress them at all, just trying to justify the fact I really had to leave. When we became very close friends later, they teased me a few times by telling me that they never believed in all the things I had told them about games. On the contrary, they had thought that I looked more like someone who owned a kebab shop, rather than a games company! Not sure whether they were pulling my leg or telling me the truth, I still don't know.

Anyway, I thanked them for the wonderful party and the conversation, and left. After my Paris trip, I also decided to throw a house party. It would be a combination of celebrating the success of Street Racer, and a house warming for my new house. In due course, I invited some of my English friends, Ubisoft marketing and PR people, my teammates and, of course, some of my Turkish friends including Erhun and Gulsun.

I thought it would be a nice mix of people at the party. We had plenty of drinks, Turkish meze, food and snacks to last through the night. We started around 8PM and my ex-girlfriend came too. By the time everyone had arrived, there was quite a crowd.

Almost Too Late to The Party

Gulsun, Isil and Turgay turned up, but well past midnight when some people were already leaving! They told me later how they couldn't find the address at first. And after trying for ages and ages, they even decided to turn back and forget about the party altogether. Strangely, they didn't have my phone number, perhaps it wasn't on the invitation.

Anyway, they explained how they wandered around near the house for ages, for maybe over an hour. Though they had contemplated going back several times, in the end they didn't give up. Perhaps having come all that way, they thought it was just as well to try and find the bloody place. Or, it was destined to be and it just had to happen that way. They had to find the house, and attend the party, there was no escaping it, so it seemed.

Anyhow, they were checking the houses as they were walking up and down Middle Road, where my house was located, to see if they could detect a party going on anywhere. Suddenly they saw a few people walking down the road, talking and laughing. In fact, a group of folks who were looking very jolly, just like party people after a few drinks. Quick as a flash, Gulsun's group asked them about the party they were looking for. Amazingly, they simply told them that they had just left my party, and it was just a few houses up the road, number 29.

What can I say? Obviously, they had to find the house, one way or the other, and find it they did. What started as a conversation at Gulsun's house continued at mine, and grew into a serious relationship, and very quickly too.

Passing of My Beloved Mum, 1995!

Life is so beautiful, and yet so cruel at the same time, like good and evil, positive and negative, plus and minus, sadness and happiness, death and birth. Perhaps one wouldn't mean much without the other, they possibly complement and complete each other. No way to avoid the inevitable aspects of life; death, the loss of people close to us is soul destroying and fills us with sadness. You need happiness to hang on and continue. As they say, life goes on and it does somehow.

It is quite remarkable how the circle of life keeps us going, the sadness created by the death of one is replaced by the birth of another. I guess all these feelings and realities help us appreciate the value of different things. We try and create a meaningful balance between things, so that we can be as happy and content as possible. Philosophically speaking, to me this is the meaning of life.

Decades before, my mum had refused to get married again after my Dad left her. In reality, Mum mostly spent her life raising me. After living in the UK for three and a half years, she spent the rest of her life waiting and longing for her grandson and me. Sadly, her body finally fell to all the hardship, illnesses and the very sad life she'd had to endure. And so she passed away, hopefully leaving all her troubles behind. With deepest sincerity, I hope there is a heaven, as she deserves to be there more than most.

My cousin Recepali gave me the devastating news on the phone. It took him a couple days to get hold of me, and as such they couldn't wait for me for the burial. Initially, I was so upset that I couldn't be even at her funeral, but not attending the funeral and the burial, probably helped me cope better. On reflection, I guess from afar, I pretended it had never happened.

And yes, life does goes on, and we learn continually to live with all the joys and sorrows that life presents us with.

On the flipside of things, Gulsun and I had started seeing and spending more time with each other. Her presence gave me so much comfort and strength, which made the loss of my mother a little more bearable.

Bringing Nasreddin Hodja into The Game

A major milestone, the success of Street Racer brought a busy period of thinking and planning. Without doubt, I always enjoyed moving onto the next original game with new ideas, new excitement and new challenges. Frankly, new is what excites me the most. But understandably, Ubisoft wanted to exploit the game on as many platforms as possible. Therefore, we kept terribly busy doing Sega Saturn (this time 8-player mode!), PlayStation, Mega Drive, PC, Gameboy, Game Gear and even the Amiga version! Harrison Bernardez coded the Sega versions, Steve Dunn doing PlayStation, Dave Cantrell PC and Allan Finlay the Amiga. I think it was Jon Williams who did the Gameboy and Game Gear.

While all the conversions were going on, I felt I could start another original game. The Hodja character in Street Racer was one of the most popular. Kids loved his special combo move that turned his car into a flying carpet, which allowed him to overtake his opponents by flying over them.

Bill Haji, who did the original Hodja character concept for me, was a brilliant ex-Disney Animator. We became very close friends and saw each other often. Driven by my desire to create new things, I wanted to make a very ambitious and dedicated game based around Hodja. And as such I asked Bill if he would do the design, and all the animations in traditional style.

Apparently, Bill told me that a famous animator he knew worked on a Hodja animated film for a long time - whilst not 100% sure; it could be the same person who oversaw the animations in the Who Framed Roger Rabbit movie. Thus, Bill loved the idea of getting involved with this intriguing character years later himself.

Very quickly I came up with an interesting concept. The game would be based around a family of four plus Hodja: an extremely ambitious adventure game, using state of the art animations and visuals. The adventure would involve the rescue of a stranded family in a parallel world, caused by Hodja's magic trick going haywire at the boy's birthday party. Mother, father, a girl and a boy, Hodja and his beloved donkey would all be in the game. As for gameplay, the player would choose and control each character as and when needed depending on the situation.

Initially, it was going to be in 2D with some amazing background graphics drawn by Bill's friend and artist, who did some of the wonderful background art in the Wind in the Willows series (sorry, I can't recall the artist's name!). As you can see, I was really going for it.

To put things into context, we are talking about 1995. Back then in the day we had very limited equipment and experience to create thousands of frames of traditional animations, and then digitise it all for cleaning and colouring on the computer. Therefore, we were all so pleased with the animations and the backgrounds. They looked so lovely that I decided the game should be in 3D. It would be perfect for PlayStation, which would be the main format and programmed by our lead programmer and friend Raff Cecco. Perfect.

I had actually started the Hodja project in 1994 while Street Racer SNES was still in development. Back then I got the Rowland Brothers (of Creatures fame) to develop the 2D version of the game.

Pains and Troubles of a Growing Business and Success

Generally, I had always enjoyed working with a small tight team, controlling everything, and making sure things ran smoothly. And I found it most satisfying when we created big products with tiny teams, as it made the achievement even more valuable.

But at that time, there was so much going on, and I needed help to manage it all. Thus, I started to look for a young and capable project manager, who would be good enough to eventually become a producer and run some of the projects himself. After interviewing a few, I eventually decided on Stephan Koenig, whom I thought was perfect for the job. He had started when we were all still working on Second Samurai, and from home.

We got on very well and he seemed very friendly and honest. Furthermore, I fully trusted him and saw him becoming my right-hand man. As a result, I shared everything with him both creatively and financially. That's how I work, and it's probably not the best way to run a business. Especially when the number of employees exceeds the small team status.

This has always been my weakness in business, and social relationships too. Fully trusting people without any reservations, and far too quickly before getting to know them properly. And it seems I cannot change either, I just think everyone will behave the way I would. Still, I learnt to live with this weakness as it mostly only causes damage to me rather than to others. I am such a softy, and it would upset me too much if my actions were to cause major problems to others. To be honest, I would find it almost impossible to live with.

In early 1995 Vivid Image was working with just over ten people, that's not a big team by any measure. But with my style of management and 100% trust in people, I can easily be blind to what may be going on in the background, and overlook some important issues.

At that point, I had shared my 3D Hodja game project with Ubisoft, and they loved it and signed a deal immediately. Everything looked perfect, and I was so happy to have another very ambitious and unique project under development with a very talented team of people. Simultaneously, we were also doing many versions of Street Racer too. Oh God, I can't remember the number of hours we all spent painstakingly getting Bill's thousands of traditional animations digitised, cleaned, coloured and put into the gaming environment. Truly, we had created a great rig for the whole thing. In fact, it was a very nice camera vertically mounted on a desk, capturing Bill's every frame of animation and transferring it all to computer.

A Small Earthquake at Vivid Image, 1995

It was a long time ago, and I honestly cannot account for all the details. Frankly, I am not sure how it started or who initiated it all, but there was a lot going on behind the scenes that I wasn't aware of. To reiterate, I cannot recall how I discovered it or when I became aware of what was unfolding in the background. All the while I was thinking everything was hunky dory, and that everyone was busy working on our ambitious Hodja game.

What I remember clearly is that some people started making demands for money and threatening to leave and so forth. However, I don't want to dwell on it too much, as these things happen at every company and at every level. Success and growth sometimes brings with it resentment and a change in attitudes. Naturally, I assume that the success of Street Racer and the amount of money Vivid Image was generating suddenly became a target point.

People always think they deserve a bigger chunk of the success, but without appreciating or realising the painstaking effort, work and risks taken before it. To benefit more from the success requires taking more of the responsibility and risks that are associated with running and managing a company.

To be perfectly honest, I always tried to be fair with rewarding people for their efforts, and contributions, and whenever possible I rewarded my team members for their commitment and their length of service. As I said, these things happen and rewards and expectations vary so much from person to person. Anyway, it was a long time ago and I put it all behind me a long time ago. So, the end result of it all was that a few of the people left the company, including my new project manager and all the critical people working on Hodja.

Of course, it was so shocking and upsetting when it happened. You go through so many different thoughts and feelings. What upset me the most was when I discovered that they had, in fact, decided to leave the company a few weeks ago. But they were pretending to be working on Hodja and trying to get more money. This fact definitely upset me more than them actually leaving. And afterwards a few people tried to join the team, but it became obvious that they were also trying to take advantage of the situation and get money from me. Definitely, you are more vulnerable after a big event like that and you cannot think clearly enough.

Truly, it was like an earthquake, and I had to live with the aftershocks too. Anyway, in the end I just decided to accept that things just happen. After spending some time with my lawyer writing letters back and forth for the source files and stuff, it was getting more upsetting. Ultimately, I just decided to let it go, and get on with the future.

I told Ubisoft what had happened and assured them that the Street Racer conversion work would go on as planned. If needed, we could simply cancel

Hodja. To be honest, I could have tried to assemble a new team to carry on with Hodja, but I was so disappointed with all the recent events that I felt it was best to forget the project all together.

Such a real shame, as it could easily have been the first ever 3D platform game. This was before the 3D Mario 64. Oh well, things happen. Of course, to me the biggest upset was with Raff leaving with the rest. But, I always felt we had a special understanding of each other, and had always enjoyed working together. Years later, in 2014, I arranged to meet up with Raff and Teoman (the original Samurai team) to discuss the possibility of working together again and possibly remaking First Samurai. It was great to see them both and they were very excited about the prospect too. And at the time they both agreed that it would be great to work together as a team again.

In fact, when I moved back to London in 2016, I setup Pixel Age Studios with Raff to remake First Samurai, and perhaps some new games. We carried on from where we had left off, and really enjoyed working together again. We never said a word to each other about what had happened. Unfortunately, we stopped the project when we realised it wasn't going as well as we had wanted. Even so, it was really fun while it lasted, but it just wasn't to be. Who knows, maybe our paths will cross again, and maybe we will still do something together?

And, Welcome Baby Sila, 1997

Generally things were going well with Gulsun and I. After the break-up of my first marriage, I was unsure about a long-term relationship, let alone another marriage. It seemed like I was just letting the relationship run its course, to wait and see how it went. We continued like this until 1996.

Gulsun's presence was such a comfort, especially after the loss of my mother, and during the brief problems I was facing within the company. After my divorce with Janet, I had lived on my own for a long time, avoiding any long-term relationships and commitments. But I did have a three year relationship with another woman and we only had a few minor problems. Overall, it was mostly enjoyable. So, the relationship with Gulsun started soon after the previous one had ended. Interestingly enough, I always enjoyed my own company, perhaps as a result of being an only child, and growing up at other people's homes, and possibly always feeling out of place and alone.

Despite some ups and downs, I was really enjoying my work, developing and producing decent games, maintaining my standing and reputation in this ever growing, and exciting industry. Upon reflection, I certainly had more ups than downs. My morale was good, but I was still afraid of commitment and the responsibility of a serious relationship. Relationships also need to be worked on, and it's not easy to share space, establish common pastimes to sustain a healthy and happy togetherness. Looking back, it seemed I wasn't just lazy about doing my studies and homework, but also about working on relationships, possibly the reason for shying away from one.

As the relationship with Gulsun became more serious my indecisiveness increased too, causing me to panic. My noncommittal behaviour was naturally causing discomfort and unhappiness in Gulsun. We started experiencing some ups and downs and some distancing too. On top of all this, I was suddenly faced with an unplanned and unexpected pregnancy too! This turned my indecisive attitude into a decisive panic! Now things got even more complicated, and I didn't even know what to think, I couldn't and didn't want to think. It was too much to bear. While I was unsure about a long-term relationship, now I suddenly had to face the prospect and reality of becoming a dad again!

Gulsun was very upset about my less than enthusiastic reaction, but nevertheless, she was over the moon about her pregnancy. With me or without me, she was going to have the baby and become a mother. She was very content and also decisive about it, my exact opposite. A very difficult process of thinking and rethinking started, I really didn't know how to deal with it, and decided to let it run its course, as I usually do when faced with big decisions. Well, I was a bit of a coward I guess. Being afraid of doing the wrong thing, you end up doing nothing!

I have to be honest that I am not sure how much we saw each other during Gulsun's pregnancy. At least I found a little comfort in the fact that Gulsun was really happy, and it seemed to be the best thing that had happened to her. She also had enough close friends around to help her get through it. At times, I may appear to be very strong and with it, a bit insensitive. On the contrary, I was really feeling sorry for Gulsun, and very sad not to be beside her during the most important and happiest time of her life.

I'm sure Gulsun would have liked to have had me around during her pregnancy. But unfortunately, I wasn't even there when she gave birth to our daughter, Sila! In fact, I was really upset about it, but I just couldn't do it. Besides, even if I were there I probably wouldn't have gone in, as I couldn't when Nej was born. Remember, I am a real coward when it comes to pain and needles. And even a drop of blood scares me and I can faint!

The truth is that Sila didn't know why I wasn't at her birth until I wrote this book. Previously, we always gave her some simple explanations, and tried to brush off her questions. However, she was never fully convinced with our answers, and she would bring it up time and time again. Now she can read it in this book and have a better understanding of that period in our lives. My heartfelt wish is that I hope she won't be too upset, and can find enough comfort to know that I will always be there for her and her brother Nej, as long as I live.

Sila was born in April 1997, with Gulsun's close friends and her nieces Isil and Isin beside her. My indecisiveness and uncertainty about things continued for a bit longer after Sila's birth. But her birth also brought new feelings and thoughts into my head, and some extra energy. Being absolutely honest, there was still some confusion about the situation with Gulsun, but by now a feeling of excitement too at the birth of our daughter. Soon after the birth, I started visiting Gulsun and Sila at Gulsun's flat in Hackney on a regular basis. Luckily it didn't last long, and I asked Gulsun to move in with me to live in our little house in Harrow on the Hill. During this time my cousin Ali Ozmen was visiting me from Turkey. It was nice that he met Sila when she was a baby.

Thankfully, Gulsun was so happy, and content, as Sila had brought so much happiness and pleasure into her life. Likewise, I was incredibly happy having Sila in my life now and starting a new family together with Gulsun. Despite the indecision at the start, we could overcome any problems we may face along the way. Plus, my work was going well and everything felt so much better. Truly, Sila was a lovely baby, it was a joy to be around her. Really, I don't remember her crying, she was always such a happy baby. Nej was like that too as I don't remember him crying much at all either. They were both happy and content babies.

Life is full of surprises. Now I had a new family, another major change in my life. Nej was back in Southampton, but he started spending more and more time in London, and finally moving in with us around 1998.

Nej and Sila always got on well. In fact, Sila adores her big brother. Nowadays, they are both in Istanbul, and see each other and spend time together quite often. Since we now live very close to each other, we recently started our weekly Burger & Poker get-togethers. In case you'd like to know, I lose a lot!

Celebrating Nej's 40th birthday! November 2020

S.C.A.R.S, Ubisoft, 1998

After having cancelled the Hodja project, we continued with the conversion of Street Racer to various platforms including PlayStation and Sega Saturn. Remember that we had created the world's first 4-player mayhem on the SNES, and now we must go one better on the next gen hardware. And we did just that by doubling it, now you could split the screen into 8 windows and play with 8 players!

Understandably, Ubisoft wanted to convert the SNES success into more revenue with the additional versions. Although I wanted to make new games, I couldn't say no as Ubisoft were trying to make the most out of their investment and publishing success. And rightly so, plus they were paying me a substantial amount of development money. In theory, I could have got third party developers for the conversion, but it would have been more trouble than it was worth.

In hindsight, the jump from 16bit SNES to 32bit PlayStation was quite a big one, and so were the expectations from the Next Gen console users. Unfortunately, our conversion effort of mainly sticking to the original design, and adapting it to the new machines fell short of meeting those high expectations. That's why I don't like doing conversions. Although we added lots of fancy, and extra modes such as micro (machines) driving mode and so forth, none of it was enough to achieve the desired impact and sales. Looking back, Sega Saturn was probably the best of the bunch.

Upon reflection, we really should have redesigned the game, and developed it from scratch to take full advantage of PlayStation's advanced capabilities. After Street Racer, we discussed a few ideas with Ubisoft, and agreed on doing a completely new and more impressive looking 3D racing game. We would develop the game for Nintendo 64, PlayStation and PC and we also decided to give it a new title too.

Nevertheless, I still wanted to do a racing game with combat, but with really impressive 3D cars and tracks. Next, I came up with the simple, but very effective idea of basing all the cars on wildcats and other suitable animals. This would automatically give us the basic characteristics of each car; weight, speed, acceleration, traction, power etc. Fantastically, it was all there provided by the nature of the creatures. And accordingly, we could design and create suitable racetracks for each car to reflect their natural habitats.

Everyone in my team loved the idea, and so did the Ubisoft people. Now we had a great game idea to develop! Henceforth, we signed a suitable deal with Ubisoft and started the engines as it were.

What I wanted was a visually more mature, serious, and generally more suitable game for the cool next gen gamer. Sony's PlayStation didn't just bring a new super-duper machine into the industry but with it brought a new type of player too. Mostly young working people in the financial sector, with more money to spend but with higher expectations too. Sadly, gameplay was perhaps taking the backseat a little, leaving the frontline to the impressive 3D visuals; this was becoming the norm with the early games.

As it happens, I was personally surprised to see that most games looked graphically amazing, but some lacked a bit in the gameplay department. Furthermore, the heavy graphics load also affected the performance; most games were running at 30fps (frames per second), as opposed to 60fps (the speed of arcade machines/games). Honestly, I was surprised that this was becoming the norm considering these were super consoles. But I guess the marketing and sales results sometimes determine the direction.

At the time, we didn't have enough artists to work on the project. Fortunately, Ubisoft had very talented artists, and they were also building a very good in-house graphics studio. I really liked the French graphics quality and style, and I thought it would be better to get all the graphics handled by the French team rather than receiving some graphical support. We would handle the programming aspect, and get some assistance with design input and feedback from Ubisoft, but they would supply all of the art.

My suggestion for the title was Vivid Racing, which I thought went quite well with the concept with interesting looking wild-cars based on wildcats. After some iteration, we ended up calling the game S.C.A.R.S. Strangely, I can't even remember what it stood for, but I'm sure we had the words super, cars, computer simulation, racing and system in there. Perhaps you could put the words together yourselves and come up with the actual title! However, I am afraid no prizes for guessing. Also, Ubisoft were going to take care of the music and sound fx. Plus, we had an exceptionally good programming team for each version; Steven Dunn (PlayStation), Jani Peltonen (Nintendo 64) and Dave Cantrell (PC). Probably Harris Bernardez was still with us too to help with all three versions.

At first, the artists initially worked from France, but eventually we rented a house for them in Harrow, near our office. In technical terms, we were really excelling on all fronts, very fancy looking 3D environments with impressive lighting and shadow effects. In addition, we also had very unique and interesting looking 3D cars with lots of special combat capabilities. Even better, our game was running at 60 frames per second too!

The Price of Technical Ecstasy

But a high level of detail and performance created inevitable space limitations in terms of the racetracks. Maybe that was one of the main reasons why other games were running at 30fps! But never being the ones to easily give up, we came up with a clever way of making better use of the limited space. To make the physical length of the tracks long enough, I decided to have the tracks spiral up and down the mountains or hilly terrains.

The tracks looked rather interesting visually, but inevitably had far too many tight corners with very few and rather short straights. All of which made driving a lot of fun for the hard core gamer, but quite difficult for the average one! To make it easier meant slowing the overall race, and cars down, which would mean taking too much away from the adrenaline. Clearly, a very difficult balancing act was needed.

On the positive side of things, it looked brilliant going around the impressively winding tracks, up and down the mountain hills, but I felt it was too difficult to appreciate it. This was largely because of the concentrated driving effort which made it difficult to engage in and appreciate all the combat elements! Both the Vivid Image and Ubisoft people seemed happy on the whole with the game, after making some more adjustments.

Since I'm not a good player, my remarks are generally to be taken with a pinch of salt. It's true that I cannot play, and perhaps cannot judge the difficulty levels properly, but watching others play, I could clearly see that there was something amiss. Instinctively, it just didn't feel right. People who were working and testing the game were happy enough, but they were too close to the game and got very good at it. What would be the initial reaction of new gamers? Looking back, I wish I had insisted on tackling the problem, but since everyone else seemed to be in agreement with it, I went along with the consensus.

Finally the day came and we submitted the game for approval to Nintendo and Sony. Interestingly, Sony had a clever hardware checker to see if the developers were doing anything fancy and cheeky with the hardware. Plus, we weren't allowed to access the hardware directly, only via the provided library routines that came with the development system.

Our programmers had mentioned to me about PlayStation having a 1K-cached memory, which is normally used for fast data access. And we weren't allowed to access it or use it directly, but our clever programmer told me that it was big enough to process the 3D cars in. That meant gaining extra performance. Thus, we did use it, and as a result gained quite bit of extra performance. But, of course, Sony's hardware tester caught our clever attempt. Luckily they let it go, as they were so impressed with the results. To be honest, I have never shared this info before, so please don't tell anyone, especially Sony!

A Pressing Concern

Eventually, we received the approvals from both Nintendo and Sony reasonably quickly. And as always, I started my round of magazine visits, first in the UK then the US. Undoubtedly, my biggest concern was how the press would receive the game.

The press played a very crucial and important role in our industry, providing a great service for both our games and for the gamers alike. Truly, they were our voice and the messenger. Because of this I always held them in a high regard. Likewise, they respected me for allowing them to come and talk to me about our work. And also for sharing all the first hand insights and details about how we did things. We always had great coverage, and I was happy with their comments and ratings. It was a very professional, and friendly relationship. We never even advertised in magazines, only once when we first setup Vivid Image.

There have been some great magazines in the UK, in the 80s and 90s; Popular Computing Weekly, Crash, Zzap!, Your Sinclair, Commodore Format, C&VG, Amiga Format, CU Amiga, Amiga Power, The One, Mean Machines, Edge and a good few unofficial and official console mags.

During my long career, I have met many great journalists and press people. I always enjoyed my time with them and even becoming friends with some. I would like to mention some of them here; Steve Merrett, Gary Penn, Gary Whitta, Dominik Diamond, Dave Perry, Julian Rignall, Stuart Dinsey, Steve James, Andy Nuttall, Stuart Campbell, Phil South, Paul Rose and Gary Williams amongst others. Sorry to those I missed out.

Back to the SCARS game, I could see that they were impressed with the technical and visual aspects, which were our trademark, but I could also sense immediately that they weren't enjoying the game enough. Obviously some fared better with it. The initial impact was brilliant, I could see their excitement, but after a while it was becoming tiresome, constantly having to negotiate tight corners, running off the road, and losing momentum. It was so sad for me to see it, as my worst fears were becoming true!

Most of all, I knew that the Americans didn't like tough games and I had feared that they would struggle even more than their UK counterparts. Truth be told, as I had feared, the reaction of the American press was even worse. Again, they really gave me a lot of time, and tried to master the game, but they just weren't enjoying it as much as they wanted. On the positive side of things, it looked so impressive that they wanted to play it, but it was just too much effort, which was taking too much away from the fun factor.

Despite all of that, the reviews weren't as bad as I had feared. Obviously, they were really impressed with our overall technical and visual achievement and, appreciated the concept and all the other features. But, at the end of the day, the reviews and the reaction of the press were nowhere near what they should have been for the game to be a big success. Even to this day, I still feel the disappointment as I write these lines.

Time For a Change

Obviously I don't know how Ubisoft felt, but for me, the failure of S.C.A.R.S to meet our expectations dented our relationship. Coupled with a cancelled Hodja project as well, I felt maybe it was time for a break. Actually, I don't remember officially discussing or saying anything, both sides just let the relationship fade away I think.

Nevertheless, I must say though that I really enjoyed my time with Ubisoft. We always got on well, and I don't remember having any problems at all. Also, they always respected me, gave me a lot of time, and looked after me whenever I visited them in Paris. Besides which I enjoyed the company of Yves, and Gerrard Guilmott, and the rest of the team. If truth be told, I would like to think that they enjoyed my company too. Over the years since, Yves and I haven't seen much of each other, apart from exchanging a few emails.

Street Racer 2 and Actor Game Engine, 1998

Time for a new start perhaps? Since we never did a proper follow up to Street Racer and didn't make good use of it on the consoles, I thought maybe I could do Street Racer 2. This way we could also achieve what we failed with S.C.A.R.S. And it was also time to write an ambitious 3D game engine, which would be in line with the expected new super consoles. With PlayStation 2 on the horizon, promising even better, and more powerful hardware, I felt we should really go for bigger and bolder games. By now, visual detail and quality was reaching another level. Therefore, we could perhaps start making games that looked and played more like interactive movies. With these thoughts and exciting ideas in my head, I appropriately named our engine Actor 3D.

With the help of my good friend Tony Adams, I managed to sign a very good deal with Eidos. Thus, we agreed to develop Street Racer 2 for PlayStation 1. With the imminent release of PlayStation 2, we had around 14 months, a very tight deadline for a Xmas 1999 release. No problem, I was used to working to tight deadlines, and always managing to deliver. We could do it again!

Marriage with Gulsun, Sep 1999

I had already become a British citizen years before. However, Gulsun wasn't yet, so it was best to get married to make things official, and to enable both Gulsun and Sila to obtain British citizenships and passports. Equally, the official marriage status would also sort out many possible problems, and any legal implications if and when we returned to Turkey.

Eventually, we decided to get married, when Sila was just over two years old. We invited a few close friends to the marriage ceremony at the Harrow registrar. Of course, Sila was also invited to attend the wedding! I remember it like it was yesterday, how she was wearing a lovely dress, and holding a bouquet of flowers and looking so excited. But not quite sure about the occasion and everything that was going on, as she was only two years old! She looked so happy and bubbly, enjoying all the attention from everyone. In fact, she was really the centre of it all.

We started the ceremony, with both Gulsun and I standing by the registrar, and Sila right in front of us. Soon after we started our solemn oath, Gulsun started to giggle and couldn't stop. It was probably the nerves and excitement rolled into one. The officer was getting very impatient, and probably already thinking this was an arranged marriage to obtain citizenship. As a result, I thought he was going to call the whole thing off! Luckily, he was very understanding about it, and eventually began laughing too. Finally, we successfully completed the ceremony and signed the book. In fact, Sila's presence was the perfect proof that our marriage was both serious and for good.

After the ceremony we all went to a local pub for some food and drinks to celebrate!

SSA (Society of Software Authors)

Let's get back to the world of video games. The rapid growth of the gaming industry started to attract top management and agency people from other sectors such as music and book publishing. Understandably, they also wanted to get a piece of the action and expand their business. Until then the most important agent representing top developers and programmers in our industry was Jacquie Lyons (Marjaq Micro), formerly a literary and/or script agent. She already had the likes of Dave Braben (Elite), Jez San (Starglider) and Geoff Crammond (Stunt Car Racer) as some of her clients.

Above all, Jacqui served her clients very well, bringing her knowledge and experience from book publishing, and getting better deals and agreements protecting IP and copyright. In truth, she was probably the first, and certainly one of the most successful, gaming agents in the UK. Although, I personally never benefited from Jacqui's services, we always got on well and remained friends. However, I worked with one of her clients, Steve Dunn (the programmer of Street Racer and S.C.A.R.S on PlayStation, so I could see first-hand how well she served and protected her clients' interests. Steve was a highly technical and capable programmer; he also did the Spectrum version of Hammerfist for us, as well as doing the conversions of Star Glider II and Virus.

During that period, the industry was growing very fast, but I didn't think most of the developers were keeping up with the growth and the required level of professionalism. I also knew that most of them weren't getting good commercial terms, and also failing to secure their IPs. Of course, as the games were becoming bigger, the project management was becoming very important too, because more and more developers were failing to deliver on time. In the grand scheme of things, the developers becoming more professional would also help the publishers and the industry as a whole at least so my good mate Jon Dean and I believed. Jon had vast experience in preparing agreements, project management, and at that particular time, he was providing professional consultancy services to a number of top development companies.

As it was a long time ago, I cannot recall the exact details, but Jon and I decided to setup an association that would help the development community. Providing standard agreements, advice and other benefits. We wanted to get the publishers involved too, as our aim was to help the entire industry and it wasn't a move against them. Basically, the idea was to create a standard agreement with standard clauses covering important terms and conditions such as advance payments, royalty statements and rates, copyright, IP, merchandising and sub-licensing etc. Each important clause would have blank sections to fill in as appropriate for each game/developer depending on the their deal points. We had an ideal approach to help the development community, especially the newcomers.

We received support from Rod Cousens, Peter Billotta and, of course, Jacqui Lyons. In due course, we very quickly set up a committee to oversee the establishment of the organisation and draw up the standard agreement. In a relatively short time, we managed to set up the 'Society of Software Authors (SSA)', registered it and started serving the sector. Together we had created a very good standard agreement as well as many guidelines.

Maybe it was too soon, I don't know, but although most of the top developers joined, the actual developers who would benefit the most were so reluctant and questioned its purpose and validity. Nevertheless, we kept at it for a while, but it was too much effort for too little progress. However, it was still the first step towards having a professional organisation for the industry, which was followed a few years later with IGDA, TIGA and others.

Agency Representation in Games

Back to the question of having an agent. Some other agencies realised the benefit of providing successful representation to top developers and decided to follow suit. Actually, I'm not sure how they found me, but I met the music agency who was involved with Peter Gabriel amongst others. At the time, I thought why not, Gabriel was one of my favourite musicians. 'Maybe I could get to meet him backstage sometime?'

To be honest I can't find any information now, so I cannot remember the names of the agency or the people. But we agreed to work together for a while. Then, they introduced me to some of their other clients to see if we could collaborate on any joint projects, but nothing much came of it. But they did invite me to a great Peter Gabriel concert at Earls Court. Even better, I was lucky enough to say hello to the man himself backstage, just as I'd hoped.

Getting All Physical With Actor 3D Game Engine, 1998-99

As I already stated, a good friend and one of the industry's veterans, Tony Adams, had helped me with the Street Racer 2 Eidos deal. In addition, he was also representing and helping the MathEngine Physics Engine software and the company who was behind it to get into the gaming sector. Back in the day, MathEngine was a very substantial dynamics simulation tool and was used in some R&D labs for important simulation projects. Therefore, Tony was trying to engage MathEngine with the game developers and publishers.

At the time, there were a couple of other physics engines coming through such as Havoc, first unveiled at the Game Developers Conference (GDC) in 2000. Importantly, these engines were becoming very popular in game development and there was always room for new and better ones.

Anyway, Tony suggested meeting up with the team, and taking a closer look at their work. Although it looked very accurate and impressive at handling all sorts of dynamic interaction, it was too slow to be used efficiently in games. As a result, we decided instead to work closely together and try and optimise their engine's performance and make it more practical and usable in games. Back then, it made complete sense to collaborate, as we were also working on an immensely powerful 3D game engine. Thus, it would be brilliant to integrate a physics engine that we knew well, as it would give us such a great advantage.

In actual fact, I had already started thinking about making games that looked more like interactive movies. Overall, that was the whole idea and purpose behind developing the Actor 3D game engine - hence the name. So, we now had two important projects on the go, developing Street Racer 2 for Eidos and also working on Actor 3D.

Things were looking good as Eidos were strong at the time and would do a great job with publishing and marketing Street Racer. And the work with Actor Engine and MathEngine integration was progressing very well too, showing the signs of something really special very early on. Truly a fantastic looking 3D gaming environment with hundreds of 3D objects with different physical attributes that could be freely interacted with.

Fantastically, my excitement was growing by the day as I could already see that I could produce a unique and ambitious game. Offering the player very realistic 3D graphics, and unlimited dynamic interaction with both the environment and the objects within it.

As it happens, I have always been a real fan of oriental martial arts movies ever since I saw the first Bruce Lee movie when I was back in Turkey in the mid-70s. My love of these movies continued in the UK with Jackie Chan and others. In fact, my son Nej and I watched so many that I lost count. One of our favourite pastimes, which we both loved, was travelling to all the local rental shops, and we would visit all of them to find any new titles. After we watched them all, we would watch our favourite ones again until they had some new ones in. Later, I continued to watch these movies with Sila too, in fact, we still do at every opportunity, and our current favourite is the IP Man series. No wonder I was involved in programming Ninja and Samurai games!

Once I knew what I wanted to achieve, first of all, I asked my team to create a very impressive martial arts dojo for a showcase demo. Then I suggested that we filled it with all sorts of different objects such as tables, chairs, and flags, and other swinging oriental things hanging from the ceiling. Plus, a big mirror on the wall, a basketball net, a pool table and even a bath tab for liquid simulation!

However, my team were resisting the throwing together of all these different things in one place. Apparently, it would reduce the realism and look wrong artistically. Nevertheless, I simply told them to think of our dojo as like a very fancy BBC props room. This was effectively our showcase and test room. Above all, our aim was to show off our engine's capability and also to demonstrate all the wonderful interactions we could have in our games. Finally, they were convinced, and everyone was doing their best to make it as special as possible to meet my expectations. We could clearly see all the wonderful and impressive stuff we could do.

So, we worked very closely with the MathEngine team for a good few weeks. They were about to attend the GDC 2000 (Game Developers Conference) in the States, where all the developers would showcase their latest and greatest work.

Accordingly, we put together a very elaborate demo. By now, I was even ripping some fancy fighting sequences from the films that impressed me, which my animators could use as a reference. The end result of all the hard work was yielding great results. It just looked and felt amazing, just going around this massive and impressive looking dojo, and just causing chaos with everything in it. You could literally interact with everything; play basketball, score goals between miniature goal posts, play pool, kick and knock over chairs and tables or even stack the tables and chairs on top of each other. You could even turn gravity on and off and see the change in movement of the objects. There were fancy lighting effects and reflections in the big mirror on the wall. Everyone was having such fun and it was so satisfying interacting with everything freely and at will.

As if we didn't have enough, I asked for a bionic rat to be included as a prop. I had it hidden under the pool table, knowing that when people found it they would click on it. Clicking on it would just set it off like a winding toy! It would then start randomly running around like mad, but at the same time knocking everything over in its path, no matter how big or small. I remember it looked so funny but also really impressive, just watching it for ages, wrecking the scene and causing complete havoc! You could also turn gravity on and off while the rat was doing its thing too! Both MathEngine and Tony were suitably impressed. The consensus was that we all felt we had something quite special on our hands.

As expected, MathEngine had a great GDC, everyone was extremely impressed with what they had seen. And it was a perfect showcase for both MathEngine and our 3D Actor game engine. A great surprise was how much the Intel people were impressed with it. At the time, Intel were working on their Pentium 4 processor, with the aim of releasing it in 2000. And, they asked for a showcase demo for them to use for the promotion of Pentium 4. How about that?!

We were absolutely delighted with Intel's request, and agreed to do a great technology demo. Of course, we added some more impressive stuff too. Truly, this would be a great opportunity to promote our engine since Intel were going to use the demo for the Worldwide promotion activities!

Intel Pentium 4 Actor Technology Demo, 2000

At that time, PC graphics cards were improving too, and we had a good relationship with Nvidia and others. As a rule, they were providing us with their latest cards and technical support, so that we could get the best out of their hardware too. In the meantime, we received a couple of Pentium 4 engineering samples from Intel. With the latest graphics cards and the Pentium 4 processor, we were pushing our engine and dynamic interaction to the limit.

We worked hard and fast, and produced a great demo. It was more like a fancy 3D digital toy in an application, and you could play with it for hours. To make it even more fun, I asked the team to add an edit and record function, so that the users could set up and rearrange the room as they wished. They could stack things on top of each other, turn gravity on and off, and start throwing things around or let the rat loose, sit back and watch it destroy the room. Also, they were able to record their action and send it to us. My idea was to implement some of this fun stuff in the actual interactive movie game that I wanted to produce.

The demo went down so well, we received a tremendous response from both the users and the industry. It was brilliant to read all those wonderful comments, which makes all that hard work and effort worthwhile. What's more, we optimised the engine so much so that it even worked fine on Pentium 3. That way more people were able to enjoy and fully appreciate it. Yes, I was fully convinced that I could indeed create my fancy and ambitious interactive movie!

Next, Intel launched the Pentium 4 processor in June 2000, and used our tech demo to very good effect for their worldwide introduction and promotion. It was lovely to hear all the wonderful praise. Intel were suitably impressed too. We were getting requests to use the engine from all sorts of companies including for medical simulation. I even remember receiving an email about Actor engine from one of the Yerli brothers of Crytek.

Intel Actor Tech Demo for Pentium 4 processor launch, June 2000

Oh No, Just When Everything Was Going So Well...

While all this wonderful stuff was going on with Actor, my other team and I were also trying to do a great job with Street Racer 2 on PlayStation 1 and PC. We had such a short time for such an ambitious game, but I thought it was going well albeit a little behind, but we could still make it by Xmas.

After a few months, and with no clue, Eidos suddenly decided to cancel all of their PlayStation 1 games, and just concentrate on PlayStation 2 instead. Let me tell you, that was quite a big, and unexpected blow. Genuinely, I was so disappointed with the decision, but there was nothing I could do about it. Fortunately, they paid quite a bit of the remaining money and that was that, no more Street Racer 2.

Thinking back on it all, it seems that certain events were happening beyond my control, no matter how hard I tried or what I did. But I find that these crises pave way for new chapters in our lives. At the time, Gulsun and I were discussing the possibility of going back to Turkey. However, if Sila were to start school in England, or if I started a couple of big projects it would mean that we couldn't go back for maybe another ten years.

When Eidos cancelled the project, I felt as if it was like a message from above. In truth, it suddenly increased my urge to go back to Turkey. After fifteen years of hard graft in the industry, I had had a few problems, but overall I had achieved more than most people could have wished. I was really happy, but very tired too. A change could do me good I thought, perhaps a fresh start, and a big challenge on a new turf...

This is from a 6-page featured interview with Paul Rose (Digitiser) for the Edge, 2000
Sharing my vision about 3D interactive movies and my plans for Actor 3D Engine

Leaving The UK...

After a few months of careful consideration, we decided to make the move and leave England. It was a huge decision. After some twenty-one years in the UK, I was now going back to my native home. I had no idea what I had missed in Turkey or what I could expect. But at least, I was armed with great knowledge and experience in gaming and if nothing else, I could kick-start the professional Turkish gaming sector.

The prospect of becoming the founding father of the Turkish gaming sector really excited me. That would make a great story I thought to myself. Coming to England without speaking a word of English, learning to program and develop games while working at a cable factory, and then programming and producing some great games, and becoming a well-known and respected name in the gaming world, only to return to Turkey, having forgotten almost all my Turkish, to start the gaming sector. All from scratch. Well, I thought I could do this, and I could pull it off somehow. And, that would be an amazing personal achievement for me.

And, what a return that would be? With these thoughts the final decision was made.

First of all, I considered selling Vivid Image and its assets including the amazing Actor Game Engine. If I am not mistaken, I even received an offer from Codemasters, but I declined and decided to keep everything. Next, I transferred all the IPs from Vivid Image to myself, closed down the company and, with that, a big chapter in my life was finally over.

I then started preparing myself for yet another big adventure filled with excitement and uncertainties…

GameX Gaming Exhibition - Istanbul, 2010

START A NEW GAME

Turkey Here I Come...Back, October 2000

So much has happened in my life, yet I only remember making a few important decisions consciously. Most things seemed to have happened and I just played along.

Returning to Turkey was one of those important decisions that I made consciously. But then again, it felt as if I had to do it, but I was just waiting for the right time or event to trigger this chain of events. In many respects, just like my dad's passing which started the series of events that led me to the UK. So, the cancellation of Street Racer 2 by Eidos caused me to pull the trigger, and I said to myself, 'That's it, I am going back to Turkey'.

Although we made such a big decision, there wasn't much dwelling on it; no real preparation or plans for business or otherwise. In fact, Gulsun and I decided that I would go alone first to get things going, set up my company, find a place to live and then they would join me in a few months.

A Fish Called Mev or (Like A Fish Out of Water)

Admittedly, I did feel like a fish out of water, quite scared, breathless, confused and anxious. My multi-tasking brain was running on turbo mode, what if this, what if that. I was almost coding my thoughts. At the same time, I could feel the excitement too, the thought of rediscovering what I had left behind. There was so much to catch up on, my Turkish, my relatives, my friends, the food, the weather, the whole lot.

Firstly, I was embarking on an exciting personal journey, which was for sure, but also, on a business level, the notion of becoming the founding father of the professional Turkish game sector was what really gave me the chills. Repeatedly thinking and saying to myself, 'now, wouldn't that be something!'

Who would have predicted that my return would set the foundation of the gaming industry in my native country? And, that I would lead and provide support to the development efforts in the crucial early years.

Life truly is a game, and I'm glad to be playing my small part. With what little information I could gather prior to going to Turkey, there wasn't much game development to speak of at the time. There had been some notable efforts in the late 80s and early 90s on the Amiga and PC, but all remained at an amateur level, and didn't get enough traction without proper publishing and business support. However, I managed to hook up with a few people who were either still trying to develop games or were interested in doing so. Clearly, I could see that there were definitely some talented programmers and artists, with good knowledge and technical ability and some experience. Early indications were promising that I could start with a very small team, and try and build it from there.

I didn't know Istanbul that well anyway, and the city had grown and changed so much since I'd been gone. Where would I live, what about the office, in fact, where do I start? So much to think about, consider and discover while contemplating all the details about the beginning of this new chapter in my life.

My Turkish had recovered reasonably well during my mingling with the Turks in London, and, of course, living with Gulsun. But I still had to brush up my language and there was so much to remember that I had forgotten. Also, just as much new stuff that I had to learn too. But despite all of this, I was in no rush. I would take my time and take it all in, slowly, but surely.

What would Nej do when he came to Turkey? I had tried to teach him some Turkish when he was young, but it was such a pathetic attempt on my part that he didn't know any. But then again, it is not called the 'mother tongue' for no reason, so no wonder I failed miserably. 'Oh well, he can learn it somehow, just like his dad learnt English' was my thinking. But when he started living in Istanbul, he never bothered because all the Turks around him preferred to talk to him in English, which suited Nej down to the ground. After eighteen years, he can now fully understand and speak it reasonably, but he still prefers his native English. I'm sure he would have learnt it well, should the situation have forced him too, but he took the easy option.

With me, I had no choice. I was compelled to learn English because I had to. My observation is that I guess the conditions and the environment we live in, can get the best as well as the worst out of us.

Finding My Way Around

After twenty-one years, I had lost contact with many friends, and I hardly knew anyone in Istanbul. Luckily, a lot of my relatives were in Izmit where Janet and I had lived before going to England. Also, it was where my mother had lived during her last years.

The first thing I did was to start visiting relatives in Izmit and in my hometown Ordu. Also, I visited the graves of my mother and father. Unfortunately, my father was buried in my village cemetery in Ordu, but mother in Izmit where she had died. So sad that they were separated even in death!

Visiting my relatives in Izmit (close to Istanbul) became a frequent thing for me, especially most weekends. It was really nice to catch up with them all and taste some of the delicious village food that I had grown up with and had missed while being in the UK.

A few times, I also visited my village and all the relatives whom I had grown up with. Of course, most of the elderly had passed away and there were so many young people, none of whom I knew. However, they were all so welcoming, and it was wonderful walking and driving around the entire village, reliving my childhood memories. It was beautiful to reflect and look back, but equally, it was very emotional too.

The excitement of starting a new adventure, which could be as important as the one I had left behind in the UK was truly enlivening. Interestingly, I felt very confident too, after all, I was going to do something that I was very proficient at. With a proven track record on an international level and having enough financial security, by the way, boosted my confidence too. If things didn't go as expected business wise, then I still had options. Indeed, I could always go back to the UK. Besides, I have always been very careful with my business, and managed to keep it afloat without ever risking my family's future or mine.

Starting From Scratch

Fully motivated, and delighted with the prospect of doing something really big for my native country, I began with the formalities of setting up a company. Of course, I had the mission to find an office and a place to live too. There were so many things to do and all at the same time, but I did enjoy multi-tasking.

The first few young game development enthusiasts who I met were computer science students at ITU (Istanbul Technical University), one of the oldest and best in Turkey. One of the students, Arkin Telli, was very excited about my return and he introduced me to all the best people that I could work with. Actually, he was a bit like Phil Harrison, who knew everyone who was into gaming. That's how my first steps towards building my first team started. Firstly, Engin Cilasun would be my first main programmer, who was a naturally gifted, highly knowledgeable, and technically adept young man. In fact, we worked together for many years. He now works at Avalanche Studios as a lead game engine developer in the USA. One could see from his first name what he was destined to do!

One of my top programmers on the Actor Game Engine was Will Cowling. He fancied the idea of coming to Turkey and helping me with the initial setup. In the course of time, he worked very closely with Engin and together they continued to develop the Actor engine. As planned, Will left and returned to the UK after about a year. Amazingly, Will now works at the Sony PlayStation UK office, as one of the lead programmers on special projects.

Before I returned to Turkey, we had become friends with Michael Armstrong of Nortel Networks, who was the R&D director in the UK. Coincidentally, he had worked in Istanbul before and loved the city. What was great was that Michael knew of my plans about Turkey, and he knew what was available in terms of state incentives, initiatives, funds and support.

There were small R&D centres at some university campuses, and one of the biggest and earliest was at ITU. With the help of Arkin, I went to explore the possibility of setting up an office at the campus, as I thought it would be great to be amongst the students. Situated there I could discover talent, take the best people on, and nurture them into professional developers.

Back to University

I had initially gone to university during troubled times and I never really enjoyed my years there. So the thought of being back at a university campus was incredibly attractive in many ways.

One of the computer science professors of ITU, Muhittin Gokmen, had himself just returned from the US. He had set up a multimedia and R&D support centre in visual computing and software development. Enthusiastically, I shared the details of my plans about the gaming sector. Immediately, he became extremely excited about it, and said he would give me a small office next to his multimedia centre to get me started. Moreover, he pleaded with me not to go anywhere else. Obviously, he thought there would be plenty of opportunity for collaboration. Bingo! I thought why not, that would be perfect. As a result, I now had a 35 square metre office, tables and chairs and all there ready to move in and start work! That was easy, I thought.

I must say though that although I did all my game development work at ITU campus, strangely enough, we never managed to collaborate with ITU in all those years.

Will and I brought with us the best PCs (including Intel's special engineering sample Pentium 4s), and 3 of the best monitors we had, to go with the computers. That was all the equipment we had to start the gaming business in Turkey. Not a bad start, I now had an office, some equipment, and two great programmers! All I needed now was to add a company and a couple of artists.

Without hesitation, we moved in promptly. Will and Engin started working on Actor 3D. It was important to develop it further, so we could make games with it. In fact, we ended up doing another demo for Intel from our small start-up in Istanbul, which was for the forthcoming Pentium 4 2.2. Really that was a nice start, as we had our first professional assignment for our new team. And amazingly it was from Intel no less!

At that time, that really made a great impression on everyone around me. The students, the professors, and whoever else was interested in us and in what we were up to. They were also impressed with my reputation, and our close relationships with companies like Intel and Nvidia.

On the flipside, it is true that the Turkish people can be very sceptical too. For a long time, they refused to believe that I actually coded or produced any of my games in the UK. Some even claimed in online forums that I was probably not even in the main team, and that I just had a small role if anything. However, it never bothered me of course, but it did annoy and upset my teammates quite a lot. To the point that a few times they even offered to beat them up for me!

Thanks to the growing retro community, where my work is often mentioned, nowadays the Turkish people appreciate my career even more. Even now I still meet quite a number of people who grew up playing Enduro Racer, Last Ninja 2, Street Racer or First Samurai. What's even nicer is the fact that these people are from all walks of life. A game is such a powerful tool, it can touch so many people, of all ages, genders, cultures, religions and reaches beyond borders. It seems our work is timeless too. Indeed, it is wonderful to see all our games being shared all the time and all over the world by the massive retro community. We are eternally grateful to them for keeping our work and memories alive!

To make an early impact and impression, I started including the local motifs and cultural elements in my work from the word go. And as such, I added the famous Maiden's Tower of Istanbul to the second Intel demo. I would continue to do this throughout my work in Turkey, to demonstrate the power and importance of gaming, and creating original content.

My objective was that I wanted to show that as the creator and the producer of my products, I could do whatever I wanted within reason. Quality content created by the successful producer could go a long way towards the promotion of the local culture and history. In addition, it was even more important to show this in my first project and with such a big, internationally renowned company too. Our work was going to be used worldwide by a global company, so this was a great opportunity for effective international exposure.

Thankfully, I obtained a lot of respect for my approach and stance. Subsequently, all the gaming and technology press took notice of my presence quite quickly and my plans for the gaming business in Turkey.

Talent, Enthusiasm and Dedication Eventually Prosper

Unfortunately, it took a while for both the public and the private sectors to realise the potential of gaming in Turkey. It was sad not to receive enough support from the big guns from the outset, but the talent and enthusiasm of the young people would be more than enough to keep me going. During that period, I was building a very strong team around me comprising of local university students who went on to create some very important work.

After many years of hard work, I can now see that it was all worthwhile as Turkey is rapidly becoming one of the most important and biggest gaming markets in the region. The three most recent major mobile game company acquisitions by Zynga and Miniclips with a total purchase value exceeding $600 million, fuelled the interest and growth of the Turkish gaming sector even further.

Peak Games, First Gaming Unicorn of Turkey

With Sidar in Istanbul, 2018

In fact, as I am writing these lines in the lockdown months of June 2020, Zynga has bought Peak Games for a staggering $1.8billion! The sale was announced around mid-Jun 2020. Sidar Sahin, the CEO of Peak Games, is around 40 years old and I first met him when I was a consultant for Turkcell, the biggest GSM operator, as their chief games advisor back in 2003. Back then, Sidar had a mobile application company and they were making mobile games for Turkcell to publish. With one of my top programmers Ozgur Soner, we developed the first online multiplayer mobile games, Backgammon and Battle Ships. What's more, Java phones were just coming to the market. So, even at that time, we could see that mobile gaming had lots of potential.

We exchanged ideas and chatted quite often with Sidar, and I knew he would go far, and he did. Just for the record, there is no way I am implying or claiming a stake in his success or achievement. It belongs to him and his team fair and square.

The point I am trying to make is that talented people with vision just need enough exposure and opportunity to shine through. Sidar and his team are a great example of this. For years not enough people believed in the power and importance of gaming in Turkey, but now with Sidar's landmark achievement, and many talented young people coming through, the gaming industry in Turkey will grow even further. Personally, I have always believed in the talent of young developers and I am confident that there will be many more big successes coming out of Turkey in the near future.

Again, for the record, Sidar phoned me a few days after the sale of his company. Just to thank me for everything I had done for him, and the Turkish gaming industry. In fact, he made my day and all my efforts worthwhile when he said, 'You are harvesting what you have sown, my friend. Any success is just as much yours as it is ours. Please enjoy and make the most of it.' It was such a wonderful gesture from him. And it really is lovely to be recognised and appreciated for your efforts and contribution.

Upon reflection, I am just glad and proud to have played a part both in the British and the Turkish gaming industries.

Sobee Studios and Campus Life at 40 Something

Surprisingly, I managed to set up my company, Sobee Studios, in a few weeks and officially started game development on 17th November 2000 at the ITU Maslak campus. For a new company there's quite a bit of paperwork and registration to do in Turkey.

Being at a university campus was great, and it was absolutely brilliant to be amongst all those bright students too. Since I couldn't really enjoy my university years, maybe I could make up for it now. There were thousands of students studying many different subjects including electronics and computer science. What was fabulous was that I spent a lot of time with them, often having lunch at the student canteen.

It was lovely sharing all my stories of the difficult times of the past. They couldn't believe some of the stuff I told them, as the times were so different, and they couldn't relate to my stories. By and large, the students seemed to be quite happy and working hard at their studies. Truth be told, they had to work hard as ITU was very tough to get into, and even harder to graduate from. Some of the country's brightest young people were there, and some of them would be working with me soon.

One thing that Turkish people really love is their bread and I mean lots of bread! In fact, the students ate even more bread because they had limited means, and that was the most inexpensive way to fill up. In the canteen, there was a set menu for each day, and it was reasonably nice food too. In fact, they even displayed the daily nutrition and calorie information. Generally, very healthy eating except for the excessive amount of bread!

It was funny to see the student food trays with mountains of bread on them as they walked to their tables to eat! I only had a couple of small pieces, which embarrassed those who were sitting with me. They would explain that it was the only way to feel completely full up for the rest of the day and even into the night. To save them the embarrassment and put them at ease, I shared an anecdote from my university years.

I recalled how my friend and I would go to a restaurant at the Ankara Coach Station, as it was the very first thing in the morning and it never closed. Also, the station was close to our school, and this is where we would take the coach to go home during holidays. Because my father had worked at Ulusoy, one of the biggest coach companies, I would get free rides. Another perk was that I also ate with the drivers, who would get nice, specially cooked food during the journey stops. That was one of the very few occasions that I would enjoy a decent meal during my youth.

Anyway, before going to school, we would stop at this restaurant to have soup for breakfast. On the whole, this is mainly a tradition of the Black Sea region, as most people there would have soup in the morning. In fact, it is extremely healthy, and especially nice to have a wholesome vegetable broth in the winter.

Since we never had much money, my friend and I would share a soup. Back in the day, all the restaurants would have bottles of water, and a basket full of sliced bread on each of the tables. At larger tables they would have several baskets of bread and bottles of water. Therefore, we usually chose big tables to sit at! Remembering how it was, it used to be either remarkably busy with many travellers, or the waiters would be too tired from working all night. This often meant that they couldn't be bothered to serve us. This would suit us fine, as we would start gobbling away at the bread and wash it down with the nice bottled water. All the time, hoping the waiters would never come to the table until we were full. Once we were reasonably sated on bread, we would get up in a hurry and walk out, saying, 'Sorry, we can't wait much longer, we will be late for our class.' In truth, I think most of the waiters probably knew what we were up to, and just turned a blind eye to our little tricks!

Back to the ITU canteen and the students loved the story, and we all had such a good laugh about it. I think, they also realised that our conditions were so much harder in comparison to theirs. Hopefully, my story may have made them appreciate what they had more.

Big Gaming Adventure Part Two

All set up at the university, we started the ball rolling in our 35m squared office. It was quite a feeling to start from scratch with just two programmers without knowing what I would face along the way. However, I guess that's what adventures are all about; discovering new things as you progress, trying to overcome obstacles, take on new challenges.

At the same time, I could see the excitement and expectation I was creating around me, especially amongst the young, and the media. Indeed, there were some game magazines, which showed a lot of interest and gave us plenty of coverage. What was even more encouraging was the attention from the serious press. Suddenly my interviews were appearing not just in all the IT magazines, but also the economic and financial ones. And not much later, my presence was becoming big news in the national newspapers, and weekly magazines. Now I was getting a lot of attention and substantial coverage. They could clearly see the excitement and buzz I was creating especially amongst the young, raising their hopes and aspirations.

And it wasn't long before I was on the telly doing many interviews. As a result, I was fast becoming a local celebrity, someone who everybody wanted to meet. Anyone wanting to do anything in and around gaming was coming to me, either for more insight and information or to be part of my team.

At this pivotal moment in time, Turkey had a real thirst for international success, and I could sense the feeling of appreciation of what I had achieved in the UK, and what I could achieve here in my own country. Everyone was continually talking about me, and my work, all of which was raising expectations way beyond where we were. All this attention and praise was great, but it was also creating unnecessary pressure, and too soon.

After all, I had only just started and had a long way to go. Consequently, it became important to manage the press attention and the high expectations building up around me. I kindly asked them to calm things down a bit. Explaining how all the attention was creating too much expectation and too quickly, which, in turn, could cause undue disappointment. Ultimately, they respected my thinking and only helped with PR whenever I asked for it. Just like in the UK, I had established an incredibly positive working relationship with most of the press. In fact, I formed particularly good friendships with most of them, frequently meeting up and socialising with them.

Settling Again in My Previous Home – Turkey, April 2001

Whilst all the excitement about my work was building up, I also had to build a new home in Istanbul too.

If I am honest, Turkey is a very dynamic country full of uncertainties and surprises. Somehow it always faces sudden economic and political crises. True to form, in February 2001, Turkey would experience one of the biggest economic and political crises in its long history. What luck I thought, I had already experienced the hard times of the mid to late 70s in Turkey before. Plus, all the changes of the 80s brought about by the Thatcherite years in the UK. At that time, I had just started living in the UK and suddenly had to face all the changes and turbulence of the new policies. And now, so soon after my return, it seemed Turkey was going to go through massive economic turmoil.

Since I had just started out, and there wasn't a game sector to speak of yet, I could just try and go about my business and ride out the storm. Nevertheless, such a big crisis could dampen people's excitement and progress. But then again, such crises could also turn our position to an advantage as some businesses and companies would be looking for alternatives. Without doubt, the gaming industry was certainly a great alternative. Furthermore, gaming just like other entertainment industries, normally benefitted from crises because during these times people will spend even more time on games. Nevertheless, Turkey wasn't yet aware of the importance of gaming, and it would take me quite an effort and also some time to create the much-needed awareness and enthusiasm for this new sector.

To give you an example of this in recent times, during the Covid-19 lockdown in the first half of 2020, the number of gamers and the time spent on gaming increased by a staggering 60%!

Upon returning to Istanbul, I had initially rented a two bed, grotty looking flat before committing myself to buying a house. First of all, I wanted to make sure of the area, and the house I would live in for years to come. As a rule, I am always incredibly careful about buying a property. It is important to make sure I can always sell it easily and at a better price, if and when I have to. It is generally accepted as a rule of thumb that you actually make profit on your property when you purchase it. This has always served me well, and I did the same thing with the first house I purchased in Turkey. Naturally, I took my time, and made sure I was 100% happy before committing.

Decision to Live in Emirgan by The Bosphorus

Eventually, I ended up renting a flat on the outskirts of Emirgan, one of the oldest and most popular districts in Istanbul. It is situated around the middle of the 20-mile long beautiful Bosphorus Straits coastline. This is also a conservation area like Harrow on the Hill, with many grade I and II listed buildings. Furthermore, it is surrounded by beautiful woods overlooking the Bosphorus, where a lot of old Turkish movies were filmed on location.

In truth, I didn't know Emirgan at all, but I fell in love with it the first time I saw it. Also, it was only a five minute drive from the ITU campus too, which

was perfect as, you know, I always prioritised having my office and home close to each other.

To this day, I still remember the reaction of the local estate agent Ismail, when I asked for a not so nice two bed flat to rent. In response, he said that was the first time a client had asked him for a bad place. Subsequently, I explained to him that I wanted a grotty place to rent, so that I wouldn't want to stay there too long. He was surprised, but equally impressed by my approach. Because of the economic crisis there were a number of houses up for sale from people unable to pay their bank loans (no mortgage system yet in Turkey in 2001).

Hunt For Our First House in Istanbul

One fortuitous day the estate agent called me and told me there was this lovely Grade II listed historical detached house in the heart of Emirgan, with great views over the Bosphorus. Apparently, it had been on sale for ages, but the owner wanted too much money for it. Unfortunately for her, she had defaulted on her payments and now the bank had put it up for immediate sale. Around that time, most banks were trying to turn all the properties they had into much needed cash funds.

Banks sold such houses on invitation, and with closed bidding, and the highest bidder would get the house. The owner was asking for $600,000 before the economic crisis. I didn't have a clue as to what it was worth or what the going prices were. With a little bit of help from the estate agent, I made the first offer of $320,000 as we thought there was a shortage of cash, plus no one would be paying much in these circumstances.

As it happens, I loved the house and really wanted to get it, but I didn't want to pay much over the odds for what I could get it for. In due course, I was short listed with the first offer and then asked to submit a second offer.

Since I was short-listed, I thought my offer must be within a good range, and not to risk losing it, I upped my offer by another $20,000. After waiting for a week and to my absolute delight, I bought the house. What a result! A beautiful, old detached house by the Bosphorus, and at a reasonable price too. What's not to like I thought?

It had been empty for several years, and in a terrible condition, but I knew I could get it all done up for around $15-20,000.

That was exactly what I had done with my last house in Harrow on the Hill. It was a 360-year-old Grade II listed detached house in a really bad condition. But I spent quite a bit of money and had it all done up but preserving all the original features. So, I would do the same with the Emirgan property.

With special planning permission I had it all done up beautifully. Amazingly, I lifted the grotty and worn out old carpet only to discover beautiful old wooden floorboards, and a lovely large pink marble floor in the entrance hall! On the outside, it was all painted in a lovely pink, with white timber windows and shutters, and a massive white double door at the main entrance. So, I had the pink paint renewed, and it really looked majestic from the main road as it was atop a small hill with no houses nearby.

Really, I felt so lucky and grateful. When I left Turkey for Britain, I was only twenty-one and I had nothing to leave behind, no house, no land, and no property of any kind - what little land I had been left by my father in the village was used by my cousins. The whole land was barely enough for my cousins, so I never claimed my share and just left it to them.

I never had a nice house of my own in my childhood to look back on with fond memories, as I grew up living with relatives. As a result, I always felt so blessed to be able to afford to live in such nice detached houses with gardens. My biggest hobby is listening to music, and quite loudly too. For me, living in a house instead of an apartment has always been such a luxury, which I consider as a gift that life has presented to me.

Sila and Gulsun's First Visit to Emirgan

During the Easter break of 2001, Gulsun and Sila came to Istanbul and stayed for a couple of weeks. I was still staying at the grotty two-bed flat as I was getting our house done up. Before Gulsun came, she always wrote to me, and mentioned how Sila would keep talking about wanting a pink house. In response, I would write back saying that she was one incredibly lucky girl as that's exactly what I had done, bought her a beautiful pink house. And I would tell her all about it; a listed building like our London house, detached with three bedrooms and on a small hill with lovely views over the Bosphorus.

Feeling very excited, I just couldn't wait to show it to them. It was quite unbelievable, Sila kept talking about wanting a pink house, and that's exactly what she was going to get. But I asked Gulsun not to tell Sila about it until they came, so we could surprise her. Because Sila wouldn't stop, Gulsun told her in the end, 'OK Sila, your dad has bought you a lovely pink house just like you want.' Apparently, she was over the moon about it and couldn't wait to see it!

Anyway, one morning we left our grotty rented flat and started walking towards our pink house, which was only five minutes away. As we were getting closer, the surrounding area and the other houses are getting prettier. I could see the excitement on Gulsun's face too, she really liked the area. Meanwhile, Sila was trying to walk fast with her little feet (she was only four years old), wanting to get there as soon as possible. She looked so happy and full of anticipation. We were going to look at the house, and then have breakfast at the lovely tea gardens by the Bosphorus just down the road.

In fact, I was also extremely excited. Can you imagine showing your four year old daughter the pink house she'd been dreaming about only a few weeks ago? And it wasn't a toy, it was the real deal!

To get to the house on the hill, we had to climb about fifty plus steps, up the winding stone stairs, and through lovely trees and bushes. Finally, we arrived at the front of the lovely pink house with its large porch. Standing there you could see the great view over the tea gardens, the Bosphorus and the Asian side too. Gulsun could hardly contain her elation, but she was just enjoying the views and checking out the surroundings, and all the details of the house. So, there I was waiting for Sila's reaction and expected delight. I was almost as excited as her!

This House Isn't Pink!

The moment had finally come. We were standing by the entrance with the key in my hand, to unlock the beautiful white wooden double doors, still waiting for Sila's reaction. In great anticipation, I was expecting a huge scream filled with happiness and absolute joy!

Then her reaction... She screamed all right but in a complete rage, kicking the main door like mad at the same time. Gobsmacked, we were stunned and shocked to say the least! The pandemonium persisted. Sila continued with her screaming and kicking, now also crying, she said, 'I wanted a pink house, this isn't a pink house, and you lied to me! I wanted a pink house!'

Flabbergasted, we were not just shocked, but angry now too at Sila's unreasonable rage, unable to give it any meaning. Perplexed, we just couldn't understand what was going on. Trying to understand and placate her, we said, 'this house is as pink as a house could get, and it's a beautiful pink too, can't you see, it's pink all over?'

No matter what we said, she just wouldn't calm down, and kept shouting and repeating, 'this isn't a pink house, you lied!' I said, 'C'mon Sila, can't you see it's a pink house?' pointing at the pink walls everywhere.

Defiantly, Sila kicked the front door even harder and said, while still crying, 'this isn't a pink house, it is a white house, can't you see?' pointing at the main door. 'I want a pink house like the one Isil has!' Gulsun looked at me with a sudden flash of light, as if to say I know what's going on here. She just said to Sila, 'OK my lovely, don't worry about it, your daddy will make it into a pink house. He will have it painted again, let's now go and have our breakfast.'

Baffled, I looked at Gulsun completely puzzled, and with a look to say, 'we can't paint it as we want, it is a grade II listed building. And it's already a bloody pink house'. I was forgetting that Sila was only four, but her over the top reaction had annoyed me. Presumptuously, I had prepared myself to celebrate Sila's delight, but all I ended up with was a complete tantrum. Oh well, Gulsun would explain what was going on I thought and so we went to the tea gardens for breakfast.

While having breakfast with Sila playing with the other kids, Gulsun told me what had happened. It had finally clicked with Gulsun when Sila kept kicking the white front door, and saying this isn't a pink house, this is a white house. Apparently, her niece Isil's flat's main door was painted pink, but only the bloody front door, not the rest of the property! That's what pink house was for Sila, and that's why she referred to Isil's flat as the pink house, and she also wanted one herself just like Isil's! Sadly, the poor thing didn't care that the entire house was painted in pink. In reality, it was only the main door that mattered to her. Well, we laughed about it afterwards. Bloody kids, I thought to myself, but angry with myself too for forgetting that kids live in a completely different world.

Of course, we couldn't make the already pink house into Sila's pink house by painting the front door to pink. But she would live in that not so pink-pink house for nine years and enjoy every bit of it. Also, Nej stayed there with us for a while when he first moved to Istanbul. But later he rented a place in Cihangir, in Taksim. His new place was more or less in the heart of Istanbul, the most popular tourist area with lots of bars, restaurants and entertainment.

Our not so pink House in Emirgan, Istanbul

Kemal Dervis of Technology

If you remember there was a tremendous amount of interest in my returning to Turkey. Consequently, I was frequently in national papers and magazines. As with most press around the world, the Turkish papers sometimes would tend to exaggerate things beyond all proportions.

After the economic crisis exploded, the Prime Minister Ecevit had invited Kemal Dervis, a Turkish economy expert working for the World Bank, to come to Turkey, and help restore the economy and stabilise the crisis.

It was quite amazing to see Ecevit, incredibly old and looking quite fragile by now, still running the country in the year 2001. He was the prime minister when I was at university in the mid-70s. That was the same period when Ecevit gave the order to send the Turkish troops to Cyprus.

All in all, Kemal Dervis was a major news headline, and everyone was talking about this man. The general opinion was, 'What a brilliant economist he was, and how he would save the economy in no time'. Everything was blown out of all proportion as per usual.

One of the major newspapers, Milliyet, did an important interview with me during the crisis and all the discussions about Kemal Dervis' magical remedies. However, it was a substantial and important interview about my plans, the importance of the gaming industry, new career, and investment opportunities. In addition to this, I also shared the important fact about how the gaming industry was immune to crisis, and, in fact, it benefitted from it, as people spend even more time playing games in such times.

Well, the young journalist was really impressed with my plans and all the valuable information I had shared with him. Also, he said he would do a great piece in the forthcoming weekend edition. It was going to be brilliant as even more people read the weekend editions. Certainly, it was a great opportunity to create awareness of my plans in these crises we were facing.What a fantastic surprise it was, I couldn't believe it when I saw the interview. Even better, there was a big headline on the front page, with a photo of me and our tiny team, holding a few CDs in our hands, and the headline read: 'Another Dervis For IT…' Wow, I could not have orchestrated a better marketing and PR stunt. Well, I thought, I had better lay low for a while to keep things on the quiet before it got out of hand. At this rate I could also receive an invitation from Ecevit to help the real Dervis!

Milliyet Newspaper Interview and Headline News, 2001
From left Will Cowling, Paul (?), Bager Akbay, Engin Cilasun and Me

Photo by Handan Aybars, 2001

Gulsun, Sila and Nej Join Me in Turkey

Our new life on the Bosphorus began when Gulsun and Sila joined me a few months later. Nej would also come to Istanbul a year or so later. We started living in our new house and the lovely area of Emirgan by August 2001.

All this attention, and news about me, was turning me into some sort of local celebrity. As a result, I became such an important figure in Emirgan too, almost a local hero. Fantastically, we were embraced and welcomed by the whole community. Absolutely everyone made us feel at home. Truly, it felt as if we had already lived there for years. Reflecting on it now, it was so nice living there. We would spend many hours in the teagardens, chatting with the locals, playing backgammon. Also, Sila played with other kids in the courtyard of the historic Emirgan mosque. Really, we had a wonderful nine years there.

Years later in 2009 we moved from Emirgan to a country house in the outskirts of Istanbul near the Black Sea region. But we continued to visit Emirgan to say hello to our friends as often as possible. They have always been very welcoming to us.

Renewal of My Turkish ID

I probably had my ID renewed in London, at the Turkish Consulate General sometime in the 80's, but apparently it was way out of date. During setting up the new company, I had to obtain a lot of official paperwork, as I had almost become an alien in my native country, after such a long time. Whenever I went to a government office or was stopped by traffic police for a routine control, I was always warned, 'You must get your ID renewed, it's way out of date'.

With this in mind, I thought it was best to get my ID sorted and be done with it. Carrying an ID is particularly important in Turkey, you must always have it with you. If the police stop you without it, you can easily get into trouble, so you get used to always having it on you! Whereas, while living in the UK, I was so relieved to discover that if you failed to show your driving licence, all you had to do was to take it to the nearest police station within five days. It's interesting that there is still no real ID requirement in the UK, what a contrast.

Anyway, back to the story and a friend was helping me with the paperwork and taking me to the different government buildings. I asked him to take me to the ID registration office first thing in the morning, as apparently there were always long queues. First, we obtained a proof of address document from the Muhtar, the local district officer. In Turkey, most official documents require a photo, and I still had half a dozen or so spare photos with me due to all the other paperwork I'd been completing.

After a while, we went to the ID place and took our spot in the long queue with about fifteen people ahead of me. There we were chatting away in the queue, as Turkish people love to socialise. In general, the conversations usually start with, 'Where are you from, what do you do, where did you do your army service, which team do you support and so forth'. If you happen to be from the same town or a supporter of the same team, you become instant best pals!

Of course, I told them all about myself, about England, the games, and what I was going to do in Turkey - the full monty. They were so intrigued that they kept asking questions, which helped pass the time, as the queue was moving slowly. Critically, you could easily lose your place in the queue, as there was no numbering system in those days. It was important to safeguard your place in the queue. Nowadays, it is so much easier; you take a number and wait to be called. And also you have to realise that whilst queuing is a given in the UK and European countries, in Turkey it is often every man or woman for themselves, and you would often have to fight your way to get on a bus or a train.

Anyway, it was almost lunchtime, and there were still about five people in front of me, so there was no chance of getting it sorted before lunch, even though there were about five counters. It was taking so long to process each application. Plus, you also had to get a birth certificate confirmation, by fax, from your original birthplace, which could take an hour or so. Remember, we are talking 2001! Then next came the printing of the fancy new ID card and sealing it off with a plastic cover etc. All in all, it was quite a process. One of the officials called out, 'we are closing for our lunch break, and will be back in an hour.' My friend said, 'c'mon let's go, we can get it done another time, as this will take all day.' I replied, 'we waited all this time, and I really want to do it today and forget about it. Let's go and have lunch and come back in an hour.' He said, 'there are four people in front of you, when we get back you have to queue up again and you will lose your place too, you may end up with ten or more people in front of you.'

After my friend's warning about the queue, I instantly came up with a cunning idea, like Baldrick's cunning plans (from BBC's classic Blackadder comedy series) before everyone left the queue. Raising my hand so everybody could see, I called out to get everyone's attention, 'My friends, I have a great idea!' They couldn't wait to hear it, after all, they assumed I was such a clever man, just back from England, and games programming and all that. One of them said, 'we're all ears brother, let us hear it.'

Composing myself and with some authority I spoke to them, 'we are all grown-ups, and very reasonable people here.' My friend was also wondering as to what I was going to say. I continued, 'before we break for lunch, please let us carefully check, and note our positions in the queue, and also note who is behind and in front of us! This way, when we get back, we can easily reform the same queue as now, otherwise we may all end up at the back.'

The reaction was amazing, 'Wow, what a brilliant idea, well done, we thought you looked like a clever man, maybe it's something they do in England...' One of them added, 'we could stick together, and convince all the newcomers to queue behind us, so that no one could jump the queue.' I said, 'absolutely, that's the idea, well done.' The best reaction was from the guy at the front of the queue. In a firm and loud voice, to make sure everyone clearly heard him, 'dear friends, please take a close look at my face, we don't want any mix-up now do we as to who is in the front? Clearly that is me, please remember that!'

My friend couldn't believe it, he said, 'no wonder people like you, you are so practical, funny and very friendly with everyone. You made lots of new friends even in the bloody ID queue!' Jokingly I said, 'it's all like a game to me, I can come up with practical and working solutions for even silly problems like this.' With the comfort of a secured position in the queue, we took our time and had a lovely lunch at an extremely popular local restaurant.

My Queuing Scheme

When we returned, it was nice to see that they had already formed the queue more or less as we had left it, over an hour ago. There were lots of new people and the queue was much longer. Calmly, I walked slowly towards my position checking the faces for good measure. My queue friends were so helpful, showing me to my place that they had kept for me. However, a few of the newcomers objected to my joining the queue near the front, thinking I was jumping the queue. Immediately my queue comrades stepped in, and sorted things out! Also sharing the fact that I was the architect of the queue scheme...

Luckily one or two people before me had not come back after lunch, and suddenly I was in third place! My friend was smiling and glad that we would get the new ID today after all.

Finally, my turn came after about twenty-five minutes of waiting, and I handed all my paperwork and four photos to the officer behind the counter. It became apparent that he was obviously watching my antics and listening to all the conversations. Curiously, he said something like, 'you seem to be an interesting person, are you an actor or something?' I said, 'no, I make games, but sometimes I act as if I am an actor.' I was so happy, feeling like a little kid that I was finally getting my new ID!

Not so fast soldier! The officer said, 'I am so sorry, but this won't do, your four photos must match the photo on the proof of address document!' I said, 'please, these are all taken within two weeks of each other.' But he replied, 'I would love to help, but sorry, there is nothing I can do as this is a very strict rule.' He suggested I went back and had a new proof of address document with the same photo as the ones I handed to him. Undeterred, I wasn't to give up easily, not now when I was so close. I said to my friend, 'let's go and get it done quickly and come back, it will only take ten minutes. Before leaving, I said to the officer, and all the others in the queue that when I returned, I would be at the front of the queue. They all said, 'no problem brother, we will let you go first when you come back.' The officer also nodded to confirm.

We collected the new address document with a matching photo and came back in no time. Straight away I made my way to the counter and started waiting for the officer to finish his current task. One or two new arrivals objected to my action but were very quickly repelled by my comrades! Next, I handed all my paperwork and the photos to the officer. After some processing, he gave me a slip of paper and asked me to go to the fax department to obtain confirmation from my hometown of Ordu. Actually, it was quite busy in the small fax room, as they were having problems connecting with other numbers. After about forty-five minutes I finally received my information, which I duly gave to the officer. 'Almost there now', I thought.

The officer said that the fax had come quite quickly. I said, 'yes, I was lucky, and I could do with some luck the way things are going.' Suddenly, as he was just about to file all the paperwork onto his tray for the final processing, he looked at me, and my fax several times, as if to make sure of something. Surprisingly, he literally exploded with laughter, and said, 'I am so sorry, but this fax won't do, it's not your lucky day, is it?' I said, 'what do you mean it won't do, what in God's name is the problem now?' He said, having difficulty containing his laughter, 'according to this fax, you appear to have died in the year 1000!' I said, 'what? C'mon, you know that's rubbish. Can't you see I'm standing here right in front of you? How can I be dead? I have never been so alive, and determined, I want to get this bloody ID today!' He said, still smiling, 'I can clearly see that you are very much alive, but the official document says otherwise, and there is nothing I can do about it. Please, just get another fax, obviously the computer made an error.' I pleaded, 'please don't send me back to the fax machine!' as if he was sending me to a jail cell, 'I just couldn't bear waiting in there again.'

I was literally begging him, 'please, there must be another way to sort this stupid thing out, can't you just initial and sign it as an error? You can see I am not dead, but at this rate I will be soon, with all the grief I'm suffering right now!' He said, 'I can't initial and sign it, but maybe the Manager can. You could ask him to do it for you, and if he signs it then I can accept it.'

Therefore, I went to the Manager, and recounted the whole tale to him. He had someone with him, who looked like a friend as they were chatting away. Clearly tickled by my story, they had such a good laugh about it. However, it wasn't a laughing matter for me as I was really getting irritated by the whole thing.

Subsequently, the Manager himself tried the fax number a few times, but all he heard was an engaged tone. In the end, he said, 'I'll sign and initial it to help you out, as it is clearly a simple error, and you look as alive as anyone!'

Mightily relieved, I thanked him, and as I was leaving, he asked me why my ID was so old. Filling him in, I briefly told him everything, about coming back from the UK and wanting to lead the establishment of the Turkish game sector. He asked if I were a computer engineer, and if so, perhaps I could look at their PCs as they were running very slowly. He asked if I could help speed up the process. I replied, 'I am not an engineer as such, but I know quite a bit about computers. I will come back the following week, and take a look, I promise.' He looked at me almost to say, 'Yeah, I've heard that before. I don't think we'll see you again.'

Finally, I received my beloved ID, and completed the company setup and registration!

True to my word, I did go back to the ID registration office the following week and checked the PCs. All of them were clogged up with a lot of unused data and programs, and were running low on disk space. Anyway, I did a little bit of maintenance, and cleaning, which seemed to help only marginally, as the machines were quite old. Afterwards, we chatted with the manager for a while and had some Turkish coffee. Gratefully he gave me his blessing and good wishes, and then I left.

Highlights of My Work and Achievements in Turkey

In the early days, we started with just two programmers and gradually built a small but incredibly talented and capable team. Fantastically, so many university students were coming to meet me, wanting to be part of our team to develop their skills. In addition to this, quite a few young developers would come with game demos, some even with finished games. It felt as if everyone had been waiting for someone like me.

Intel Actor Technology Demo 2, 2002

Towards the second half of 2001, Will Cowling and Engin Cilasun were working on the Actor Game Engine, and developing the second Intel Pentium 4 2.2 technology demo. We were adding new features and functionality to the engine, as well as making it even more impressive by trying some more new and fancy stuff.

Webcams were very new and primitive at the time, but I saw it as an opportunity to try something different. In our engine you could interact with the backgrounds, and all the objects at will using the mouse controller. But I thought it would be great if we could manage to use our hand as the controller to pick, move and throw objects around. At that time, Engin was experimenting with edge detection and shape recognition for fancy collision stuff. He was really into visual computing and as a result, I always asked him to try out new things.

First, I asked him to have a go at detecting hand movement via the webcam to see if we could interact with the scene with our hands. He loved the idea, and tried a few things, but the webcam resolution and feedback were not quite up to the task. All in all, it was just too slow, and made it difficult to detect and track hand movement.

Since I would never give up on a good idea, I kept thinking about different ways to do it. The next day I brought to the office three of Sila's fabric hairbands, red, blue and green. Then, I asked Engin if he could put one on his finger, and instead of detecting the movement of the whole hand perhaps he could just detect and track the colour on the finger. After some coding and experimenting, Engin said the idea was brilliant, as it worked quite well. Together we did some more tweaking and it did exactly what I wanted. In fact, we could pick up, hold and throw objects around at will. It felt really nice doing all this fancy stuff using our hands. We did it so that you could open and close your fingers to either push or hold the object.

The pace of development in technology and hardware is mind-boggling. Nowadays, you can detect anything even with mobile phone cams. Currently, there are technologies based on colour detection for motion-capture and amazingly fast and efficient face detection and recognition even in crowded places…

Perhaps my only regret about returning to Turkey in 2000 is the fact that I couldn't do my fancy interactive movie project. Even now, I still haven't seen anything like what I had intended to create then. Maybe next time?

As it happens, I received a message from Will Cowling in late 2019. He now works at the Sony Europe PlayStation, London offices on special projects. What's more, Will told me that they were working on interactive film technology. Their first project using it was 'Erica', which was about to be released on PS4. In addition, he fondly remembered our Actor engine, and how I had wanted to produce an interactive movie some twenty years earlier. Also, he said that he had the Actor engine up and running, and it still looked quite impressive.

Although I was sad about not being able to realise my ambition to create an interactive movie back in 1999, it was nice to see that the idea was still valid, even more so now that Sony was working on a similar idea with a dedicated team.

Intel Actor Technology Demo 2 for Pentium 4 2.2Ghz

Dual Blades, The First Console Game From Turkey, 2002

A computer science student, Galip Kartoglu came to me with a very nice fighting game that he had developed for PC. The game was called 'Slashers'. I could see instantly that he was exceptionally talented. Amazingly, it was a very playable game with lots of fancy moves, original characters, and great graphics. Nevertheless, there wasn't much hope of making any money on the PC version as game piracy in Turkey was well over 90%. So, I suggested to Galip that we should develop the game for Nintendo Game Boy Advance (GBA). Well, he was chuffed about the fact that his game was going to be on the GBA console. Also, we changed the name to Dual Blades. Plus, I managed to sign a deal with an American publisher, Metro3D to market the game globally.

Unfortunately, development licences were not being granted to Turkey at the time by either Nintendo or Sony, but due to my past relationship and connection with Nintendo, I was granted special permission with my Vivid Image company label. Anyway, we received a development kit from Metro 3D and Galip did a great job. All in all, we finished development in about six months or so. Then, Metro 3D published it in 2002 in the US and Japan - a real milestone as this was officially the first professional game to be published globally out of Turkey. It received great reviews, but unfortunately Metro 3D couldn't provide enough marketing and promotional support.

Interestingly, years later, Galip released an updated version on mobile and Steam under the original title Slashers as an independent developer.

Online Football Manager, 2003

Another exceptionally talented student that came to me early on was Ozgur Soner. Basically, he was studying computer science at ITU, and had started programming at an
early age. Also, he did it all on a Spectrum too just like I had many moons ago. Therefore, he had a special respect and admiration for me as a Spectrum lover. During that period, he had developed a small role-playing game (RPG) game and was also working on an online football management game. For over a decade I worked with Ozgur up until I left the company in 2013. Truly, he is a very talented and reliable programmer with a wide range of skills. We worked very well together because we had a similar synergy to that which I had with Raff Cecco.

In 2003, I was also contracted by Turkcell, the biggest GSM operator in Turkey, as their game consultant. My main role was helping and guiding them with their efforts in mobile gaming. At that point, Java telephones were just coming out. Mainly, I was exploring what games and apps we could develop for the ever-growing mobile market. Remember we are talking seventeen years ago! Who would have guessed then that the mobile game sector would command half the revenue of the entire industry in 2020? Obviously, we were on the right track.

After some reflection, I thought simple multi-player games would be great on mobile (casual games, as they are known today) as people could have a quick play while out and about. Groundbreaking really when you think that Ozgur and I even developed multi-player backgammon and battleships games back in 2003! Back in the day, we were getting into online gaming, and I could see the importance of it. Noticing that South Korea was leading the field, I thought I should develop online games with my team too. We were looking at developing simple mobile games as well as an ambitious MMORPG (massively multiplayer online role-playing game).

Eventually, we released online Football Manager with Mynet, the biggest news portal and tabletop games publisher of the time. Fabulously, it was a huge success and we had hundreds of thousands of gamers. As you may know, Football is a big craze in Turkey like in many other countries. On that basis, we also did a mobile version.

An important landmark in the Turkish game development, we released the world's first online football management game at the end of 2003. To put this into context, it was well before the famous Championship Manager going online!

Turkcell Years 2003-2004

Turkcell, the biggest GSM operator, was very aggressive and ambitious. With a visionary and innovative team of people, I felt I could make a great contribution to their efforts. They really valued my input and welcomed my ideas. As is the case with big corporations, for one reason or another, many great ideas never get turned into products. Sometimes it is near impossible to create collaboration between big companies, and many sound projects never even make the starting line.

One example was this great card game idea I had at the time. Collectable cards were so popular. Turkcell had an exceptionally good marketing team and a dedicated service just for the young, which was simply called Young Turkcell. Also, they had millions of subscribers and were selling millions of scratch cards for pay-as-you-go customers. However, people were just throwing the cards away after using the codes. What a waste I thought, as we could turn them into collectable cards, and make a great card game.

The idea was that we used the star signs as the basis for the cards. Everybody had a star sign, young and old. With rising/descending, female/male, plus adding four elements (earth, air, fire and water), we could simply create so many different and interesting characters. Our graphics guys designed beautiful cards, all with many different attributes and characteristics including weapons and powers.

In addition, we would be able to get the cards promoted by big food brands such as Doritos. In fact, Turkcell was already working very closely with many major brands for cross promotions. Everybody loved the idea including the top management. My team and I spent ages in meetings and planning, but for whatever reason this project never materialised.

In fact, I had another remarkably simple idea that could have been the first of its kind in the world. SMS was becoming immensely popular and SMS dispatch and server capacities were quite adequate too. Therefore, I devised an SMS version of Bingo where one million people could play Bingo live on TV. The idea was to send people their bingo cards via SMS (25 random numbers). Then they could purchase up to five cards each. Just after the countdown for the New Year, the game would be hosted and broadcast live on a popular TV channel. Played by millions and watched by many millions more. Again, everybody loved the idea and Turkcell really wanted to do it. A three-bedroom flat was the big prize to be won!

It was back in 2003 and quite revolutionary. Most people thought it was technically impossible to allow one million people to play live Bingo on national TV as it would be impossible to send that many SMS messages. With Ozgur, we simulated the game in advance and put it on a server. On the night we would simply playback the results we had already created, but in real-time on TV.

We had several meetings with ATV one of the biggest TV channels, but in the end Turkcell and ATV couldn't agree on the commercial terms.

As I am writing these lines, I feel sad about it. Such a shame really, both ideas are still viable and even more doable today. Those who may be interested in pursuing the ideas are welcome to go for it. I wouldn't mind at all; it would only make me happy.

Billiards Magic With Semih Sayginer, 2004

Just as I did in the UK, I was constantly trying to come up with good
ideas that would create an impact.
But now I was putting more empha-

sis on online gaming. To add value to our creations, I was also trying to engage local celebrities, and sports personalities, who would also help with marketing and PR activities.

Although never being good at it myself, I always loved watching snooker, a brilliant game of natural talent and skills. My favourites were Alex Higgins and Jimmy White. Years before, Archer Maclean had developed a great snooker game with Jimmy White, published by Virgin Interactive.

I thought I could do something similar in Turkey with billiards, which is immensely popular. Through one of his friends, I convinced Semih Sayginer, a three times World Billiards champion, and such a naturally gifted player to come on-board. In fact, Semih was very similar to Higgins and White. Anyway, he worked with us very closely, and together we created a great online multiplayer billiards game in about eight months.

Again, we published it on Mynet portal in 2004. It was an instant hit, reaching hundreds of thousands of gamers in just a few weeks. Everybody loved the game, and it became so popular with thousands of people who had never even played computer games before. Because we were effectively creating the game sector in Turkey, anything I produced was a first, and thus attracting a lot of attention and praise from all quarters.

A couple of shots from an early demo of Billiards Magic

The Istanbul Game, Turkey's First MMORPG, 2004

Having built up quite a bit of confidence from the success of two online sports games, I thought perhaps I could start developing a big online game. Maybe even a fully blown massively multiplayer online game with RPG (role playing) elements, played by thousands online and concurrently? What better than having the game set in historical Istanbul too? My gut feeling was that Turkish gamers would love it as it would be in Turkish, with local motifs, traditional characters, and features. Surely, everyone else would be equally impressed too and we would get lots of attention and coverage across the country?

My company Sobee was almost into its fourth year and with only a team of six or seven people. Simply put, embarking on a MMORPG game was quite an undertaking. To start such a massive project with such a tiny team was extremely ambitious and perhaps a bit crazy too, but I always enjoy a bit of a challenge.

At the time, World of Warcraft had just been released, a game developed by over 120 people. Also, South Korean developers were doing quite a few MMO games too. Putting Turkey amongst the early developers and publishers of MMO games would be quite an achievement I thought.

My small team was also trying to enhance the capabilities of the Actor engine too and bring it up to date with the current hardware. Furthermore, doing an MMO game meant we also had to develop server-side stuff too. In reality, it's almost like developing two games at once. Nevertheless, we started the development of Istanbul in earnest in 2004, with a tremendous feeling of excitement and self-belief.

Ultimately, my desire was to base the game on old Istanbul, and one of our team members brought in an old map of the historical quarters of Eminonu. The map was incredibly detailed and had many landmark buildings, including Sirkeci Station (the train station that was home to the Orient Express), Grand Bazaar, Topkapi Palace and Ayasofia amongst others.

The map was based on old Istanbul from the 1950s, which was perfect. Old Istanbul was much prettier and less built up. Since we were going to model the whole area one to one and use the actual textures from photos, our game could also serve as a reference point to the old city.

When I officially announced the project and shared some early concept art and 3D models, the reaction was just tremendous. The level of interest and curiosity was unbelievable, to such an extent that I was constantly giving interviews to magazines, and newspapers. In addition, I also had lots of TV appearances on all the major TV channels. All in all, we created a massive buzz. After all, we were working on Turkey's biggest and first ever MMORPG game! Also, it was completely in Turkish and featuring the beautiful city of Istanbul. What's more, the gamers were also extremely excited about the prospect of finally playing a big game developed by the Turks and fully in Turkish.

All the interest and excitement in the Istanbul game also raised expectations, which made our job even tougher. But somehow, we pulled out all the stops and managed to release the Beta version in December 2006. To be honest, it was a bit earlier than I would have liked. This date is accepted as the birth of the game and has been celebrated by the diehard gamers every year, ever since. Unfortunately, I had to leave the company and the game behind in 2013, and it just did not get enough support from Telekom. Despite all the problems and the lack of support, thanks to the undying love of the gamers, the game is still active, and will be celebrating its 14th anniversary in 2020 - one of only a handful of games to have lived and remained active in its teens.

Every day I still get many messages from Istanbul gamers, begging me to either rescue the existing game or create an all-new version developed from scratch. I must say, it's so tempting!

Looking back, there have been many memorable events that took place in the game over the years. The world's first ever real-time virtual in-game protest is definitely worth sharing.

Actual screenshots from the Istanbul MMORPG, 2004

Discovery Chanel Documentary on Istanbul MMORPG by Guven Catak, 2011

Wonderful Istanbul Game Music by Emre Yucelen

Real-Time Virtual Protest by Gamers

The MMORPG gamers amongst you will know that there are different races of characters to choose from in such games. We had three in ours: warriors, healers and magicians.

For such games, it is crucial to have a fine balance between the different races. This is to ensure that all gamers equally enjoy the game, as this is one of the hardest things to get right in MMORPGs.

As it happens, we had made a small mistake in our code, and the magicians had a slight advantage over the others. As a result, the warriors and healers were complaining about the apparent and unfair advantage of the magicians. After all, the magicians already had special ability to do fancy stuff from afar. And on top of that, we had inadvertently given them extra power rendering them almost unbeatable. This was the claim, but my team kept dismissing it, saying that they checked the code and couldn't detect any errors.

But I have always sided with my gamers, as they were our bread and butter, and the main reason for making games. Therefore, I asked the team to go into the office with me and work on the problem. And lo and behold, after spending a good few hours, the team found the problem. After all that, it turned out the players were absolutely right in complaining and their claims were completely justified. Accordingly, we fixed the problem, and fully tested everything. In case of any possible problems over that weekend, I had told the team to update the servers early Monday morning when we would be back to work.

As usual, I turned up to work on Monday at around 9:30, but only to see the whole team waiting for me in a panic. They told me that now the magicians were complaining about the changes we had made. In fact, they had organised a massive protest inside the actual game! Unbelievable, what I witnessed was out of this world, I had never seen or heard of anything like it before.

The change we made in the code was justified but resulted in the slight reduction of magician's powers. As a result, they decided to organise a big protest rally against us. What is even more flabbergasting was that they were to hold it inside the game! Imagine thousands of gamers connected to the game from various parts of the country, all at the same and in real-time. And marching in the game and protesting against us!

For good measure and better impact, they had even taken off their clothes, remaining in just their underwear! In fact, they had set a proper route for the rally with a start and finish, just like in real life. The game was based on a real place and they used all the landmarks and streets for the actual route. It was unbeliev-

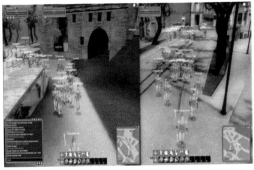

Thousands marching in real-time in Istanbul MMORPG

able! It was quite remarkable and a brilliant example to clearly demonstrate the absolute power and importance of games in so many different aspects.

Afterwards, it took me ages to convince the magicians to accept that the changes were fair and necessary!

I Can Football, 2007 (World's First 11 vs 11 Soccer Game)

Albeit with many difficulties, we had achieved a massive milestone with the Istanbul game, and showed what can be done with local talent. Now into my sixth year after returning to Turkey, there were already other developers coming through too. One of the earlier ones showing signs of great things to come was Teleworld (Mount & Blade fame).

In hindsight, I was right about the potential of Turkey's gaming talent, and it felt fantastic to play a leading role in the early years. What's next, I thought? Now armed with all the knowledge and experience we had gained from the Istanbul game, I had to attempt something even more impressive.

Soccer is widely recognised as the most popular game in the world by far. Although, there were already two big games on the market, namely FIFA and PES, neither did full multiplayer. By that, I mean up to 11 vs 11, where you have every gamer controlling one player/position, including the goalkeeper, just like the real thing.

Now that would be impressive if I could pull it off. When I first suggested it to my team, they were really shocked by the magnitude of the project. As ever, it didn't take me long to convince them. In fact, after I shared with them what I had in mind, and discussed some ideas, they couldn't wait to get going!

By now, my son Nej was already living in Istanbul and working at Sobee making design contributions to our games. He is particularly good with ideas and creating technical documents very quickly. Therefore, Nej and I worked together to create the general framework, the controls, the game mechanics and so on. Unfortunately, I made a big mistake of allowing the team to write a new dedicated engine for the footie game, I Can Football. Admittedly, our Actor 3D was getting on a bit, and was overly complicated for the soccer game. Looking back in hindsight, I wish we had used a third-party engine and concentrated all our limited resources on the actual game development. Had we followed that route, we could have finished the game quicker and possibly achieved better results far easier.

While supporting the Istanbul game, I now also had another big online game project under development. We were making great progress and I could see that it was a viable idea. Everyone could see that it would work, and the gamers would love it. To be honest, I can't even remember the Internet speed back in the day, it was 2007, but it wasn't very fast for sure. The game looked great technically, the team did a great job with network programming and all the optimisation needed. We could have thousands of football matches on each server concurrently. There were many features such as waiting rooms, global and private chat rooms, in-game chat, and full 3D with multiple camera angles.

After some discussions, I managed to sign a deal with Vestel, a consumer electronics giant, and part of the Zorlu Group. Vestel manufactured TVs even for some of the big European and Japanese brands. This meant the collaboration was perfect for the game. We did the first launch towards the end of 2008 at a very nice venue, with all the major sports journalists in attendance. As a matter of fact, our launch and promotional events were on a par with those I used to see when I was attending shows in the UK and America!

Before signing the game to Vestel, I also had some preliminary discussions with Codemasters too. But they didn't quite like it. Upon reflection, I think we shared the game at such an early stage that they couldn't appreciate the potential. Who knows how things could have turned out had they published it?

Anecdotes From Istanbul and I Can Football Games
Game Masters

In massively multiplayer online (MMO) games, the community management is very crucial for maintaining and attracting the continued interest of tens of thousands every day. This is one of the most important subjects even in mobile games with tens of millions of gamers.

Without doubt, gamers are the most impatient and the fastest consumers of all. They can play nonstop and finish games in no time at all. In addition to this, some gamers can start demanding new levels and updates only a few weeks after a game's release. What's more, since there are so many games to choose from, it makes the gamer an even harder customer to retain and please.

As a result, designing games has become even more important. You need elements and features such as regular missions or tournaments to keep the gamer engagement and interests alive.

On the whole, I have always sided with my gamers and even fought my development team many a time to accommodate player demands and wishes. After all, we make games for them and their continued happiness and satisfaction, which in turn, keep our games going and generating revenue too. It is no different to other service industries in some respects. A good restaurant will have lots of returning customers if it provides both very good food and also excellent service.

Making the gamer really own and feel a part of the game is paramount for its longevity and success. Thus, I always asked my gamers for ideas and suggestions for improvements in our games. Most of the ideas they suggested would have already been thought of or planned by us, but I always made sure the gamers were credited for some features. That pleased them no end and made them part of the game. They owned, supported and at times defended our games even more than we did.

GM Dida

Since I hardly play games, I never spent too much time in our games. However, I used to go in and spend time observing the behaviour and enjoyment levels of our gamers. As a matter of fact, I used GM Dida as my nickname and pretended to be one of the Game Masters (GM), but none of the gamers knew that it was really me. In no time at all, I became the most popular GM of the whole bunch. In fact, we had three or four official GMs employed by us and the rest of the GMs were volunteers, chosen from the thousands of gamers who applied for the posts. Incredibly, at one point, being a voluntary GM in our Istanbul game was the most sought-after career in the whole of Turkey!

Some days we would get hundreds of applications and it was so difficult to sift through it all and make the right choice. It was absolutely amazing the way that some applicants would beg me to give them the GM position. Of course, when I say me, I actually mean my secret identity as GM Dida. In order to keep the demands made to me at a minimum, I would remind them that I was not a top-ranking GM, and as such had no authority to make decisions. To avoid disappointing them completely, I would always add, 'Of course, I could recommend the right candidate'. The virtual world is absolutely amazing, as behind different nicknames and masks we can all play different roles and pretend to be someone else. The gaming environment provides the perfect arena to execute our hidden abilities and release our inner selves. There's no limit to what or who we can be while roleplaying...

By and large, the main GMs were generally the bad cops. Not necessarily by conscious decision, but it was usually natural human instinct. People seemed to enjoy having the power of authority and would exercise it at every opportunity, as if to show who the boss was. Mostly they would punish gamers for bad behaviour, such as swearing or attempting to cheat. Generally, they would be silenced, so they couldn't communicate in game or they would be banned from the game for a period. Of course, the GMs were mainly carrying out their duties to maintain law and order as it were, but at times they did overreact.

All the suspended and banned gamers would come to me, the GM Dida, begging to be let back into the game 'on parole' and reinstated. As usual, I would say I had no authority, but would ask the other GMs to consider their parole. Provided, of course, that they apologised and changed their behaviour and more importantly promised never to misbehave again. Accordingly, I would note and track the behaviour of these gamers. If they seemed to comply with my demands and I could see enough improvement in their behaviour and attitude, then I would ask my GMs to lift the bans!

This simple, but carefully orchestrated and executed relationship with my gamers, made me the most popular GM. In a nutshell, I was the good cop. As a result, they would always look forward to seeing me. Also, they would share with me their problems with our other GMs, suggesting ideas and asking me to pass on their complaints and other messages to the real me too! In return, I would always bring messages from the real me and pass it onto the gamers, but always keeping my true identity hidden. Frequently, I would send them my best wishes and especially ask for their support and good behaviour. In fact, the real me would always finish the message with, 'I am asking for good behaviour for your own sake, it is your game and for your enjoyment. I don't even play games!'

It was so wonderful to witness and experience the reactions from the gamers. A simple hello or thank you message from the real me for their continued support and good behaviour would make them so happy. Believe me when I say that I could almost feel their happiness and excitement from the warmth of their replies.

They had no idea that GM Dida was me, but I connected with them through it. After writing this book they all now know of course! On reflection, I am so glad that I reached so many gamers, which have turned into lifelong connections. So much so that I keep getting messages from them every day. Most of the gamers started when they were around eight or nine years old and some fourteen years ago. Nowadays, quite a number of them are at university studying computer science and looking to make games themselves. During my university visits for game development talks I seem to meet quite a few of my gamers. In fact, I meet many gamers everywhere, as they are from all walks of life. In fact, some of my gamers are successful developers themselves making their own games.

Honestly, I cannot tell you how wonderfully touching and gratifying this is. It gives me so much hope, energy, and fulfilment.

GM Dida is in The Army!

Since becoming a part of the Telekom Group in 2009, I was busier than ever before. There were so many projects to manage, continually running around and not being able to spend time in our games. As a result, I had been absent from both the Istanbul and I Can Football games for a considerable time. The gamers were getting very upset not seeing their favourite GM Dida for weeks and wondering if something bad had happened. They kept asking after me, everyday hundreds of gamers would want to know my whereabouts.

Our GMs would pass me the gamers' messages saying hello and showing concern about my absence. It went on for weeks like this and our GMs were having difficulty convincing the gamers with simple answers such as 'he's busy with testing, he's doing this, that and the other'. In the end, our GMs begged me to either spend a little time in the game or provide a more convincing explanation for my absence. It really had become a big issue!

Realising that it would be a few more weeks before I could go in the games and mingle with the gamers, I came up with a simple solution. I simply suggested to my GMs that they post a message in the game forums: 'Important Announcement – GM Dida is in the Army to complete his military service.' Well the reaction was incredible! All the gamers were shocked but found the reason for my absence perfectly reasonable and acceptable.

It was amazing to witness their reactions and read their lovely, heart-warming messages of good wishes. 'Good luck to him! Hope he completes it without any trouble! Let's hope he won't be sent to the borders to fight the terrorists. God speed and see you soon GM Dida…'

Goalkeeping in I Can Football

Being the world's first ever 11 vs. 11 online soccer game, we captured the interest of hundreds of thousands of gamers in no time. Football is the most popular game in Turkey as it is in many other countries.

Goalkeeping is a difficult thing in such a game as the goalkeeper can easily mess the game up. Instead of kicking the ball into play, they can simply leave their goal, take the ball and try and score a goal themselves!

To avoid the risk of this happening, I decided to have the goalkeeper as a computer player for a while. This way we could have decent goalkeepers and adjust their skill levels to balance scoring and match results between teams.

The gamers just loved the game. It was just like the real thing. We had one gamer controlling each of the 11 players and playing only one position. Initially, everyone would be where the ball was, chasing after the ball, keeping the ball and never passing it with everyone wanting to score! This was classic and natural juvenile behaviour, which we all did as kids. Gradually, the gamers educated each other. 'C'mon, where are you going, stay back! For God's sake, just pass the ball. I promise I will pass it back and help you score. C'mon people, everyone stay in their positions.'

It was great to see and experience the whole process. As the gamers improved, so did the team play. We would soon start seeing wonderful matches between teams. I love football, and to observe and suggest improvements, I did play quite a bit in the early days. We used to have Development vs. Gamer team matches. It was so nice to see how quickly the gamers would pick up and become so proficient at the game. Then, they would start destroying our Development teams to embarrassing levels!

After several months, I could see that the gamers were really enjoying the game and playing properly. Plus, they were helping the newcomers as well.

Once I was happy with the progress of the game and the gamers, I felt it was time to include the Player Goalkeeper. Prior to one of our Development vs. Gamer matches, I asked my team to put me in goal! As usual, the match started but this time with me in goal. Nobody noticed as I had turned my player name off (all gamers could easily turn their own name tags on and off too). So, I appeared to be just like a computer goalkeeper, as I started with no name. But I kept doing silly things, such as instead of kicking the ball into play, I would start dribbling my way towards the opponent's goal!

The reaction was just out of this world. No one was playing the normal game, as they were all watching my antics and trying to take the ball away from me. They were chatting away and asking questions like mad at the same time; 'What the hell is going on? What happened to the goalkeeper? Why is he behaving so silly?'

Suddenly, I switched my nametag on. Now they could see GM Dida on the goalkeeper. Honestly, I will never ever forget their reaction, it was simply priceless; 'Oh my God, it's GM Dida in goal. They have opened up the goal for manual control by gamers. Please Dida, I am begging you, let me have a go. Just put me in goal for 10 seconds!'

Afterwards, to become a goalkeeper in I Can Football was probably the most important thing at the time amongst the gamers. So much so that I was even offered bribes to let them go in goal, just for a bit!

As I always say, the power, importance and the depth of games still isn't quite realised as a whole in societies. Some of the incidents, activities, behaviours, and interactions could be the subject for many PhD theses. Eventually, we did open the goal to everyone and just as I had guessed, initially no one stayed there and instead they ran around the field just for the fun of it. But in time, it did get much better and mostly by gamers' own initiative and intuition. In fact, games can be great tools and vehicles for education and behavioural change.

Generally, we ensured that we had computer-controlled goalkeepers in important matches, such as the ones broadcast on NTV Spor TV Channel during the World Cup in 2010. Otherwise, we left it to the gamers to switch it on and off as they pleased.

First Encounter With Vestel, 2004

In case you're wondering how I convinced Vestel and got them into the game, here's a brief background. In my first years back in Turkey, I was receiving a lot of press attention and coverage. As a result, many influential, and respected technology experts and business people approached me too. Obviously, wanting to find out what I was all about and possibly see if they could get a piece of the action. One of them was Cengiz Ultav, a board member of Vestel.

Vestel had just started a defence company to manufacture unmanned space vehicles, in 2004. Cengiz knew that we could produce 3D visual simulations, which they would need for their defence work. And he also knew about my attempts to develop a big game for the Turkish Army, similar to America's Army. For this reason, Cengiz asked me to help them with their defence project. I thought it was a perfect project to develop and so I said yes to Cengiz. Accordingly, I assembled a small and dedicated team to do the R&D work for a full 3D map of Turkey.

All the top programmers wanted to work with me, so it wasn't difficult to find good people. My good friend Erdal Yilmaz (then a Major in the Turkish Airforce with a PhD in visual computing!) was the main man behind the R&D. We got to know each other in the first year of my return to Turkey. He later retired from the Air Force and joined my team. In fact, much later he headed my Ankara office doing special projects and mostly mobile games, in 2010! So, I could see then that mobile gaming was coming, and it was going to become big. In actual fact, I had already seen the signs for mobile gaming back in 2003.

We called the project Kanava after Erdal suggested it (meaning map/ mapping, a term used by the Turkish Air Force). In a relatively short time, we managed to map all of Turkey using satellite images and a digital elevation map. We had another great programmer who helped for a while, Rupen Meskitoglu.

Our achievement was quite impressive, as this was well before Google Earth. Added to that, it was amazingly fast, just like a game environment where you could fly around from one end of Turkey to the other.

While developing games I also tried to convince many officials, companies, and institutions about creating powerful products. The idea was that I could use the knowledge, experience, and performance capabilities from the gaming work. In truth, it wasn't too difficult to create many products, services, and simulations in many areas such as defence, health, education and earthquake. In fact, I really wanted to create an important earthquake simulation for training, rescue, public awareness and to gain lifesaving knowledge before, during and after earthquakes. In these times, it is actually quite sad that earthquakes are still the biggest threat in Turkey, and the region.

Of course, I also spent a lot of time and effort convincing the Turkish authorities to create game-based learning content and present it to millions of pupils online. To put it into context, I am talking about mid 2000s!

With that in mind, I was really sad to see that we still didn't have any decent online educational content to use during the Covid 19 lockdown!

Kabus 22, 2006

During those days, there were many talents knocking on my door, bringing to me their game ideas and projects. However, there were two incredibly talented brothers Yasin and Yakup who were like a small team. In many ways, they were just like the West Bros who developed Street Racer for me in the UK. Yasin was an exceptionally talented programmer, who had just started university doing computer science, and Yakup was a brilliant artist, a high school dropout. Just like the whiz kids in the early 80s of the UK gaming scene, most of them had left school to pursue a games career.

Basically, I decided to help them with their First-Person Shooter (FPS), a lovely looking famous Resident Evil influenced game. Very well coded with great visuals. Accordingly, I produced the game, and convinced Vestel to distribute it through their retail shops! The game was called Kabus 22 (Nightmare 22), and was received very well by the gamers, selling thousands of copies. Very impressive for Turkey.

Besides that, we even managed to license the game to a Russian publisher with English language support, and it was released in Poland and Russia. Even today I get many messages from the gamers asking for a follow up.

My Good Friend Jon Dean's Istanbul Visit, 2007

While working on I Can Football, we reconnected with my good friend Jon Dean. At the time, he was one of the Executive Producers at EA Sports. In due course, we exchanged a few emails where I also shared with him our achievements with the Istanbul game, and the world first I Can Football. Suitably intrigued, Jon decided to pay me a visit in Turkey!

Jon and I met in London, 2017

At first, we thought we could discuss the possibilities of working together again. Wouldn't that be wonderful, if nothing else it would be great to see each other and catch up. Actually, I also thought that EA could perhaps set up a development studio in Turkey. Clearly, Turkey was already promising real potential in terms of talent. Plus, the government had started providing funding incentives and tax breaks in technology centres.

In fact, Ubisoft did this better than any other publisher, having successfully operated development houses in many countries from Romania to India.

It was great to spend a couple of days with Jon in Istanbul. I introduced my small team to him. During his visit, I showed him all the work we had done, including, of course, I Can Football that we were working on. Truly, he was impressed with our achievements and the quality of my team.

Back in the UK, Jon and I had worked together on many projects many moons ago. So, in that respect, we both fancied the idea of doing a project together. The timing was perfect too as all major publishers in the West were also going online. With our online gaming knowledge, and experience, it made complete sense to work on an online project.

Their Tiger Woods Golf game was one of their most successful sports franchises. Jon suggested it would be great to develop an online version. Wow I thought, what a great project! It was right up our street and would be a perfect project to do. Thus, Jon was going to provide us with all the assets including the source code. How exciting for me, my team and the Turkish game sector as a whole. Doing such a major collaboration with a top publisher for a top game and all from Turkey.

My team were thrilled about the prospect, and so was I, maybe even more so. We had to go through some security checks. Jon told me that there were some formalities, which had to be carried out. He had already seen our offices, now some 100 square meters, and within the compounds of ITU Technology Centre with particularly good security measures.

A security expert from the UK visited us, and it turned out that he had played some of my old games (Last Ninja and First Samurai). He said, 'You are one of my heroes.' It really felt nice, as it always fills me with happiness to meet one of my gamers. In fact, I still meet people who had played my games many decades ago. It is so gratifying to have touched so many people with my work around the globe.

After the inspection, the security expert indicated that he was very happy with the security measures, and that he would send the EA management a very positive report.

Although we received the security clearance, after a while it became obvious that the EA lawyers had objections. They insisted that we couldn't guarantee the safe keeping of the source files in Turkey. Sadly, they advised that it was too risky for EA to sign! Such a bummer really, the lawyers put a stop to the whole thing. And with it destroyed our excitement and the chance of a great achievement at a global level!

Of course, Jon was also extremely disappointed, but unfortunately, there was nothing he could do about it.

Citroen C4 Robot Game, 2008

Citroen C4 Game
Trailer

Despite the EA blow, things were going very well. In a relatively short period of seven years and starting from scratch, I had managed to build a very capable development studio. Bearing in mind that we achieved it all in a country with no game sector yet, this was a massive success in everyone's eyes.

My team and I had been enormously proud of our work up to that point: Intel Actor Demo 2, Dual Blades, Football Manager, Billiards Magic, Istanbul MMORPG, 11 vs. 11 I Can Football, and Kabus 22. Not forgetting the mobile multiplayer Backgammon and Battleships games as early as 2003. With all of this in mind, our Sobee Studio was a name to be reckoned with. Everyone was talking about us, and everybody wanted to work with us. Plus, we were also influencing and inspiring lots of new developers.

There was a real buzz around us, it seemed like things could only get better.

One day, Cem Sermen, one of our lead programmers on I Can Football, told me that the General Manager of Citroen Turkey wanted to meet up. Basically, he wanted to discuss doing a promotional game. Citroen C4 Robot was very popular at the time, with many videos of the Robot doing break dancing and other fancy transformation animations.

He was very keen to have something incredibly special and eye catching. In response I told him that he had met the best man for the job. Also, I made it clear that I would not do a simple advergame (at the time major brands were using simple games for marketing, based on Adobe Flash), which was extremely popular in those days. Additionally, I also informed him that if he were to provide decent funding, then I would develop a great racing game. It would be in glorious 3D with a fun driving experience using both the C4 car and the robot.

Obviously, he was very keen and serious about it, so we agreed on the spot. Accordingly, I promised to create a great 3D racer, which could be used as a showcase product for Citroen Turkey and France too. Furthermore, other countries could also use it should they so wish.

To get the ball rolling, Yasin, Yakup, Nej and I put together some ideas. As ever, I wanted the racetrack to be set in Istanbul. And thus, we fully modelled the Bosphorus Bridge, and included the Marmaray. This undersea tunnel connecting the Asian and European parts which wasn't even built yet!

Well I can tell you that the team did a great job and the end product was really impressive. With a great and fun driving model, and fantastic graphics, it really looked the business. I even had the Robot race on skates both on the road, and on top of the roadside barriers. It was a lot of fun transforming between the car and the robot at will and driving around the wonderful track.

The Citroen CEO was thrilled! So was the French Director who came to Istanbul to see the demo. He couldn't believe our achievement. Within weeks of its release, it reached over 900 thousand gamers.

Unfortunately, this success was not to endure because of a change in leadership. It was such a shame what happened next; the Citroen CEO left the company soon after the release. Then, even worse, the new CEO dismissed the whole project as a gimmick and didn't want to take it any further! In life, vision is such an important asset to have and without it we are blind. What a blow it was, especially knowing that other Citroen subsidiaries asked for a localised version.

Still, it was a great product to have under our belt. Even tens of thousands played and loved the game outside of Turkey. Anyway, I had plenty of other things to do. Onwards and upwards, I thought.

The Sale of Sobee to Turk Telekom, 2009
Another Big Change Beckoning

We had been working within the ITU Technology Centre complex since 2004. Although there were other technology and software development companies, because of the popularity of our games, and the PR I was getting, it made me the centre of attention. Everybody was having coffee and a chat with me whenever possible.

To be honest, it's in my nature, and I always give people a lot of time, and share my insights. Also, I was using my popular status to encourage other companies to interact and create synergy with each other. That was the idea behind the Technology Centres where I was playing an ambassador role.

Most of the people working at the Centre were playing our games, especially Football Manager and Billiards Magic. They loved the billiards game and would organise tournaments amongst themselves. In addition, they were also playing with their friends and relatives across the country and with those in Germany too. Actually, I think online gaming is so powerful, as it really expands the interaction and socialising to a different level and scale. At the same time, it succeeds in removing physical boundaries as well as cultural, religious, and language barriers too.

There was a software development company, Innova, which had been recently purchased by Turk Telekom. Plus, I knew Aydin Ersoz, the CEO very well, and we often would have coffee and a chat. If I am not mistaken, a few years prior to this time, they had even considered investing in my company. One day while having coffee, Aydin asked me if I would like to meet up with the advisors to the Turk Telekom CEO, Paul Doany. Sure thing I said, as I had been thinking about collaboration with or at least getting investment from a big company. The timing was good. It was 2009 and things were really maturing in the Turkish gaming sector.

On balance, Telekom would be a perfect partner as they had over twenty million subscribers (fixed line and mobile combined), and they were also the main internet provider. Paul Doany had become the CEO after the recent privatisation. In a short time, he had already bought a couple of technology companies to expand the group's operations.

It was almost the end of 2008. Their advisors met me in my office. In due course, I gave them a full presentation of my work in the UK and in Turkey plus my future plans. Thankfully, they were impressed. Also, they told me that they would report to their CEO and would get back accordingly.

Only a couple days later, the advisors informed me that Paul Doany was extremely interested. Next, Paul asked his top management team to meet me for further discussions. Straight away we arranged another meeting with the advisors plus the VPs of Technology, Operations and Marketing.

There we all were in the meeting room, just as I was about to start my presentation. However, the advisors asked if I would be kind enough to wait. Apparently, Paul the CEO had decided to join the meeting at the last minute. With pleasure I said, even better. Surely, Paul hearing all about my work plans first-hand would be much more effective.

Eventually, Paul turned up after half an hour or so, ordered some drinks and I started with my presentation in English, as Paul didn't know any Turkish. Similarly, Paul had studied and lived in England for some time, so we had some common ground.

During my talk Paul was listening to me with real intent and care and making positive remarks along the way. He was clearly very impressed and praised me for my achievements in the UK. His presence in the meeting really pleased me, as I wasn't sure how well the VPs would understand or pass on the information. After I finished my presentation, he just asked me a few questions about my company and the team.

Next of all, we left the meeting room, and Paul asked for five minutes with his advisors. While they were chatting, I was also chatting with the VPs. Although they seemed to be impressed, I wasn't sure if they had sufficiently comprehended my work and plans.

Soon after though, Paul came back and asked if I could show him around the office and allow him to meet the team. By all means, I said with pleasure, and showed him our small office and our even smaller team! After seeing the size of the team, he was even more impressed with our achievements. After which he greeted and talked to each team member in turn. A very clever man indeed, as he put everyone at ease and showed genuine interest in what they were telling him.

We walked out of the office. Suddenly, Paul just turned to me and simply asked, 'Would you like your dreams to come true?' My simple and direct reply was, 'Who wouldn't?' After that he wrote his mobile number down and handed me his business card. Then Paul told me that he would call me in a few days, and then left.

'Gosh, that was quick, what just happened?' I thought to myself. Subsequently, I told the team that the meeting and the presentation had gone very well. Equally, that the CEO was impressed with our work and with the team. Moreover, I also added that the CEO would get back to me soon. Clearly, I could see the excitement in their eyes.

So many thoughts rushed through my mind; excitement, delight, selling and working for someone else, a big corporation, could I manage, wondering and worrying all at once. My multitasking brain at work... Let's see what happens, I thought.

As I stated before, as if I didn't have enough on my hands with the game projects, I was trying to do other useful applications too. Another such project I was creating was some 3D city modelling work with a big IT company. In fact, the projects were for a few major Istanbul municipalities, using Google Earth. Initially, we were doing all the 3D modelling with our 3D mapping technology Kanava. However, since then Google Earth had come out with better satellite images and bigger support. Therefore, why not use Google Earth, I thought, as it would make things easier. To me, it doesn't matter where the technology comes from; it is the content and the underlying functionality that matters most.

And we were generating really nice 3D city models with layers of information; historical buildings, landmarks, hotels, parks, planned new projects. Also, we were including every single building with simple, but accurate 3D representation. People could find their houses and plots of land, plus get all the relevant information such as poll tax, gas, water and electric bills. This was around 2008-2009.

It was a really comprehensive and useful application that could be continually developed and enhanced. Some mayors were very pleased with what we had done and were showing off their applications on TV. One of the Mayors even picked up an award in Europe for innovation.

And The Telekom CEO Calls

Back in 1985, I was waiting for my first important call from Tony Rainbird of Telecomsoft (British Telecom). And 24 years later, I was waiting for another important call, this time from Paul Doany of Turk Telekom. How interesting is that? Parallels between the two!

As promised, Paul called me in a couple days, and invited my wife and I to dinner. Paul was staying at the Kempinski Ciragan Palace, one of the best hotels in Istanbul, as he hadn't rented a place yet. We had a lovely meal there with him and his wife.

He was always very direct, and not one to waste time and mince his words. In fact, he made me an offer for Sobee on the spot, there and then, and said that he could close the deal very quickly. He also wanted me to continue working there but as an employee. The offer was within his executive power, and we could sign without getting the board involved.

However, it certainly wasn't a lot of money, considering my track record and achievements. But it was still a very good offer under the circumstances. More importantly, Sobee would be the first games company to be acquired in Turkey, and that was nothing to be sneezed at, I thought. Normally, I would never rush things, but I felt that if I dwelled on it too much then I would probably bottle out and not go ahead with it at all.

I thanked him for believing in me and making an offer so quickly. 'Obviously, it's not a lot of money considering my illustrious career', I added. And I continued by saying, 'Under the circumstances, and what Telecom could add to my efforts it was a good deal.'

To make the offer more attractive and compensate me for proposing less than the expected cash offer, I also suggested that he could offer me a lot more in the way of salary. Immediately, Paul said, 'Sure, not a problem with that at all, I can up the salary as per your request, but the cash offer is the limit.' While we were at it, I also confirmed that I would keep the company money in the bank and any funds which were due in the next 6 months from Government incentives. Again, without any hesitation Paul said it was fine.

And that was it, sold, done deal. After some twenty-five years on my own, I was about to start a professional career rather than being my own boss. Again, as Paul promised, we closed the deal in a couple of months, and Sobee became a Turk Telekom group company in March 2009.

By the way, Paul told me later why he had decided to come to my presentation at the last minute. He explained that he was already convinced with the advisors' report. Plus, he was worried that his management team may not see the potential and be as enthusiastic. To avoid the possible risk of this happening, he decided to attend the meeting himself. See the presentation and make the decision there and then. Otherwise, who knows, perhaps it could have dragged on much longer, and possibly the sale would never have happened. Clever man.

I signed over all the work we had done in Turkey but kept all my IPs I owned in the UK. We remained in our offices for a few months longer, but with my suggestion and encouragement Turk Telekom created a big office space at the campus. Eventually, it became Turk Telekom's R&D centre with Sobee and Innova occupying the offices along with the Telekom R&D team. The R&D team was headed by Enis Erkel, with whom we became good friends. All in all, we had created such a great synergy and had planned for so many wonderful projects in the future.

Sobee Studios in 2009. This is the core team who I did all my work with in Turkey

Screenshots from R&D and special simulation projects

Sobee Becomes a Big Player, 2009

With Paul Doany

Now with Turk Telekom behind me, I could only go forwards. The sky was the limit! Now, I could undertake even more ambitious projects as I had the CEO's full support. Also, Paul had made his full support clear to everyone, and instructed his top people to unequivocally support me too. Brilliantly, I was so welcomed by both the top and middle management. It seemed like all the thirty thousand plus employees were excited too. Everyone was talking about Sobee and I within in the Group.

Telekom was also benefiting from my popularity with the press and all the media attention. Truly, Sobee's acquisition was news everywhere and I had many interviews and TV appearances.

There was a computer exhibition called Compex, which was turning its attention more towards games. Now that I was part of Telekom, I signed an agreement with the organisers. As a result, Sobee became the main sponsor for the entire show, which now became GameX.

As the main sponsor and partner, we rented almost one third of the space. It was just so amazing, as Sobee was suddenly in the mainstream. Our stands were almost as impressive as those of Sony and Nintendo. We even built a small stadium as a stand for I Can Football and did a massive launch at the show. In addition, Telekom was one of the main sponsors for the major football teams Galatasaray, Fenerbahce and Besiktas. That meant that we had all the top players visiting our stand, and our gamers and visitors were just ecstatic. There had been nothing like it ever before! All in all, we were so thrilled and enormously proud too with the overwhelming attention and interest.

Even better we also had a big stand for our beloved Istanbul game. It was so crowded that no one could believe their eyes. It was lovely to meet our gamers; most of them were so incredibly young, only around ten years old. Some had come with their parents, and there were many girl gamers too, which was wonderful! In all sincerity, I was so pleased to see all these different people who I was touching and bringing together through my games.

What was absolutely fantastic was that they were happily mingling with each other, exchanging their experiences and battles in the game. Most of them were becoming friends for life and later some would even get married.

What touched me the most was the fact that our gamers were from all walks of life. Young and old, male and female, police, soldiers, and I even met several religious clerks at the show! Now, everyone could see the importance and power of the games with their own eyes. Something I had been talking about for years and, incidentally, still do.

Sobee is in The Premier League With Man United

What a great start we had had, and I tried my best to build on it, and forge ahead with plans. The following year, in 2010, we managed to sign a special deal with Manchester United to include them as an official team in I Can Football.

It was also the year of the World Cup. We managed to strike an incredibly special deal with NTV Spor, the biggest sports TV channel in Turkey. NTV Spor didn't have the live broadcasting licence for the World Cup, so instead we offered them a world first with our I Can Football game. Basically, the chance to broadcast our online live games fifteen minutes before the actual World Cup games. We would form two best teams out of tens of thousands of gamers, which would represent the World Cup matches played on the day.

Furthermore, we set up special servers at NTV's headquarters to broadcast all sixty I Can Football matches. Gaming was at its very best. Amazingly, the world's first 11 vs. 11 online footie game was broadcast live on national TV, which also was a first. Tremendously, the reaction of people was fantastic, as millions of people were watching our matches live on TV! Even the taxi drivers and the people I mingled with in Emirgan were talking about it. And remember that this was well before eSports became really big. I already had big plans for eSports myself. Only the following year, I would become the founding president of the World's first-ever Turkish Digital Games Federation!

For the I Can Football World Cup contest, we gave the player of the tournament an Audi 3. In fact, I personally presented the keys on a live program on NTV. What's more, Turk Telekom also won 'the best content' award in London's Communication Awards that year.

Incredibly, Sobee was fast becoming the darling of the group, and things were looking exceptionally good. Truly, I was really making good use of the power, position and the reach of Turk Telekom.

SuperCan, Turkey's First Kids' Hero & Marvel, 2011

When I first went back to Turkey from the UK for my army service in 1991, one thing had caught my eye. It was a TV game played via fixed line telephones in real-time. It was a simple kids game called Hugo, not Turkish, and I think it was probably licensed from Denmark. Nevertheless, it impressed me that some entrepreneur had the vision to bring Hugo to Turkey.

It was such a new thing, kids playing a game from home, using the dialling keys of the home phone. Also, it was watched by hundreds of thousands, maybe millions of people. From what I remember BBC was either just starting or about to start to do something similar, so Turkey was ahead of the game. Well done Turkey I thought to myself.

Alas, when I returned to Turkey at the end of 2000 for good, I still saw that Hugo was being played rather than a Turkish home-grown game. For God's sake, I thought, at least you could have created a local game after ten years! I cannot tell you how disappointed I was.

Immediately afterwards, I promised myself to create a kids' hero that would become a role model for kids in Turkey. In fact, I wanted to create something really popular and make games, comic books, informative and educational short animation films and so on.

But I had been so busy with other projects that my hero had to wait until after I joined Telekom. In fact, way back in 2001, soon after the major economic crisis, I had met an incredibly famous comic book artist, Salih Memecen, who is also from my hometown Ordu. Subsequently, we became good friends. He had a couple of lovely characters, Zeytin (Olive) and Limon (Lemon) with many published books. They were exceedingly popular and loved by kids. In fact, my

GameX Istanbul, 2011

daughter Sila loved those books too, so much so that she would always have one under her pillow before going to sleep.

At some point, I designed a lovely little TV game that involved cleaning the Bosphorus Straits. Using our Actor game engine, we created an early prototype, which looked very impressive. With a lovely 3D character and a speedboat whizzing around on the water, negotiating obstacles and waves. The artist Salih was

Early Demo, 2001

already working with one of the top TV channels ATV. So, it made sense to do the project with them, but for some silly reason we couldn't reach an agreement.

In short, they wanted the game for free, insisting that they wouldn't even share any advertising revenue, let alone paying for any of the development costs. That's why I thought it would be absolutely crazy to sign a deal with them! Mental!

Anyway, winding forward to 2010, with Telekom now backing me, I could create something special with a big impact - a project that would capture the imagination and the full attention of the wider public not just the gamer, as well as government officials and departments, educational institutions, parents and of course, millions of kids. As a matter of fact, I always believed in the importance of winning over kids because once you have them on your side then you also have their parents and siblings too.

In 2010, soon after joining the Telekom group, they were building a Kids Portal with lots of animations and other popular content. It looked like a perfect opportunity for me to get involved. Also, I noticed some content was from Marvel too. Straight away, I thought, 'Wow, that's impressive and interesting'.

In my mind, I wondered if there could be some sort of collaboration with Marvel. As always, I was aiming high.

Anyway, the team behind the Kids Portal were extremely excited to collaborate with Sobee. What's more it was Ismail Bayazit and Ozleyis Pamir who were responsible for the Portal. Together we had several very productive meetings. Even better they were delighted with my work and incredibly supportive of my future plans. Instantly, we decided to collaborate, and I shared with them my idea. Realising my vision, my plan was to create a kids' hero for Turkey. In return, they loved the idea and promised me full support.

As dates go, 23rd April is an important date in Turkey because it was on 23rd April 1920 that Ataturk opened the Parliament of the newly formed Turkish Republic. Ataturk, who spent almost all of his short life in battles and wars, declared the date of 23rd as a day of celebration for kids. With a great vision and message; 'Peace At Home, Peace In The World.' Such a powerful message and even more relevant today!

Well, back to the story, and Ismail and Ozleyis had a lovely animation film made in the States using Marvel's heroes. Turk Telekom used the film as part of the 23rd April Kids Celebrations. There was a lovely Turkish kid in the film who caught my eye, Can. Immediately I thought he would make a great kids' hero. There you have it, literally that's how the SuperCan character was born.

I told Ozleyis and Ismail that I was going to create a beautiful game for millions to play. In addition, I asked them if I could in anyway use Marvel characters in the game, in some capacity. Anything would do, they can be SuperCan's friends or make brief appearances here and there in cameo roles. Even just in a few cut scenes at the very least. In response, they said they would investigate it and discuss it with their American partners. Immediately, I started working on the game. The development team consisted of the brothers Yasin and Yakup, plus Nej and I. Basically the same team as we had for the Citroen C4 Robot game.

Appropriately, I decided that the first game would be about protecting the environment. And also, it would create awareness about the importance of recycling. It could be a perfect example to show the importance of games, entertaining and educating at the same time.

After long discussions and negotiations, we managed to convince Marvel to allow us to use their heroes in our game. Casting my mind back, I remember spending a couple of hours on the phone with the Marvel lawyer. Somehow, I managed to persuade him that we would do a great job with the game. Also, that I was a renowned developer and they could fully rely on my ability. In the end we included Spiderman, Ironman and Hulk in the game with lovely animations in cut scenes. In addition to that, we did all the graphics for the heroes in-house and managed to get Marvel's approval in no time at all.

What a scoop that was! In all honesty, I don't think anything like this had ever happened before or after in Turkey or anywhere else for that matter? Incredibly, Disney bought out Marvel only a week after we had signed the agreement! Subsequently, I met with the managing director of Disney Turkey, Sinan Ceylan, and I never forget what he told me. He said, 'I don't know how you pulled it off, but if you had waited for another week, no way could you have got that deal from Disney!'

Truly we did a great job with the game; gorgeous graphics, and lots of lovely levels with many game modes. Plus, as I had hoped, everybody loved the concept of preserving and saving the environment from the evil robots. What's more we were also teaching kids the importance of recycling via the game. In the end we reached millions of kids within a couple of months, and it was a huge success. Besides which it was so satisfying to receive many letters of praise, gratitude and congratulations from all quarters. They came from many walks of life, families, state departments, educational institutions, and many others. It was just as I had hoped for.

To top it all, we even brought Marvel's heroes to Turkey on a special invitation by SuperCan to take part the in the 23rd Children's Celebrations in Istanbul. It was unreal, how we welcomed the heroes at the Istanbul Ataturk Airport with SuperCan. Thousands of kids and their families came to join us, and it was so beautiful to see. Only Telekom could have pulled off such a big PR stunt, so my decision to join them was justified. If truth be told this was why I wanted their position and reach in my projects: for the betterment of society and the wider impact.

And next of all we took SuperCan and the Marvel heroes to the Asian side of Istanbul. We had a lovely cortege of open top busses with SuperCan and his famous hero guests, driving through the famous Bagdat Caddesi. The reaction, attention and interest was just out of this world. One of the policemen on duty told me that it was the biggest crowd he had ever seen in the fifteen years he had served in the area. There must have been more than fifteen thousand people there.

Everything was moving along as I had hoped and planned, and so many projects lined up for SuperCan. What a great start, which I could only build on. Immediately, I started working on the SuperCan 2 game plus on a series of educational two-minute short animations too.

In addition to that, I was exploring creating customisable online digital SuperCan magazines and, of course, discussing many merchandising deals with the likes of Carrefour, Migros and other major brands!

Everything seemed to be looking good for Sobee and me.

SuperCan welcoming the Super Heroes for the 23rd April Children's Day Celebrations

SuperCan Game 1 Trailer   SuperCan Game 2 Trailer   Major News on TV

Untimely Departure of CEO Paul Doany, 2011

Soon after the successful release of SuperCan and the addition of Manchester Untied to I Can Football, the sudden departure of Paul Doany was a real blow. Without doubt, Paul was fully behind my efforts, and his presence and vision was crucial. That was the only way of getting the necessary and important support from Telekom.

At the time, I was also getting the support from all the regional managers across the country. To promote gaming and our vision, I was visiting universities and giving talks. It was brilliant meeting thousands of students and sharing my knowledge and vision with them. All these activities also benefited Telekom, with everyone praising the company for supporting my important mission to help Turkey become an important player in the region.

Perhaps, all this attention towards me may have caused some resentment amongst other group company CEOs and some of the top management people too? Soon after Paul's departure, it was so easy to see the change in attitude. Nothing specific, but generally speaking, the decision-making process had slowed right down. Whenever I requested something, it would take ages for it to happen, or sometimes never materialise at all. Some of Paul's important people had also left, which additionally affected my position and the level of support I was getting.

Not long after Paul's departure, I had also heard on the grape vine that some of the board members were against the purchase of Sobee. But Paul had gone ahead with the deal and did it within his executive powers. Undoubtedly, this probably caused some resentment with other board members.

Suddenly, our bright future looked very cloudy. It was fast becoming obvious that life after Paul would never be the same for Sobee and I. In the post-Paul set up, we now had two CEOs: one for Turk Telekom and another for the Telekom Group. This also slowed the decision-making process.

As ever, I did my best to continue with my projects and plans for another year or so, but it was getting harder and harder.

For months we couldn't launch our I Can Football 2 game in the UK. Incredibly, Man United had given us an opportunity to launch the game at Old Trafford, fifteen minutes before a home game. Can you imagine that? An opportunity you couldn't even pay to get? My team and I were so excited about it, but for some reason the CEO kept cancelling the launch. Eventually after a few cancellations, I got an email from the Marketing Director of Man United simply saying, 'Sorry Mev, this is both unreasonable and unacceptable, if it doesn't happen at the next available home game then they can just forget about the whole thing."

Unfortunately, we never took the opportunity and that was that. The game was never launched, and it was just left to die. It was unbelievable, soul destroying really. It was downhill from then on and my eventual departure seemed inevitable!

Despite all the negative vibes, I still tried to keep things going. In fact, I even started working on an all-new MMOFPS (first person shooter instead of RPG – role playing game), as a follow up to the Istanbul game. This time we would expand the game's environment to include Anatolia, with its rich and diverse history and culture. In addition, SuperCan 2 was also under development.

As well as our Istanbul office, I also had an office and a small team in Ankara. Our office was situated at the ODTU Technology Park (Middle East Technical University, probably Turkey's best). My good friend Erdal Yilmaz was heading and running the Ankara office. It was in 2010 that we built a team in Ankara with Erdal with the aim of mainly concentrating on mobile games. At

Life Is A Game

the time, I could clearly see that the mobile sector would become huge. After all, I was involved in it way back in 2003.

Now we were making several SuperCan based mobile games. Additionally, we were creating some innovative and useful educational content, and projects with SuperCan. We even got approval and funding from a European R&D initiative on a couple of big projects we submitted with the Telekom R&D department headed by Enis Erkel.

Despite the negative atmosphere and uncertainty, I was going full throttle, with the hope that the Board and the CEOs would change their attitude towards Sobee and provide full support again.

Turkish Digital Games Federation, 2011

Another particularly important project I was working on was the establishment of the World's first Digital Games Federation. Despite a lot of time and effort, it still took me over one and half years to reach my goal. My good friend Erdem Celik (Google, Facebook) was my right-hand man on the project, and provided valuable help and support.

My objective was to make the Turkish gaming sector more professional and provide help and support to developers. The Federation would become an important bridge between the Government and the sector. Furthermore, it would encourage universities to start game design and coding courses, provide support for game based educational initiatives and projects and create public awareness of this rapidly growing and important sector. Lastly, it would entice big corporations and businesses to invest.

Of course, the main objective was to promote and support the emerging eSports, which I thought would be one of the biggest developments in gaming. As everyone now knows, eSports indeed has become a big thing, and continues to grow. Gaming events are now surpassing music festivals, and thousands of players and teams are competing for big prizes and awards. eSports is also providing all new career opportunities for the talented youth, becoming a successful gaming broadcaster on Twitch, or becoming a YouTuber, or an Influencer. And for exceptionally talented gamers there's the opportunity of becoming members of successful eSports teams.

Also, there is all the fame and fortune that comes for the successful gamers. We now have the Messis and Ronaldos of the eSports world.

With the Federation, I also wanted to create collaboration at an international level - the first objective being the formation of a confederation in Europe and then globally. Using my UK network and standing, I also hoped to bring two countries closer together via games. Equally, to work on social responsibility projects, where we could bring the schools of both countries together via eSports events and competitions. And I also wanted to encourage more female presence in gaming.

In support of developers, I even contacted my good friend Mike Gamble of Epic Games to provide special incentives and support with their Unreal Engine. It was great that he kindly came to Istanbul and attended the GameX exhibition to announce the collaboration.

As you can see, I had many projects in the pipeline during that period and the Federation was founded with these aspirations.

After I left Telekom, I asked Baris Ozistek of Marble Games to stand for the Presidential elections of 2013. He duly accepted and was elected as the new president, but for reasons still unknown to me, then the Minister of Youth and Sports didn't approve of his election. The result was that the Federation was left dormant for seven years. Eventually, the subsequent Minister of Youth and Sports established a new Federation in 2018.

Dropping Out of The Game...

It was becoming obvious that the Board wasn't going to change its attitude towards Sobee and me. Things really came to head for me, when I heard rumours that the Board had decided to merge Sobee with TTNET, a bigger company of the Group. Clearly, that meant killing Sobee!

The group CEO officially told me about the decision. But he kept trying to assure me that nothing would change much in practice. And as such, he wanted to convince me to stay on and continue to run things as before. Since I was already having difficulty running things, I thought I would have even more difficulty under TTNET.

For a good few weeks, I kept coming up with great ideas and projects to collaborate with TTNET instead of merging. But soon it became clear that they just wanted to go ahead with the merger and in reality, TTNET did not want to collaborate and were just stalling.

All the rumours and uncertainties were also creating unease amongst the team members. In addition, there are always those who would try to take advantage of this kind of situation and Sobee was no exception. Indeed, my right-hand man was plotting to leave with the top members of the company. Even worse, he even knew about the merger before I did.

This was all too much to bear, and I just wanted to leave as soon as possible. Thus, I officially left, after several months of fierce and sometimes, painful negotiations with Turk Telekom. Suddenly, I parted with my beloved Sobee, leaving all my games and gamers behind in May 2013. One of the saddest moments in my life…

Just When The Turkish Gaming was Ready to Skyrocket

What was really heart-breaking for me was the fact that my personal career was taking a beating while all seemed to be going so well for the Turkish gaming industry. After the sale of Sobee to Turk Telekom in 2009, a number of important international players were making serious moves towards Turkey. A lot of big companies were showing interest in the Turkish gaming market such as Zynga, Riot Games and PayPal.

I remember having many meetings with the representatives from all three, as the President of the Turkish Digital Games Federation. In fact, we were the first gaming company in Turkey to integrate the PayPal payment system in our MMO games.

Nicolo Laurent of Riot Games, then the VP of International Business and now the CEO, had a meeting with me not long before setting up an office in Istanbul. If I recall correctly Nicola actually offered me the job of running their Turkish office, but I kindly declined due to my existing position with Sobee. Eventually, Hasan Colakoglu was appointed to head the Istanbul office and I must say Hasan did a great job and is now the VP International (Europe and Emerging Markets).

Unfortunately, PayPal was forced to close down its operations in Turkey, but both Riot and Zynga are growing their business and presence in Turkey. Netmarble, Tencent and other major players are also investing and growing their interests in Turkey.

Game Over, May 2013...

Due to an unplanned and undesired interruption, my illustrious and long career abruptly came to an end! It was really painful, and left a massive void in my life, which I still haven't been able to fully recover from. Truly, it was a huge blow to my career and to the continued success of Sobee.

What broke my heart even more was the fact that it happened just when Turkish gaming was about to skyrocket. Telekom's untimely and unwarranted decision dropped itself, and me, right out of the game!

And so, after many decades, many teams and many great projects, my game development journey was finally over... It is a shame really, as I still had a lot of energy and game 'credits and lives' left in me.

Alas, it was 'Game Over' in my game of life!

Online Gaming Academy, 2013-2015

I am incredibly lucky to have enjoyed a long career spanning over thirty years, and two countries. Upon reflection it was a career with plenty of excitement, jubilation, and drama. However, my retirement really felt weird, and I didn't know how to deal with it. At first, I thought I would just try and have a well-deserved break. Rest a bit, spend more time with my family and friends, and just see how it all panned out. Plus, it wasn't as if I was desperate to get a job straight away because I had enough savings for the rest of my life. If I so desired, I could take it easy, and help young developers around me, just to keep busy and useful. Actually, this is something that I have always been doing and which I enjoy very much too. To me, giving is a beautiful thing to do and in fact, I find it very satisfying and fulfilling. Giving to others gives me strength and energy.

To be perfectly honest, starting a new company was certainly out of the question. Surely, that wouldn't be challenging or exciting enough. So far, I had done so many things, and perhaps achieved more than most people would in a lifetime. In that respect, I felt that I had nothing left to prove. I was just going through so many different thoughts. Obviously, it was a natural process of coping with the new situation.

After enjoying a bit of a break and taking it easy, but constantly thinking of ideas in the back of my mind, I thought I should set up a gaming academy. Since I always enjoyed helping the young, sharing my knowledge, experience and insights, it would be perfect. As always, I was thinking big, as it had to reach everybody across the country. Something on an exceptionally large scale, now that would be challenging and exciting.

With university visits I could see the potential, but I also wanted to reach out to the middle and high school kids. Surely, the earlier you catch and nurture talent the better. With a massive young population in Turkey, I could help tens of thousands. More importantly, I wanted to reach and discover talent in rural and deprived areas too. Even to go as far as the remote villages because God knows what gems there could be there to unearth. Surely, the technology was there to do it too. All I needed was some will, desire and a good team of people. It was right up my street; I was the right person to lead this great initiative.

An online gaming academy would allow me to achieve my objectives. Surely, many people and institutions would support me. Who wouldn't want to be a part of something like this and work with me? To cut a long story short, after many months of meticulous planning and preparation, I assembled a core team of great people. And in earnest, started discussions with a few major universities. The universities were extremely interested, but the slow progress was becoming so frustrating with all the bureaucracy. I had even shaken hands with the president of a university, who literally begged me not to have talks with any others. But sadly, he changed his mind at the last minute, after having waited for months!

Frankly, it was so annoying, and I had reached the point where I'd had enough of wasting my own time, and I wasn't going to waste anymore. Although it was truly soul-destroying, after all that effort I decided to give up on it. In the end, I was worried about taking the whole thing on my own shoulders and carrying the responsibility alone.

After careful consideration, I decided that I should give up trying to do something to fill the void that was created after leaving Telekom. Maybe it was high time that I had a break away from Turkey? Really tired and disappointed, it started to bring me down. At that time, my daughter Sila was already in England, doing her A levels and my son Nej seemed happy and content enough to be in Istanbul.

In the end, I decided to have a chat with Gulsun. After some deliberation, we both decided that it would do us good to get away from it all. Just leave it all behind and find a lovely place in Europe to live for a while. I could recharge my batteries, and return with newfound energy and enthusiasm, should I decide to do so.

Before leaving I wanted to at least see if I could rescue something from the efforts I had put into the formation of the Academy and set up a gaming and eSports agency. My plan for the academy was to train and teach young people how to produce actual games, rather than help them learn programming. Since I had founded the Digital Games Federation and could see the importance of eSports, I also wanted to have training for eSports. What I intended was the formation and running of eSports teams, training about how to become a good gamer, how to improve social media and broadcasting skills to become a better Twitch broadcaster, YouTuber and Influencer.

At that time, a few really competent people who wanted to help me and become a part of the academy, agreed to set up an agency with me. So, with all these other experienced people we formed the agency with equal shares and responsibilities.

Even though I was leaving Turkey, my son Nej would represent my stake, and work in the company as he could contribute to it too. Additionally, I would help them remotely, allowing them to benefit from my network, as well as arrange and set up meetings with important companies. It was the perfect solution: a digital world and a digital business which I could easily be part of remotely. Well, at least for a while anyway.

Leaving Turkey... Again, 2015

Although my gaming career was abruptly stopped, life goes on and the adventure of life continues. But where does all the time go?

Amazingly, thirty-six years had passed since leaving Turkey for the first time to move to the UK. That was way back in 1979! Yet now I was doing it again, but admittedly under completely different circumstances and conditions.

The first time going to the UK seemed to be a complete twist of fate, whereas this time it was my conscious decision. Nevertheless, some of the events leading up to the decision were out of my control. Plus, I wasn't certain about where we were heading.

First of all, we needed to rent our house, but however hard we tried we couldn't find anyone who wanted to rent it for months. Although it's on an immensely popular estate because of the British International School nearby and convenient for ex-pats, we had no luck. It seemed like everything was going against us. That's how most of us feel I guess, especially when we feel down on our luck.

In the end, I said to Gulsun, 'sod this, let's just go whether we let it or not, surely, we can let it somehow later, we don't have to be here.'

Gulsun is from Adana, a big city in Southern Turkey, where it's very warm generally and extremely hot in summer. With that in mind, she didn't want anywhere cold such as London, so Britain was off the radar. After a lot of exploring and comparing, Barcelona was the clear winner by a long way. Excitedly, we booked our one-way flight for the 5th May 2015, and rented a small flat via Airbnb for a month. We would be able to find a proper place while we were exploring the city.

As luck would have it, just one week before our departure we found a tenant for our house. As the saying goes, we must never lose hope, as things can't go wrong all the time. Even a broken clock gets the time right twice a day as the Turkish saying goes!

Perfect timing too, as our South African tenants moved in on the same day we left. Even better was that it was a company let and they would pay in USD, and the tax stoppage too. Excellent on all counts, as our Istanbul rent money would roughly cover the rent due in Barcelona. Plus, we had done our homework and checked all the living indexes of the potential cities. Overall, Barcelona's cost of living wasn't cheap by any standards, but it wasn't much higher than what we had experienced in Istanbul.

Zekeriyakoy house, Istanbul

And Now For Something Completely Different

There was quite a bit of excitement and apprehension in the air, as I was about to enter unknown territories and waters. Still, it felt good to get away from it all, and enjoy Barcelona. In fact, Gulsun had been there before with Sila, and loved it. And from the little I had read, it looked very promising indeed. It had wonderful food, wonderful weather, and wonderful architecture, in a word... wonderful.

So much to discover, enjoy and take in...

We let our house fully furnished, as such we only had to spend a few days to box our personal belongings and store it all away in the large loft space. Then, we just packed two small suitcases each, with some clothes and essential bits and pieces. Plus, a couple of kilograms of homemade red pepper paste, a must have ingredient for a Turkish person away from home. We wouldn't leave home without it! It's a bit like the Brits taking tins of baked beans and tea bags with them while going on holiday abroad! All done, we set off to start yet another journey! Without knowing what was waiting for us, we embarked upon our Spanish adventure!

Please remember that I was embarking on a new adventure soon after the massive disappointment of unwanted interruption to my successful career. Coupled with the subsequent failure to start the gaming academy after two years of intense effort. Overall, I moved to Barcelona with the hope of getting over my huge disappointments in the so-called dream city. Time would show how this chapter would play out.

Finally, in Barcelona, the Airbnb flat was in Gotic, the heart of the old city. Gotic looked remarkably interesting with its narrow streets and very old buildings. The flat was in the middle of a very narrow long street. On our day of arrival, the taxi dropped us off with our luggage at one end of the street. We could clearly see a 'no entry' sign. However, the driver approached the one-way street from the wrong end, and he mumbled something in Spanish or Catalan, and then drove off!

Well, neither of us knew Spanish or Catalan and we didn't even have a simple dictionary. Immediately, I thought we could use our phone, so there was no need for a dictionary. Then the penny dropped; I realised we didn't have any mobile data either! Unfortunately, we weren't at all prepared for our new adventure. Here we go, no language, no mobile, no communication, no nothing. There I was thinking to myself, 'I've been here before!'

God only knew what plans the Gods of the Game of Life had made for us.

With two suitcases plus a couple of shoulder bags each, we couldn't take everything with us and walk to the flat. Furthermore, there was no means to call or send a message to the landlord. After a quick think, I asked Gulsun to wait at the bottom of the street, while I walked to the flat with a couple of suitcases. After a few minutes walking, I found the building where our flat was. But I couldn't work out which floor or the flat number, as there was no clear indicator on the buzzer. It looked like a four or five storey building, with four separate buzzers. Also, there was a small bar café on the ground level, which was shut.

Suddenly I noticed there was a young man looking out of the window of the first floor flat. Hoping to get some help, I told him that we had rented one of the flats here but couldn't tell which. However, he didn't seem to understand most of what I had said but must have guessed that I was a tourist tenant. Next, he indicated the number four on his fingers, presumably telling me the flat number.

Anyway, I rang the bell a few times but nothing. My new neighbour made a few hand gestures, presumably saying no one was there. At the time, I didn't want to risk ringing the other bells and disturbing my new neighbours before even moving in.

While I was walking to the flat, I had seen a corner shop just a few yards back from the building. I must try the shop I thought, get some water, and maybe borrow his phone for a few seconds.

The shopkeeper appeared to be either of Pakistani or Indian origin, and therefore, I thought, he would most likely speak English. So, I walked in and briefly explained everything. Then I asked him if I could use his phone. I told him that I was from Turkey, thinking if he were a Muslim, he may be more helpful. That worked I thought, as he confirmed he was a Pakistani Muslim. While handing me his phone, he said that I could use it, but I would have to pay. Although I was surprised by him asking for money, I said, 'Sure', thinking it would only cost a couple of euros at the most.

Immediately, I called the Landlord's son, as I had dealt with him while booking the place and his father didn't speak a word of English. Apparently, the landlord was waiting for our call. He only lived twenty minutes away, and he would be at the flat soon. Great news indeed! At least the landlord was on his way and we could carry the rest of the luggage and wait for him by the building.

A Sour Start to Our New Adventure

Subsequently, I thanked the shopkeeper, took two small bottles of water out of the fridge (they were one euro each), and handed him a ten Euro note. Waiting for the change, he simply said, 'Thank you, this should be enough for everything'. Wow, what a so and so I thought, he really took advantage of me. That was way over the top and unnecessary, which really pissed me off no end. Truly angry, I wanted to say a few words to vent, but then I thought better of it and just walked out. Nevertheless, it was his loss, as we could have shopped there quite a bit, but we didn't after that.

On reflection, it was a good job I told him I was from Turkey, otherwise he may have charged me double, I joked to myself.

Anyway, I ran back to Gulsun, and helped her bring the rest of our stuff to our new place. Then, I told her what had happened with the shopkeeper and we just shook our heads and started waiting for the landlord.

In the grand scheme of things, it was only a small thing, but I guess it is all those small things that give life meaning. Furthermore, we are not used to that kind of thing, as something like that could never happen in Turkey. Except for some dodgy taxi drivers who are known to overcharge the tourists or try and take longer routes than needed! And some Turkish shops in tourist areas are famous for overcharging tourists, but most corner shops would not even think about taking money for a very short call. Let's move on now and continue the Barcelona tale, as we now had a city to explore and enjoy. We would soon forget this had ever happened, I mumbled to myself.

Anyway, the Landlord soon arrived, a very friendly looking old man, and very welcoming too. Greeting us with just a simple hola, he then helped with our suitcases and we walked into the building. At first glance, it was a tiny entrance with no apparent lift, in fact no lift at all upon closer inspection! Oh well, we started climbing up the very narrow winding staircase with tiny steps. We could only just fit with the suitcases.

Oh dear! To make matters worse, our flat was on the top floor too. 'Never mind, we won't do much shopping, that's for sure', I thought.

Once inside the property, he showed us around the flat, the utensils, cooker etc. Actually, he was rambling on explaining a few things then it suddenly dawned on him that we couldn't understand a word he was saying. So, he straightaway called his son! Speaking to the son he gave us the lowdown on everything, in a nice and straightforward manner. After talking to the son, we thanked the landlord, and he left. My immediate thought was 'Let's just ignore the little niggling things like no lift etc. and discover the neighbourhood. First things first, let's get the mobile phones sorted.' Remember I have always been a pragmatic problem solver, so sorting the practical stuff out first is always the priority.

In a short time, we started wandering around this very old and lovely quarter we were now living in. It was full of small shops and lots of eating-places. A few streets up from our flat, we found a mobile shop with photocopy and Internet service. There were a few young people behind the counter, again looking Pakistani or Indian. In fact, it seemed most corner shops were owned or run by them. We said hello, and the guy by the cashier asked how he could help in a friendly manner and speaking in very good English. So, in response, I just told him that we needed mobile data and SIM cards for our phones. Also, I explained that we intended to stay for a long time. Then, he recommended the most suitable and cost-effective SIM card and completed all the settings for us too. And Bob's your uncle, now we were in business!

What a relief, and how important bloody phones have become in modern life. Nowadays, we are lost without them, and how did we ever manage before?

The shop assistant had excellent customer service skills and a friendly attitude, which I thanked him for. Also, I shared what had happened at the other corner shop. He was shocked and very angry too. In the end, we just agreed that there were many petty people everywhere, and that it had nothing to do with race or religion. After that brilliant experience, we mostly used this shop for all our mobile needs and for faxing some official documents to Sila's school in the UK.

Welcome to Barcelona, 2015
But, First Some Reflections or A Bit of Self-Analysis

Lately, I have really started to think that my life has been like a game. Who knows, after reading my book perhaps you may agree, and possibly think the same about your own life?

Sadly, I don't ever feel in full control of things, as if life puts me in an environment with certain rules and conditions and then expects me to find my way around. Then, you make decisions for better or for worse, facing obstacles along the way some of which you overcome. However, some obstacles you try to avoid, but sometimes only to face even bigger ones. Ultimately, we always try our best to find the right path for our own comfort and happiness. But just like in a game, we can fail often and instead of happiness we experience sadness. Instead of embracing success we can end up facing failure.

Somehow, we try and learn from both successes and failures to go further and achieve better results. Without really thinking about it, we repeat this almost every day and to various scales. In short, we are trying to perform our roles as best as we can. And yet we are not all great actors, besides which even great thespians don't perform at their best all the time. Indeed, they have bad days, just like writers having a writer's block or songwriters not finding inspiration.

As I have already admitted, I am a lousy gamer and so crap at computer games. In my later years, I have started to think that perhaps I am also a lousy player (actor) in real life. The reason being I find it difficult to make decisions, I let things linger, all of which tends to amplify problems and make situations worse. Although I have achieved a lot in terms of my work, I still feel very much a failure in realising some of my own expectations. Even though I always have high expectations, sometimes I'm at a loss and don't even know what to expect from life.

Furthermore, I can never seem to relax or ease my mind or loosen up. I am always so serious. In fact, I am probably the last person in the room to act the joker. However, the funny thing is that I can also be such good company amongst friends. Sadly, most of the time I just cannot help it, and constantly think about lots of things simultaneously, even when I am focused and concentrated on one thing. That's why I always have problems going to sleep. In fact, I have to tire both my mind and eyes to sleep. What's even worse is that I can never go back to sleep if I wake up in the middle of my sleep cycle. This is why I have always wanted to live in quiet, peaceful areas, mostly on the outskirts of cities.

It seems I am such a worrier too; any small failure or niggle can bother me and upset me. As a result, my mind is always full of little annoyances and niggles, which is very tiring. In truth, it really drains a lot of energy from me. Luckily, I seem to have quite a good reserve of energy, which seems to keep me going both physically and mentally.

In a way, I am both a warrior and a worrier. Going to the airport much earlier than needed just to avoid the possibility of missing my flight is a classic example of something I do. Then, I will spend most of the time with one eye on the bloody departures panel!

Once I remember going to Didim (Turkey) with my good friend Nejdet Pamuk, who is the exact opposite of me. He was checking his mails, making calls, and yet there I was constantly warning him about our flight! Despite all that worrying and anxiety, we ended up missing our flights. Yes, I say flights because we bought new tickets for another flight, but somehow, we mixed the flight numbers up and missed the second flight too!

Incidentally, Didim used to be an extremely popular destination with the Brits, with so many buying houses and settling there, but after the economic crisis of 2018 in Turkey, most of them sold off their properties and left.

My friend Nejdet has a lovely sailing boat in Didim. Even though we missed our flights and had many other problems with the boat, we still had a superb time and a really good laugh about it all.

Obviously, I am not at all happy with my uptight nature. Despite all my best efforts, I don't seem to be able to do anything to change it. It is likely that some characteristics are engraved in our DNA and there's nothing we can do to get rid of them. Somehow, we learn to live with them. The real shame is that other people around us have to live with them too!

It's becoming more and more obvious as to why I found myself in a big void after the sudden and unwanted interruption to my successful career. Being constantly busy with my work and achieving success and recognition would help me to stay more relaxed. Suddenly, I had so much more thinking and worrying time on my hands. As a result, my worrier nature came to the fore and the warrior nature didn't help much. It felt like I was all-alone, in a small boat, on stormy waters just trying to stay afloat, constantly fighting strong currents and winds...

Adventure in Catalonia 2015...Wandering and Wondering Begins

With a low state of mind and mixed emotions about my future, we started our new adventure in the city of Barcelona.

For a long time, Gulsun has had a bad back, and climbing the stairs to our Airbnb with the weight of the luggage suddenly dawned upon us. 'What a terrible thought having to climb these stairs every day for weeks! Well, it was only temporary, and if we are lucky enough, we could find a nice place and move in as soon as possible'.

We started wandering around the lovely city, finding our way around and looking for 'to rent' signs or whatever the equivalent in Spanish or Catalan was. Equally, we were also hoping to find estate agents, but it wasn't like Britain or Turkey. There weren't many around that we could see or find easily. How strange I thought for such a popular city. Oh well, we had nothing else to do, but just look around and find suitable areas that we liked.

The first few days were great, we couldn't care less about the stairs or any other small niggles. We were really enjoying this wonderfully lively city, with lovely weather, food, and it was full of character. So much so that I was falling in love with the city and couldn't get enough of it. There were beautiful buildings and well-designed wide roads with plenty of pedestrian walks and in fact, they had more space for the pedestrians than the traffic, which was brilliant.

We were just walking and walking, which was great for burning off all those calories from the wonderful food. We were out and about all day until extremely late, arriving at the flat absolutely knackered. We would get a few hours' sleep until we were woken up early in the morning by noises coming from everywhere.

As I have mentioned, I am extremely sensitive to noise, and Gulsun knows it too. I absolutely hate it in fact, and I can never ever get used to it. Luckily, I have lived in detached houses, and quiet areas.

Living in the city of Barcelona most probably meant living in a flat no matter how nice. But I could cope with it for a while since I wasn't even going to have my HiFi system with me. Our plan was to enjoy the city for a time, and then move to a lovely quiet village on the outskirts, half an hour or so from the city. Then, we would be able to rent a lovely house, and bring my HiFi from Turkey. That was the plan anyway.

The Gotic quarter of Barcelona had incredibly old houses, and our building had really thin walls. We were on the top floor, but what appeared to be an old lady was living underneath us, with a dog that barked nonstop. In fact, the silly thing barked at everything that moved. It barked when people were leaving or entering the building or whenever the bell rang. To be honest, that seemed like its hobby. As if the dog barking wasn't enough, the old lady herself was on the blower the whole time. Talking very loudly, almost as if she was complaining about things, or having arguments with her kids? Actually, we didn't have a clue, as we didn't know Spanish or Catalan. Luckily, she would go to sleep around midnight, but was up by 7am, so we had at least some peace and quiet from her. But the dog, it would bark all the time and anytime, it didn't care what time it was!

So, the scene was set and our first Friday night/early morning gave us a real glimpse of the noise problems that we would face in the coming weeks and months!

Welcome to The Noise Nightmare...

That first Friday night it was around 3am when we were woken up by loud and constant chattering and laughter. Honestly, it was so loud that it was as if they were inside our building. First, I thought maybe someone was having a party next door. That's how loud and disturbing it was. We were completely shocked, and both looked as if we had just woken up from a nightmare.

To make matters worse, the windows had no double gazing and all faced the street. As we looked out, we could see a group of people standing outside the bar smoking, with drinks in their hands, just talking and laughing. Imagine a very noisy British pub with loud music, and people raising their voices to be heard over the music!

Oh my God, this was a complete nightmare! Although, I wished it was a nightmare, as at least it would go away when I woke up. Also, with a nightmare you are not likely to have it every night. In stark contrast, this noisy nightmare was to be with us as a permanent fixture every night and every morning.

Absolutely, there was no way I could go back to sleep, even if they all started singing nursery rhymes. Well, I thought to myself, if you can't beat them join them! So, we decided to get up and just go for a walk, as far away from our building as possible. We would make use of the time and discover different parts of the city. In fact, it was the best time to find quieter areas at night. Even more horrifying though was that it was only the first week of May, and there would be more tourists and even more noise later in the season. Even the thought of it depressed me!

Let me fast forward to 2019. I was back in Istanbul, in my country house on the outskirts of Istanbul, Zekeriyakoy. A very built-up village nowadays, but almost all estates have semi or detached houses with gardens. For some reason, a lot of the new people who moved onto our estate, all came with dogs! Most of them young couples with young kids, wanted to make the most of the gardens and living in the village. Suddenly, neighbours with dogs surrounded me.

As you may know, when one dog starts barking the others follow suit. What is even worse is that they keep barking as if trying to outdo each other.

This went on for days and weeks. Some of the neighbours worked and during the day the dogs were let loose in the gardens. Barking away at anything that moved. Meanwhile, I was home working on my book. As it was a largish estate, there were always people about, especially security guards or gardeners. This meant each time someone walked past these houses, I would endure quarter of an hour of nonstop barking. Really this was enough to drive me mad or off the estate!

The estate management tried to resolve the problem, but to no avail. In the end, I decided to leave the estate, as the barking became unbearable for me! Now I live in a rented flat in a twenty-three storey high-rise building. Luckily, the big round corner flat is on the top floor in the district of lovely Kadikoy, on the Asian side. It is so quiet as I have no neighbours as such. Also, I even brought my HiFi system, so I can listen to music without bothering anyone. Now you can see how sensitive I am to noise, as it drove me out of my detached house and into a flat!

Let's get back to the game and hit continue. Now, we had desperately upped our efforts to find a place quickly, but also making sure it was in a relatively quiet area. Thus, we established some red lines. Basically, we were looking for a lovely old principal building from the early 1900s. In addition to this, if possible, on the top floor, and as it could get very hot in the summer it shouldn't be south facing. In contrast, it wasn't like being in the UK, where having a south facing garden was so important to get as much of the little available sunshine as possible.

Hunt for the Noiseless Flat

So, there we were walking around all the different quarters and getting to know the city. After all, discovering the city was partly why we were there. In the meantime, not forgetting to taste the lovely local food, which was utterly delicious. And there were so many places to try too.

The El Borne area looked very nice, perfectly situated, close to Gotic, the Beach, Ciutadella Park and the Zoo. It was one of the most popular and busiest of the districts, but we discovered a couple of quieter areas and noted them for closer inspection.

In truth, Barcelona isn't a big city by any stretch, and you could walk from one end to the other within about an hour. This meant it was lovely the way you could just stroll around everywhere. In a way, all this nonstop walking was really tiring, but at least it helped us get a couple of hours sleep.

Well, there was this relatively big new district called Eixample. It had newer buildings and exceptionally large roads running across each other both ways. Besides that, it was remarkably close to the famous Avinguda Diagonal road, which cuts across the entire city diagonally. Hence, the name.

We had started searching Google for any rented property and estate agents. Of course, only a few had English support, so we had to rely on Google Translate to make sense of most of the sites!

Even so we found an ad for a two-bed apartment flat, which was awfully close to our flat. Fortunately, it just took a few minutes to walk there to check it out. It was on the main road that runs along the shore, a lovely old building with nice cafes nearby. Gloriously, it seemed to have lovely views over the sea, the marina and the beach! 'A perfect match at last. We could be in luck', I thought.

Upon arrival, we asked the doorman about the flat and he let us know a few things, but as it was in Spanish we didn't have a clue what he had said. Luckily, two ladies and a tradesman were walking out of the building at the same time and the doorman said something to them while pointing at us. So, we said that we wanted to see the flat, and it turned out that the older lady was the owner and the younger one the estate agent.

Great we thought and then we all went up just one floor. Upon first inspection, it seemed they were renovating it. In actual fact, it would be finished by mid-June at the latest and be let fully furnished. It was €2,200 per month. After a brief chat with Gulsun, we decided to take it and made an offer on the spot. Sooner the better we thought, it looked like a reasonable property with newly installed double-glazed French windows. More importantly, the area didn't look like it would be busy or noisy during the night. On the spot, I offered €2,000. Then, we exchanged contact details with the estate agent. She said, the owner would think about it and get back to us.

We were really excited, worst case scenario we would just pay the asking price if needed. With the 'finding a flat saga' seemingly out of the way, we could now just enjoy the city. After all, this was the main reason for coming to Barcelona.

The estate agent phoned me the next day, and told us that they had a few other alternatives. We thought, 'why not? The more the merrier while waiting to hear from the owner.' On the way to the estate agent's office, I saw a let sign near a very posh and historical five-star hotel. It seemed like an incredibly quiet street in Gotic. Upon closer inspection, I could see that there was a doorman outside, and I simply asked if we could see the flat. Again, there was no understanding of any kind due to the language barrier.

Damn all these different languages, it was making life so complicated. As luck would have it, a young girl walked out of the building, who happened to be the estate agent. Apparently, she was checking the particulars and was about to add it to their website. It was a newly decorated and fully furnished flat. To me, it looked really lovely and seemed very quiet too. Seizing the opportunity, we had a quick look, but the main bedroom opened into the living room. This is something we would discover later that lots of flats would have. However, this appeared to be one of Gulsun's red lines. Therefore, another red line was added to our list of definite No-Nos. In contrast, I personally didn't mind it at all, but Gulsun just hated it and wouldn't have it.

Although we seemed to be in luck with finding places and estate agents reasonably quickly, the places we found always had a snag or a major problem. We were already having our patience tested, but we had only just begun!

The Land of The Landladies

Undoubtedly, the flat hunting was proving to be a problem. So, in due course, I called the estate agent about the renovated flat by the shore. Apparently, the owner was interested in our offer, but wanted to secure the rent payments. 'Sure, no problem just let me know what she needs', I said.

First of all, we had to sign a guaranteed bank letter for twelve months' rent. But to my dismay, I found out that there was a high bank fee to pay for such a letter. Almost in the region of a couple thousand euros! No way would I pay those bank fees, but I would be happy to sign the letter if they paid the fees. To simplify things, I suggested that I could pay six months in advance to put her mind at rest and then pay the rest monthly. She accepted it. Great, it looked like we had secured the flat.

In our short dealings with them, we had already realised that there was something peculiar about the attitudes of both the owners and the estate agents. They would say things, which we would discover to be false, or the homeowners would change their minds at the last minute for no reason.

To be on the safe side, we decided to continue looking for alternatives just in case. Besides which, we didn't know what sort of furniture the owner was getting, as she refused to give us any details. What's more, there were other small things that we ignored for the sake of quick completion. Near the end of May, while wandering around different areas, we also found more estate agents and more flats too.

The attitude of the owner was really strange, as she refused to give us info about the furniture and also, she would not give a definite completion date either on the refurbishment. As a result, we started getting quite agitated. This led to us nit-picking over the flat details too, as if asking for trouble!

To make matters worse, the owner suddenly insisted that we paid twelve months upfront! Since we were already shying away from the flat anyway, the owner just made it easier for us to change our minds. Gulsun said the bathroom was too far from the bedroom. She also pointed out that we might not like the furniture either. We were nearly into June and yet, after all that waiting, we suddenly decided to find another flat instead!

If you have an itch for something and then ask for it, you shall get it or so the expression goes. Obviously, I was asking for it! Now the plot was thickening and the gameplay getting more complicated! The more areas, and more alternative flats we saw the more confused we became. We were having real difficulty making our minds up. There was always one major thing wrong, maybe we had too many red lines. Of course, the reddest line was the noise factor followed by the main bedroom opening into the living room. But these were closely followed by too much sun in the afternoon, old building, minimum of two beds… Sometimes, the ad would say two-bed flat, only to find that it was only one. As a rule, inaccurate information was almost the norm. In time we stopped getting excited about the ads before viewing the places.

It seemed as if we were looking for something that didn't exist or was at least rare in Barcelona. The whole thing started getting to me. After all, I was already feeling low and I had come here to relax and ease my mind. All of these problems were mounting and slowly driving me mad. But at the same time, they were making me even more determined to find what we were after! It was crazy!

As we were running out of time, the attitude of the locals was getting to us too. They never did any weekend viewings, and sometimes they couldn't get the keys from the owners. At other times, no viewing was allowed if the flat was already occupied, and we were asked to wait until it was vacated! In Istanbul, it's mainly the weekends when people view properties, but not in Barcelona!

We were getting quite agitated and desperate. As a result, I decided to up the ante and told Gulsun we should start looking for flats in the €4-5,000 range. Perhaps this would increase our chances of getting what we wanted. At the time, Gulsun thought I was being silly, and we should just continue to look for something more reasonable. But I felt that we were losing control of the situation. It is a fact of life that when frustration sets in, desperate measures must be taken.

The clock was ticking. We only had a week left at the Airbnb flat. I cannot remember ever having a decent night's sleep at all to this day, but, in this sodding flat I just couldn't go to sleep, full stop! And we were still nowhere near to finding a place. Our landlord knew we were very unhappy with the noise, and having problems finding a place. But he offered for us to stay at the flat for longer if we couldn't find a place before the 5th June. And added that we wouldn't have to pay. Although I wouldn't want to stay there even if he offered us money on top, but it was still nice and considerate of him. What a lovely man. Somehow, we had to get out of the Gotic flat before either the noise or the lack of sleep killed me!

Finally in Luck...

After searching for ages, we finally found a place. Even better still, it was in our favourite El Born district, and it was on the quietest street too. A fantastic old building converted from an old nuns' house. It was a truly lovely flat with two large en-suite bedrooms and a huge living room with an open kitchen. Finally, in luck I thought, as it seemed to tick all the right boxes. Our patience and resilience had paid off. But yes, there's always a but, and this time was no exception. There was one major problem, which crossed one of our red lines. Lo and behold, the main bedroom opened into the living room, Gulsun's principle red line!

It really wasn't a big problem, as there was another large en suite bedroom. Also, it was on the other side of the kitchen, which we could easily use as our main bedroom. Nonetheless, Gulsun was really put off by this, as she was concerned about when friends visited or Sila stayed with us.

By far, this was the best flat we had seen and to me it looked perfect. An even bigger bonus was that a large living room meant that I could even bring my hi-fi system, and possibly stay here longer than one year. That's how much I liked it. It was simply perfect in every possible way and within walking distance of all the wonderful places.

On the same day, we had seen another house near the Diagonal Ave. and Gaudi's famous Casa Mila. It was a three-bed flat and none of them opened into the living room. But, it was on one of the busiest roads in the city, Mallorca, plus, no double-glazing on any of the windows. We would definitely have major noise problems, which was my major redline. To be honest, it wasn't even comparable to the El Born flat. But Gulsun liked the Mallorca flat much more, as it had three bedrooms and none opening into the living room. In addition, it also had a closed kitchen.

A Lovely Flat in Lovely El Born, On a Quiet Street Too...

Obviously, Gulsun could see my serious concern about the noise and apparent preference for the El Born flat. She also accepted that El Born was nicer as an area. Also, it was a beautiful old building, with a much bigger living room, and more importantly, the street was really quiet. Besides which El Born was such a lovely area, which was buzzing with tourists, and within short walking distance to the beach too. Additionally, it was surrounded by wonderful cultural and historical buildings, and eating places such as El Xampanyet, the Piccasso, Mercat del Born, Zoo Barcelona, Parlamanet de Catalunya and Parc de la Ciutadella. It was already our favourite district.

Finally, Gulsun agreed that the El Born flat was a better option despite the main bedroom problem. She also agreed that there was another large en suite bedroom that we could use.

Great I thought, as we decided on the El Born flat! The asking price was €2,300 per month, which even included a car park space. Without much delay, I made an offer through the Irish estate agent. My proposal was €2,100 per month, and the owner could keep the parking space and rent it separately, as we didn't need one. Clearly, the owner could easily get €200 per month for it separately. Accordingly, she accepted my offer, but said she would double check with her husband, and confirm the next day, which was Saturday.

Finally, we had found what we had been looking for and I cannot tell you how happy I was. Also, we were able to move in a few days too, which was perfect. In the end, it all seemed to fall into place. Our hard work and patience seemed to have paid off.

Nonetheless, I could see that Gulsun wasn't entirely happy as her heart was set on the Mallorca place! But to make me feel better, she kept saying that the El Born flat was nice, and we would be happy there.

Finally, we were so relieved and happy. In fact, we celebrated our new flat with a nice meal and some good wine in El Born. Afterwards, we went back to the Gotic flat. It was well past midnight and Gulsun went straight to bed.

However, I decided to check my mails. As usual, my mind was multitasking like a supercomputer. Yes, we had definitely made the best choice, but Gulsun seemed very disappointed about not getting the Mallorca place. For some reason, she really loved that place for all its faults and, despite the bloody noise. Three bedrooms and a separate kitchen seemed much more important to her. Actually, she perhaps expected many friends to be visiting us. Inwardly, my mind was all over the place, and I just couldn't stop thinking about it. The more I thought about it, the worse I felt for Gulsun. It was really bugging me; I just couldn't get it out of my head.

In the end, I thought maybe I should make an offer on the Mallorca flat. Gulsun could be right, as it was also quite a nice flat despite a few small faults, and in a nice area too. As far as the noise was concerned, I could ask the owner to install double-glazed windows.

Yes, I should make an offer for the Mallorca flat and surprise Gulsun in the morning! Clearly, I was asking for it, sufficed to say that I was itching for it. And perhaps it had to happen. Well, 'Life Is A Game' and it seems I am not always good at making the right decisions or choices. Who is?

Before going to bed, I shot an email to the estate agent for the Mallorca place with an offer of €2,000 per month. Quite relieved with the fact that we had found a flat after all the trials and tribulations.

Although I did like the El Born flat much more, I decided I could live with the minor faults of the Mallorca one…

Looking For Trouble, Not Just a Flat

Thus, the next chapter of our adventure was set in motion by my action. All I could do was to sleep on it, and wake up to all that was about to unfold.

As usual, I woke up early, *(correction)* I was woken up by the usual noise! After a quick shower, I started killing time on the computer. Around 9:30, I got the email from the estate agent confirming the acceptance of my Mallorca offer. Wow, that was quick! Straight away I told Gulsun that our offer was accepted. Initially, she seemed quite happy, of course thinking I was talking about the El Born offer. Pleased as punch like a kid, I said joyfully, 'The offer for the Mallorca flat was accepted, which I made after you went to bed'. She was absolutely delighted, even more so than I had expected. It was so obvious that she really had set her heart on that flat. I was so relieved by the decision I had made for Gulsun's sake.

Hopefully, we could now quickly complete the formalities and move into our new flat soon. The timing was perfect too. A famous French writer was currently occupying the flat and was going to move into his own flat in a wonderful building next door. It was being renovated and would be ready in a week at the most. No problems, we could easily wait that long. We could even move into a hotel for a few days should we have to. The difference was that it wasn't like we were moving into a house, as we only had a couple of suitcases each.

To ensure smooth completion, I paid the €2,000 deposit to the estate agent's account. By the way, I had managed to open a bank account with Catalunya Caixa (now BBVA). It was with the help of a Greek origin bank clerk. He was into games and even knew the Last Ninja and First Samurai games. We became instant friends, and he was always so helpful to us with our banking needs.

The world of politics seems to treat the relationship between the Turks and Greeks as enemies. On the contrary, I have always had great relationships with the Greeks. In fact, we have more in common than differences, and share so much history and culture too. Shame on those who created the conflict in the first place and who are still trying to keep it going!

Gladly, we were almost there now as we were only waiting to sign the tenancy agreement. Even the date was set, and I could move in on the 7th June. The reason I say 'I' is because Gulsun had planned to be in Istanbul for the forthcoming elections of June 7th, 2015. All in all, we had agreed on everything, two months deposit, rent etc. The signature date of 4th June was set with Gulsun leaving for Istanbul the following day.

The Big Day!

I couldn't sleep from excitement, well, couldn't sleep from noise anyway, but was up even earlier on that Thursday. It was a big day.

Around 9:30, I received a WhatsApp message from the estate agent. It was a short message and didn't look very clear as to what it said, but it didn't look good. Although the estate agent's English was okay, she would sometimes make big mistakes. As such, I thought maybe she misplaced a word or something. In a state of panic, I double-checked and reread the message several times. Surely, this couldn't be true, there must be a mistake. It simply said that the owner had changed her mind! Absolute calamity!

No way, I thought, no, this couldn't be true. But I did already warn you about the homeowners suddenly changing their minds, and that was exactly what she had done.

In the aftermath of the news, Gulsun and I felt utterly devastated, and we just sat there, completely numb and speechless for ages! Really there's no way to accurately describe how I felt. The whole sky seemed to collapse in on me.

Suddenly, I thought 'I hope the El Born flat is still available'. Without hesitation, I immediately called the Irish estate agent. In response she said she would speak with the owner and get back to me. Suddenly, it crossed my mind that all the owners were ladies. Moreover, they were all being really difficult and tough too, which I found most unusual.

Apparently, the owner said we could still have the flat, but she would only accept the full asking price of €2,300 now, and no garage! In reality, she probably raised the rent guessing our desperation. Let's be frank, €200 per month is not small change, but for God's sake, after what had just happened, 'just accept and take the flat!' were the words ringing in my head. Besides, we could afford it and I had really liked the place. It was my first choice anyway. More importantly, it would help us recover from the Mallorca shock.

Really Asking For It!

Nevertheless, we defiantly refused to bow to the pressure of the situation. It was a question of principle. How dare she take advantage of our situation? In fact, the reality of the situation was that she was only doing what was right for her, albeit perhaps a bit unfair. In any case, Gulsun wasn't too keen on it. However, when one reflects on situations like these in life, the important issues can often hang on the smallest of things. But sometimes it seems we fail to think things through properly.

It was so obvious we were asking for trouble, yet again. In response, we said we would think it over for a couple of days. As if we didn't have enough problems, now we were playing the tough customer!

In hindsight, I think that the shock was so massive from the Mallorca flat that our brains probably stopped functioning properly. We weren't thinking logically. Yet I was a successful programmer and capable of thinking almost as logically as Mr Spock of Star Trek. Clearly, we should have simply taken the El Born flat, as there was absolutely nothing to think about. Instead, we were leaving ourselves wide open for even bigger shocks.

The next day, with a clearer mind, I called the estate agent and simply said, 'Okay, we accept the asking price and would like to move in as soon as possible.' She said, she would get back to me after talking with the owner.

Well, it didn't take her more than ten minutes to call back. Then she dropped the bombshell and gave me the devastating news. Apparently, late yesterday afternoon an American writer had seen the flat and immediately fallen in love with it (just like I had!). What's more, he rented it on the spot for six months with an offer of €3,000 per month, all paid upfront!

Normally, things could only get better, but in our case, it seemed things could only get worse. We were experiencing shock after shock. However, these shocks weren't like the aftershocks from an earthquake. Each shock felt like a new earthquake.

The stark reality was that we had to pull ourselves together and start all over again, from scratch. But now, we had completely run out of time. We had to leave the Gotic flat, as there was no way I could stay there any longer.

And as a result, I decided to find a hotel, and stay there for a bit to recover. Almost as if I needed a sanctuary. At least we could get some decent sleep and recover from all the shocks and blows. In all fairness, maybe we should change our tactic and just find a much better Airbnb place first? After that we could then continue with the flat hunting. It may be easier to find a short let for a few weeks or even months. It could give us the time we needed to find something we really liked again. No more rushing, just taking it easy and enjoying the city too. These were the thoughts prominent in our minds.

But the tourist season was hotting up, and the places were becoming even scarcer. This in turn made our flat hunting even harder.

It seemed like everything was working against us. The game master had raised the game level even higher. Of course, our indecisiveness as to what to do was making things doubly worse. The thoughts going through my mind were, 'What a mess, when will this nightmare end? How long will it last?' To put things in context, we had only been here for five weeks, and experienced nothing but problems and troubles. Ironically, we had come here to relax and recuperate from the untimely and very upsetting career interruption. But I was far from relaxing, instead I was getting even more depressed.

Nevertheless, we kept going somehow, finding more estate agents, expanding our search area for more alternatives for a quicker result. All this extra effort and different alternatives was causing even more confusion if anything. At that point, we just couldn't keep up with it all. By then, we had almost seen every estate agent in the city. Everybody knew us now and was apparently talking about us too. Suddenly, we were becoming the talk of the town.

Remember, I was also looking for a nice quiet hotel to stay for a few days. That was proving hard too, as most hotels were filling up fast. We were truly getting fed up with searching and looking for places to live. Instead of the places to eat and visit!

By now, estate agents were getting fed up with us too. With our peculiar demands and redlines; too noisy, too much sun, rooms opening into living rooms, too modern… We were becoming too difficult to handle. But luckily there were two estate agents who were patient and helpful. One was a middle-aged Catalan lady, and the other a young Mexican girl.

After Losing The El Born Flat, About to Lose My Mind

All in all, it took a couple of days to find a hotel, which wasn't too far from our favourite El Born. Likewise, it was also very close to the flat I loved so much but failed to secure! To avoid encountering noise, I had specifically asked the hotel to give me a quiet room. But, lo and behold, it was full of noise, noisy air-conditioning, and a continuously running noisy fan in the bathroom with absolutely no way to turn it off! At the end of my tether, there was no way to escape from the bloody noise. Conversely, the more I wanted to get away from it the more I seemed to walk into it.

Pleadingly, I begged the receptionist to change the room the next day for a quieter one. Luckily, the new room was much better and, at last we managed to get a few nights decent sleep.

On another positive note, our friendly young Mexican estate agent was really trying to help us. In fact, she spent a lot of time with us and we were seeing each other almost every day. Genuinely concerned, she could see our desperation and was really feeling sorry for us. Thus, she helped us view quite a few flats, but each had something majorly wrong or missing. Truthfully, we were running out of options and luck and too many of our own self-imposed redlines weren't helping our cause either.

After having seen a number of places, we decided to have lunch and re-evaluate our options. We were finding fewer places to view; we had seen almost all the properties on the market! Really tired, fed up and clueless as to what to do next. During lunch, the Mexican girl said, 'I cannot believe your luck, but maybe there is a reason for it all. So many things going so wrong all the time it must mean something. Maybe there is a message behind it all and, perhaps the city just doesn't want you here. It wants you to leave!'

From the look of things, maybe she was right!

Years before, Gulsun had lived near a railway line in Hackney, London, and she was used to quite a bit of noise, however, even she couldn't cope with the level of noise in Barcelona. Believe me when I say that there was no way for us to get used to it, as there was so much of it and from so many different sources; traffic, bars, tourists…

Our hearts and minds were still with El Born. So much so that we were still looking around there too. Honestly, it broke our hearts each time we walked past the lovely flat that the American writer was enjoying. Several times, I wondered if I should have a word with him and ask him to leave a few months earlier!

Pleading Banners

In El Born there were so many banners hanging from the windows of the flats. Adorning the banners were messages written on them in huge letters; 'Please be quiet and consider the neighbours!' Hilariously but tragically, the locals were literally begging the noisy tourists to keep it down a bit, so they could get some sleep! That's how bad it was. So, at that point, I could clearly see that I wasn't exaggerating the noise problem at all! It seemed, even the locals were desperate and helpless about it.

One fine day, we saw an ad on the Irish estate agent's web site for a three-bed flat in the heart of El Born. It was in a lovely old building and looked very nice on paper. Straight away, I called her, and she instantly said, 'Mev it's not for you, it would be much too noisy there, in fact, it's the noisiest square in the area.' Nothing to lose, I said, 'Could we at least view it since we were staying at a hotel close by?' She replied, 'well, I did warn you, but sure, you can see it of course. I will arrange it.'

There was no escaping the inevitable. The wheels were set in motion; the fate, the stars, the planets were all lined up. The route was laid out in front of us, and we were walking towards it or it was beckoning us forth! Whatever it was.

Soon after, we met at the flat and the owner (yes, another lady owner) was there too. In fact, she lived in the opposite flat, so she owned the whole floor.

I thought to myself, 'What's with all these landladies? They are out here to get me!' So far, more than 90% of the owners had been ladies.

Since the owner was already living there, I thought it couldn't be that bad. In fact, she even had a young kid. That day we did the viewing, it was around lunchtime and the area was rather quiet. No through traffic, only the dustcarts and occasional delivery people. Probably all the noisy tourists were fast asleep from the previous night and recuperating for the coming night. In addition to this, I could see even more banners begging the tourists to keep the noise down at night. They were across the square from the flat! A clear warning!

On the positive side of things, the owner was genuinely nice and friendly towards us. Furthermore, it turned out that she was an architect and, in the construction business with her husband. She informed us that the rent was €2,000 per month, and we said we would think about it, and duly left. It was a nice spacious flat in an old building with beautiful floor tiles.

Becoming Inspector Clouseau

Doing our detective work, Gulsun and I visited the area after midnight to inspect it for noise. By now, we were becoming noise experts. Not that it was helping us much, as we were still considering a flat in the noisiest area! Even worse, it was really buzzing with overly crowded numbers of tourists. People inside and outside bars, drinking, smoking and nonstop talking. No wonder the neighbours were begging for quietness. Regardless of the banners, nobody seemed to care one iota! As far as they were concerned, they were here to enjoy themselves and that was exactly what they were going to do!

Anyway, we observed the area a little more. Just walking up and down the lovely, lively, and bubbly square. Sitting on the banks and trying to measure the noise level. Continually thinking and evaluating; yes, it was noisy, but the flat was on the third floor with three bedrooms. As a compromise, we could always sleep in the back room if the noise got too unbearable. It didn't have double-glazing, but it did have big timber shutters, which could block out some of the noise.

It was clear that we were trying to think positively and convince ourselves to take the flat! It was incredible how pathetic and almost helpless we were with our thinking. How quickly we had forgotten about the bloody noise in the Gotic district? Even crazier, this square seemed ten times worse! To the point that even the local residents were crying about the noise! In truth, we were so tired and fed up with it all. So much so that we just wanted to end the flat hunt there and then. Really, we were ready to just face the music so to speak. Well, I mean face the noise in this case!

Nevertheless, we were so scared and confused, which meant we couldn't decide on anything. Beaten and exhausted by sleep deprivation, we were tired of looking, tired of thinking, just bloody tired full stop. Determined to the last though, we continued with our observation and inspection of the area a while longer. Basically, we were trying to see when and if the crowd and the noise would start to die off. Really, we were racking our brains for anyway that it was going to be okay to rent the flat.

In fact, if truth be told, we were not making sure of anything. We were just working hard to take the bloody flat and be done with it. Come what may we were ready to take the plunge. Just play along and see what happened. In life sometimes wonder wins over fear! Looking back now, it was so obvious that we shouldn't have even considered the flat. But there we were, more than considering, actually trying our bloody best to take it.

Taking The Plunge

Finally, the decision was made; enough was enough, no more looking anymore. As a result, we said yes to the flat and decided to just enjoy the place and the area.

Accordingly, I made an offer of €2,000 per month, which the owner accepted immediately. The main bedroom faced the square and was partitioned into two sections. The section farther from the window was like a darkroom, which seemed to be quieter. In effect, this meant that we could sleep in that part of the flat, if the front section were too noisy.

Immediately, I put my thinking hat on, and decided to put my game design skills to some use. Accordingly, I suggested to the owner to put sliding doors in the dividing wall, so that we could open and close them as needed. This way we could get some light in the back section too, and use the entire space as one big room during the day or whenever we wanted.

Amazingly, the owner loved the idea and said she could get it done in a couple days as she had builders working on another site. Curiously, she asked me if I were an architect or something. No, but I told her I was a game designer. She said, 'Oh, that's where the logical approach comes from'. As planned, we were going to be in the UK from 12th June for a few days visiting our daughter Sila for her graduation. With that in mind, I told the owner that she could get the doors done after we had moved in.

We had seen so many flats and prices by now that I thought this flat was priced at €2,200. By making an offer of 2,000, I thought that I'd knocked €200 off the asking price! In actual fact, I only realised after we had signed the tenancy agreement the real price. It turned out that I had offered them the asking price, which is no wonder why she accepted on the spot! Negotiation was one of my strengths normally, but while negotiating with so many problems and obstacles, I failed with the rent offer!

Frazzled by our tumultuous searching, my clear thinking had deserted me, and I had completely lost control. Clearly, I was not playing the game of life well at all. Well, I did say I wasn't good at playing games! The roles in this situation were not easy either, testing me to the fullest. Thus, I began to think that perhaps I was being punished. Maybe we should have listened to the Mexican girl and left the city, which didn't seem to want us?

Priority wise, we had to be in the UK for Sila's graduation from Backswood School, Hastings, on 12th June. Yet we moved into the flat on 11th June. Truly, I don't know how we managed that calamitous timing! In fact, we didn't really manage anything, we were just moving along without properly thinking during those days.

In the meantime, Gulsun's planned short visit to Turkey for the June 7th elections fell by the wayside. She was going to join me in London from Istanbul, but she didn't want to leave me to face all the difficulties on my own. Firstly, we had to get her London flight sorted, but we couldn't find any available seats on my flight. In the end, we got her a ticket on a flight two hours before mine. The night before we thought we could get up early and go the airport together. Also, I would kill the two hours at the airport on my computer.

Despite everything that had thwarted us, we were really excited, as we were going to move into our first Barcelona flat. We took a taxi from the hotel and loaded up our four suitcases, and other bits and pieces. As per usual, there was no access to the square for vehicles, so the driver parked as close as possible. Furthermore, he was nice enough to give us a hand with our luggage, and I tipped him accordingly.

Finally, we had moved and settled into our El Born flat. Even better the nice owner had left a lovely bowl of fruit for us and in it were two big mangos and one big pineapple! How nice of her I have to say. That night, we ate the lot over the course of the evening, and they were delicious. That evening we decided to get out and get lost in the crowd of buzzing tourists, who, in fact, would be our neighbours for the coming weeks and months. Just as well I thought that we should get acquainted.

Next, we feasted on a nice meal followed by a few drinks in the favourite local tapas bar, El Xampanyet. By the way, the square where the flat was in was called Passeig del Born. In case, you decide to visit it after reading the book.

True to form, the square was so busy and alive. We were just walking around and enjoying the lovely atmosphere, thinking what a place to live, holiday every day! Surely this would be worth any level of noise? We had nothing else to do and therefore we could just mingle with the crowd and the noise all night. Afterwards, we would then go to bed extremely late, just like the others. We were going to live here for a long time, so we may just as well live like a tourist every day. In any case, we had come here to relax and enjoy. Frankly, that was exactly what we should do I thought. We were flying to London tomorrow morning anyway. In which case a couple of hours of sleep would be enough.

Our First Night (Mare) in El Born!

The first night was an utter nightmare, and in comparison, the Gotic flat was a sanctuary. That's how bad it was! We went to bed around 3:30, and the plan was to get a few hours' sleep. After that we would get up, have a quick shower, and set off for the airport. We only had a 20-minute walk to the Aerobus station, in Placa de Catalunya.

Unfortunately, this was not to be because there was no way for us to go to sleep. Mind-numbingly loud, the unprecedented level of non-stop noise, the constant roar of humming and buzzing, was like a herd of bulls charging towards us and we had nowhere to run, trapped in our flat. To be fair, the estate agent had warned us.

Gulsun and Sila in our El Born Flat on Passeig del Born, also known as The Centre of Noise!

The signs were there all along for us to see, but we were completely blind and deaf to it all. 'Please be considerate to your neighbours', 'Please keep your noise down!' 'Please let us sleep!'

Huge banners were everywhere, and yet we chose to ignore them and now, we needed an even bigger banner ourselves. But it was clear that the banners weren't helping, no matter how much pleading was on them! Therefore, the defunct banners weren't going to help us either!

With no double-glazing, the big shutters both outside and inside were only 10-20% effective. No sliding doors yet, but we could try the dark side of the room. At least there was another dividing wall to reduce the noise. Thankfully, there it seemed to be a bit quieter. Even though we could still hear the noise, it seemed more bearable. In many ways, it was like a small sleeping sanctuary from the noise. Nevertheless, it was almost five in the morning before we could go to sleep. At least we could get a couple of hours. This was how desperate for sleep we were!

Alas, it was no more than forty-five minutes or so before we were woken up! This time though not by the outside noise, but by heavy thudding footsteps above us. Obviously, it was a wooden floor, but the noise was so loud and disturbing that it sounded as if they were wearing clogs or high heel shoes! In such an annoying and repeating pattern, it would stop for a bit and then start again, stop, and start… almost as if someone were doing it out of spite to punish us. Bloody hell I thought, it was like we were being tortured!

Then, thank God it stopped. Maybe that was it, probably happens for quarter of an hour every morning I thought, which we could cope with. But, not so fast cowboy, no rest for the devil. Thudding footsteps stopped, but now the heavy furniture was being dragged around. There were big sofas, a dinner table, chairs, and all sorts of other things and each making a horrible squeaky surface noise! It was almost as if they were moving in and rearranging furniture. Tragically, there was no way to sleep. Oh my God, I could cry. Our first night in our first flat had been a complete and utter nightmare!

If truth be told, the Mexican girl was right, and she had rightly warned us about this. Obviously, the city didn't want us and, we were being punished for resisting it!

As if the outside noise wasn't enough to drive us insane, we now had this horrid noise coming from above, and so early in the morning too. During the only time we could sleep, we were subjected to screeching furniture noises. While hoping that moving of furniture would stop and give us a much-needed break, to add insult to injury then a woman started talking on the phone! But it was like she was shouting rather than talking, and with a very high-pitched annoying voice too. Of course, it was in Spanish or Catalan, and she was really enjoying the conversation, laughing, shouting constantly. We could hear every word so clearly. Good job we didn't understand any of it. Perhaps she was telling the other person how she was annoying us and ruining our sleep.

'For God's sake, what's happening?' I despaired. Not a wink of sleep, confused, fed up and drained of all energy. We looked so pathetic, fragile and helpless. I could easily break in half.

Clearly, I was getting a damn good beating from life, but still trying to stay in the ring and on my feet to save the last ounce of sanity. Feeling so desperate, and tearful. How did all this happen, how did I allow it to happen? As if I were going to go mad, I could weep my eyes out.

Undeterred, we managed to pull ourselves together, showered and dressed. With suitcases ready, we just stood there looking at each other totally puzzled. How could we live here like this for a year, and this was only the first night? Even worse, we had only signed the agreement yesterday! How I wished time travel really existed, just like the Time Travel game we had produced in 1990. Simply to go back and change the course of yesterday! It felt like I had just received a life sentence. No way could we get through this soul-destroying situation.

Somehow, we managed to regain our senses, picked up our suitcases, and set off for the airport. Multitasking and taxing my brain; I would sort something out, as I was good at coming up with solutions. Without doubt, I would come up with something to fix this problem too. Meanwhile, I was constantly trying to console us both. Soon after Gulsun's flight left. There was some time before my flight, so I got myself a big mug of Americano, and started thinking again. Surely, I must do something soon, as there was no way we could get through it in one piece. Staying in that flat would definitely drive me nuts.

With many thoughts and fears in my mind, I started writing an email to the Irish estate agent. 'I know you kindly and strongly warned us about the noise, and we didn't listen to you. And clearly, we should have done. We have made a huge mistake and no way could I last there more than two months tops. Please help us! The owner seems to be a nice enough person, and I am sure she would understand. Don't worry, I will make it extremely easy for her to accept. Basically, I will pay for two more months of rent in advance, so that's three months of rent paid in total. That should cover the work she has planned for the double door. Besides, it's a good idea and would benefit the future tenants too. She would have three months to find another tenant. In the meantime, I will try and find a place and vacate the flat as soon as possible.'

Also, I added to the email the fact that we were on our way to the UK for a few days and then I hit send.

When I landed in London, the estate agent had already replied, informing me that she wasn't very hopeful, but my offer seemed quite reasonable, and she would share it with the owner.

Blissful and Quiet Few Days in England!

What a contrast, like day and night, England seemed so quiet and peaceful. We could feel the stark difference. And all the suffering and torture we endured in Barcelona was still so fresh in our memories. Of course, we were in Hastings, a much smaller city, but I know that London is full of quiet streets and cul-de-sacs even in the central parts.

Enjoying sanctuary from the sleepless nights, we forgot all about the noise and enjoyed our time with Sila. It was nice to celebrate with her as she finished her A-levels successfully. Funnily enough, we had been to Hastings when Sila was only two years old and spent a good few hours on the beach.

That day it was cold, windy and the sea was very grey, typical seaside weather. But Sila loved playing in the sand and throwing stones into the sea with me. Life is full of surprises. Who would have known that years later Sila would come back from Turkey, and do her A-levels there in Hastings, England?

Back in Barcelona and Back to Noise!

It wasn't all doom and gloom. We did also enjoy our times in Barcelona!

After a lovely and well-deserved break, we were back in the lovely city of Barcelona. And we were ready to continue our adventure from the save point like in games. Overall, we were more relaxed, having regained some of our strength and energy in the UK.

In anticipation, I checked my emails as soon as we landed in Barcelona. Wow I thought, I couldn't believe my eyes, what an understanding and compassionate person! The owner had accepted my offer. Suddenly positive thoughts took over; maybe things could get better after all? Accordingly, I paid the three months' rent up until the 12th September. To show my appreciation, I also promised the owner that we would vacate the place within two weeks of her finding a new tenant. Worst-case scenario, we could stay at a hotel or find an Airbnb place for a while. Nothing could be worse than what we had presently.

Renegotiating the end of the tenancy agreement was such a relief. And yet it was a like a game of Snakes and Ladders as we were back to square one, flat searching. Watch out estate agents, here we come again, back on the market and on the hunt! Fortunately, we had no pressure other than to save ourselves from the current noise as soon as possible. Therefore, we could suffer a bit and take our time to make sure we get it right. Famous last words.

Time passed. We must have spent weeks looking. Now, we were in high season, and there weren't many places to find! Just like a game; as we were progressing through the adventure, the levels were getting harder. Our indecisiveness coupled with less will power and energy were making it harder to make our minds up.

After a while, Sila came and joined us too. She was also trying to help, but her attitude was to take the first place she liked. Personally, the noise problem had scarred me so much that I wasn't making any decisions at all. If I am perfectly honest, I was becoming so picky to the point that we were not agreeing on anything. Now there were three of us, wanting three different things. Hence, the pressure was mounting alongside my indecisiveness. Sometimes we would view a place and then go, 'Come on let's make a decision, and be done with it.' But last minute I would chicken out.

Although we were discovering new places, quieter areas, the rent was rising to €5-6,000. To be honest, the whole thing was getting out of control again. Also, there were confusing property ad details too because so many of them were inaccurate or contained false information. Upon viewing a place, some things were different to what we had assumed. For instance, we would see an ad for a lovely big loft, only to find that it was an open plan ground floor flat. A loft conversion in the UK is completely different.

Before long, the estate agents were talking about us again. 'Our Turkish friends are back on the hunt!' It was getting harder to find a fully furnished place, so we decided to expand our search horizon by including unfurnished ones too. The thinking was that we could just get some basic furniture from IKEA. Like I said, the gameplay was becoming harder and more complex, and so much more to do, and tackle. As a result, the decision-making was getting more complex too. It was becoming impossible!

Generally, Sila was okay with the noise, as she never slept much during the night anyway. Therefore, we tried to sleep in her room at the back of the flat once or twice. But this time the bloody pigeons woke us up with their early morning ritual of non-stop cooing!

Alas, there was no escaping from the noise and the suffering it caused. Despite all of this, we were still trying to enjoy all the other aspects this wonderful city offered. Lovely weather, food, walks, the beach, but we couldn't make the most of it yet.

Becoming Neighbours With Gaudi!

After seeing almost all of the available flats, we made a firm decision on a flat in the Eixample area. It was near the Diagonal Ave., and the famous landmark building of Gaudi's La Padrara (Casa Mila). Our flat occupied the whole of the Principal Floor of a magnificent old corner building. The principal floors are the master apartments in a building and much larger in size.

Generally, they have the highest ceilings and ours was over four-metres! There was a large living room with

Our lovely Principal Flat

wonderful columns and beautiful large tall windows with painted glass. The owner himself had lived there for a long time and it was beautifully decorated, furnished and well kept.

We were over the moon. We didn't much care about the noise that was coming from the busy main road into our large bedroom. In the end, we bought some earplugs and that solved the problem to some extent. Besides, there were two other rooms and the lovely living room with comfy big sofas to sleep in if needed.

The owner was living in Mexico and the flat was managed by a property management and letting agency. Instantly, I became very friendly with the manager and he was immensely helpful with things that needed fixing or replacing. However, things were so slow in this beautiful city. In fact, it was unbearably slow, inefficient and people were just indifferent to the urgency of matters. Incredibly it took three months to replace our TV, and almost as long to replace the noisy electric hob!

Later, we would discover that the manager was on holiday for the entire month of August! Nevertheless, we were slowly trying to put up with it all and just accept the way things were in Barcelona.

As is customary in Barcelona, most markets and restaurants would be shut between four and seven in the afternoon, something we could never get used to. What's more on particular days, markets would close after certain hours. We lost count of the number of times we would walk to this lovely big local market, only to find it was closed. Every time the same reaction, 'c'mon not again.' Of course, the reaction was also about our failure to remember the days and the times it was open. It is a good job we were really enjoying our long walks by then.

Finally, the day came, and we moved in on 1st of August and, really enjoyed living there. The owner had made a small part of the big principal floor into a studio, where his son lived. We also made friends with him. Generally, the noise was acceptable, and we didn't have much trouble with it. Apart from the occasional cleaning of the office floor above, it was fine. Also, it was much better after the management agency had a word with the office people. Although there was also some noise coming from the neighbouring hostels, they were quiet after midnight.

So, all in all, we were happy in our new home, and we just tried to enjoy the beautiful city of Barcelona with what little energy we had left…

Barcelona in Summary…

Finding a place to live turned into a nightmare, to say the least, but it was mainly our fault, and of our own doing. It is a compact and remarkably busy city with very large roads, which run across and parallel to each other. That means there's always this continuous and horrendous traffic noise. Being exceedingly popular and relatively small makes it both crowded and noisy.

Despite all the small niggles and troubles, we loved every bit of the city and thoroughly enjoyed it. Fantastic weather! In fact, possibly the best you can get anywhere in the world. Even during the hottest season, it never gets unbearable and has hardly any humidity. There is a wonderful variety of food, lovely places to visit and lots to do. Furthermore, everyone seems really relaxed and content, and nobody seems to bother anybody else.

And the jewel in the crown of Barcelona - the lovely, clean blue flag beach in the heart of the city, which is nearly four miles long! It's very well designed and planned and very hygienic too. The beach is cleaned each and every day. Truly there is much to see in and around the city with many wonderful places to visit.

Would I like to live there again? Certainly. With all my hard-earned knowledge and experience, I would probably live in a small historical village near Barcelona. But then again, that was exactly what I had planned. Maybe better luck next time.

What Barcelona Experience Taught Me?

This is what I learnt from the Barcelona experience. No matter how nice and lovely a place is, unless you're happy and content within yourself, you will never be happy enough wherever you are. It was clear that I was running away from frustration and unhappiness caused by the sudden pause to my long career. Topped off with the failed attempt of forming a gaming academy.

How can you run away from your problems when they are very much part and parcel of who you are? Our problems are within us and we carry them with us wherever we go. They are our luggage in life. What a shame there is no luggage drop off point for our problems! Maybe there is, but so far, I have failed to find it. Please let me know if you know of one!

Barcelona is beautiful, but ultimately, they were utterly new surroundings for us. Plus, a new language (two in fact, Spanish and Catalan), culture and lifestyle. In the end, I discovered that having too much of a good thing didn't work long-term. To think that one could live like a tourist every day is a misguided fantasy. In reality, I wasn't content within myself and I felt empty and useless. Gradually, I started to fear that I might never make games again or do meaningful and impactful things. This is the worst thing that could happen to someone who had been producing and creating for decades. And that was exactly what had happened to me.

That was the stark truth and reality I was facing.

Towards the end of our stay, I tried to make myself available to the large and successful game development community in Barcelona. Ubisoft had a sizeable presence in Barcelona, but I never attempted to contact or visit them. It seemed like I was almost scared to try things. It was quite terrifying to think that I was lacking self-confidence, something that I had always had in spades. When you start losing confidence, then fear and anxiety start to fill the void.

Too Little Too Late

However, I was invited to make a presentation at the Game BCN, a game and start-up incubation centre, which was supported by the local Catalan Government. Really, I cannot tell you how much I enjoyed sharing my knowledge and experience with the 9 start-ups. It was something I had been doing for years in Turkey. Even better was the fact that they were really impressed with my work and all the insights I shared. It was lovely to discover that they already knew some of my work from the 80s and the 90s.

Quite a few of them asked me to mentor them. Amongst the nine, I decided to mentor one, which I really enjoyed doing. Overall, I believe I made a meaningful contribution to the game. Also, they were so happy and grateful for my guidance and insights, which they always recognised and acknowledged. For the record, the game was STAY by Appnormals. It was a superb concept, with a great story supported by lovely pixel art. In fact, we are still in contact with Inaki and Danny, the founders of the studio.

Unfortunately, it was too little and too late to keep me in Barcelona. My destiny was set, as I had already decided to move on. Equally, Gulsun was feeling it too, as she wasn't very happy either, missing her language and close friends. In addition to this, she was missing all the meaningful and important work she was doing in Turkey at Mor Cati, a very important women's organisation.

Becoming A Chef

After the long and energy draining flat hunting, Gulsun wanted a long break and to go back to Istanbul. She stayed in Turkey for the whole month of September.

As usual, I was doing my daily walks of fifteen thousand steps. Just wandering around, discovering new areas plus attending a few jazz concerts. But after a while, the daily routine started to bore me. More than anything, I was really missing my music system, as I usually enjoyed a few hours of intense listening each day. Listening to music is an important part of my daily routine and nourishment.

To me, and probably to many more, 'music is food for the soul.' Which brings me to the lovely couple I met and became friends with in Barcelona. One thing that I found very disappointing was the lack of hi-fi shops. Astonishingly, there were only a handful and they didn't seem to carry many of the major brands either. This really had shocked me as London was brilliant for it and, even Istanbul had several great shops. To be honest, I had expected at least a few major ones in Barcelona.

By complete chance, I discovered a very big hi-fi shop in the heart of the city, 'Supersonido'. It was run by Ernesto and his German wife Caroline. Funnily enough, they had opened the Barcelona branch in May 2015, at the same time of our arrival. In fact, it was a twenty-five year old family business out of Bilbao.

God, I was so happy to discover their shop, like a little kid. Totally engrossed, I spent quite a bit of time there and listened to plenty of music. Ernesto couldn't speak English, but Caroline did. We became instant friends and saw

With Ernesto at Supersonido

each other quite often. It was marvellous as we really enjoyed their friendship and the wonderful food they introduced us to at their favourite tapas bars.

After Gulsun had gone, I started to get bored with the same food, almost always eating out. Suddenly, I realised that I had missed some of the traditional Turkish food that I loved. Surprisingly, there weren't any decent Turkish restaurants in Barcelona either. All that time, I had also completely forgotten about my homemade yogurt and cornbread. In a eureka moment, it suddenly occurred to me, 'What could be better than doing some good old home cooking? That would be a great way to pass the time and enjoy some homemade wholesome food.'

In The Kitchen

We had a lovely little kitchen in the flat with all the utensils I needed. Yogurt and cornbread were easy enough, as I managed to find maize flour from the local shops. Just as in the UK, most of the corner shops were owned by the Pakistanis and were open twenty-four hours, which was brilliantly convenient.

But the biggest challenge was to attempt some serious traditional Turkish and Georgian dishes that I love. Conveniently, I went

Beans, Cornbread and yogurt all by me

through dozens of YouTube videos and found some favourites to try out. Any ingredient I couldn't find, I would simply improvise and replace with something appropriate.

It was such fun, and I was really enjoying cooking and creating some very tasty food. First, I thought maybe I had missed Turkish food so much that it seemed to taste nice. With that in mind, I invited a Turkish friend to try out some of my home cooking to see if it was as delicious as I thought. The friend in question had been living in Barcelona for years. Incidentally, he supplied cooking equipment to restaurants and was bit of a gourmet himself. Besides that, he even had a Turkish restaurant of his own at some point. Of course, it goes without saying that his Turkish wife was cooking a lot of traditional Turkish food at home. Anyway, he tasted my Turkish beans with meat, along with some cornbread and yogurt. Fabulously, he absolutely loved it all and, seemed to be genuinely surprised. Even better, he repeatedly complimented the food and me, declaring that it was delicious. Well, that gave me a lot of encouragement and I tried to create lots of different dishes.

Subsequently, I cooked many dishes for many friends, who visited us from Turkey. They also loved my food and were sufficiently impressed by my cooking. As a matter of fact, I have been cooking at home ever since. And, constantly kidding my friends and myself with the idea of opening a small place; Mev's Eats. Who knows and why not?

Of course, I must not forget about the moka coffee, which I first tasted in Barcelona and have been consuming ever since. When I first saw the moka coffee maker in the kitchen, I didn't know what it was. In no time at all, I learnt to use it and enjoyed lots of moka coffee. Instead of milk, I mostly have a bit of Baileys Irish cream whiskey with it, which I used to have in my black coffee.

In the end, I bought my own moka coffee maker in London, and have been using it all the time. One of my treats of an evening, especially after a meal, is to brew a big mug of moka coffee. My magical recipe is this: I put some Baileys in it, and have it with hazelnuts, bitter chocolate and a couple of Annas original ginger thins.

Such a great combination, which I would highly recommend you try. You can thank me later when we hopefully meet someplace and sometime for a book signing!

With family and friends in Barcelona

Bye-bye Barcelona, London is Calling!

We had planned to stay in Barcelona for around 3 years or so, but after just short of a year, I wanted to move on. Despite all that was great about Barcelona, I just wasn't happy with myself and, wanted a change, which hopefully would help me obtain some fulfilling occupation. Likewise, Gulsun wasn't incredibly happy either. With that in mind, we decided to look for a new home and, for a better and more meaningful life.

This time neither of us wanted a new adventure filled with unknowns and further disappointment. Hence, we unanimously decided to play it safe and go somewhere where we would be more familiar with the surroundings, the people, the language, and the culture. Effectively, we were looking to be within our comfort zone.

In hindsight, I am not 100% sure, but I think Gulsun wouldn't have minded going back to Turkey. But for me, there was no way that I could go back, not after twelve months. Especially since I was feeling just as bad as when I had left a year ago, if not worse.

London was calling...

Gulsun had many friends in London. With no language problems, she could spend quality time with both English and Turkish speaking friends. Of course, she could get involved in the local women's organisations too or work with children as she had done before.

As for me, I would be going back to my own backyard, back to my own turf, as it were. The very place, where I had already lived for over twenty years and where I had learnt almost everything about game development. It was my theatre of dreams where I successfully developed some notable games that are still remembered and loved by many even today. Plus, I had many friends to reconnect with. Also, there were so many team members and colleagues I had worked with. So many possibilities, so much more than any other city could offer.

On balance, there seemed to be only one destination that would fit the bill right now, good old London...

London Here I Come, Again, 2016!

Yes, under the circumstances, London was the obvious choice for our next destination. Furthermore, our daughter Sila was now studying at Leeds College of Music. Being in London would mean seeing her more often and spending more time together. Nej was still in Istanbul but he could visit us easily.

Here we go again, house-hunting time! I had sold my wonderful old house in Harrow on the Hill, so there was no home to go back to. Basically, I had to start all over again as I had done nearly forty years ago! But this time at least I could speak the lingo and find my way around London with ease.

Now, where would we live in London, so many choices? We came in February 2016, for a short trip and a quick look around to establish the possible districts.

Our tenancy agreement in Barcelona was expiring at the end of July 2016, but I wanted to move by mid-May. However, Gulsun and Sila would stay on for a couple of months, as they wanted to visit Madrid and a few other cities in Spain that we couldn't see before. Once I set my mind to something, I just have to do it. Thus, I decided to leave Barcelona and it had to be done as soon as possible. In truth, it was like an opportunity for me to get rid of all my worries. I was running away again…

The two cities cannot be more different. London is so much bigger, yet so much quieter and with more choices on either side of the River Thames. Nevertheless, we didn't want to live too far away from the town centre as we did before with Harrow on the Hill. From Harrow it used to take over forty-five minutes on the Metropolitan tube line, so it wasn't very practical or easy to go into town.

Trying hard to leave all the negative feelings behind, we short-listed a few districts Gulsun and I fancied as far apart as Greenwich and Highgate. The most important thing was that we weren't too keen to be too close to the hustle and bustle of the city centre. With that in mind, we set a travel time limit of 20-25 minutes by tube or 45-50 minutes bus ride to central London.

One of the great benefits of living in Barcelona was the daily average of 15,000 plus steps. What a great way to discover places in a city and to stay fit. To be honest, I hadn't really seen much of London when I lived there in the late 80s and the 90s. But this time with nothing much to do and plenty of time to kill, I was determined to discover and visit all the interesting places, which London certainly has plenty of. Not just the city itself, but also all the wonderful villages, parks and woods surrounding it.

Initially, we decided to stay in Greenwich for a week or so. Gulsun's niece Isil was living there and was also working at the Greenwich University as a lecturer. This meant we could her see her too after many years apart.

In The Greenwich Meantime!

To begin with, we stayed at a nice small hotel right in the centre of the village. I loved the whole place. It was such a lovely little village full of character. Right by the River Thames and with amazing views over the London landmark buildings and Canary Wharf, with gorgeous sunsets almost every night, and lots of people especially coming to capture the lovely images.

As happy as Larry, I thought I could live there because I loved Greenwich and instantly took a liking to it. Just as I did with the El Born district in Barcelona. And as a result, I thought there was no point in doing much searching elsewhere. However, there was no harm in checking out a few other alternatives too. Plus, it would be a good excuse to wander around the city. We could have a nice walk around and discover new places too. Henceforth, we spent a couple days checking out a myriad of places along the south side of the River Thames, including London Bridge and beyond.

We found a couple of estate agents in Greenwich and very quickly arranged a number of viewings to get a feel for what sort of flats they had to offer. The prices ranged from £2,200 to £2,700 per month for two-bed furnished flats. It was clear in our minds that we were definitely looking for furnished or at least part furnished. The reason being we didn't want to buy furniture yet, as we didn't know how long our second coming would last. As we were getting to know Greenwich, I was beginning to like it even more with its lovely park and observatory, village market, riverside walks and pubs. Not forgetting the amazing historical buildings.

One day we saw a two-bedroom, modern flat in a newly built complex right by the river, and my favourite Waitrose supermarket. It had the most beautiful views ever over the river, with ceiling to floor windows all around the round fronted flat, including both bedrooms. In addition to that, it also had a balcony, which stretched along the width of the flat with full height opening glass panels! The views were just stunning!

Thankfully, the asking price was £2,600 per month, which was well within our range. Without any doubts, I really fancied it myself and was ready to make an offer on the spot. Also, I clearly remembered all the horrid experiences of Barcelona and therefore didn't want to miss the opportunity. On the downside, it had an American style kitchen, which put Gulsun off a bit, plus she thought the rooms were on the small side with limited storage space. Having learned from experience, I thought to myself, 'Here we go again, asking for trouble, as if she hadn't learnt lessons from before'. However, my lips were sealed, and I didn't say anything, but I really liked it. 'I will try and get this flat', I thought.

We checked many other places along the river and went to Highgate to look at some semi-detached houses with gardens. What a lovely place! Highgate could be a serious alternative too.

After seeing some more places and flats, we went back to Barcelona. Also, I left my number with a few estate agents with clear instructions as to what we were looking for. We stipulated a few important things setting some red lines, but the lines weren't as rigid or as red as in Barcelona. Lessons learnt, perhaps. Pretty soon they were going to send on any other interesting flats for us to evaluate. Then, we could come back to view all of them and hopefully choose the best one.

Eventually, I came back to Greenwich to check out a few flats that we had short-listed from many different agents. If I am honest, I was afraid of spending a lot time going through endless alternatives. Intentionally, the first thing I did was to view the first flat we had seen (The one I liked by the river). Unsurprisingly, I liked it even more on my second viewing. After seeing a few others here and there mostly by the river, I decided that the Greenwich flat was perfect and we should not miss the opportunity. With my firm conviction, I convinced Gulsun that it was the best flat for many reasons. Besides, Greenwich was such a lovely village to live in too. Many lovely walks and places around it, we could even walk via the Thames foot tunnel to Canary Wharf. The Wharf was now a beautiful financial quarter with lovely walks, restaurants and cafes of its own.

Full systems go! I made an offer, which was accepted very quickly and we signed within a week. The great news was that I could move in on 15th May, as that was when the current tenant was moving out.

Wow, that made a change! Easy and quick and a lovely flat to boot! A sign of better things to come perhaps.

Second Coming to London, May 2016

Here I was in London again. The beginning of a new adventure and the start of a new beginning… Amazingly, after some thirty-seven years, I would be making another start in the UK. But this time in completely different circumstances. The first one lasted over twenty years, but only time would tell how long the second one would last.

Feeling more in control of things and avoiding any unnecessary risks, I managed to rent the first flat I had seen and liked. My mind went back to Barcelona and wondered what would have happened had I done the same and rented the first flat I liked in El Born. Of course, I will never know. My thoughts wondered about what London had in store for me instead.

The flat was on the first floor of a 12-storey modern building with an oval front, like an Admirals tower. Hence the name of the building, Admirals Tower! Stunning and awe-inspiring, the views over the river and London city were just out of this world. Wow, I couldn't believe my luck. Truly, it didn't matter whether it was sunny or rainy, it was always beautiful just the same.

With feelings of nostalgia, I remember how the sunsets were just gorgeous with beautiful vivid colours. Also, the vista was changing into many different shapes and shades, as the sun went down. You couldn't take your eyes off it. Every day I was taking so many pictures with my iPhone and finding it difficult to choose which one to share on social media.

The flat also had clear and beautiful views of the Gherkin and other modern buildings. So many great places nearby too! All in all, I was having a lovely time rediscovering London, especially walking to Canary Wharf, or taking the DLR (Docklands Light Railway) to Bank station, the heart of Central London.

Sunset view from the Greenwich in its full glory! With Admirals Tower building on the left

The view from the actual flat! Both pics taken with my iPhone, 2016

Reconnecting With Friends and Work Colleagues

Straight away, I started making contact with some of my old chums, whom I had kept in touch with, and also, some of my team members, and Turkish friends, who I hadn't contacted for over sixteen years.

Everyone seemed to be very pleased about my return, and some even hinting at my possible comeback to the UK gaming scene. How nice and gratifying I thought, I must have left a lasting impression on people around me. After a horrid twelve months, it made me feel incredibly good and I enjoyed the warm reception and welcome.

In a short time, I managed to meet quite a few of my old buddies, to name but a few: Jon Hare, Charles Cecil, Will Cowling, Raffaele Cecco, Charles Hasdell, Mat Sneap, Hugh Binns, Doug Hare, Mark Cale, Sean Brenan, Gary Williams, Rod Cousens and Shahid Kamal Ahmad.

Strangely enough, we had never met with Shahid before when I lived in the UK, although we almost started at the same time in the gaming industry in the mid-80s. But many moons later we met for the first time in Barcelona, and it was an instant friendship! So, we met a few more times in London.

Of course, I hooked up with some of our Turkish friends too. My good friend Erdem Celik, who was previously with Google, was soon to start at Facebook in London. It seemed that the London decision was good for social connections. If nothing else, I would definitely have a much nicer time in London. For starters, I had a much better beginning than in Barcelona, that was for sure.

Revisiting Southampton, My First UK Hometown

Without much delay, I decided to visit Southampton too, my first home in the UK back in 1979. It would be good to see my sister in-law Carol and her husband Roy, and their kids too. God, the kids must have grown up by now, both older than my son Nej who was now 40 himself! Besides that, I would definitely see my good mate Brian Marshall, the lovely guy who did the amazing and crazy sonics for my early games. He was still living in Southampton.

Of course, I would reconnect with and see Janet, my first wife and the reason for my first coming to the UK. Unfortunately, my father in-law George had passed away a few years earlier. My mother-in-law was still alive, well only just. Sadly, she was extremely ill and staying at an old people's home, bed ridden.

Reconnecting With Janet

We had always remained in touch with Janet and asking after each other from time to time. Sadly, Janet couldn't see much of Nej or hear from him for years. Nej had been living in Istanbul and Janet never had a chance to visit. However, they exchanged emails or phone calls, but it's never the same as seeing each other. Unfortunately, this was making Janet very sad, but she had accepted it however difficult it was. Kids don't really understand the love of their parents until they themselves become one. There is no doubt that Nej loves his mum, but sometimes life makes things too difficult for us. Living thousands of miles apart is doubly harder.

With Janet in Southampton, 2016

Janet was now living in Kent on a riverboat. She had never remarried, and I am not even sure if she had a steady relationship. To be honest, we never really talked about it, but she knew about my second marriage and my daughter Sila. In truth, Janet is a very considerate and kind-hearted person and she always asks after them.

Janet told me about her mum on the phone. Basically, she was visiting her in Southampton a few times a month and staying there with her for a few days. Luckily, her elder sister Carol was still living in Southampton and so could visit more often.

Anyway, we arranged to meet up in Southampton at the nursing home where her mum was. This way I could see them both. It was really nice to see and catch up with Janet, but very upsetting to find her mum looking so poorly and completely bedridden. Poor thing was in a bad state and was being fed by the nurses too. It was terribly sad to see her like that after so many years. Without doubt, life can be so cruel and unforgiving at times. Aging is inevitable, but to spend one's remaining life bedridden and helpless is surely the worst thing. Life is so precious and even in the worst of conditions, it seems we want to experience life to the best of our ability until our very last breath.

To be honest, I wasn't at all sure if she even remembered me when Janet introduced me. Janet had told me that her only favourite enjoyment in what was left of her life was a cup of tea, and a few Mr Kipling Angel Slices! To make a small contribution to her remaining enjoyment, I had brought a few packets of Mr Kipling cakes with me. She seemed so pleased when Janet told her about it that her eyes lit up. It seems that as we grow old, we become like kids again. The story of Benjamin Button is definitely true in spirit.

With Janet's instructions, I even made a cup of tea for my mother-in-law Doris; not too hot, and with plenty of milk. She really enjoyed me feeding her with her tea and her favourite Mr Kipling slices. She loved it and you could see it was something she very much looked forward to - probably the only thing. How sad, really. That was the only little bit of pleasure she was able to enjoy; the rest just seemed like suffering as she was holding on to her dear life. Making the most of the time I had there, I visited the mother in-law and met with Janet several times...

Meeting With Brian Marshall, Carol, Roy and The Kids

On my last visit to Southampton, I wanted to walk around some of the important and familiar places. It felt really weird to say the least. So many memories gushing through my mind and so quickly that I just couldn't keep up with it all. The first port of call was our council flat and the St. Marys College, where I had taken my English lessons. Followed by the areas, and the houses where I had lived. Somehow, I failed to go and see the STC cable factory. Shut and dismantled a long time ago, perhaps there was nothing much to see anyway.

Most importantly, we arranged to meet up with my friend Brian in the afternoon. It was so lovely to catch up after so many years. We ended up spending several hours together at his place, reminiscing over a nice couple of cuppas. Brian also visited me back in London.

Next up, my plan was to meet up with Carol and her family for an evening meal. There was a new shopping complex outside Southampton where we met, near Southampton Airport. Thankfully, Brian drove me there, so we talked even more on the way. It was quite emotional for all of us. Both Carol and Roy were genuinely very happy to see me, as were the kids. Their daughter Jennifer had come with her partner. In addition to that, their son Michael had come all the way from the Isle of Wight where he now lives. Reunited together, we talked for ages over a lovely dinner. We had so many memories to reminisce about and so much new stuff to share too.

Truly, Roy seemed extremely happy to see me, which pleasantly surprised me. In fact, he told everyone how they followed my success, and how proud they were of me. That made me so happy. The English normally aren't as emotional as the Turks, and don't really show their true feelings. Because of this emotional distancing and coldish stance, it's hard to tell how much the English people like or appreciate you. Therefore, it was so heart-warming to hear them say all those wonderful things about my work and me. Especially as they were sharing it with their son in-law and making me feel like a family member once more which was so nice.

Of course, Roy also talked about how he helped me get the job at the cable factory. Also, how I managed to learn programming all by myself. Well, it was quite an emotional thing and my eyes got a bit watery. Michael was also married with two kids, and had become a successful writer with a couple of published books under his belt.

Unfortunately, dear Roy (RIP) passed away in late 2019. Such a sad and sudden loss, I do hope he is happy wherever he is.

From left Me, Sean, Roy, Carol, Jennifer and Michael, 2016

With Brian Marshall in London, 2016

Vivid Image team in 1995-96 from left; Robby, Harris, Mark, Allan, Charlie, Neil, Lee and me.

Meeting and seeing many friends in London, 2016-2017

Bringing Janet and Nej Together

Without doubt, it was clear to me that Janet would love to see Nej. Accordingly, I arranged for Nej and his girlfriend to come and visit us in London for a few days. Previously, they had also visited us in Barcelona. The big day came and Janet and Nej met up in London and spent some time together. She was so happy to spend time with her son. Afterwards, Janet was grateful to me for arranging it. Truly, the love of a mother for her child is like no other, as I know so well from my own mum.

A few months later I also arranged for Janet to go to Istanbul to see both Nej and the city itself for a week. Symbolically, it was the very city where we first met, and which she loved very much. Therefore, she was over the moon about it. She told me afterwards how much Istanbul had changed, and unfortunately for the worse. Also, she said that she remembered it being so lovely, whereas now it was overgrown, overcrowded and way too noisy. Sadly, that's how most of us think too. Istanbul was so much more beautiful before, and most people miss the old city of Istanbul…

Now Back in London. Could I Also Make a Comeback?

As I started meeting with friends and my ex team members, I also started thinking about a possible comeback - and why not? What better place to do it than in London? Everyone I met was asking if I was thinking about making a comeback. Some were even declaring that they would be more than happy to join me should I setup a team.

All this was fuelling my appetite. Soon after, I found myself seriously discussing the idea of setting up a company around a compact team. We could start with a remake of my own classics, Street Racer or First Samurai.

First, I had met Charlie Hasdell, who had just left Sony PlayStation Europe (London Office) and seemed to be very enthusiastic about the prospect of working with me again. Charlie did his industrial placement at Vivid Image in the early 90s, and I gave him a fulltime position as a game designer after his graduation.

One of the top people, Will Cowling was working at Sony as a lead programmer. He told me that Sony was laying off some more people and, he would be very happy to join us too. Incidentally, it was Will, who had come to Turkey and helped me in my first year. As a result, I felt it would be great to have Will again right from the beginning.

However, I decided to make sure no one took undue risks and sensibly I suggested to Will that he continued at Sony. Initially, he could spend some of his spare time with us in the evenings and at weekends. Apparently, there was a possibility that he may be laid off too. Being naturally cautious, I decided to see how things would go.

This warm and enthusiastic reception was invigorating and was encouraging me even more. After careful consideration, I suggested that we should do a remake of Street Racer, and probably on mobile. Furthermore, we would do it with Unity or Unreal game engine. That would mean that the game could be released on many platforms including consoles. After all, I had even developed my first game on three platforms.

Becoming a BAFTA Member

By the way, we were having our meetings at BAFTA (195 Piccadilly). The UK gaming industry had come a long way since I had left it back in late 2000. And now, we even had BAFTA Games. Lovely Jubbly I thought, as Dell Boy (Only Fools And Horses TV series) would say.

Will and Charlie were members through Sony, and they were signing me in as their guest. Surely, I thought, I should become a member myself, as I did do my little bit for the UK gaming sector in the 80s and 90s. Both Charlie and Will said that I deserved to be a BAFTA member more than most. With Will's recommendation I applied and became a member within a few weeks. Wow, it felt really good to be a BAFTA member. Suddenly, I found myself back in the UK gaming scene again and really feeling a part of something.

Honestly, I must admit that I thoroughly enjoyed my BAFTA membership and spent a lot of time there. Mostly, I had my meetings there. I loved it so much that I even invited a few non-gamer friends to have lunch at BAFTA. They were impressed and enjoyed the lovely atmosphere and the food. Incidentally, they serve a lovely breakfast and lunch at BAFTA. Even better is the fact that members are also able to go to premiere screenings. In addition, BAFTA also does a great job with awards and provides mentorship and support to young budding game developers and designers.

Super Street Racer

Pierre-Luc Vettier is a real fan of the Saturn Street Racer. He really wanted to develop a new version with me, but it just wasn't to be for one reason or another.

After a lot of brainstorming, I came up with the name Pixel Age Studios and everybody seemed to like it. So now we were all set, and we could set up a company too. Firstly, we were going to prepare a nice Kickstarter project and go for small community funding. Equally, it would be good for marketing and PR too. To keep things simple, I suggested we called the remake Super Street Racer, as in Super Street Fighter. Next, Charlie tried out a few logos. We even did some preliminary character graphics too.

However, everyone was working remotely because I decided to see how things would work out. Initially, two to three of the new people had crucial roles in the team, but I had never worked with them before. This meant we didn't know each other at all and this situation worried me quite a bit. Also, the other downside was the fact that I always found remote work inefficient, especially with small teams. This is because I am very much a hands-on producer and enjoy working closely with my team and this also raised a few concerns.

Unfortunately, we also experienced some major differences about ideas and approaches with the new members. More so, I could clearly see that I could have serious issues with managing them effectively. I had offered the initial team an equal say, equal responsibility, and equal equity too. Which in the long run could have made my task of managing the product and the team even harder.

With these negative thoughts in mind, it seemed too risky. And I didn't want to fall out with people who I didn't even know yet. So, I thought better of it and decided to give it up before going too far. Clearly, it disappointed and upset people, but there was no way I could do something for the sake of doing it. Already feeling vulnerable, I needed to be 100% sure and comfortable about it, and I wasn't. I decided that it was better to upset or disappoint people right at the start, rather than fall out big time much later down the road. That could have had far worse consequences.

Being semi-retired myself, I wasn't taking any major risks, but apart from Charlie they were all going to leave their jobs. There was absolutely no way I could risk other people's futures and livelihoods.

Unfortunately, that was the end of Super Street Racer. The race was finished before it had even started. Of course, I was really sorry about the decision, but deep down I knew it was the right one. To be honest, I was really upset and sad myself, as I really wanted to make a new start, but it wasn't to be.

How About Super Samurai Instead?

In the meantime, I also had several meetings with Raffaele Cecco and Teoman Irmak. It was great to reunite as the original First Samurai team. In fact, we had first reunited sometime in 2014, when I was still living in Turkey. Back then we had discussed the

Concept work for Super Samurai by Ozan Civit

possibility of remaking First Samurai again. It would be just the three of us, maybe one or two more artists to help. A small compact team, just like the good old days. They loved the idea then. We were all extremely excited about the prospect of resurrecting one of our classic games. Perhaps, this time it would achieve the success it surely deserved, but never received due to the demise of Mirrorsoft.

After two years, we started seriously discussing the project again. This time, it would be under Pixel Age Studios. We would do it from scratch but try and maintain all the important elements and aspects that made the original such a classic. Of course, as always, we would add some fancy and exciting new stuff too, which we were very capable of and good at doing. In addition, this would be much more manageable, as the original team had worked together before for years. Even more importantly, we had mostly worked remotely then, and could easily do it again with all the new technology and facilities available.

In the 90s, Teoman had worked from Birmingham and he was still living there. So, he would simply do the same again. Raff had mostly worked from home too even though he was living in London. Nowadays, he was living in Leicester, but that was inconsequential as we could meet up occasionally in London, Birmingham, or Leicester.

Collectively, Raff and I loved the idea and got so excited about it. But for some reason, Teoman didn't appear to be enthusiastic at all. There was no sign of his drive and passion of two years earlier, but complete negativity. In fact, he kept telling us about his recent bad experiences and failing very badly. Moreover, that he didn't want to take any risks again. There was no risk, as we were planning a Kickstarter to raise some funds. In addition, I assured them that even if the Kickstarter campaign failed, I would fund the project myself to create a demo.

No matter what we said or what assurances we gave, he wouldn't have it. We just couldn't convince him. He just wouldn't budge an inch. It was a real shame. If only we could have tried, as Raff and I were certain about pulling it off.

However, it was clear that the original team was out of the question in terms of graphics. Sometimes, we can feel that something isn't going to happen, and on this very occasion, there were signs everywhere. But then again, when we want something so badly, we also tend to turn a blind eye to things, and pretend they are not happening.

It was almost as if Teoman's negative approach made our attitude even more positive. As a result, Raff and I decided to accept and respect Teoman's decision but go ahead with it ourselves. Besides, we had always enjoyed working together, and it would be great to do it again after so many years. Likewise, Raff had been out of games for a long time too, making some professional web stuff and selling it online. He said he really missed game development and would love to make a comeback too.

Thus, Pixel Age Studios came to be with us both as directors and shareholders. Along the way, we would find a talented artist or two and give it a go. Raff and I we met up a few times in Leicester and in London. We were really having fun coming up with lots of ideas. Chatting away, we were discussing how we could make a game special and impress everyone as we had before. It would be our last foray perhaps.

As an aside, I had also visited Mat Sneap and Hugh Bins at their Eight Pixel Square mobile company in Derby. It was nice to see them too. Prior to the Derby visit, Mat and I had also met up in London. It was really nice to hook up again after so many years. It was Mat who did the graphics for the excellent C64 version of our First Samurai. Previously, we had discussed the possibility of remaking some of my old IPs. Therefore, my visit to Derby was a follow up meeting. At the same time, I also met with Raff, who came up to Derby from Leicester.

Full of enthusiasm, Raff and I started looking for an artist, who would love to work with us and fully commit to the project. Having great graphics was an integral and important part of a quality game, something both Raff and I put a lot of importance on. Hence, I really had to find a good artist, who could meet our expectations and deliver the quality we always craved.

Frankly, that was why we really wanted Teoman with us in the team. One hundred percent we knew we could rely on him to deliver the goods. Finding a top artist really proved difficult and took a long time too. Suddenly, I found myself experiencing similar problems with finding an artist, as I had done with finding a flat in Barcelona!

Eventually, we managed to sort out some background graphics, which we thought would be decent enough for the Kickstarter campaign demo.

Fabulously, Raff learnt to use the Unity game engine in no time at all. Without a shadow of a doubt, he is one of the best programmers I have ever worked with. Hitting the ground running, he quickly started producing wonderful stuff. In fact, it was going very nicely, and we were coming up with some interesting ideas. Somehow, I even managed to find a very gifted artist in Turkey, who did some lovely concept work from our brief. In addition, he also designed the new main character. As we wanted to bring the game up to date with the current quality of games, we felt it should look 3D, but play like a 2D game. That meant that the game should have a fast, fluid, and flowing gameplay with impressive 3D visuals. Yet again, we found a very decent character modeller and animator in Turkey for the main character.

Overall, Raff and I were reasonably happy with the graphics although they could have been much better. We spent a lot of time making the demo really stunning, and it did look impressive. We also received some help from a veteran UK artist for the background graphics. Also, Raff added some fancy graphical effects to jazz it up a bit too. Eventually, we put together a nice Kickstarter project, which we announced and kicked off in early November 2016. The initial reaction was incredibly positive.

We soon found out that there were so many Kickstarter projects. What's more, I would soon realise that promoting a campaign to reach enough people was more important than the actual project itself. In the first few days, we got exceptionally good backing, mostly from my own network, and some people even pledging for £500 rewards. Very quickly we reached over £10,000, but it became clear very quickly that reaching the target of £90,000 would prove extremely difficult.

Next of all, it quickly transpired from many of the comments that the retro community were refusing to accept and support the project as it was. Basically, they simply stated that it looked too 3D and that they were expecting a re-mastered original! Sadly, that was probably the biggest blow to us. Looking back in hindsight, we should have done a little bit of research and a survey prior to launching the campaign. This would have helped us establish what the retro community and gamer expectations were.

Under the circumstances, it seemed futile to continue with the campaign. Overall, it was proving too hard for me; staying up every night, trying to rally people to back us. In truth, it was so tough, and I just couldn't see myself struggling for another twenty days to hit the target.

In the end, to save me from a punishingly hard task and the risk of possible embarrassment, I decided that we should simply cancel the campaign.

In all honesty, the retro community didn't embrace what we wanted to do and to reach new gamers would require a bigger and a more professional campaign. As a result, I discussed the situation with Raff and told him that despite my best efforts it would be too difficult to hit the target set. The eventual failure would have been soul destroying for us both. Accepting that there was a high risk of not hitting the target with the Kickstarter, we decided to gracefully cancel the project incredibly early. So many people were really disappointed, but everyone respected our decision. Most of them are still waiting for us to develop a game.

Despite accepting the reality of the situation, it was obvious that we really wanted to develop this game and didn't want to give up. Nevertheless, we cancelled, but decided to forge ahead with the development ourselves. Perhaps we would create a demo, and then try and find a publisher. However, that wasn't very realistic and practical really. Raff wasn't working and he was spending all his time on the game and not producing any of his web stuff. This made me feel really uneasy as he was working on the demo without pay. To make things a bit easier, I offered to pay Raff towards the demo. Raff only reluctantly accepted, and we continued for another few weeks. But now, Raff wasn't too comfortable about only me taking the financial risk.

Besides, we weren't happy with the graphics either. They just weren't cutting it, and nowhere near our expectations. This in turn meant that we couldn't produce something that we would be proud of. In the past, we had always been proud of our work. As such, we didn't want to put our legacy at risk with a game that we weren't 100% happy with.

It was so obvious that things weren't going the way we wanted, but we really wanted to do something together. We weren't ready to give up and we tried to keep going although we just weren't getting anywhere.

How About Going Mobile Instead

Maybe we could do a mobile game instead, it could be relatively easier and quicker. We would just give it a few more weeks and see how we get on. Truly, we were still trying to stay in the game, well, in fact, trying to get back in the game to be precise. Also, I came up with a simple, one-touch, easy-to-play game mechanic. The underlying idea was that anyone should be able to play, plus it had some fancy puzzles and obstacles to negotiate by using some physics too. All the while, Raff was brilliantly coding lots of ideas. Similarly, I also immensely enjoyed inventing interesting and fun ideas. Together we could really make a fun mobile game. Apart from which, mobile gaming was the way to go anyway. At that time, it was already commanding half the revenue of the gaming sector.

Basically, I came up with a character based on Wiggly Polliwog (a tadpole). Raff loved it, and we ended up calling the game Polliwog. As ever, Raff was producing levels and trying out new things very quickly, while I was testing, tweaking controls and suggesting ideas. We became excited again, it seemed we both needed to succeed somehow. 100% we were not giving up and kept trying different things to keep going. It wasn't the most professional way to go about things, but it showed how much we wanted it to happen. Eventually, we found someone to help with the graphics, but it was proving too difficult to get what we wanted. It was just too much work for the results that weren't satisfactory for us.

After a while, we both felt that we were probably going to spend more time than we should on it. Raff also didn't feel comfortable about getting paid out of the company, which I both appreciated and respected. The bottom line was that Raff had a family to support and it was best for him to find a nice and secure job with decent pay. Shortly afterwards, Raff found a particularly good job, which wasn't surprising with his ability and experience. With a fulltime job, Raff couldn't spend enough time on the game, and it would not be practical to carry on.

And that was that. Although we both wanted to make a real go of it, it just wasn't working out, no matter how hard we tried. It just wasn't meant to be…

The cumulative effect was that it really made another massive dent in my confidence. Very soon after I started thinking that I would never make games again, and that that was it for me. To be honest, I couldn't believe it. In fact, I didn't want to believe it. Although, I still had so much energy and so many good ideas, I just wasn't making a success of them. Clearly, something wasn't right, and I didn't have a clue as to what it was.

How could Raff and I fail? It was so hard to accept and swallow, but that's how it was, the harsh reality. We tried but failed. Not for the lack of talent or experience but failing to go about it the right way probably. In truth, it was ill prepared and possibly half-baked. It seemed that I wasn't getting to where I wanted to be, as if I was going in the wrong direction. In contrast, at times it felt like if I just kept going, I would reach my destination eventually.

In the end, the reasons didn't matter really. The result was that we didn't get far. With that in mind, it was inevitable that now I had to call it a day. In short, that's what we did. We threw in the towel.

Where would I go now from here? I was at a loss, with no direction and nowhere to go. Again…

Back to Istanbul, 2018

No one around me could fully comprehend what I was going through or how I felt. Not that I shared my plight with many people, but even if I did, no one would believe it. Gulsun was the closest person to my sufferings. She could clearly see that I wasn't at all happy. From time to time, I tried to open up to her and try to explain how I felt. However, I wasn't sure if she could quite understand what I was going through. However hard she tried, she couldn't make any sense of it, no one could. On paper, I was somebody with such a successful and respectable career and in theory I could do whatever I wanted.

Unbelievably, it had been over five years since the career interruption. Even now, I was still not doing anything meaningful and satisfactory. Simply put, it felt like I was in a big void, free falling. There was no way to find the exit out of where I was. The best approach to find my way out of this abyss was to avoid it completely. Just run away from it. Clearly, I couldn't stay in London like this. It was time to move on again.

After the Barcelona experience, I wasn't willing to take any risks, as I had neither the will nor the energy. What I needed was another safe house, like a fugitive drug lord on the run! More than ever I also needed a safe bet of a project to keep me occupied and fulfilled.

Yes, I should just concentrate on completing my book, which I had started writing in Barcelona. Obviously, this was probably going to be the first and only book that I would ever write. Presumably, just like songwriters, writing books also needed inspiration, the right mood and the right state of mind or all three at once.

It seemed that writing my story would allow me to reminisce over my old memories and channel my thoughts into creating something worthy. Surely by writing a decent and reasonably interesting book, it would mean another opportunity to make a mark and a lasting impression? For a while I worked on my book, but on and off, as I wasn't very comfortable being in London. Maybe I should go back to Turkey again? It could be better and possibly easier to finish the rest of the book there. Besides, it may be better to release the Turkish version first anyway I thought. While working on the book, I could also continue to provide free mentorship and guidance to young developers. In all sincerity, this is something I have always enjoyed doing and, it is nice to be respected and appreciated, which I get in spades from young people. It gives you a sense of purpose and a reason for being.

Everyone likes to be liked and receive a bit of flattery. But receiving unconditional praise and appreciation is truly wonderful.

After just less than two years in London, I decided to move on again. A lovely flat, amazing London, friends, nice walks, relaxed and comfortable life, but none of it was enough to make me feel happy and content. Back on the run again like a fugitive from my inner turmoil, running away just like I did from lovely Barcelona, now I was fleeing from lovely London, my second home. It seemed I had to make a move, but I couldn't see one step ahead of me. It is utterly amazing how chess players can see so many moves ahead. Wouldn't it be nice to be able to do that in life? But then again, I am not very good at chess either.

So, I was on the move again, but where could I go this time? In a similar fashion to how I came to London from Barcelona to a safer and more comfortable destination, Istanbul now seemed to be the only viable alternative to seek refuge in.

Our tenants had just vacated the house in Istanbul, so I could just go back, and get it all repainted and ready to move into. Following that, Gulsun would come later as she did from Barcelona to London. Frankly, it seemed unfair on Gulsun, as I seemed to be dragging her along with me, but she wasn't 100% happy in London either. Perhaps I would be doing her a favour too?

In the end, I spent a couple months in the summer of 2017 in Istanbul working on my book and getting the house ready. I don't want to bore you with the details of more troubles, but I must share this incident, which occurred during the painting and decorating of our house. This is just to give you an idea of how bad things had become. Also, a lesson in how things can get even worse when you think that couldn't be possible. It would suffice to say that that there was a shooting incident. However, it didn't involve me and luckily, I wasn't there at the time of the incident. Let me just leave it there…

Although I was just trying to concentrate on my book, there were always people coming to me for help with projects. Many diverse projects including games, but the common recurring factor was that they were always having problems of some kind. It was crazy, as nothing was working out no matter how hard I tried. Constantly, I had been having problems, facing obstacles and troubles, all of which felt like I was being tested continuously for character and strength.

There were many different projects that I was involved with, and although I was making considerable contributions to all of them and some were achieving significant success, right towards the end, for one reason or another, I would either walk away or be left out. Out of all the projects that I really regret not being able to pursue, it was with Ulas Karademir and Unity that I regret the most.

In the end, I decided not to do anything with anyone, just to work on my book and also to continue helping young developers.

They say that time is the best healer, but it hasn't worked for me so far. Unfortunately, I still feel like a lost soul. I went back to London for a bit longer. Subsequently, we vacated our lovely London flat in February 2018, and moved back to Istanbul once more…

My Left Ear!

When things go downhill there's no avoiding troubles on the way. In June 2018, feeling quite down and out, Gulsun, Sila and I went to my cousin Recepali's youngest daughter's wedding in Izmit. It was a big reception with food and music and lots of dancing.

In a five-star hotel but with a one-star music system, the noise was blaring out of the hidden speakers. They had some huge speakers covered in black sheets; you couldn't see where they were but you could certainly hear them from a mile away!

After the meal everybody started dancing and the Turkish people love it, they could dance for hours nonstop. I love it too and did quite a bit of it myself when I was young. All my nieces and nephews insisted that we join in the fun. We duly obliged but I was hanging by the corner of the stage just trying to get in the mood. But I could feel the awfully loud and distorted music, I should say noise, but I just stayed there without realising I was stood by one of the speakers! I do listen to loud music and have been to so many really loud rock gigs from Thin Lizzy to Metallica, but this was just terrible. Little did I know that I was so close to the ugly thing that I was damaging my left ear without knowing it.

It was gone midnight when I was on my way back home to Istanbul, and suddenly there started a horrible ringing and resonance in my left ear. Thinking something loose was rattling in my door or Sila's door, who was sitting just behind me. I was checking my door pocket but there was nothing there to rattle. Then I kept asking Sila to check hers repeatedly. The poor thing said, 'Dad there's nothing here to cause a rattle', and by then I even removed everything from the door pocket! I was driving, desperately trying to get home as soon as possible to get away from this awful constant ringing, which was driving me potty!

I arrived home and jumped out of the car, hoping to free myself from the awful experience. Oh no, this can't be, the bloody thing is still there, it's actually inside my left ear!

I would soon discover that the overly loud distorted noise destroyed some of my hair cells (sensory receptors) in my left ear! Apparently, it is these hair cells that detect and amplify sound waves. God, this is the worst thing that could have happened to someone who listens to music every day!

Unfortunately, the dead hair cells can only regenerate in chickens, but humans' remain dead for good! It's been nearly two years now, and the only thing I can do is learn to live with it. Using all my logical skills, at least I found a solution that greatly reduces the problem when listening to music but when I am out and about, just walking, driving or on public transport it can badly cause ringing and discomfort. The environment and ambient sounds can trigger my tinnitus.

What's worse is the fact that quite a few hair cells are dead, which cover a wide frequency range (mostly midrange, 250Hz - 2kHz). From my limited research this is what happens. The brain doesn't know or accept dead hair cells, so it puts a sound of its own in place of the missing cell. That's why I get random sounds in my left ear, which don't exist in the original source. My right ear hears the sound as is whereas on my left ear I get ringing, hissing or resonance. It's so annoying to say the least and ruins the experience of quality music listening and becomes very uncomfortable in noisy public places or in social gatherings. Some high frequency sounds are the worst, as they produce a horrible echo as if I'm in a glass room.

I only listen to digital music these days, streaming from online sources. I use my computer to listen to music, and YouTube and Netflix for movies and videos. I solved the problem to some extent by finding an Equaliser plugin whereby I managed to identify the sounds in the frequency band that cause problems. Then with careful tweaking and adjustment I managed to reduce the volume of those sounds to acceptable levels. It doesn't completely eradicate the problem but reduces the level where I can still enjoy listening to music and it doesn't change the overall tone of the original music. I am hoping to turn this into an R&D project to incorporate a custom equaliser with a hearing aid device, so that I could use my solution when I am out and about too.

Searching the net, I discovered that ringing in the ear, tinnitus and other hearing related problems are widely spread, affecting millions of people world over. I wanted to share my experience in case it could help anyone who suffers from similar problems. I do hope I can develop my in-ear solution as a product that can be widely available and can be customised to everyone's specific needs.

If after reading this, any of you fancy the idea and would like to contribute to the project then I'm all ears!

Life Is A Game

I spent the best part of the last three years writing my book and mentoring young developers whenever and wherever I could. In fact, I started writing the Turkish version of the book, 'Hayat Bir Oyun', in Barcelona early 2016.

In August 2015, I was invited to attend the Amiga 30 UK, to celebrate the thirty years of the Amiga computer. Before going to the Amiga event in Peterborough, I had a dinner at my friend Erdem Yurdanur's London house with his wife. Erdem is a remarkably successful entrepreneur with many successful investments, one of which is Massomo Games (Head Ball 2- Kafa Topu 2). A successful Turkish mobile company which was sold to Miniclips for several hundred million dollars. In fact, Erdem knows me from when I was in the UK in the late 90s. He also always knew of my work and achievements, but never the details of how it all started. So, over the dinner I shared some of my life story with him and his wife Ayse. They were absolutely gobsmacked with what they had heard. Erdem's immediate reaction was, 'Please, you must turn your story into a book asap and Barcelona is the best place to write it!' As it happens, I had been thinking about writing for a long time, but Erdem's enthusiasm and pointing to Barcelona being the perfect place was what made me pull the trigger. As a result, I would like to thank Erdem once more for the nudge!

The journey of writing Hayat Bir Oyun started in Barcelona, continued in London and was finally completed in Istanbul. The book was eventually published in January 2020. The reaction and reception were way more than I could have ever expected. Generally, Turkey isn't known for being much of a reading nation and as a result my publisher didn't have huge expectations. However, recognising my work and fan base they agreed to print three thousand copies on the first run.

From the beginning, I knew that it would be mostly me promoting and selling the book. Using all my social media and network reach, I encouraged everyone to buy it. Surprisingly, the majority of people were reading it on one sitting and I was getting heart-warming feedback from my relatives, friends and in particular my gamers.

The majority of gamers had started playing my games when they were in primary school. Some of them now were at university studying computer science and aiming to write games like me. In this respect, they found my story absolutely fascinating and inspirational. There are twelve-year-old readers who started making games after reading my book. Due to that I am wholeheartedly delighted that I wrote the book.

To promote it I was running from one event to another. Giving talks, meeting my gamers and doing lots of book signings at universities. Amazingly, there were constant invitations from many universities in many cities. God it felt amazing, what a great feeling.

Suddenly, I was back in the field, back in action and all because of my book. In fact, I was over the moon and so glad to have written it. Actually, it gave me a new lease of life. Even game companies started organising events for me. Furthermore, they were also buying lots of books to give out to the attendees. At long last, it felt so satisfying as I was selling hundreds of books at each event. The warm reception and reaction was just out of this world.

It felt so good to be back amongst all those youngsters, who had admired and respected me over the years. Due to feeling very low in myself, I had actually thought that they had forgotten me. On the contrary, I was being welcomed with open arms and, these young coders were literally begging me to make games again.

In no time at all, we were on the second edition with lots of bookings planned for a multitude of events across numerous cities. That was exactly what I had planned and wished to do; travel the country with my book. It was much more than I had expected, as I was inundated with invitations. The overwhelming response to my book gave me so much energy. Truly exhilarated, I felt so tireless and excited to meet them all and to embrace all the love and affection of thousands. In addition to all of this, I had planned a number of gamer get-togethers with my gaming community too, which delighted them.

COVID-19, Testing Times For All

Suddenly, the dreadful Covid-19 hit us. It was very sad to see how a virus made the entire world helpless and confused. Immediately, I cancelled all my events. Upon reflection, it is quite remarkable how I never caught it myself, as I mingled with thousands of people in many cities. On a mission, I was travelling from one place to the next for weeks. Who knows, maybe I caught it and recovered from it?

Although there was partial lockdown in Turkey, I decided to self-isolate and stay home continuing to promote my book online. Soon I started giving online talks to many universities, sharing my experience and also talking about my book.

Just like in the UK, now so many people in Turkey were asking me to stage a comeback and make games again. Suddenly, my failed online gaming academy project was also back on the agenda. Everyone was talking about online education! A lot of people, who read my book, discovered my intentions and plans about the academy, and realised how important a project it was. They were repeatedly stating how it would have been perfect in this lockdown situation. In fact, several gaming companies and organisations started to collaborate to start an online academy. They asked me to help them with it, and I told them that I would.

Anyway, I am just enjoying the ride at the moment. I am getting lots of lovely messages from my gamers and young developers. I will always consider the possibilities in front of me. Currently, I am promoting my book, and reaching more readers each and every day. To be honest, I can't wait to get back out there again, once things return to normal.

There's Good In Every Evil

During lockdown and self-isolation, I decided to write the English version of my book. Initially, I had actually planned to get it translated. Nevertheless, I must say that it was a good job that I ended up writing it myself. Due to the different cultures and the use of the language, it very quickly became obvious that I had to almost rewrite the entire book. In fact, that's exactly what I did.

Luckily, once I start something, I really give it all I have and work non-stop. As a result, I managed to finish the first draft in just over three weeks! My fingers and neck were sore at the end of it! After two readings and corrections, my friend Jamieson Lee Hill helped with making it more elegant and flowing.

Incidentally, I am delighted to say that he loved the book and immensely enjoyed reading it several times. He was so inspired he even wrote a poem dedicated to me!

Another wonderful thing was that Michael Holley, my English nephew, did the proofreading for me. Ever so grateful to him.

Writing the book has been a wonderful journey for me, which started in Barcelona, continued in London and finished in Istanbul. I cannot tell you how gratifying and fulfilling it is to have written Life Is A Game. It has been worth every second and moment I spent with it. With all my heart, I will forever treasure every second you have spent reading my book. I do hope to meet you sometime someplace…

As I Leave You...

I have poured my heart and soul into Life Is A Game; I do hope my story inspires a few people, as nothing would please me more.

I thank you from the bottom of my heart for reading it, and I very much hope you have enjoyed it as much as I enjoyed writing it.

My sincerest hope is that you achieve everything your heart desires in life!

Finished.
Barcelona, London and Istanbul, 2016-2020

With Nej (1982) & Sila (2019)

To live like a tree one and free,
And like a forest brotherly,
This longing is ours…
NAZIM Hikmet

The following poem was written by Jamieson while helping me edit Life Is A Game. He was inspired by my views and feelings on life. I liked the poem a lot and decided to put it in the book, I hope you like it too.

The River

Pause a while,
Stop the cycle of torment
For you are unique,
Let your sorrow and anxiety
Flow away with the river of life.

The cycle of thoughts
Cartwheels through highs and lows,
And the worries that spin inside
Are but rapids in the river of life,
Learn to flow through and beyond them
Though the currents are strong
And hope can slipstream away,
The river will always continue on
New horizons will take us past grief, loss and pain.

Pause a while,
Stop the cycle of torment
For you are unique,
Let your sorrow and anxiety
Flow away with the river of life…

Jamieson Lee Hill (aka The Bard of Malvern)